ARTIFACTS AND ORGANIZATIONS

Beyond Mere Symbolism

LEA'S ORGANIZATION AND MANAGEMENT SERIES

Series Editors:
Arthur Brief
Tulane University
James P. Walsh
University of Michigan

Associate Series Editor:
Sara L. Rynes
University of Iowa

Ashforth (Au.): *Role Transitions in Organizational Life: An Identity Based Perspective*

Bartunek (Au.): *Organizational and Educational Change: The Life and Role of a Change Agent Group*

Beach (Ed.): *Image Theory: Theoretical and Empirical Foundations*

Brett/Drasgow (Eds.): *The Psychology of Work: Theoretically Based Empirical Research*

Darley/Messick/Tyler (Eds.): *Social Influences on Ethical Behavior in Organizations*

Denison (Ed.): *Managing Organizational Change in Transition Economies*

Elsback (Au.): *Organizational Perception Management*

Early/Gibson (Aus.): *New Perspectives on Transnational Work Teams*

Garud/Karnoe (Eds.): *Path Dependence and Creation*

Jacoby (Au.): *Employing Bureaucracy: Managers, Unions, and the Transformation of Work in the 20th Century, Revised Edition*

Kossek/Lambert (Eds.): *Work and Life Integration: Organizational, Cultural, and Individual Perspectives*

Lampel/Shamsie/Lant (Eds.): *The Business of Culture: Strategic Perspectives on Entertainment and Media*

Lant/Shapira (Eds.): *Organizational Cognition: Computation and Interpretation*

Lord/Brown (Aus.): *Leadership Processes and Follower Self-Identity*

Margolis/Walsh (Aus.): *People and Profits? The Search for a Link Between a Company's Social and Financial Performance*

Messick/Kramer (Eds.): *The Psychology of Leadership: Some New Approaches*

Pearce (Au.): *Organization and Management in the Embrace of Government*

Peterson/Mannix (Eds.): *Leading and Managing People in the Dynamic Organization*

Rafaeli/Pratt (Eds.): *Artifacts and Organizations: Beyond Mere Symbolism*

Riggio/Murphy/Pirozzolo (Eds.): *Multiple Intelligences and Leadership*

Schneider/Smith (Eds.): *Personality and Organizations*

Thompson/Choi (Eds.): *Creativity and Innovation in Organizational Teams*

Thompson/Levine/Messick (Eds.): *Shared Cognition in Organizations: The Management of Knowledge*

ARTIFACTS AND ORGANIZATIONS

Beyond Mere Symbolism

Edited by

Anat Rafaeli
Technion, Israel

Michael G. Pratt
University of Illinois at Urbana–Champaign

LEA LAWRENCE ERLBAUM ASSOCIATES, PUBLISHERS
2006   Mahwah, New Jersey   London

HD58.7
.A765
2006

o57670125

Lawrence Erlbaum Associates, Inc., Publishers
10 Industrial Avenue
Mahwah, New Jersey 07430
www.erlbaum.com   .

Cover design by Kathryn Houghtaling Lacey

Library of Congress Cataloging-in-Publication Data

Artifacts and organizations : Beyond mere symbolism / edited by Anat Rafaeli,
Michael G. Pratt
      p.   cm. — (LEA's organization and management series)
Includes bibliographical references and index.
ISBN 0-8058-5036-8 (alk. paper)
  1. Organizational behavior.   2. Symbolism in organizations.   I. Rafaeli, Anat, 1954–
II. Pratt, Michael G.   III. Series.

HD58.7.A765   2005
302.3'5—dc22   2005040029
                                                                        CIP

*To West Quad
and All of the Collaborations
Her Walls Enabled.*

Contents

Series Foreword   xi
James P. Walsh and Arthur P. Brief

Preface   xiii

List of Contributors   xv

Introduction: Artifacts and Organizations: More Than the Tip of the Cultural Iceberg   1
Anat Rafaeli and Michael G. Pratt

PART I   KNOWING ARTIFACTS

1   Managing Artifacts to Avoid Artifact Myopia   9
   Iris Vilnai-Yavetz and Anat Rafaeli

2   Organizational Artifacts and the Aesthetic Approach   23
   Antonio Strati

3   Studying Physical Artifacts: An Interpretive Approach   41
   Dvora Yanow

4 Perceptual Biases and Misinterpretation of Artifacts   61
   Kim Elsbach

PART II   ARTIFACTS AND KNOWLEDGE

5 Cartoon Displays as Autoproduction
   of Organizational Culture   85
   N. Anand

6 Artifacts and Knowledge Negotiation Across Domains   101
   Paul Carlile

7 Linguistic Artifacts in Organizing and Managing   119
   Ann Cunliffe and John Shotter

PART III   ARTIFACTS, BRANDS, AND IDENTITY

8 Brand Life in Symbols and Artifacts:
   The LEGO Company   141
   Majken Schultz, Mary Jo Hatch, and Francesko Ciccolella

9 Employees as Animate Artifacts: Wearing the Brand   161
   CV Harquail

10 On Logos and Business Cards:
    The Case of UK Universities   181
    Yehuda Baruch

11 Fine Fashion: Using Symbolic Artifacts, Sensemaking,
    and Sensegiving to Construct Identity and Image   199
    Rossella Cappetta and Denny Gioia

PART IV   ARTIFACTS AND LEGITIMACY

12 Fred's Bank: How Institutional Norms and Individual
    Preferences Legitimate Organizational Names   223
    Mary Ann Glynn and Christopher Marquis

13 Stuff Matters: Artifacts, Social Identity, and Legitimacy
in the U.S. Medical Profession   241
Marlene Fiol and Ed O'Connor

14 Artifacts, Articulation Work, and Institutional Residue   259
William N. Kaghan and Michael Lounsbury

PART V   TOWARD FUTURE RESEARCH

15 Artifacts and Organizations: Understanding
Our "Object-ive" Reality   279
Michael G. Pratt and Anat Rafaeli

References   289

Author Index   313

Subject Index   321

Series Foreword

Every now and again you run across a book and say to yourself "I wish I had written that!" This is such a book. Rafaeli and Pratt (and their many colleagues) have opened our eyes to a world we see every day. Ask your average organization and management scholar what he or she knows about artifacts and we bet that you will hear about Schein's model of culture and little else. Taking nothing away from Schein's influential contributions to our understanding of culture, we really think you should read this book. Yes, the authors further our understanding of culture and yes, they offer us a whole lot more. Artifacts are ubiquitous and generally overlooked. Do not overlook this book. It houses a wonderful collection of really stimulating theoretical and empirical papers. We suspect that we will be reading and rereading this book for many years to come.

James P. Walsh
University of Michigan
Arthur P. Brief
Tulane University

Preface

As a book on artifacts, we felt it only appropriate to dedicate the book to one: "West Quad"—the aging dorm-turned-un-air-conditioned offices that once housed the Department of Organizational Psychology at the University of Michigan. More important, it was the place more than a decade ago where we first met and first collaborated; and the place where we developed our fascination with organizational dress and—more broadly—organizational artifacts. What a treat it is to be writing a preface to yet another artifact: a product of our collaborative curiosity—a book about artifacts.

Since our time in West Quad, we've been frustrated with the paucity of good up-to-date resources considering the uneasy relationship between artifacts, organizations, and organizational scholarship (see our introductory chapter for some rare exceptions). Nearly 2 years ago, we embarked on the creation and editing of this book in the hope of generating a resource to fill in this gap that we and others have sensed. We feel a lovely sense of accomplishment as we see the book in print. We hope the book will be put to good use by all students of organizations—be they academic or practitioner. Although the authors are primarily academics, we feel certain that there are useful insights here to inspire effective management of and through artifacts.

Obviously we cannot nor should not take full credit for the contributions the book might make. We wish to thank our peers at the University of Michigan—the birthplace of our working relationship—as well as our many colleagues in our home and other institutions who, over the years, have provided us useful examples, insights, criticisms, and suggestions in various formal or informal conversations. We thank Lillian Bluestein for her dedicated editing, and Israel Bravo, for handling the endless updates to the book web page. This web page was critical in helping authors get a glimpse of other parts of the book while they were working on their own chapters.

And of course we thank our families. We thank Sheizaf and Trudy (our spouses), who acted as "sounding boards" and who tirelessly sought and found examples of artifacts and artifact stories—many of which appear in various parts of the book. Our beautiful children Sella, Agam, and Ofek (Rafaeli), and Lucas, Mikaela, and Jacek (Pratt) cannot be thanked enough—though they are not artifacts, they are the best things we feel we can produce in this lifetime.

—*Anat Rafaeli*
Michael G. Pratt

List of Contributors

N. Anand
London Business School

Yehuda Baruch
University of East Anglia

Rossella Cappetta
Bocconi University

Paul Carlile
Boston University

Francesco Ciccolella
The LEGO Company

Ann Cunliffe
The University of New Mexico

Kim Elsbach
University of California, Davis

Marlene Fiol
University of Colorado at Denver

Denny Gioia
Pennsylvania State University

Mary Ann Glynn
Emory University

C. V. Harquail
University of Virginia

Mary Jo Hatch
University of Virginia

William N. Kaghan
Touro University International

Michael Lounsbury
Cornell University

Christopher Marquis
University of Michigan

Ed O'Connor
University of Colorado at Denver

Michael G. Pratt
University of Illinois at Urbana–
    Champaign

Anat Rafaeli
Institute of Technology
Technion, Israel

Majken Schultz
Copenhagen Business School

John Shotter
University of New Hampshire
    and KCC Foundation, London

Antonio Strati
University of Trento

Iris Vilnai-Yavetz
University of Haifa, Israel

Dvora Yanow
California State University at Hayward

INTRODUCTION
Artifacts and Organization: More Than the Tip of the Cultural Iceberg

Anat Rafaeli
Michael G. Pratt

> *A billboard just outside Austin, Texas, bears the image of a silhouetted Coca-Cola bottle on its side with the caption: "Quick. Name a soft drink." The image reveals the iconic nature of the soft drink that fills the famous contoured bottle. "Unmistakably Coca-Cola. Unmistakably American."*

If you stood before this billboard, how would you react? Would you notice the seductive contours of the bottle? Would you be able to link the silhouette of one of the only merchandizing packages to have its own patent (http://www2.coca-cola.com/ourcompany/historybottling.html) to its famous contents before seeing the name, "Coca-Cola"? Would you notice the writing on the billboard at all—and just be thankful that the structure provides shade on a hot Texas day? For one of the authors, the sign would evoke memories of an eccentric grandmother who served every meal with a Coke, and who would consider you a traitor if you drank Pepsi. For the other, it would evoke thoughts of how Coke has become a household word around the world. This billboard is an artifact. It is a product of an organization. It is a public statement of a company, but also holds private meanings for viewers. It can be appreciated for its beauty and for its function. It can also powerfully represent a corporation across the world. In fact, it is difficult to imagine the organization this billboard represents without also imaging its artifacts.

The authors in this book are united by the recognition of a core irony: that artifacts in organizations are highly visible but overlooked. Their chapters illustrate that artifacts are ubiquitous in organizational life. Artifacts prevail in how we decorate our offices (see the Elsbach chapter), the language we use (Cunliffe & Shotter), the logo-embossed business cards we carry (Baruch), and the cartoons we display on our doors (Anand). Artifacts can be seen in the name of an organization (see the Glynn & Marquis chapter), its employees (Harquail), its products (Schultz, Hatch, & Ciccolella), its buildings (Yanow), its processes (Strati) as well as its contracts (Kaghan & Lounsbury). Artifacts can represent people (Anand; Elsbach; Harquail), organizations (Baruch; Strati; Yanow), and professions (Fiol & O'Connor). They are everywhere (in fact, you are looking at one right now)!

Despite (or perhaps because of) their prevalence, Schein (1990) viewed artifacts as the most superficial "layer" of culture. But such a conceptualization dilutes our understanding of how potent artifacts can be. Artifacts, we suggest, are neither superficial nor pertinent only to organizational culture. They do much more. They are relevant to a rich and diverse set of organizational processes within and across multiple levels of analysis. Artifacts are shown to be integral to identity, sensegiving, and sensemaking processes (Elsbach; Cappetta & Gioia), to interpretation and negotiation (Carlile; Yanow), to legitimacy (Fiol & O'Connor; Glynn & Marquis; Kaghan & Lounsbury), and to branding (Harquail; Schultz, Hatch, & Ciccolella).

We hope that this volume will lead students of organizations to embrace the full complexity and richness of artifacts. We encourage a recognition of the potential power of artifacts in evoking aesthetic and instrumental considerations, and not just symbolic ones (Vilnai-Yavetz & Rafaeli; Strati). And we seek to inspire those who focus on artifacts as symbols to delve deeper into the complexities of artifacts-in-use, for individuals, organizations, and institutions. For example, we encourage exploring the subtleties and complexities of artifacts in enacting legitimacy, branding, and identity (Baruch; Cappetta & Gioia; Elsbach; Fiol & O'Connor; Glynn & Marquis; Harquail; Kaghan & Lounsbury; Schultz, Hatch, & Ciccolella). More generally, we suggest artifacts are vessels for transferring knowledge (Anand; Carlile; Cunliffe & Shotter), and we provide methodological tools to unlock that knowledge (Yanow).

Some of our chapters are empirical; others are primarily theoretical. Empirical pieces employ various methodologies. Some chapters relate to processes of learning and adaptation (Carlile; Shotter & Cunliffe). Others draw heavily from institutional theory (Anand; Glynn & Marquis; Kaghan & Lounsbury). Still others contribute to prevailing conversations about identity in organizations and corporate brands (Cappetta & Gioia; Elsbach; Fiol & O'Connor; Schultz, Hatch, & Ciccolella). A real hodgepodge, one might say. However, such diversity is intentional. As we discuss in our concluding chapter, the volume seeks to communicate that artifacts are much more than what is currently recognized in organizational research.

OVERVIEW

The four parts of the book address various aspects of what we know about—and what we know through—artifacts. Together the full set of chapters challenges the field to move beyond a narrow conceptualization and understanding of artifacts in organizations.

In Part I—Knowing Artifacts—we advance the understanding of how to view and understand artifacts. In chapter 1, Iris Vilnai-Yavetz and Anat Rafaeli call for a move to the study of artifacts outside of the exclusive domain of symbolism and culture—suggesting that artifacts should be conceptualized as having instrumental, aesthetic, as well as symbolic dimensions. Integrating a wide range of literatures on artifacts, this chapter argues that a focus on only one dimension may lead to artifact myopia whereby students and managers of organizations run into problems of oversimplifying how artifacts function in organizations.

Chapter 2, by Antonio Strati, calls attention to the aesthetic dimension of organizing, while also focusing on behavioral elements of artifacts-in-practice. Using a student performance as an organizing example, Strati reminds us that artifacts may be ephemeral and evanescent because they are created in practice, and may phase out or change as time passes or the context changes. Whereas Vilnai-Yavetz and Rafaeli suggest looking beyond the symbolic, Strati reminds us of the dynamic element of artifacts. As he notes, even organizational artifacts that are physical and tangible objects, "are not static, immutable, and determinable once and for all."

In chapter 3, Dvora Yanow incorporates insights from the interpretive approach to other methodological frameworks for studying artifacts as she reminds us how important it is to keep in mind the researcher and the researched. Drawing on her analyses of organizational space, Yanow argues for the importance of understanding design vocabularies, design "gestures," proxemics, and decor.

In chapter 4, Kim Elsbach continues by focusing on the self–other distinction in artifacts and the perceptual differences between artifact displayers and observers. Building from her research on physical markers, she argues that the unique nature of artifacts as visually salient, relatively permanent (and thus repeatedly observable), and visible apart from the displayer leads to systematic differences or perceptual biases in how displayer and observer view artifacts in the work setting.

Part II of the book—Artifacts and Knowledge—shifts gears to how artifacts are used in organizations as a means of disseminating information.

In chapter 5, N. Anand positions artifacts as elements of the autoproduction of organizational culture. Anand offers an analysis of an artifact
many of us have seen—cartoons displayed by university professors—and
argues that these cartoons can communicate multiple types of identity
messages, including in-group similarity, divisive social issues, public, idiosyncratic characteristics of displayers, and comedic relief from social,
psychological, or physiological controls.

Chapter 6, by Paul Carlile, presents artifacts or "the material world" as
something that "mediates human activity;" he begins to unravel one paradoxical element of artifacts: their ability to erect boundaries within organizations and knowledge communities (by maintaining functional differences among members), and their ability to traverse these same divisions.
Carlile identifies the concept of "boundary objects," which are artifacts
that help resolve this paradox, and argues for three characteristics that
boundary objects must possess to serve in this capacity.

In chapter 7, Ann Cunliffe and John Shotter embrace a philosophical
approach of "artifacts and knowledge" by focusing on "knowing" (as opposed to "knowledge"). Knowing, they argue, is an implicit type of "fluid"
sensemaking process that is grounded in everyday experiences. Cunliffe
and Shotter focus on linguistic artifacts (such as words, stories, and metaphors)—suggesting that they are at the heart of communal understanding, conversation, and "relationally responsive" interactions.

Parts III and IV of the book discuss information or knowledge that artifacts can disseminate. Part III—Artifacts, Brands, and Identity—illustrates
how artifacts are used in the construction and imposition of identity by organizations, employees, and other stakeholders. In chapter 8, Majken
Schultz, Mary Jo Hatch, and Francesco Ciccolella draw upon their experience with the LEGO Company to illustrate how artifacts help link corporate vision, culture, and image for employees and other stakeholders. In
the process they depict that as an organization's emphasis shifts from
product branding to corporate branding, there is also a shift from a tangible artifact (e.g., a LEGO brick) to the ideas the artifact represents.

In chapter 9, CV Harquail extends the connection of artifacts to identity
in suggesting that organizations engage employees as artifacts as part of
the branding process. Discussing cases of organizations that make employees "wear the brand," Harquail delineates both intended effects and
unexpected complications of employee branding.

In chapter 10, Rosella Cappetta and Denny Gioia integrate the themes of
organizational identity, image, and employee branding with sensemaking,
presenting artifacts as critical to relating stories of "who we are" as an organization. They suggest the importance of studying "defining artifacts"—artifacts that are centrally related to an organization's identity. Ideally, an organization uses artifacts to create a coherent cycle of sensemaking and

sensegiving to both members and nonmembers. Problems arise—as they illustrate—when organizational image and identity are not aligned.

Part IV—Artifacts and Legitimacy—connects artifacts to issues of institutionalism. In chapter 11, Mary Ann Glynn and Christopher Marquis adopt a multilevel approach in an empirical study of organizational names. Names function as a "shorthand" cue that affects perceptions of organizations. But they find that individuals vary in their preference for institutional conformity, thus challenging whether isomorphism necessarily legitimates for all audiences. The chapter contrasts the value of symbolic isomorphism (which legitimates) with creativity (which distinguishes), embedding artifacts in a blend of institutional and individual forces. This chapter helps illustrate when and why artifacts function as potent carriers of meaning and how individuals may vary in their responsiveness artifacts.

Chapter 12, by Marlene Fiol and Ed O'Connor, considers how and why legitimacy emerges, how it is maintained, and what factors lead to its erosion. They use key artifacts as a way to visibly trace the path of the establishment and subsequent decline of legitimacy in the U.S. medical profession. Drawing on visible artifacts that have been both reflective and constitutive of changing social realities within the medical profession, they illustrate the potential for artifacts to embody contradictory social meanings.

Chapter 13, by Michael Lounsbury and William Kaghan, ends Part IV by integrating themes raised in various other chapters. Lounsbury and Kaghan suggest that artifacts, like actors, are not only reflections of an institutional reality—hence merely upholding or reproducing institutionalized understandings—but can also extend, modify, adapt, and sometimes directly challenge current understandings. Local modifications that artifacts convey are, in turn, often fed back into the broader institutional field, sometimes leading to modifications of existing templates and prevailing institutional beliefs.

We conclude our book with our own vision of future research directions. Our subtitle for this chapter, "Understanding Our 'Object-ive' Reality," highlights the fact that artifacts profoundly influence our understanding of organizational reality. People come to know organizations by the artifacts they keep. We note that artifacts are both physical and social constructs. We also suggest that artifacts need to be considered according to how enduring they are, how many senses they engage, what they "say," how they can be viewed, and how they may be interpreted differently from different perspectives, such as that of a displayer versus a perceiver.

We named this book, *Artifacts and Organizations*. We hope that by the end of the volume it will be clear how intimately tied these two notions are; that organizations, such as Coca-Cola, could not exist apart from their artifacts.

I

KNOWING ARTIFACTS

What are artifacts? How should they be analyzed? What perspectives can be taken on viewing artifacts? The first part addresses these questions by examining a broad range of issues regarding how to view artifacts. *Vilnai-Yavetz* and *Rafaeli* (chap. 1) call to move artifacts outside of the exclusive domain of symbolism and culture. *Antonio Strati* (chap. 2) then focuses on the aesthetic dimension of artifacts and on the behavioral elements of artifacts-in-practice. *Dvorah Yanow* (chap. 3) continues by focusing on methodologies of studying artifacts. *Kim Elsbach* ends the section with a focus on perceptual differences between artifact displayers and artifact observers.

1

Managing Artifacts to Avoid Artifact Myopia

Iris Vilnai-Yavetz
Anat Rafaeli
Technion-Institute of Technology, Haifa, Israel

Israel's national public transportation company recently tried to repair its suffering from increased competition by adopting a new physical image: It began a public relations (PR) campaign that was symbolized by painting its buses a dark green (Rafaeli & Vilnai-Yavetz, 2004a). The color was chosen by management as a symbol of environmental friendliness. However, responses to the color were far from positive, and referred not only to the symbolism of the color. The dark green bus was described as too dark for the hot Middle Eastern climate in which it needs to transport passengers. It was described as too dark for a public transportation vehicle, so dark that other drivers and pedestrians on the road cannot see it. It was described as a wrong green—a specific hue that symbolizes military camouflage, hospitals, garbage trucks, and terrorist groups. And it was described by some people as simply ugly—unaesthetic. We studied what we have come to call "The Green Bus Case" in depth (Rafaeli & Vilnai-Yavetz, 2003, 2004a, 2004b), and these studies led us to the development of a conceptual framework that we believe can help managers avoid the damage of the green-bus mishap.

Building on the green-bus case, we suggest that assuming something is only a symbol may be a case of artifact myopia—not recognizing the full complexity of an artifact and its implications and potential implications. We believe that any symbol is better viewed as an artifact, and artifacts, as we argue next, require broader attention than the imagery that they seemingly represent as symbols. Awarding artifacts the breadth of attention they deserve, and recognizing their full potential influence, can help avoid managerial myopia in the management of artifacts.

PHYSICAL ARTIFACTS IN ORGANIZATIONS:
A DEFINITION

Physical artifacts are defined by the Oxford dictionary as "artificial products, something made by human beings and thus any element of a working environment" (Hornby, 1974, p. 43). Gagliardi (1990) added to this definition that artifacts are always perceived by the senses and that they have certain intentions, aiming to satisfy a need or a goal. Research on organizational artifacts, building on Schein (1990) and Trice and Beyer (1993), has considered intangible notions, such as names (Glynn & Marquis, chap. 12, this volume), language (Cunliffe & Shotter, chap. 7, this volume), and contracts (Kaghan & Lounsbury, chap. 14, this volume). In this chapter we focus on tangible notions, concentrating on organizational artifacts that are *inanimate objects introduced by organizational members into their organizations.* Artifacts can include colors (Frank & Gilovitch, 1988; Sassoon, 1990), dress and accessories (Rafaeli & Pratt, 1993; see also Fiol & O'Connor, chap. 13, this volume), furnishings (Baron, 1994; T. R. V. Davis, 1984), buildings (Nasar, 1994; Yanow, 1998; see also chap. 3, this volume), offices (Hatch, 1990; see also Elsbach, chap. 4, this volume), stores (Cappetta & Gioia, chap. 11, this volume), vehicles (Hirschman, 2003; Rafaeli & Vilnai-Yavetz, 2004b), windows (Leather, Pyrgas, Beale, & Lawrence, 1998), cartoons (Scheiberg, 1990; see also Anand, chap. 5, this volume), logos and emblems (Heskett, 2002; McCall & Belmont, 1996; Stern, 1988; see also Baruch, chap. 10, this volume; Schultz, Hatch, & Ciccolella, chap. 8, this volume), and more.

Given this definition, organizations are one big conglomerate of physical artifacts. Stripping an organization of its artifacts is removing all physical evidence of its existence. Yet our understanding of *what artifacts really are* remains limited at best. Are they but a collection of physical matter? Most artifacts are more than that. Artifacts allow people to do things, and inspire people to feel or react a certain way. Our goal in this chapter is to propose a model for analyzing physical artifacts, and to illustrate how this model can help prevent what we call "artifact errors" or "artifact myopia." Our presumption is that a systematic model for analyzing artifacts can significantly enhance the understanding of artifacts and facilitate effective artifact management.

THREE DIMENSIONS OF ARTIFACTS:
INSTRUMENTALITY, AESTHETICS,
AND SYMBOLISM

A systematic analysis requires understanding the dimensions on which artifacts may vary. One key problem in most prior research, however, is the unstated assumption that artifacts can be classified into distinct categories. Scholars who have written about artifacts as symbols (Hatch, 1997b; Ornstein, 1986; Pondy, Frost, Morgan, & Dandridge, 1983; Schultz, 2000), for example, tend to focus on and elaborate this specific aspect and may not consider additional dimensions on which artifacts may vary. A symbolism focus may provide an elaborate view of one of the dimensions; but we suggest that it may still reflect a certain form of artifact myopia if the full complexity of organizational artifacts—including additional dimensions, such as instrumentality and aesthetics—are not considered with sufficient care.

There are some hints in current theory that artifacts can embody conceptually distinct and independent qualities, for example, Frost and Morgan's (1983) suggestion for a "real-ization" of symbols and artifacts. Canter (1977) and Lang (1988) similarly suggest that places evoke both actions and feelings. T. A. Markus (1987) suggests that buildings can vary in form, space, and function. Hershberger and Cass (1988) identify multiple factors on which buildings can be evaluated, including utility evaluative and aesthetic evaluative. Yet these and similar efforts still analyze distinct aspects as having distinct implications. In Markus' analysis, for example, the form of a building is considered "design" rather than "function." In Goodrich's (1982) analysis the office environment is considered an instrumental cue, not a symbolic cue. Thus, current models maintain the implicit assumption that an artifact is to be categorized into one distinct category. We suggest this to be a narrow view, arguing that artifacts can have various qualities simultaneously, so any categorization necessarily leads to some form of myopia.

An important exception to this discrete approach is presented by Strati's (1992) "aesthetic approach" to artifacts, which argues that classifying artifacts into aesthetic objects and functional objects is inaccurate and misleading, because any artifact is likely to load on both factors. Strati illustrates that although a picture is typically classified as "aesthetic" and a chair is typically classified as "functional," chairs and desks have aesthetic properties and pictures have functional properties. A picture of a boy on a door, for example, has the important functional property of informing people that behind this door is the men's (rather than women's) toilet. Important to note, such pictures can be aesthetic or unaesthetic, though equally functional. Thus, aesthetics can be separate but also complementary to function. As with pictures, degree of functionality and a degree of aesthetics can characterize any artifact, with no clear positive or negative correlation between the functionality and aesthetics of an artifact.

This argument—of separate and complementary dimensions of the same artifact—is the core assertion of this chapter. Based on Rafaeli and Vilnai-Yavetz (2003, 2004b), we describe next three specific dimensions essential to analyses of artifacts: instrumentality, aesthetics, and symbolism. We then suggest that artifact myopia, where the three dimensions of an organizational artifact are *not* considered, represent artifact errors of organizational members.

Instrumentality. The instrumentality of an artifact refers to the extent to which the artifact contributes or hampers performance of individual task or accomplishment of individual or organizational goals. Instrumentality is the impact of an artifact on the tasks or goals of people, groups, or organizations. Instrumentality can be high, or positive, if the probability of attaining a goal or accomplishing a task is increased by the presence of an artifact. Instrumentality is low, or negative, if the presence or the qualities of an artifact dampen or decrease the same probability.

The key to instrumentality is that people and organizations have goals to accomplish, and artifacts can be evaluated according to whether they help or hinder the accomplishment of these goals. Canter (1977, 1997) aptly illustrates instrumentality of physical places or environments, with some places suggested as highly instrumental to local goals whereas others dampen accomplishment of desired goals. Gibson's (1979) ecological approach suggests that what people perceive in the environment are "affordances," namely the extent to which the environment supports or hampers desired activities. Nielsen (1994) referred to the "usability" of artifacts as a critical feature, and Flanders (2002) suggests identifying "web pages that suck" to "help identify whether a Web site succeeds or fails at its main mission—effectively communicating what it's about and what product or belief they're trying to sell" (p. 135).

Building on Shumaker and Pequegnat (1989), two models of impact of artifacts on efficiency and productivity can be suggested. In a model of "direct influence" the artifact directly supports or disturbs performance. If the artifact is a physical workstation, for example, it can hamper performance due to bad location or damaged or inappropriate equipment. If the artifact is an organizational Web site, it can facilitate performance through a good design (Nielsen, 2000). In a second model, of "indirect influence," an artifact can cause stress or other emotional reactions, which in turn hamper performance.

Garling and Golledge's (1989) review of environmental psychology consistently emphasizes the key role that individual perception of an environment can play in facilitating performance in this environment. Thus, instrumentality is one dimension for assessing artifacts. However, this is only one dimension relevant to such assessments. Our review of the literature suggests two additional and essential dimensions—aesthetics and symbolism.

Aesthetics. A second essential dimension, suggested by Rafaeli and Vilnai-Yavetz (2003, 2004b), regards the aesthetics of an artifact. Aesthetics is the sensory experience an artifact elicits. Nasar's (1994, 1997) typology of environmental cues echoes the idea of aesthetics as a key factor. Strati (1992, 1999; see also chap. 2, this volume) played a central role in rejuvenating the importance of aesthetics to organizations, and connected architectonic aesthetics and organizational experiences. Gagliardi (1990), Dean, Ramirez, and Ottensmeyer (1997), and Ramirez (1991) further position aesthetics as an essential, but independent, dimension in assessments of artifacts. Eisenman (2004) suggests aesthetics as factors that, separate from instrumentality, can determine product and organizational success.

Aesthetics is separate from instrumentality, but cannot be divorced from it, because aesthetics is judged in the context of the tasks or goals of the context of an artifact. In the example of a picture of a boy on a door, the same picture can be considered pleasantly aesthetic when on the door of the men's bathroom, but considered tacky and unaesthetic when appearing on a news Web site. Similarly, expectations of aesthetics from a logo of an auto shop, for example, are likely to be very different from aesthetic expectations for the decor of a boardroom, although both logo and boardroom are important organizational artifacts.

In product design, aesthetics is often an important criterion, occasionally at the cost of instrumentality, or performance of important goals. As Postrel (2001) describes, the good looks of the Apple computer "Power Mac G4 Cube" did not make it a successful product, most likely because its instrumentality was not up to par—it did not perform as well as its price demanded (see also Eisenman, 2004). However, as Postrel noted, aesthetics is not always easy to plan:

> Everybody from industrial designers to city planners claims to be looking after our aesthetic interests, and there is ample anecdotal evidence that, on the margin, people do put a higher premium on the look and feel of things than they once did. But aesthetics doesn't come in neat units like microprocessor speed, calories, or tons of steel. Style is qualitative . . . it is hard to be assessed. As a general matter, aesthetics sells, not just in computers but in other goods and services.

A classic case of aesthetics taking a lead over instrumentality is with the design of cellular telephones. Ergonomic considerations recommend a certain angle of a telephone headset, but such angles produce bulky and less aesthetic cellular phones. The industry has navigated toward the more aesthetic even if less functional telephones (Yun et al., 2001).

Symbolism. The bus company with which we opened this chapter as well as many organizational theorists focus primarily on the symbolism of organizational artifacts (Trice & Beyer, 1993). Clearly symbolism is a dimension of artifacts, but, based on Rafaeli and Vilnai-Yavetz (2003, 2004b) we suggest it as a third dimension, which acts in concert with and independent of instrumentality and aesthetics.

Symbolism regards the meanings or associations an artifact elicits. Csikszentmihalyi and Rochberg-Halton (1981) illustrate that even simple or mundane things such as chairs and tables have meanings. Trice and Beyer (1993), Stern (1988), and Schein (1990) consider artifacts as symbols representing the values of organizational cultures. A similar perspective is presented in this book by scholars who study the process of shaping and presenting personal and social identities via artifacts such as cartoons (Anand, chap. 5, this volume), buildings (Yanow, chap. 3, this volume), fashion stores (Cappetta & Gioia, chap. 11, this volume), and logos (Baruch, chap. 10, this volume; Schultz, Hatch, & Ciccolella, chap. 8, this volume).

Ornstein (1986) and Elsbach (chap. 4, this volume) empirically illustrate that the physical layout of an organization reliably elicits associations of certain qualities. Advertising campaigns are the most vivid context in which such symbolism is used (Aaker & Myers, 1987), to the point of using symbolism to create desired identities (Aaker, 1994; Avraham & First, 2003; Hirschman, 2003). Hatch (1990) reports attitudinal and behavioral responses to offices as products of meanings that individuals attribute to the work environment.

Importantly, however, attributions made to an artifact are not necessarily those intended by the organization. Key to symbolism is the process of observation and interpretation by observers, and as Elsbach (chap. 4, this volume) notes, misinterpretation of observations can and does occur. Observers can make unexpected inferences and attributions based on their own associations, rather than those intended when an artifact was selected or presented. Thus, artifacts can have both intended and unintended symbolic consequences (T. R. V. Davis, 1984; see also Elsbach, chap. 4, this volume). Gagliardi (1990) focuses attention on views of corporations afforded by symbols and artifacts. Berg and Kreiner (1990) discuss physical settings of organizations as "symbolic resources."

In short, as we asserted earlier, three dimensions are essential to understanding artifacts and to effectively managing them in or for organizations: instrumentality, aesthetics, and symbolism. Failing to recognize these three simultaneous dimensions can lead to artifact myopia and to various artifact errors, as we discuss later.

Why These Three and Only These Three Dimensions?

Perhaps we recognize only three dimensions but are there more? A review of the diverse bodies of research on physical artifacts reveals three clusters that are the foundations of these three dimensions. A first cluster is technology and human factors engineering, which discuss how artifacts relate to task performance, clearly attending to instrumentality (Helander, Khalid, & Tham, 2001; Howell, 1994; Nielsen, 1994). A second cluster is architecture, product and industrial design, and the fine arts, which focus primarily on aesthetics of artifacts (Berleant, 1988; Gagliardi, 1996; Nasar, 1997; Strati, 1999; Takahashi, 1995). A third cluster is advertising, communication, and especially semiotics, which focus on the symbolism of signs and artifacts (Aaker & Myers, 1987; Avraham & First, 2003; Hirschman, 2003; Swartz, 1983). This marriage of multiple disciplinary perspectives appears to capture the breadth and depth of views on physical artifacts, supporting the three dimensions as essential to capturing the full complexity of physical artifacts.

The idea of three dimensions of the physical artifacts is supported by the classical conceptualization of the characteristics of architecture (Vitruvius, 1934, 1960). The Roman architect Vitruvius, whose work is considered to be one of the classic foundations of architecture, noted that building design must offer durability (or firmness), convenience (sometimes labeled commodity), and beauty (which has been labeled delight). Durability was defined by Vitruvius as a good structure that holds up an artifact under all conditions; convenience was defined as what makes a building comfortable (Vitruvius, 1960). Thus, durability and convenience (or firmness and commodity) together comprise what we have termed instrumentality. Delight, according to Vitruvius, is what makes a building more than just a shelter. It may be an intellectual delight, a visual delight, or other form of delight, but it brings something more to the building than just functionality (Vitruvius, 1960). Here we find similarity to the aesthetic and symbolism dimensions.

Furthermore, these three dimensions together can be viewed as creating a philosophical "whole" by integrating a behavior, sensory, and cognition, or hands, senses, and mind. Norman (2004) similarly refers to behavioral, visceral, and reflective aspects of designs. Instrumentality relates to "doing," thus either facilitating or hindering behavior. Aesthetics are tied to the senses or to visceral reactions. And symbolism builds on associations, as it is "all about message" as Norman (p. 83) states, so necessarily relies on cognitive processes. The three dimensions therefore suggest theoretical "completeness" because they tap and integrate the fundamental distinctions in scientific thought between doing, sensing, and thinking.

Empirical analyses tend to verify that the three dimensions are distinct. Lavie and Tractinsky (2004) confirmed that a factor analysis separates between factors of instrumentality and aesthetics in judgments of Web sites. Tractinsky and Zmiri (2004) confirmed that a factor analysis separates three factors—which can be identified as instrumentality, aesthetics, and symbolism—in a factor analysis of perceptions of "skins" of interactive applications such as Microsoft's Media Player. They showed that instrumentality accounted for 45% of the reasons people reported for preferring a certain appearance of an application over an alternative appearance, whereas aesthetics accounted for 39% and symbolism accounted for 5%; in this study only 10% of the preferences could *not* be accounted for by one of these dimensions.

In our empirical work we confirmed the model in an analysis of employee perceptions of office design (Vilnai-Yavetz, Rafaeli, & Schneider-Yaacov, 2005). In a qualitative study, narratives of informants about office design echoed the three dimensions, and in a quantitative study, survey data of 148 office employees confirmed the three separate dimensions. These analyses also provided initial insights about the relationship between the three dimensions and key dependent variables such as employee satisfaction and self-reported performance.

That the three dimensions can always be applied in an analysis of an artifact does not necessarily mean that all discussions of an artifact must necessarily discuss all three dimensions. In any specific context, one or more of the three dimensions may be ignored for whatever reason. But this does not negate the idea that all three dimensions can be applied in considerations of all artifacts or all organizational contexts. For example, it may be that some dimensions operate in a fashion similar to the "hygiene" job factors as defined by Herzberg (1966), so that only artifacts that are disagreeable for some reason are noted, whereas acceptable levels of a dimension are not noted.

For example, in the case of employee attire as an artifact, when attire hampers performance, employees may comment on it. Flight attendants and waitresses have complained about having to stand up for a long time in high-heeled shoes (Hochschild, 1983; Steinem, 1983). But instrumentality was barely mentioned in the analysis of Rafaeli, Dutton, Harquail, and Mackie-Lewis (1997) of the attire of office employees and the analysis of Pratt and Rafaeli (1997) of nurses' attire. It may be that when uniforms are reasonably instrumental for the job employees forget about instrumentality, taking it for granted that they can perform in the presence of this artifact.

Similarly, researchers may choose to focus on some of the dimensions, ignoring others. For example, Vilnai-Yavetz, Rafaeli, and Ramati (2004) report on a study of the attire of bank clerks. Presuming that bank employees can perform their tasks wearing attire that ranges from jeans and a T-shirt to a formal suit, the study examined only two dimensions other than instrumentality—aesthetics (clean vs. dirty attire) and symbolism (professional vs. unprofessional attire). The study finds that these two dimensions can predict the extent to which customers desire to interact with a bank clerk.

The key point is, therefore, that all three dimensions may be relevant to any artifact. For effective artifact management all three dimensions need to be considered at least initially, in order to fully understand the meaning and implications of introducing or using a specific artifact.

ARTIFACT MYOPIA AND ARTIFACT ERRORS

Management of artifacts can rely on the three-dimension model to recognize the full complexity of the potential influence of an artifact and hopefully to avoid artifact errors. Errors occur, we suggest, because of artifact myopia by managers or designers of artifacts. Artifact myopia occurs when only one or two of the three dimensions are taken into consideration in artifact planning, selection, or implementation. Artifact myopia may also occur when invalid presumptions are made about a certain dimension.

Artifact myopia is the case where perception errors lead people to view artifacts in a certain way and to assume that this is the only way an artifact should be viewed. Because of self-projection biases, managers may fail to recognize how others might see the world (Stanovich & West, 1998). Artifact myopia means failing to recognize individual differences in artifact perception or alternative artifact influences, both of which can easily compromise artifact decisions (Kaplan & Kaplan, 1983).

Managers may fail to recognize the full set of constituents to whom an artifact applies, or may fail to recognize the full set of issues an artifact may influence. Different constituents may hold very different perceptions of the same artifact, and as Rafaeli and Vilnai-Yavetz (2003) argued, even seemingly trivial artifacts may apply to a broad set of organizational constituents. Moreover, a certain artifact may influence alternative tasks or goals very differently. To illustrate, a certain fashion of employee dress may be interpreted differently by employees and customers. As illustrated by Steinem (1983), dressing up women as Playboy bunnies can promote sales to certain customers, but can alienate certain employees. Similarly, as described by Raz (1997) and Van Maanen (1995), costumes of Disney employees may be interpreted as playful and fun by customers, but may be hot and uncomfortable as well as humiliating to employees. Focusing on only one set of constituents may lead to a focus on only one dimension, and to a failure to realize the importance of additional dimensions (Artifact Error I) or to a failure to realize additional aspects of the same dimension (Artifact Error II).

Artifact Error I: Failing to Recognize the Three Dimensions of an Artifact.   Artifact myopia may lead managers to overlook some of the three dimensions in their consideration of a certain artifact. Typical myopia, for example, is a focus on instrumentality while overlooking issues of symbolism or aesthetics. The historical case of the Edsel car, which was manufactured and marketed by the Ford auto company in 1958, is considered a benchmark of design failure, although the car ran properly. Its failure has been attributed to aesthetics and symbolism. Some people argue that the Edsel car manifests universal standards of ugliness. Others argued that it had a grille that looked like a female vagina (Wernick, 1994). The bottom line is that the Edsel as a product was a failure in the United States, although as far as engineering and human factors were concerned (i.e., instrumentality) it could run just fine. Instrumentality is also a typical focus in the design of wait queues, where time taken to reach a service provider is presumed to be the only key variable. However, as Rafaeli, Barron, and Haber (2002) as well as Rafaeli, Kedmi, Vashdi, and Barron (2004) report, symbolism—or the associations a wait queue elicits—appear to be key. In these studies, wait queues that symbolized unfair waits (by including multiple short lines rather than one long but single line) produced unpleasant feelings of injustice even though their instrumentality (i.e., the objective waiting time) remained identical.

Artifact Error I may also involve ignoring instrumentality and symbolism and referring only to aesthetics of an artifact. A recent case is the Power Mac G4 Cube of Apple Computer, which was canceled barely a year after it was introduced; the machine was introduced as "the coolest computer ever" and one observer called it "a test of the aesthetic revolution in computing" (Postrel, 2001). The cancellation was because the tiny, elegant computer had not been selling well. However, this case suggests that glamorous is not in itself a sufficient criterion for computers to sell, because this computer could not compete in the market place with less glamorous but more powerful, or instrumental, machines.

Artifact Error I may also take the form of a focus only on symbolism, with little attention to instrumentality. For example, Vilnai-Yavetz, Rafaeli, and Schneider-Yaacov (2005) described a case where office design focused primarily on symbolism and official status of employees rather than on the instrumental needs of employee jobs. Lower level secretaries in the offices they studied had smaller and more crowded desks than higher ranking managers, although the former needed more desk space to handle larger amounts of paperwork. The size of the desk, thus, symbolized the higher organizational status of the managers, and ignored the functionality of the desk to its incumbent.

Artifact Error II: Failing to Recognize the Full Complexity of an Artifact Dimension. Even if all three dimensions are recognized, artifact myopia may lead to an error if the full complexity of any of the dimensions is not recognized. A key to Artifact Error II seems to be incomplete identification of relevant constituents, so that the full breadth of each of the dimensions of an artifact can be recognized. Artifact planning, selection, or implementation must consider instrumentality, symbolism, or aesthetics of an artifact with consideration of all the constituents and all the possible interpretations that the organization wishes to consider.

Artifact Errors II are most easily recognized with respect to symbolism. Symbolism errors occur when planning or selection of an artifact presumes only one type of meaning and ignores other plausible associations. Raz (1997), for example, describes what he called a "communication failure story" (p. 206) and we would label a cognitive symbolism error. According to Raz, a sign for a toilet in Tokyo Disneyland confused park guests because, "The toilet has an English sign saying 'rest rooms' and in Japanese 'rest' stands for 'resuto' (restaurant)" (p. 206). As Raz notes, park guests do not realize the sign symbolizes toilets. The error occurred because the multiple meanings of the sign were not sufficiently considered.

The brief story with which we opened this chapter also describes a symbolism error; green was selected because it was presumed to be associated with environmentalism and green ethics (Bansal & Roth, 2000). But the choice was a symbolism error because it (green) may also be viewed as symbolizing garbage trucks, terrorist groups, marijuana, or emergency rooms in hospitals (Rafaeli & Vilnai-Yavetz, 2004a).

Artifact Error II may occur with instrumentality if an artifact is instrumental to the goals of some constituents, but not to others. Service forms, service stations, and other artifacts of relevance to service delivery may be useful and convenient to employees but not to customers, or vice versa. Consider, for example, the kindergarten employee who needs to sit on furniture that was selected to meet the needs of the clients—young children. Sitting on tiny chairs near colorful tiny tables can produce pain and damage to the back, neck, and shoulders of kindergarten employees (Gibson, 1979). Similarly, modern and posh office buildings may fit the needs of employees and customers, but not attend to the special needs of handicapped employees or customers. This would be an example where not all the aspects of instrumentality were considered.

Why Worry About Artifact Myopia?

Artifact myopia and the resulting artifact errors are critical to organizations because they may lead to compromises in performance. As Eisenman (2004) explicitly notes, and Norman (2004) implies, failing to recognize the full complexity of artifacts can dampen financial success of organizations.

Performance compromises may occur if certain constituents and their goals or perspectives are overlooked in the design, selection, and implementation of an artifact. Artifacts that fail to consider instrumentality, for example, in a case of Artifact Error I, can clearly dampen performance if they do not meet important organizational goals. The goals may be of internal constituents (e.g., employees), but also of various other constituents who are somehow influenced by an artifact. For example, web designs that may be highly aesthetic but difficult to navigate compromise performance and have been argued to turn away customers from e-commerce (Rust & Kannan, 2002). Similarly, the failure of the Power iMac computer has been attributed to instrumentality oversights (Postrel, 2001). And Elsbach (chap. 4, this volume) argues that misinterpretations of office decor and employee dress may dampen performance through a negative influence on employee cooperation and teamwork.

Undesirable artifact effects may also occur because of a misalignment in the decoding of artifacts, where the effects on target persons are different from that intended in the introduction of the artifact (Rafaeli & Vilnai-Yavetz, 2003). For example, the green bus, in the story that opened this chapter, was intended to evoke positive emotion through environmental-awareness associations (Bansal & Roth, 2000). But environmentalism is only one of the associations that the green bus elicited, and alternative associations brought about different and not necessarily positive emotions. Moreover, the desired positive association of environmentalism produced negative emotions in some constituents, who saw it as a hypocritical act of the organization (Karliner, 2001). Such artifact errors can be costly to organizational PR and to financial performance of organizational stocks.

Relationships Among the Three Dimensions?

Our analysis suggests that artifacts should be viewed in an integrated mode involving three dimensions—instrumentality, aesthetics, and symbolism. It further suggests that artifact myopia, or a failure to recognize the full complexity of artifact dimensions, can produce various errors and undesirable outcomes. However, our premise—that the three dimensions are of equal relevance to all artifacts—may be a bit myopic itself. It may be that particular dimensions may become more or less salient as a function of context. A painting seen on a museum wall may signal that aesthetics are relatively more important than when the same painting is seen on a food tray or a place mat; in the latter context instrumentality may become salient. Similarly, Fiol and O'Connor (chap. 13, this volume) refer to the black bag or white coat of medical professionals as symbols of professional identity; these could also be perceived as instrumental working tools. In Baruch's analysis (chap. 10, this volume) of corporate logos, it can be seen that although the logo has an important instrumental objective of transferring explicit knowledge about the organization, its most salient and central role is communicating tacit organizational messages, through symbolism.

But the relationships among the three dimensions might be even more complicated through second-order effects. Cappetta and Gioia (chap. 11, this volume), for example, analyze the fashion industry and talk of beauty and ugliness (aesthetics) as an instrumental tool for transferring symbolic messages. Based on their claim, we would like to suggest that there may also be additional implications to the dimensions; second-order effects of an artifact would be aesthetics or symbolism evoked by the instrumentality, aesthetics, or symbolism of an artifact. For example, both aesthetics and instrumentality may themselves be symbols that trigger associations of efficiency or effectiveness. Prasad (1993) illustrated such dynamics with instrumentality and symbolism of office technology. Such second-order effects do not contradict the current three-dimension theory, but rather enrich it by suggesting first- and second-order implications of artifacts (Lakoff & Johnson, 1999).

First-order effects involve the artifact directly. Second-order effects occur when first-order effects themselves have an instrumental, aesthetic, or symbolic quality. Through such second-order effects aesthetically pleasant service reception areas, for example, might be viewed as symbolizing great customer care (Bitner, 1992). Aesthetics may become instrumental if more aesthetically pleasant customer service areas produce greater customer satisfaction and greater revenues. Similarly, through second-order effects, symbolism may become instrumental if it contributes to the task at hand. Employee uniforms symbolizing professionalism may, for example, help customer service employees do their job (Rafaeli & Pratt, 1993).

SUMMARY

A view of any artifact through only one lens (or dimension) can be misleading, or as we labeled it here—*myopic*. Yet professional training often creates a context that leads to a focus on primarily one dimension. Ergonomics focuses and develops a deep respect for instrumentality. Marketing professionals typically operate in a context that emphasizes symbolism. And designers often focus on aesthetics and creativity. As we have shown elsewhere (Rafaeli & Vilnai-Yavetz, 2004b), both experts and nonexperts recognize the three dimensions. Expertise is evident in the elaborateness with which experts consider the particular dimension that is relevant to their expertise. Experts use more elaborate language forms, and can provide a lot more detail in their assessments of an artifact. Expertise is therefore important in recognizing the complexity of a particular dimension of an artifact. But because artifacts are necessarily multidimensional, effective artifact management in organizations requires recognition and integration of multiple lenses and dimensions to avoid artifact myopia.

2

Organizational Artifacts and the Aesthetic Approach

Antonio Strati
University of Trento, Trento, Italy

There is by now a substantial body of organizational literature on artifacts, and it has gained accreditation among organizational theories as the crisis of the rationalist and positivist paradigm has deepened (Hatch, 1997b; Strati, 2000). And since the pioneering works of Fred Steele (1973) and Franklin Becker (1981), it has also developed in relation to aesthetics (Gagliardi, 1990; Ramirez, 1991; Strati, 1992; Turner, 1990). Toward the end of the last century, the *pathos* of organizational artifacts highlighted by study of aesthetics and organizations was flanked by Michel Callon's (1980) sociology of translation—thereafter termed "actor network theory" (Law & Hassard, 1999)—and in particular by Bruno Latour's study (1992), which treated artifacts as "missing masses" from socio-technical analyses of organizational phenomena. The status of the artifact has also been changed from that of a tool to an actor in organizational dynamics by the analyses conducted within "workplace studies" (Heath & Button, 2002), as well as those on "cooperative learning" and "participatory design" applied to information systems (Ciborra, 1996; Ehn, 1988).

Organizational artifacts, even when they are physical and tangible objects, are not static, immutable, and determinable once and for all; on the contrary, constructionist, phenomenological, and interactionist analyses have shown the extent to which they are mutable and constantly self-innovative—all the more so in the case of information technology artifacts (Suchman, Trigg, & Blomberg, 2002). In short, at the beginning of this new millennium, organizational artifacts depict contemporary Western societies as some sort of *"postsocial* environment" (Knorr Cetina, 2003) in which they mediate the social relations among people to an ever-increasing extent, and in which they themselves transmogrify into transmutational objects.

The aesthetic approach, actor network theory, and the three strands of inquiry comprising workplace studies, cooperative learning, and participatory design, therefore, all emphasize the importance of the organizational artifact in the everyday lives of organizations. They stress symbolic interaction and the social and collective construction of reality. They pay close attention to socio-technical detail and to the micro dimension, conducting qualitative analysis of organizational phenomena, the constant changeableness of organizational artifacts, and the time span in which they arise and spread. By contrast, these approaches differ in the extent to which they attribute to nonhuman objects a capacity for action on a par with that of humans—actor network theory in fact theorizes the capacity for action of the organizational artifact and the scaling back of exclusively human action—and also in their conceptions of the centrality of knowledge and aesthetic experience. Nor do actor network theory or the workplace studies, cooperative learning, and participatory design approaches view the organizational artifact necessarily in terms of pathos—although some attention is paid to this aspect (Whalen, Whalen, & K. Henderson, 2002).

In order to illustrate the importance of aesthetics in the understanding of the organizational artifacts, I deal in this chapter with the production of an artifact that was particularly evanescent and equivocal because of its ephemerality and its nature as action-in-being. The artifact in question was a "performance" (Guillet de Monthoux, 2000, 2004; Hamilton, 2001; Höpfl & Linstead, 1993; Mangham, 1996; Nissley, Taylor, & Houden, 2004) produced for a female student's degree. Its antecedents were her work for two courses during which "by accident" recordings of discursive practices in work routine and study of Weber's bureaucracy coincided with "discovery" of an art installation in the civic gallery of contemporary art. The student's desire to do something different therefore arose in an extrauniversity context—the gallery—and was prompted by the mingling of various kinds of experience: her experience of academic study acquired while recording the conversations in the organizations, that of classroom learning, and her artistic experience in the art gallery.

The "Iron Cage" performance described in this chapter was therefore "situated" within a set of complex organizational dynamics where it was the pathos of the artifact-performance that set them in relation—due to the pleasure that the performance provoked, the enthusiasm that it aroused, the desire that it stimulated, and the imagery that it evoked—to the "différance" (Derrida, 1967) that distinguishes every individual, the heterogeneity of material artifacts, the multiformity of organizational processes. Indeed:

- It was the aesthetic dimension of the artifact, initially imagined but not yet existent, that stimulated the senses and the taste of the students and teachers on the two courses in sociology of organization and sociology of work, and the creative process that was thereby "improvised" (Montuori, 2003).
- It was aesthetics that connoted the organizational interaction when the artifact-performance was enacted in the faculty.
- It was aesthetic pleasure that translated the ephemeral organizational act of the performance into the collective construction of what I call, following Baudrillard, the artifact-simulacrum of the performance: to wit, the multimedia product that ensued from it and that constituted the material artifact of further organizational interactions (university lectures and conferences).
- It was aesthetics that distinguished the organizational communication (L. Putnam, Phillips, & Chapman, 1996) brought into being by the performance.

AESTHETIC APPROACH AND PERFORMANCE

The aesthetic approach (Strati, 1992, 1999) examines the artifact in its "being-in-use" in organizational settings, emphasizing material knowledge and "practice" in the study of organizations (Nicolini, Gherardi, & Yanow, 2003). The approach concerns itself with tacit knowledge (Polanyi, 1962), as well as with the being-in-use of artifacts and the aesthetic and artistic pleasure that they arouse (Jauss, 1982). Art and aesthetics furnish a language with which awareness of "knowing how"—and at the same time awareness that one's knowledge is impossible to explain scientifically—can be both expressed and studied without violating the character of tacit knowledge by having perforce to translate it (Serres, 1974) into explicit knowledge. For the aesthetic approach, the organizational artifact has pathos (it is "art" and not just "fact") just as organizational life is not only *logos* (which concerns its ontological definition, its essence, its "nature") but also *ethos* (which comprises its unwritten principles, its moral codes, its deontologies, and the constant regulation of its legitimacy) and pathos, that is, its dimension of feeling, perceiving through the senses, judging aesthetically.

Hence, everyday organizational routine comprises artifacts that are beautiful to use, graceful to the eye, or grotesque, kitsch, or repellent—and to which the language-in-use of organizational discursive practices attaches labels evocative of the aesthetic categories of beautiful, ugly, sublime, gracious, and so on (Strati, 1999). There are artifacts that are desirable or repulsive, artifacts born from our desire for knowledge, and artifacts that spring from our desire to "give form"—in that every human "forms" something (Pareyson, 1954)—and that is thus "formative." There are artifacts that arouse aesthetics feelings (and obviously emotions as well) these being not independent effects, separate and distinct from the artifact itself, but rather qualities expressive of the style that characterizes it. And there are artifacts that constantly transmute because they are observed in organizational and work practices—that is, observed in their being-in-use within organizations.

A chair, for example, acquires multiple forms and meanings in an organization (Strati, 1996): It may be a power symbol or an artifact on which to sit, a decorative item or an improvised table, a stepping-stool or a jacket hanger. The artifact "chair" does not have a well-defined ontological status that determines its organizational action; rather, its identity changes according to the interaction in which it is involved, and it sometimes assumes more than one identity. But the aesthetic approach maintains that the interaction is based on the perceptive-sensory faculties and on the sensitive-aesthetic judgment: The chair can be touched with the body and the hands; it can be smelled (albeit not deliberately); it can be heard as it creaks; it can be appreciated for its shape and style, or even for the sense of the sacred that it evokes by virtue of its workmanship and history.

It is therefore sensory knowledge and the sensitive-aesthetic judgment, and not solely ratiocination, that sets the artifact in organizational dynamics and processes. And just as the artifact has multiform and transmutational identities, so the human body, as well, is never the same from one moment to the next—as we know from medicine and biology—and never from one social interaction to the next, as we know from the social sciences, and also from art: Consider the portraits by Francis Bacon or Pablo Picasso, or the three-dimensional transformations of the human body in computer art.

The artifact discussed in this chapter is very different in nature from a chair. Nonetheless, evident are its heterogeneity and its aesthetic construal as a dialogue for noncausal knowledge (Cairns, 2002; Strati, 1999). Aesthetic knowledge of the chair springs from practice: that is, observing, imagining, or using a chair when it is in-use or in dis-use. The performance-as-artifact further enhances practice in organizations: It exists when it is in action, to the point that the opposite, its nonbeing in action, necessarily entails its nonexistence. Artifact and action are closely intertwined in performance, in the sense that the latter exists in the moment when it is enacted, when it is social, work, and organizational *practice*. In other words, whereas when the chair-artifact is not in-use it is still the outcome of organizational interaction and work, this is not the case of the performance-artifact, which is an artifact-in-action and for this reason ephemeral, evanescent, elusive, and also—as in the case of the "Iron Cage" performance described shortly—hybrid: A human being and heterogeneous materials are con-fused in it, highlighting the complexity of experiencing as well as simultaneously aesthetically understanding an organizational artifact. A performance "evokes" by means of complex action in which corporeality goes beyond the logical-rational intelligibility of the semantic content of the heard sound, of the observed gesture, and of the artifacts that interact with the body—beginning with the organizational space in which the process takes place. Sounds, body movements, and heterogeneous artifacts "evoke" and stir the emotions by their beauty, ugliness, rhythm, style, and artistic language.

It has been pointed out (Strati & Guillet de Monthoux, 2002) that performance is an expressive style that is difficult to convey in a written text. The script is only one component of the whole. It does not entirely account for the performance: In fact, Steyaert and Hjorth (2002) note that, although the script "creates 'evidence' of organizing aesthetics', . . . it is not without a sense of loss that we relate to the text, having performed the play" (p. 769). In what follows I first describe a performance artifact as it was "acted" within the organizational interactions that it had brought into being. Then, in the following section, I analyze what happened before and after the action in question. The organizational meaning of the performance was not that of artistic creation, but rather the meaning of a teaching device used at a university. It concerned, in fact, the confluence into a "dialogue in act" of a visual and oral counterpoint among:

- Practical knowledge in organizations as discussed during a course on the sociology of work, the focus of which was organizational learning. The course program included practical exercises where the students recorded discursive practices in organizations.
- The norms underpinning the Weberian ideal type of bureaucracy discussed in a course on sociology of organizations.
- A work of art exhibited in a civic art gallery and consisting of an installation divided into two parts: one rigid, solid, and stable, the other melting into soft sinuous movement, which, however, did not deprive the installation of its structuring character.

THE PERFORMANCE AS AN EPHEMERAL ORGANIZATIONAL ARTIFACT

Let us suppose that the reader wants to observe directly, but by means of his or her imagination, the performance that I describe. I refer to a style of organizational ethnography (Strati, 1999) that is used for qualitative empirical analysis in organizational settings much more frequently than has been documented. In order to undertake an ethnographic study of this kind, the participant observer puts him or herself in the place of one of the actors in the process and "constructs" the action and the scenario. But she or he does so on the basis of an activated knowledge that is entirely personal in that it is rooted in his or her personal experiences and based on his or her capacity for imagination and empathy.

The reader should therefore choose a point of observation. This may be very different from the one that I am about to describe, but let us assume that the prompts that follow will suffice to satisfy his or her desire for knowledge. Let us suppose, therefore, that one dreary morning in spring the reader finds him or herself in a small city in northern Italy, in the medieval surroundings of the city center and close to one of the most beautiful cathedral squares in Europe. Standing a few dozen meters away, in one of the main streets, is the university faculty building in which the performance will take place. Outside the faculty building, under persistent drizzle and a gray sky, groups of students are holding a protest meeting with banners, megaphone-amplified slogans, and chants. The reader threads his or her way through the demonstration and enters the faculty building, finding him or herself in a large lobby. On the left is the porters' lodge fitted out as if it were an audiovisual recording studio; on the right is an installation executed by an well-known Italian artist. The reader crosses the lobby, goes up three steps flanked by two large pillars, and follows the temporary signs giving directions to the conference venue. The reader skirts the broad staircase leading to the two upper floors, passes through a large covered courtyard, and heads toward the Main Hall. There the reader takes a seat in a room tiered like a Greco-Roman theater. From his or her seat the reader can see that behind and above the speakers' dais is affixed a large screen on which appear, in sequence, slides of the entrance to the faculty, the room of a German university, and the Main Hall in which she or he is now sitting. The reader listens to the welcoming address and those announcing the theme and context of the event. The reader then leaves the Main Hall and returns to the lobby and to the installation erected therein. She or he is unable to get close to it, however, because of the large number of people assembled to watch the performance. Instead, the reader climbs the main staircase to a vantage point from which she or he can watch and listen.

What the reader hears is a playback of conversations recorded in organizational settings. A female student enters the installation and from its interior, by way of counterpoint, recites phrases taken from the Italian version of the sociologist Max Weber's writings on bureaucracy. The phrases uttered by the student alternate with recordings collected by herself and some other students in the same course for the purpose of studying work and organizational practices in a variety of settings: a railway station, a supermarket, a dance school, and other settings besides. The reader thus witnesses a dialogue between the recorded voices recounting present-day routine in organizations and the live voice reciting the phrases from Weber inside the installation. Merged with these voices is the visual language of the installation, that of the student inside it, and that of the organizational space of the faculty, made up of human bodies and heterogeneous materials, in which the performance is positioned. The reader watches and listens to the performance, but also to the "noise" of the context in which it is taking place. The reader notes that television camera crews are filming the student and the audience, and watches as students enter the lobby, fold their umbrellas, hush their voices and, stooping so as not to block the view, make their way through the watching crowd. The reader can also hear the increasingly distant voices of the demonstrators. Twenty or so minutes pass. The reader then sees the student come out of the installation and, reciting the phrases over again, head toward the Great Hall, accompanied by a lecturer and followed by the audience. The reader thus reenters the lecture hall as enthusiastic applause covers the noise of the participants returning to their seats. One of the speakers briefly introduces the German academic—visible on the screen thanks to the teleconferencing system—who comments on the performance. He is followed by the panel of speakers: lecturers from the faculty, the director of the city gallery of contemporary art, the artist. At the end of the morning, and amid resounding applause on conclusion of the conference, the reader returns to the lobby and inspects the installation—now empty, as is the space surrounding it—and listens to a recording made of the performance that is now being played back at low volume.

The vocal dialogue transcribed in the script that follows was only one aspect of the performance, therefore, for it combined with the "visual" of the installation and of its setting in the university organizational space.

The installation (see Fig. 2.1) occupied a large area to one side of the entrance lobby. It was constructed from materials whereby its linear architecture shifted from rigid and square shapes to fluid and sinuous ones. Thus, although on the one hand the "iron cage" structure gave the impression of solidity, on the other it seemingly melted and collapsed on itself. The squared part of the structure was entirely covered with transparent material and contained a door to the interior. The base of the installation was initially rectangular but then soft, curved, and irregular in shape. The transparent material covering three of its sides created a sharp separation between interior and exterior. But also when the linear structure—the installation's skeleton—became soft, flexible, and bare, it still separated the interior from the exterior and kept the visitor outside the area of the installation or internally to it.

The installation interacted both with the discursive practices of work in organizations and with the norms of the Weberian ideal type of bureaucracy (Fig. 2.2), translating itself into the nonhuman protagonist of a

FIG. 2.1.   Loris Cecchini's installation *Density Spectrum Zone 1.0*. Copyright 2003 by L. Cecchini. Courtesy Gallerie Continua. Reprinted by permission.

FIG. 2.2.   The student Anna Scalfi performing in the entrance to the faculty. Photograph by P. Cavagna. Copyright 2003 by P. Cavagna. Printed by permission.

trialogue among practical knowledge, social science, and art. On conclusion of the performance, the installation was still a protagonist: Though deprived of human presence, it set itself in relation to voices that repeated, over and over again, the following:

A woman queuing at the station [excerpts from taped conversations in organizational settings]: . . . *because the one behind . . . his train is leaving but he can't go. It's the lady asking as many questions as she wants, of course. But this is also a ticket office and behind her there are people queuing because they need to buy tickets. There isn't an information office anymore, there's no window where you can get information only. This is reorganization as the train company does it, they just cut staff. They cut staff in smaller stations or they ask you to dial this or that telephone number at a rate of . . . 6 or more cents a minute . . . because they're those very expensive numbers, those which used to cost 1400 lire and now cost 60 cents, you're charged on connection. If you go on the Internet it's free, for those who can connect, that is, it's really crazy . . . and a simple thing like the information office has just gone.*

Student [who has in the meantime entered the installation; excerpts from Weber, 1922, English translation: 1978, pp. 956–1005 and 212–226, and in Mayer, 1956, pp. 125–131]: Modern officialdom functions in the following manner: There is the principle of official *jurisdictional areas*, which are generally ordered by rules, that is, by laws or administrative regulations. This means: The regular activities required for the purposes of the bureaucratically governed structure are assigned as official duties.

At the supermarket: *bip bip bip 77, 78, 79 . . . 79? 80?*
—*It's me.*
—*Yes, please Ma'am.*

Student: The authority to give the commands required for the discharge of these duties is distributed in a stable way and is strictly delimited by rules concerning the coercive means, which may be placed at the disposal of officials. Methodological provision is made for the regular and continuous fulfilment of these duties and for the exercise of the corresponding rights; only persons who qualify under general rules are employed.

A woman traveler and a male clerk at the station: *How can the PC keeps track of the previous one?*
—*I don't know. I don't really know much about computers . . . I was never trained, I only issue tickets.*
—*Please?*
—*For technical stuff you need to go to an engineer.*
—*Without reimbursement you do the . . .*
—*Ah! The change . . . eh!*

Student: The principles of *office hierarchy* and of channels of appeal stipulate a clearly established system of super- and subordination in which there is a supervision of the lower offices by the higher ones. Such a system offers the governed the possibility of appealing, in a precisely regulated manner, the decision of a lower office to the corresponding superior authority.

A woman clerk at the tax office: *If you want, we can check in detail how the payment was made, if it was late and so on. It is very likely that the government will send you, maybe in five years, an order to pay interest because the tax was paid too late. Please consider that the tax is debited directly on . . . OK, the sum clearly goes to the government, instead the government can ask you to pay a penalty. So just to inform you of this I thought it appropriate to let you know . . . by law we have to do it, just in case you receive the penalty notice . . . because it's not one hundred percent sure we are dealing with the specific issue of payments here.*

Student: The management of the modern office is based upon written documents, which are preserved in their original or draft form, and upon a staff of subaltern officials and scribes of all sorts. Office management, at least all specialized office management—and such management is distinctly modern—usually presupposes thorough training in a field of specialization. Official activity demands the *full working capacity* of the official, irrespective of the fact that the length of his obligatory working hours in the bureau may be limited. The management of the office follows *general rules*, which are more or less stable, more or less exhaustive, and which can be learned.

A woman client and a male clerk at the station: *So you want a complete reimbursement? No, no, I'll cancel the transaction because they won't, I'll cancel everything . . . OK, OK, I'll make a complete reimbursement and then do it all over again. I'll do, I should do something else, but I'll do it anyway, when do you need it for? I'll cancel . . . I'll get the seat free and then I'll make a brand-new reservation. Only for the reimbursement, however, and nothing else, then he'll find it, but only for the reimbursement.*
—Any problems?
—Yeah, because it won't accept the change, should I do this way?
—How come the change can't be made?
—Well, let's say that the system is not perfect, let's say
—Please?
—I said the system is not perfect, sometimes it happens that . . . for the 27th you said?

Student: The decisive reason for the advance of bureaucratic organization has always been its purely *technical* superiority over any other form of organization. Bureaucratization offers above all the optimum possibility for carrying through the principle of specializing administrative functions according to purely objective considerations. Individual performances are allocated to functionaries who have specialized training and who by constant practice increase their expertise. "Objective" discharge of business primarily means a discharge of business according to *calculable rules* and "without regard for persons." The peculiarity of modern culture, and specifically of its technical and economic basis, demands this very "calculability" of results.

Woman teacher at the dance school: *Please girls, one hand on the bar . . . stretch in the air and press toward the floor, bend and lift your heel, and down, and stay, and . . . Stretch, and "rond," don't stop, don't stop, continuity, stretch back, the heel brings the leg forward, stretch from far and back.*

Student: When fully developed, bureaucracy also stands, in a specific sense, under the principle of *sine ira ac studio*. Bureaucracy develops the more perfectly, the more it is "dehumanized," the more completely it succeeds in eliminating from official business love, hatred, and all purely personal, irrational, and emotional elements which escape calculation. This is appraised as its special virtue by capitalism.

Clerk and an elderly customer at the supermarket: *bip bip bip 77, 78, 79 . . . 79? 80?*
—Me
—Yes, please Ma'am.
—Here, look, the other day I got a piece of cheese . . . goat cheese, good, really good, but I can't remember which . . . I think, that's it, IS it?
—Is this too much?
—No, there's too much rind.
—Too much rind?
—Oh dear, I'm already too old without . . .

Student: Where administration has been completely bureaucratized, the resulting system of domination is practically indestructible. The individual bureaucrat cannot squirm out of the apparatus into which he has been harnessed. The professional bureaucrat is chained to his activity in his entire economic and ideological existence.

A woman clerk at the tax office: *If you want, we can check in detail how the payment was made, if it was late and so on. It is very likely that the government . . . will send you, maybe in five years, an order to pay interest because the tax was paid too late.*

Student: The whole administrative staff under the supreme authority then consists, in the purest type, of individual officials . . . who are appointed and function according to the following criteria: They are personally free and subject to authority only with respect to their impersonal official obligations. They are organized in a clearly defined hierarchy of offices. Each office has a clearly defined sphere of competence in the legal sense. The office is filled by a free contractual relationship. . . . Candidates are selected on the basis of technical qualifications. . . . They are remunerated by fixed salaries in money, for the most part with a right to pensions. . . . The office is treated as the sole, or at least the primary, occupation of the incumbent. It constitutes a career. . . . The official works entirely separated from ownership of the means of administration and without appropriation of his position. He is subject to strict and systematic discipline and control in the conduct of the office.

Woman teacher at the dance school: *And stretch in the air, and press toward the ground, bend and lift your heel, and down, and stay, and . . . Stretch, and "rond," don't stop, don't stop, continuity, stretch back, the heel brings the leg forward, stretch from far and back.*

<u>Student</u>: In that case every single bearer of power and command is legitimated by that system of rational norms, and his power is legitimated insofar as it corresponds with the norm. Obedience is thus given to the norms rather than to the person.

<u>A woman traveler and a male clerk at the station</u>: *Let's do it again with a different date, can you tell me your name and surname? What should I put in the notes? No, it says I must put it here*
—Listen, but you solve the problem instead of reimbursing it maybe you can convert it into a different ticket to . . .
—Yeah, yeah, I'll make you out a new ticket, it doesn't matter. The system doesn't allow the date to be changed
—The system doesn't allow the change? Date . . .
—If you sign here, then I'll make out another one for the other date, good, good, then we are even, 7 and 28, 7 and 28, here it is
—Thanks.

<u>Student</u>: The purely bureaucratic type of administrative organization . . . is the most rational known means of exercising authority over human beings. . . . The whole pattern of everyday life is cut to fit this framework.

<u>At the butcher's shop</u>: *Cooked beef is, is 1,67, 167, ground is 4,74* [noises], *3,61, 2,47 for sausage*
—Thanks, that's all
—Is that all, madam?
—I'll let you know right away: 2, 3, 4, 5, 6, 7 times, yeah.
—A bit more and that'll do.
—Thanks and good day.
—Bye and thank you again.

<u>Student</u>: Already now, rational calculation, is manifest at every stage. By it, the performance of each individual worker is mathematically measured, each man becomes a little cog in the machine and, aware of this, his one preoccupation is whether he can become a bigger cog. . . . it is horrible to think that the world could one day be filled with nothing but those little cogs, little men clinging to little jobs and striving towards bigger ones. . . . This passion for bureaucracy . . . is enough to drive one to despair.

<u>Woman teacher at the dance school</u>: *Please take care with these movements because otherwise they become mechanical, and end themselves and they become . . . sort of sad. Please, let things start from within, from your soul, from your body, from your heart. And always filter, always, mind, heart, body. You.*

The voice of the woman queuing at the station returns; so does that of the student reciting Weber, and the dialogue between sound artifacts and visual artifacts resumes. But now lacking are the gestures and the gaze of the participants in the event, although there are now those of the people intrigued by the unusual audiovisual artifact placed in the faculty lobby. By moving, using his or her empathic capacity and imagination, among the places of the organizational event, the reader has familiarized him or herself with three of the four organizational spaces in which it took place. These spaces were the following:

1. The faculty lobby in which the installation was positioned, together with the equipment for real-time transmission via Internet and the amplification and recording equipment. The morning light illuminating the scene filtered through the three large glass doors of the entrance, and through them passed to and fro students, lecturers, university personnel, and the television and newspaper reporters. On the opposite side of the lobby, three steps and the broad staircase leading to the upper floors constituted "natural" vantage points for watching the performance. On the side not occupied by the installation, the porters continued with their normal work, given that the performance did not interrupt the faculty's usual activities but was supplementary to them.

2. The Main Hall, equipped for teleconferences and video recording. This was the place where the event began. The attendees were welcomed by the chairman; the two lecturers explained what the event was all about. Then the image of the German academic appeared on the large screen behind the speakers as he commented on the event via teleconference from his university in Germany. It was the place in which the performance was discussed by the Italian lecturers, the German academic, the director of the civic art gallery, the artist, students who had helped with recording the workplace conversations, and some members of the public. It was also the place where the event ended: (a) the performance finished with applause for the female student who had led them vocally through it like the magic piper of the Grimm brothers' fairy tale; (b) both the off-line conference and the teleconference concluded.

3. The street outside the faculty where the students were holding their demonstration, and then moved away from the front entrance so that their banners, slogans, amplified voices, chants, and noise no longer disturbed the performance.

4. The screens of computers logged on to the faculty Web site, both internally and via Internet, and on which events in the lobby or the Great Hall could be watched. Although this place of the performance was obviously a space accessible to anyone, it was not utilized by the reader, by the participants, by the student who did the performance, or even by any of the speakers except for the German academic.

But what led up to the performance? And what happened subsequently to it? This is examined in the section that follows, whereas the conclusions consider the new insights that originate from the performance for the aesthetic understanding of organizational artifacts.

THE PERFORMANCE: ARTIFACT-IMAGERY,
ARTIFACT-EPHEMERON, ARTIFACT-SIMULACRUM

I have said that it was the aesthetic sentiment, and the strong emotion aroused by the installation, that fused the student's learning acquisitions from the two courses together. Yet this could not have been anticipated, given that it had not been the artist's intention to represent the sociological problematic of work practices and/or Weber's iron cage. Amid this tangle of sentiments, the performance was—as March (1994) might put it, discussing the "garbage can" model of the organizational decision-making process—a solution looking for a problem: "I could recite the Weber excerpts from inside the installation," the student suggested: "I've studied drama." Should she have been allowed to continue with a study project of such entirely exceptional nature in the faculty—for which, that is to say, there were no socially legitimated practices? The factors that eventually weighed in favor of the performance were the following: (a) the social legitimacy in the faculty of the sociological study of organizational aesthetics as a research topic and an academic subject; (b) the student's past artistic experience, also professional; (c) the fact that there were two faculty courses, rather than only one, involved in the event; (d) the aura of "practice" that surrounded the performance and chimed well with study of organizational practices; and (e) the intention to go ahead step-by-step, seeing how things developed. After all, two of the student's examinations were at stake, and her exploratory work on "what would be beautiful to do" could be assessed as a monographic supplement to the core syllabus.

The occasion that stamped a "style" on this organizational process was the rehearsal of the performance in the art gallery after closing time. The dean of the faculty attended the rehearsal, together with the German professor teaching the course in sociology of art. The dean was impressed by what the female student was trying to do. He understood and admired her work, although everything possible went wrong: The voice recordings were incomprehensible; the student missed cues and forgot part of the script; the emotional support provided by her fellow course members (who had also furnished their own recordings of organizational discourses) did not translate into adequate technical support; the space in which the installation was exhibited was too cramped; and to top it all, the acoustics were dreadful. Despite all these problems, the rehearsal was a success: not because of what could be seen and heard, but because of what was evoked in the lecturers, the dean, and the director of the gallery, viz.:

1. the student possessed the qualities required by the performance: a fine voice, command of gestural communication, and an ability to arouse emotion.

2. the multivoice discourse, the diversity of the work settings in which the voices had been recorded, the swirl of students around and within the installation, all together created a dialogic action with the artwork.

3. the vocal counterpoint between everyday practice in organizations and Weber's sociological reflections was interesting and suited to the faculty's institutional context.

This highlights the aesthetic knowledge on which the lecturers and gallery owners drew: They "felt" that the performance had the potential to become such—in the sense that they had perceived it aesthetically without actually hearing or seeing it. So certain of this perception were they, in fact, that the idea was mooted of organizing a small-scale conference around the performance in order to enhance its value as a didactic innovation. The episode of the rehearsal was thus translated into a course of organizational action of much greater organizational weight: creating space for the innovation in the faculty's teaching program, starting collaborative relations between the faculty and the art gallery, and constructing a scientific debate by holding a conference.

It was thus that the installation entered the university. It was too large to be placed in the Great Hall without removing some of the seats. The only feasible space was the faculty's entrance lobby, the equipping of which to accommodate the performance required involvement of the faculty's IT (information technology) center, the university's multimedia laboratory, and an external technician. But compared to the Great Hall, the lobby had one special advantage that concerned the concept itself of "performance": It did not isolate the performance from the quotidian context, embalming it as a specimen of theatrical recital. On the contrary, precisely because of the lobby's nature as a space through which people entered and left the faculty, even if they did not participate in the performance, it exalted the latter's significance as practice in complex organizational settings. Moreover, the entrance lobby symbolized the temporariness of the performance-as-artifact.

This latter consideration introduces the theme of the ephemeral and of the reproducibility of artifacts. What remained after the performance? The simulacrum of it did (Baudrillard, 1978, 1997), "constructable" from materials that were heterogeneous because they were artifacts from different organizations. These materials were:

- Accounts of the performance published in the local press and broadcast on the local television news.
- The audio and video recordings available at the faculty's web page.
- The audio and visual recording of the teleconference.

- The films and photographs taken by professional television film crews and press photographers, as well as the amateur ones taken by friends and students.

These were the multimedia materials that—enhanced by the memories that they evoked—the student reworked for her degree thesis (Scalfi, 2003), which consisted of a written text and a hypertext CD-ROM. While the student was preparing her thesis, a second artifact was constructed (Gherardi & Strati, 2003): a film of the performance in VHS, DVD, and CD-ROM format, with subtitles in English. The last feature was the quality of the artifact that completed, closed, and stabilized the continuous translation and transmutation of the performance through organizational negotiation. There have, in fact, been no subsequent stagings of the performance and it has been used in its actual form at international conferences—for which purpose the English subtitles were added—and on courses in sociology of organizations and sociology of work (for which the English subtitles are superfluous, given that the courses are taught in Italian).

NEW INSIGHTS INTO ARTIFACTS AND AESTHETICS

The first insight gained from the performance is that its script emphasizes (by default) the importance of the material cultures and artifacts required by its being-in-act for its aesthetic, emotional, and symbol-evocative enjoyment (H. S. Becker, 1982; Fineman, 2000; Linstead & Höpfl, 2000; Rafaeli & Pratt, 1993; Strati, 1999) through the senses (Baumgarten, 1750–1758), through the imagination (Vico, 1725/1968), through taste (Kant, 1790/1968), and at the level of formativity (Pareyson, 1954). But those who rely on writing (as I do in this chapter) are able to evoke the aesthetic that gave rise to the performance by illustrating the artifact as "situated in the practice" of the interactions that it engendered and that themselves imbued it, as well as the scenarios that it depicted and configured for the future.

A second insight furnished is that aesthetic experiences are not invariably of the same intensity, the same strength; they do not have the same capacity to mobilize and connote organizational interaction. It was an aesthetic experience that catalyzed the student's motivation to produce the artifact-performance: It did so because, regardless of the artist's intentions, the artwork in the gallery evoked Weber's iron cage of bureaucracy for her. When the structure of the installation became sinuous and austere, it reminded her of what she had discerned in the recorded workplace conversations: namely, that it is practice that prevails over rule; practice consisting not only of regulations but also of activities that, too, have social legitimacy but are at odds with the regulations, and that indeed circumvent, flout, and make a mockery of them.

Another insight is that, with her initially vague intent to "do something," the student communicated an aesthetic sentiment and an emotion to her fellow students, teachers, and other actors in the performance. They were thus involved, not in "doing" art, but in giving new form to academic work, even though the catalyst had been an aesthetic experience. In other words, this was not a matter of "forming for the sake of forming," as happens in art even at the dilettante level, but of the more general aesthetic experience theorized in Pareyson's (1954) phenomenological and hermeneutic philosophy as "giving shape" to something that does not yet exist in that particular form and corresponding to the interpretative activity of the persons involved. In the case illustrated here, "shape" was given to a dialogue performed visually and vocally and constituted by languages both academic and organizational, as well as being artistically expressed by the installation and the performance.

Described in these terms, it may appear that the process was entirely straightforward and that it uncontroversially yielded only positive outcomes. Instead, mention should be made of certain aspects that show how the beauty of artifacts may conceal the imperfections of the organizational process by which they have been constructed (Strati & Guillet de Monthoux, 2002). In particular:

- The artifact-performance had been socially and collectively constructed by several actors who from time to time gave new form to it, also collectively, in often anarchic and random manner.
- It highlighted the faculty's lack of technical equipment and professional expertise (an outside technician had to be called in), revealed the underfunding of the multimedia laboratory, and led to negotiations whereby, for example, the expense of the recording engineer was shared between the dean's office and one of the teachers.
- It provoked fierce conflict in the multimedia laboratory, because of the professional jealousies caused by the fact that some of the audiovisual technicians, having initially perceived the performance as a minor student work, did not want to participate. Once the performance had grown from a minor event into an artifact that gave professional visibility, they found themselves excluded from it, and clashed with their colleagues who had instead been involved in the social construction of the artifact.
- It disappointed when it was addressed along a single dimension: that of the artist student's performance (as it was perceived by the newspapers, e.g.), Weber's iron cage, practice in organizational life. From heterogeneity and multidimensionality, from evocation on several levels, although constituted of numerous performances, the performance was, to paraphrase Marcuse, reduced to a "one-dimensional artifact."

3

Studying Physical Artifacts:
An Interpretive Approach

Dvora Yanow
California State University, Hayward

> *Built spaces, decor, and so forth "are all symbolic objects . . . which refer to the manners and morals . . . and express the significance of the people and their way of life . . . , [evoking] sentiments about who they are and . . . justifying [a] vision of the [meaning] of their world."*
> —William Lloyd Warner (1959, pp. 44–50 *passim*)

> *It should be noted that I did not count these behaviors or measure them. For I am interested in their meaning, and . . . the meaning of an event is in its relationship to the larger picture, not in the qualities of the event itself. . . . I must know, to derive meaning, exactly how each behavioral unit fits in relation to the others in the larger system. So I shall not present charts and statistics, but only simple descriptions, and later abstractions not unlike those that every clinician makes. The advantage is that* I can retrace my steps and tell exactly how each is derived.
> —Albert Scheflen (1966/1974, p. 184, emphasis added)

One day, during the second phase of a study of the Israel Corporation of Community Centers (Yanow, 1996), I set out to interview the Director of the Community Center—called a *matnas* (accent on the second syllable)—in a place I'd never visited before. As I entered the city, I told myself to head toward the area of the City Hall and the open-air market and to look for a "*matnas* kind of building"—although in that moment, I could not have spelled out the elements of that form. I found the Center in minutes.

What does it mean to talk about "a *matnas* kind of building," and how did I recognize what one was? And why is this important for research? Embedded in this story is a set of ontological and epistemological presuppositions concerning meaning and its communication. These, in turn, shape the methodological considerations which a researcher might engage in studying built space, as well as other physical artifacts; and these considerations themselves direct one to certain methods of inquiry rather than others. Research methods and research questions are intertwined: Methodological presuppositions concerning the ontological status of social "realities" and their capacity for being known are embedded, often without conscious attention, in research questions and research methods alike. Inquiry that starts from the presupposition that human meaning suffuses the artifacts of our creation and that those artifacts enable us to communicate meaning—research that asks not only *what* artifacts mean but also *how* they mean—draws, implicitly if not explicitly, on interpretive methodologies and methods.

These reflect theoretical developments in the social sciences of the last half of the 20th century which have signaled a shift toward the study of meaning (e.g., Fischer & Forester, 1993; Hiley, Bohman, & Shusterman, 1991; Rabinow & Sullivan, 1979, 1985; Van Maanen, 1995). Most of these center on "taking language seriously" (White, 1992)—exploring how language enables the construction of the social world. Yet in contexts of "doing," language rarely works alone to communicate organizational meaning. Research in nonverbal communication suggests that words convey as little as 7% of the meaning in an interpersonal exchange (Mehrabian, 1972). The rest is conveyed through two other categories of artifacts: acts and objects, the physical artifacts we create in organizational (and other) contexts and vest with meaning and through which we communicate collective values, beliefs, and feelings. Among physical artifacts are the spaces in which words are spoken and read and in which organizational members act and interact, as well as the objects that populate those spaces, to which words refer and that acts engage.

Built spaces, their appurtenances, and other physical artifacts are still not widely attended to in organizational studies, over a decade after Gagliardi (1990) noted this absence (a point made also by other authors in this volume; see Yanow, 2003, for an analysis of why this might be so). Likewise, methods for accessing and analyzing object-data in organizational studies have also not received much directed attention. Even those scholars who have attended to physical artifacts (e.g., F. Becker & F. Steele, 1995; Hatch, 1990) rarely reflect explicitly on their methods, let alone on the methodological presuppositions these entail. The absence of such reflective methodological work is understandable—so much of our sensemaking of and response to built space and other artifacts is tacit knowledge that is made explicit only with great difficulty (Polanyi, 1966)—but it has contributed to the sense that interpretive analysis more generally, and the analysis of physical artifacts specifically, are not systematic.

This chapter lays out some of the presuppositions underlying an exploration of objects as central actors in the communication of organizational meaning(s) and then suggests some of the methods by which that might be done. Such delineation illustrates various ways in which this research is, indeed, systematic (Yanow & Schwartz-Shea, forthcoming, offers further evidence). Because the focus is on meaning-centered research, both presuppositions and methods are interpretive, rather than those informed by positivist philosophies. As the category of organizational objects is quite large, the discussion will treat primarily one element: built space. The methods discussed here lend themselves to the study of other objects (and, indeed, also to acts and language), but little attempt will be made to extend the discussion to them more broadly.

METHODOLOGICAL PRESUPPOSITIONS: THE SCIENTIFIC CHARACTER OF INTERPRETIVE METHODS

Interpretive approaches to social science research may be traced to a set of philosophical arguments that developed largely in Europe in the first part of the 20th century, engaging the presuppositions characterizing contemporaneous logical positivism and 19th-century positivist thought. Interpretive and positivist methodological underpinnings differ in their ontological and epistemological presuppositions concerning the character of the research topic's reality and its knowability. These implicate certain procedures of discovery (which themselves then serve to undergird truth value claims). Interpretive scholars—in hermeneutics, phenomenology, and other approaches—hold that a human (or social) science needs to be able to address what is meaningful to people in the situation under study in ways that accurately reflect human knowing processes.

The presuppositions entailed in analyzing physical artifacts in organizations derive largely from two concepts. From hermeneutic scholars comes the notion that artifacts (by which they meant human creations, such as novels and other writing, and by extension, paintings, architecture, etc.) may be "read" to discern the meanings embedded in or projected into them in the process of their creation. And from phenomenology comes the concern with situation-specific local knowledge derived from the lived experience (or "life world": *Lebenswelt*) of members of the setting under study—that is, the meaning(s) they made of those experiences, including in interactions with physical and other artifacts (for further discussion, see Hatch & Yanow, 2003; Yanow, 1996 [chap. 1], 2000 [chap. 1], and the references there).

Both approaches reject the idea that such understanding can be achieved through objective, unmediated observation (indeed, they reject that as even possible conceptually). They draw instead on the Kantian notion that knowing depends on a priori knowledge, and they hold that understanding rests on a process other than that restricted to one or more of the five senses (which was critical positivism's claim). Knowing is an interpretive process: Something "beyond" the senses—the prior knowledge of Kant's argument, termed variously weltanschaaung, frame, lens, paradigm, worldview, mind, consciousness—intervenes to order and shape sensemaking of sense-based perceptions.

Procedurally, such as in the form of participant observation or ethnographic methods, a synthesis has emerged that focuses study on both content *and* form: studying both meaning (the values, beliefs, and feelings of lived experience) and the artifacts that embody meaning—not only language (the original focus of hermeneutic analysis), but also acts and objects (or physical artifacts). The latter development is in keeping with later hermeneutic arguments that argued for treating acts as "text analogues" (C. Taylor, 1971; see also Ricoeur, 1971). Ontologically constructionist (or constructivist) and epistemologically interpretivist—although for the sake of brevity, commonly called "interpretive," echoing "the interpretive turn"—such meaning-oriented approaches are characteristic of space studies in the fields of human and social geography, planning, political and some other philosophy, and semiotics (e.g., Casey, 1993; C. Cooper, 1976; M. Edelman, 1995; Goodsell, 1988, 1993; Gottdiener & Lagopoulos, 1986; Jackson, 1980, 1984; Kirshenblatt-Gimblett, 1998; Lasswell, 1979; Meinig, 1979; Noschis, 1987; Preziosi, 1979; Rapoport, 1976, 1982; Zeisel, 1981; cf. Goodman & Elgin, 1988).

One of their central presuppositions concerns the hermeneutic relationship between meanings—values, beliefs, and/or feelings—and artifacts. The two stand in a symbolic relationship: The artifact is understood to be the more concrete representation of the more abstract, underlying meaning(s). To access organizational meanings, then, one seeks to identify the artifacts commonly used in that organization and to inquire into their significance in organizational terms, to organizational members and/or others (Yanow, 1996, 2000).

As the projections or embodiments of meaning, artifacts are not completely external to the world of their creators or of others engaging them (including researchers), and so their meanings must be interpreted. This is a second central presupposition: Meaning cannot merely be perceived and grasped. Inquiry, then, constitutes an intentional "reaching" for the other's meaning, through "sustained empathic inquiry" (Atwood & Stolorow, 1984, p. 121). Interpretive researchers would typically not seek an understanding of, say, the meaning of a workspace to employees through a survey, seeing survey instruments as reflective more of researchers' prior assumptions than of members' understandings, and as limited in their ability to explore nuances of understanding.

Interpretive researchers, then, are dealing with a double hermeneutic: Their knowledge claims come from interpreting *others'* firsthand experiences (themselves "primary" interpretations) as these are narrated to or observed by them (including reading about them as a form of observation), as well as from reflective sensemaking of *their own* experiences of others' "worlds" (and there are subsequent interpretive "moments" in the writing and in the hearing or reading of the report; Yanow, 2000). Both researcher and researched are situated entities: The meaning making of and meanings made by both are contextualized—a third central presupposition—by prior knowledge, including of history and surrounding elements (other events, other experiences).[1] This has several implications for the character of interpretive research and its practices.

First, presupposing the context-specificity of meaning implies that social "reality" may be construed differently by different people, because of the different "a prioris" they bring to present-day events and circumstances: different personal backgrounds, education and training, experiences, and whatever else has gone into creating an individual's prior knowledge. Even collective meaning is taken to be specific to the situational or cultural context of the group, whether at departmental, organizational, or industry level (see Berger & Luckmann's, 1966, discussion of intersubjectivity). Living in a social world of potentially multiple "realities" and multiple interpretations means that a researcher needs to be aware of the wide variety of "users" of an office space, both near and far (e.g., readers of an annual report containing photographs of headquarters) and must be very cautious about assuming that its design carries the same meaning for all of them. The green color of the bus (Vilnai-Yavetz & Rafaeli, chap. 2, this volume) and the physician's black bag (Fiol & O'Connor, chap. 13, this volume) are examples of other objects embodying divergent meanings.

Second, researchers' interpretations are provisional, subject to corroboration, or refutation, by members of the situation under study, typically through direct inquiry, whether formally convened or informally initiated. Given the context-specificity of artifactual meaning and the possibility for multiple meanings, researchers must treat this provisionality seriously. Inferences are also held up for confirmation or disconfirmation against evidence from other observations, documents, and/or conversations. One of the interesting procedural deliberations in interpretive analysis arises when the researcher's interpretation of events, supported by data and analysis, conflicts with situational members' interpretations.

---

[1]This position is shared by critical theorists and echoed in feminist "standpoint theory" (e.g., Hartsock, 1987; Hawkesworth, 1989; cf. Jacobson & Jaques, 1990). It is in this sense that research writing, itself, constitutes a way of "worldmaking" (the phrase is Nelson Goodman's, 1978; see Yanow, 2000, chap. 6, on this point).

Establishing the trustworthiness of inferences is one of the central areas of debate and development within interpretive research. Though generalizing about processes of meaning making and interpretation, interpretive researchers reject generalizing about the specific meanings of specific artifacts. Interpretive research posits evaluative criteria, in keeping with the need for research to be trustworthy, but that conform with its own philosophical presuppositions (rather than reliability and validity, which emerged from positivist presuppositions; so Whyte, 1943/1955, e.g., had "Doc" review his findings; see Erlandson, Harris, Skipper, & Allen, 1993; Schwartz-Shea, forthcoming).

Third, the constant tacking back and forth in ongoing comparison between the nonverbal data of objects and acts observed and "read" and members' explicit pronouncements, whether in formal or informal speech (including interviews) or in writing, points to one of the strengths of interpretive research: its utility for studying situations in which the meanings of words and deeds are not congruent (described by Argyris & Schon, 1974, as the tension between espoused theory and theory-in-use). In this sense, physical artifacts are a form of deed: a nonverbal enactment of underlying values, beliefs, and/or feelings, which they represent.

When "reaching" for another's meaning, whether as participating situational actors or as nonparticipant researchers, we observe and engage people initially at the most grounded level of lived experience—through what they do and say, including the artifacts used in these—rather than inquiring at the level of abstraction. (A discussion of the meaning(s) of those experiences and artifacts could well move to a higher level of abstraction, but it would always be grounded in the details of lived experience.) Instead of asking the executive director, "What do you value?" we might observe what she is wearing, what kind of car he drives, what sorts of items he displays on his desk, how she acts with her colleagues. We infer meaning(s) from the more directly observable, more tangible artifacts.

It is useful, procedurally and methodologically, to distinguish between methods of accessing data and methods of analyzing them. Accessing object-data is typically done during the "fieldwork" phase of research. Although analytic reflection on these data is not entirely separable from the activities of accessing them, directed, systematic analysis takes place during the "deskwork" phase (typically after leaving the "field" of study, using whatever methods are appropriate). Further analysis often takes place during the "textwork" phase, in which the focus shifts to the preparation of research reports. In actuality, analysis begins with the very framing of the research question and continues on during daily fieldwork and well into the process of writing up findings; during deskwork and even textwork phases, the researcher may even discover the need to return to the field to access additional data. But the distinction between methods of access and methods of analysis highlights the differences between "qualitative" and "interpretive" work (Yanow, 2000).[2]

To think about "accessing" data comes closer to what interpretive researchers do than "gathering" or "collecting" data. In field research, the data themselves—events, experiences, situational actors, conversations, documents—stay in the field (or should!). Unlike the botanical or archaeological or Colonial origins that appear to provide "field" research with its metaphorical roots (and which have at times fostered contemporary legal and ethical contestation over items removed from the field), organizational data are not brought back to the researcher's lab for analysis. What are (legally, ethically, morally) brought back are one's notes (on observations, interactions, conversations, organizational texts), photographs, recordings, or perhaps copies of original texts.

ACCESSING SPACE DATA: CATEGORIES FROM LITERARY ANALYSIS

In general, artifactual data are accessed using one or more of three inquiry processes:

- Through observing (with whatever degree of participating; see Gans, 1976).
- Through talking to people (conversational or "in-depth" interviewing).
- Through identifying, locating, and closely reading or viewing research-relevant documents (e.g., primary data such as memos, correspondence, quarterly and annual reports, web pages, and the like, and secondary data such as contemporaneous newspaper accounts) and/or other materials (e.g., photographs, films, maps, etc.).

---

[2]"Qualitative" methods have increasingly been coming under pressure to conform to the evaluative criteria of quantitative methods—reliability and validity—even though these criteria grew out of a science marked by positivist presuppositions. As researchers yield to these pressures (e.g., adding the trappings of "large-n" surveys to "small-n" case studies), qualitative methods resemble less and less the traditional field studies characteristic of Chicago school–style anthropology and sociology (e.g., H. Becker, Geer, Hughes, & Strauss, 1961; Dalton, 1959; Kaufman, 1960; Whyte, 1943/1955). There are now, in effect, two modes of doing "qualitative" research: one that increasingly conforms to positivist ontological and epistemological presuppositions, and one that adheres to more interpretive presuppositions. Both of these may access data in similar ways, but they part company in their modes of analyzing data. Today, we increasingly have a tripartite taxonomy: quantitative, qualitative-positivist, and qualitative-interpretive.

(Fieldwork also entails taking notes on or recording these in some fashion.) Participant-observer and ethnographic studies typically combine the first two or all three (e.g., Feldman, 1989; Ingersoll & Adams, 1992; Kanter, 1977; Kunda, 1992; Orr, 1996; Rosen, 2000; Van Maanen, 1978, 1991; Yanow, 1996). Space-data are often accessed initially through observing and engaging or using the spaces and their props firsthand and observing others' uses, with interviewing and/or reading to check the researcher's provisional inferences.

"Interviewing" has a specific meaning for interpretive researchers: Unlike survey research, it denotes talking to people in a more conversational mode, with no attempt to minimize or eliminate so-called "interviewer effects" (in keeping with the third presupposition, these are accepted as given). It is also known as "in-depth" or "unstructured" (or sometimes "semistructured") interviewing, although those labels position it as a marked term against the unmarked, "normal" case of survey questionnaires, rather than naming it for its own special qualities (as Schaffer, forthcoming, does, e.g., in naming it "ordinary language interviewing"). Moreover, unlike survey researchers who translate word-data into numbers for purposes of statistical analysis, interpretive researchers accord epistemological legitimacy to interview-generated word-data and retain them for analysis in that form.

Researchers need to identify both potential sources of space (and other) data and processes for accessing them. Burke's categories (1945/1969; see also Feldman, 1995; Gusfield, 1989) for literary analysis, rooted in drama, are useful for thinking about where to find meaning-focused data in an action context. He proposed analyzing human action in terms of the "scene" or setting, as well as the agent, act, agency, and purpose (corresponding to the where, the who, the what, the how, and the why of the episode or event). He thereby enacts a hermeneutic treatment of acts and spaces as text-analogues.

Burke's category set implies a sixth element, made explicit in later "reader-response theory" (e.g., Iser, 1989): audience or reader. This, too, applies one of the central presuppositions discussed previously: In according agency also to audience members, meaning-in-action is seen not only as what was intended by the initiator of the communication but also as entailing interpretations made by the "receiver" (see, e.g., Neuman, Just, & Crigler, 1992). More recent communications theorists have similarly critiqued the earlier, overly simplistic sender-receiver-noise model along agentic, interactive-interpretivist, and/or constructionist lines (see, e.g., L. L. Putnam & Pacanowsky, 1983). According agency to readers-audience members of intended, "authored" meanings—such as the users of an architect-designed office complex—in light of the inherent possibilities for multiple interpretations focuses attention on constructed meanings and the possibility of tensions among situational members' interpretations, something that needs to be explored in any interpretive research. The categories can help a researcher think about where to look to access data in a spatial study.

An extended example, drawn from the research that is the source of the opening vignette, illustrates several of these issues. That study of the Israel Corporation of Community Centers (Yanow, 1996) drew on all three modes of accessing data; those acquired through one mode suggested inquiry to pursue through the others. So, during the second phase of research, at the same time that I was reading memos, correspondence, annual reports, and other written materials in agency archives to see how founders and others talked about agency purposes, I was engaged in extensive conversational interviewing with agency founders and staff and observation of Center (*matnas*) activities. The first phase, some years earlier, had consisted of extended participant observation, during which, among other activities, I used the buildings in various ways: walking through and past them between town centers and market places; entering, ordering a coffee, and sitting in the lounge area to drink it; visiting the library, offices, classrooms, and other areas; talking or dancing or partying with other staff and visitors (clients-customers, other agency professionals, volunteers, etc.) in these spaces, and so forth; all the while watching and listening to others, residents and visitors of all ages, occupations, race-ethnicities, and other "classes," who entered and engaged the space, talking with them about what they were doing there and what they thought and felt about that—in short, by "in-dwelling" with others in very noncompartmentalized ways, following the dictates of my role as community organizer. "Engaging" with the built spaces also entailed engaging with other physical artifacts in them, such as the furnishings, paintings, books, Center programs, and so on (as well as with acts—e.g., the act of soliciting residents' views on program offerings—and language—the metaphor of the Community Center as "functional supermarket," e.g.; Yanow, 1992).

As I embarked on the second phase of the research, then, I felt I was intimately familiar with the buildings from a functional design perspective, but I had not thought much about them as an artifact communicating meaning. Reading in the archives one day, I came upon copies of a few letters written by the then-chairman of the board that referred to the design of the Center buildings. These letters made reference to overall scale, building materials, specific design elements (kinds of rooms, e.g.), and the fact that useful models for community center construction existed in the United States. Not long after that, I set out to conduct the interview about which I wrote at the beginning of the chapter.

This observational experience of locating a never-before-seen building by looking for a "*matnas* sort of space" led me to the reflection, some days later, that the design was, in fact, both distinctive and common to *matnassim* (plural) in different locales. Trying to make explicit to myself what that distinctiveness entailed led me to review the chairman's letters and to consider that his comments were not solely articulations of his personal aesthetic sensibility and values, but rather that he was expressing the intent shared among agency founders to embody and to convey, through the design of the agency's built spaces, certain collectively held values, beliefs, and feelings. I subsequently found articulated in letters written by other board members the same relationship among specific design elements, underlying meanings, and intentional communication to a broad spectrum of "readers" of these built spaces, confirming my provisional interpretation. Two of these letters, in particular, linked these meanings to intended changes in client behavior.

These "organizational" meanings, held collectively by board members and agency staff (and, as I came subsequently to see through other sources, by agency-relevant publics near and far, including would-be clients), comprised the agency's identity and its desired image and were being expressed, in speech, in writing, and in acts, as well as through built materials, to several different, very specific publics, among them clients, other agencies (local, national, and international), and potential donors (also local, national, and international). Here, as I came much later to see, were enacted both hermeneutic and phenomenological principles concerning the artifact-meaning relationship in the context of the life-world of the agency and its collective "Self."

Subsequent conversations (including formal interviews) with founding and later board members, Community Center staff, staff of other agencies, local residents, more distant publics, and others confirmed this desire and intent and indicated how these intended meanings were perceived and understood by others (Yanow, 1996). All of this generated word-data for subsequent deskwork, when I began to make sense of the observations, conversations, interactions, correspondence, and so forth in a more explicitly analytic mode. It also corroborated my provisional sensemaking that organizational meanings were being communicated through the buildings themselves. But how was this happening?

ANALYZING SPACE DATA: NONVERBAL CATEGORIES

There are many modes of interpretive analysis through which space data, as with other physical artifacts, may be approached. They may be analyzed using ethnomethodology, semiotics, symbolic interactionism (see, e.g., Feldman, 1995), or some other focused method, or in a more general social constructionist approach seeking to establish the ways in which spatial elements communicate organizational and other meanings (see, e.g., Goodsell, 1988; Stein, 2001; Yanow, 1993, 1998). As experiencing and sensemaking of built space initially invoke bodily and affective responses rather than cognitive and linguistic ones, insights and categories from research in nonverbal communication are useful analytically in suggesting how meaning processes unfold.

Analyses of nonverbal communication (e.g., Mehrabian, 1972; Weitz, 1974) have generated a set of categories, several of which lend themselves to analyzing settings:

- A "vocabulary" of design elements and construction materials (corresponding to the nonverbal categories of physical characteristics, such as height or body type, and personal decoration, such as clothing, jewelry, etc.; it is analogous to Rafaeli and Pratt's, 1993, "attributes of dress" category).
- "Gestures" that constitute affect and status displays (corresponding to the nonverbal category of facial movements and hand gestures that do the same).
- Design proxemics (measures or indicators of distance and the spatial "bubble" surrounding specific buildings or other spaces).
- "Decor" itself.

The discussion of these analytic categories that follows rests on the following hermeneutic understanding of built spaces. As with other objects, built spaces may be literally mute, but they have their own "language" of design elements through which they articulate properties, identities, values, and so on in a nonverbal way. Much in the way that humans communicate through nonverbal means, built spaces (and other objects) communicate their artifactual meanings nonverbally, through these design elements. And much as some people are more adept than others at "reading" nonverbal human behavior, some are more attuned to "reading" built spaces and other physical artifacts (although enhancing one's abilities is possible in both instances). Analysis of design vocabulary is contextual—glass as a building material may imply one meaning in a warm climate, another in a wintery one—and, hence, often comparative, sometimes explicitly so. A building, a courtyard, a reception area is analyzed in light of the concern, explicit or implicit, "As opposed to what?" Comparative analysis focuses attention on similarities and differences with respect to adjacent and/or surrounding spaces.

Our bodies serve us in interpreting spatial meanings in two ways. First, it is not just that we experience built spaces and other physical artifacts initially through nonverbal, physical means (seeing the award plaque hanging on the wall, and perceiving its shape, color, size, etc., before reading the text; feeling on and through our bodies the mass and scale and "airiness" and lighting characteristics of the oversized, glass-paned entryway into corporate headquarters before focusing on the specific materials). More than that: In many respects, the design of built spaces appears to recapitulate human bodily experience. Lakoff and Johnson (1980) captured this in their analysis of the orientational aspect of a considerable part of American English, as expressed through its metaphors: up–down, front–back, central–peripheral, and so forth. "Up" is associated with control ("He's at the *height* of his power," p. 15); more of something is "up," as the pile gets taller ("My income *rose* last year," p. 16); and "status is correlated with (social) power and (physical) power is up" ("He has a *lofty* position," p. 16). "These spatial orientations," they wrote, "arise from the fact that we have bodies of the sort we have and that they function as they do in our physical environment" (p. 14; see also Casey, 1993, p. 75). To the extent that acts and language are interrelated, our built spaces may "embody" meaning in a quasi-literal as well as a figurative sense. Examples of this follow later.

Researchers' understandings of designed space draw on human bodily experience in a second way. Because of the nonverbal character of spatial communication, in particular, including furnishings, as well as of other physical artifacts, and because of the highly tacit nature (in Polanyi's, 1966, sense) of members' knowledge of the meaning(s) being communicated, researchers commonly use their own responses—affective, behavioral, and especially kinesthetic—as proxy for others' interpretations in formulating provisional inferences about how buildings mean (Yanow, 2000). As Van Maanen (1996) notes with respect to ethnography, "the self is the instrument of research" (p. 380).

Design Vocabularies. Design vocabularies include such things as shape, height, width, mass, scale, the quality of light and dark; materials (glass, wood, cement, stone, shingle) and their color, tone, texture; landscaping (use of water, fences, types of plant materials); and so on. The historical or aesthetic reference points of architectural design (e.g., classical Greco-Roman columns, modernist styling, Japanese materials) and the values, beliefs, or feelings they represent and evoke would also be included here, as would the appurtenances, furnishings, and other "props" populating the spaces. Hospital designers, for example, are increasingly attending to paint colors in halls and rooms, centrally located solaria with plants, lighting, and other elements that affect patients' and visitors' feelings and well-being.

In trying to understand the significance of the Community Center design to clients and potential clients at various socioeconomic levels living in different parts of town, I compared *matnas* buildings with those of other agencies, public and private, intended to serve similar purposes in the same locale (so, the same geographic and socioeconomic context); with other public buildings serving various purposes; and with surrounding residences of various types. The contrast highlighted the features that were unique to the Center buildings, both externally—size, scale, mass, materials (glass, stone), siting—and internally—ceiling heights, furnishings (upholstered armchairs), decorative elements (reproductions of Impressionist paintings).

As with hospital spaces, other buildings' design vocabularies may affect acts (encouraging entrance, e.g.) as well as feelings. Stein (2001) notes how classroom design and school hallways shaped students' movements and comportment. In the Community Center case, Center spaces markedly contrasted with the settings of residents' everyday activities. With such contrasts a built space frames an activity that is not ordinary life—in this case, one of extreme social difference. The effect on residents, removed from the immediacy of the everyday, was to create a receptivity to the organizational meanings represented in these design elements—a socioeconomic and cultural identity that might be theirs some day, as Warner's words (the first epigraph) imply. Although local residents could not afford Community Center materials or furnishings, they could participate in Center programs. The act of entering the Center building and engaging what it contains becomes the symbolic equivalent of acquiring what the building represents—the values, beliefs, and feelings that the Center buildings embodied: the buildings' "cultured, spacious, restful atmosphere," in contrast to their surroundings, "would belong to the world of a higher level of expectations, which would serve as an example of what could be the legacy of its visitors" (chairman of the board, Annual Report, 1973).

Design "Gestures." In the language of spatial design, to speak of gestures is to focus on how a building relates to its surrounding spaces, built and otherwise. Design may be used to suggest relationships, whether affirming or negating: Recapitulating the roof line or materials or colors or aesthetics of a nearby building "gives the nod" to spatial predecessors (whether historical or present) by using complementary design elements; ignoring those elements and using contrasting ones that bear no relationship to them "turns the back" on the new neighborhood. Contrasts of height, mass, quality of materials, and the like may denote or connote not only historical referents, for example, but constitute, in this context, status and/or authority gestures, which are often attributed to the organization that arranged for the design and construction or the retrofit or to the occupying organization, even if it was not the responsible party. A marked height differential, for example, might be seen as the designing organization conveying a "hands off" unapproachability.

In cultures in which quantity is an indicator of status, design entailing expense or height is read with similar meaning. So, for example, in the United States, the larger the office space, the greater the number or the costlier the quality of furnishings, the better the quality of construction materials, and/or the higher the office floor, the higher the rank (typically) of the office's occupant relative to others in that occupational grouping—including of the occupant's secretary relative to other secretaries; and vice versa. As rank is commonly correlated with power, this spatial association is what makes for the seeming anomaly and ensuing surprise at the discovery that persons with lesser rank and its spatial and other artifactual associations—the ground-floor receptionist, the mail sorter in the basement, tech support on the lower floor, or the janitor whose "office" is a closet—may be centers of organizational power (in these cases, due to their respective commands of information, in some cases correlated with physical location). An organization that designs and constructs a new building that "towers" over its surroundings or, comparatively, over others in its industry may be read as intending to signal its higher status relative to those neighboring organizations or competitors.

Interpretations of the meanings of building gestures echo those of physical bodies and the cultural values attached to their various parts. It is common in the United States, for instance, to "read" the top floor office as a symbol of its occupant's high status with n the organization. Humans "embody" vertical, erect bodies; Western society values reason and the rational, which are seen as brain activities; brains reside at the topmost position of our bodies; and so we position "quarters for the *heads*" of our *corpora*tions and *organi*zations—those at the heights of hierarchy (itself part of this conceptual configuration), control, income, and therefore economic, social, and organizational power—at the tops of our buildings. Such correlations play out in community and residential planning as well. In class discussions (as related in Yanow, 1996), students familiar with Oakland, California, topography and socioeconomic conditions will note the local distinction between the wealthier "hill dwellers" and the poorer or working-class "flatlanders." Some correlate this privileging of "up"- or "top"-ness with God's "residence" in the heavens.

Others from non-U.S. cultural backgrounds often interpret spatial meanings differently. An Indian student noted that executive offices in Indian organizations are more typically located on the ground or second through the sixth floors (or were, at least, in the 1980s when these particular observations were made). With little, no or inconsistent electricity and nonexistent or unpredictable elevators, office space on floors easily accessible by foot is more desirable than a grand view (Mazumdar, 1988). Here, too, however, there is a possible body-centered, cultural or meaning-focused explanation for such a design choice, drawing on Hindu traditions. The Upanishads relate that the center of human consciousness lies just below a hand's span from where the lowest ribs converge. Also, according to the legend, the world (in the form of a lotus blossom) sprang from Vishnu's navel while he slept. For a culture that locates the soul in the center of the body and values it (rather than the head) as the source of humanness, it makes less sense for corporate headquarters to be at the heights of buildings (Yanow, 1993).

A Ghanaian confirmed his analysis, indicating that there, also, having one's office on the highest floor would signal that the occupant is of relatively low status. She further noted that only poorer Ghanaians lived in the hills because hill residents had to walk longer distances from the downtown markets, carrying heavy bundles on their heads. Moreover, in Ashanti culture, she said, gods are in the earth as well, and libations are poured to them on the ground. Her American classmates' association of height with the heavens and God and human social status perplexed her.

Design Proxemics.   A third category of analysis parallels Hall's (1966) notion of proxemics—the social and personal spaces between people, and our perceptions of those spaces, that implicitly and tacitly shape human behavior and interaction. In the context of built space, proxemic analysis looks at the spatial relationship of a building (or part of one) to others in the immediate area. As with spatial gestures, this is a relational view that sees built spaces in the context of their surroundings. Whereas gestural analysis examines elements internal to the design itself (whether materials or aesthetics), proxemic analysis considers siting and spacing—the shaping of space through voids ("negative space," or absences) and "intrusions" (or presences). These would include such design elements as setbacks (from the street or pathway, from the sides, at the back), spatial surrounds (open, inviting spaces; narrow, dark alleys; walls or other barriers), and the approaches and activities encouraged or prohibited by these (a broad, open expanse with glass doors might encourage passersby to enter, whereas other design elements might signal that only those who have business inside should enter).

Much as Hall (1966) found that people feel uncomfortable with strangers encroaching on their "personal" space (18 inches to 4 feet, in the North American norm), a sense of discomfort may arise for those who traverse passages between buildings that they experience as too close to each other or who maneuver in office spaces that are too constraining of movement, and so forth. The discomfort may be experienced by onlookers as well. Conversely, a room that is too large for the activity it contains may also be experienced as uncomfortable by those gathered in it (e.g., a hall designed to accommodate 120 people being used for a meeting of 15).

The command of space—especially when a built area leaves large amounts of surrounding property unbuilt and open to view—is often read as a statement of power, much as is a human body that takes up space with an erect posture.[3] Lasswell's (1979) analysis of government buildings and Mosse's (1975) of the Third Reich's architecture focused on the ways in which they took up space vertically and were relatively isolated from surrounding buildings horizontally. Traditional museum and other public building design entails the visual–physical experience of standing at street level and looking upwards toward the entrance. The height is imposing, especially when added to the typical (or stereotypical) museum's or court's or agency's massive and visually impenetrable facade. Visitors often experience this feeling of monumentality as distancing, rather than welcoming.

Decor.   Lastly, built spaces may be analyzed with respect to their "decor" or furnishings, using that term broadly, to encompass not only desks, chairs, and other furniture proper, but also displays of artwork, family photographs, jokes, and cartoons (cf. Hatch & M. O. Jones, 1997; Anand, chap. 5, this volume), signage, and the like. Even uniforms could be considered an element of decor (such as at Disneyland; Van Maanen, 1991): One might argue that "personal decor," in the form of the general dress code, including hairstyles and facial hair, rather than an aspect of personal, individual choice, was externalized, objectified, and collectivized as part of the organizational decor communicating organizational meanings (cf. Pratt & Rafaeli, 1997; Rafaeli, Dutton, Harquail, & Lewis, 1997; Harquail, chap. 9, this volume).

Of the four categories, this is the one that has been most commonly addressed in organizational studies. Company practices developing manuals that stipulate the allocation of desks, chairs, credenzas, works of art, plants, and the like by quantity, size, and compositional materials to organizational members at different hierarchical ranks have been widely noted (e.g., F. Becker & F. Steele, 1995; Doxtater, 1990; Hatch, 1990; Rosen, Orlikowski, & Schmahmann, 1990; F. I. Steele, 1973, 1981).

These four categories are usefully distinct for analytic purposes: Each focuses analytic attention on different ways in which built spaces communicate meaning(s), and the analytic separation imparts some conceptual and procedural systematicity to such studies. In practice they may overlap, as when a pronounced setback from adjacent buildings is read as a gesture signaling higher status (either because it represents a command of wealth, or because it imitates human posture and command of space, or both) or an office building relates to its surroundings through the inter-

---

[3]In many cultures height and broad shoulders, in a man, are signs of physical power and financial or social stature. I cannot demonstrate that built space is correlated with masculinity, only that building design, especially in the corporate and governmental organizational worlds, invokes status symbols associated with culture-specific masculinity. But see Kemper (1990) on the association of testosterone, an erect spine, and a feeling of mastery in men.

play of design vocabularies, gestures, and proxemics. In the Community Center case, analysis of the meanings conveyed through design gestures, proxemics, and decor supported the assessment of the meanings communicated through materials and other design vocabularies.[4]

MAKING SENSE OF SPACES

The systematic character of interpretive space analysis lies in the sustained inquiry over time that is characteristic of these studies, which produces myriad "observations" (in the sense in which that term is used in large-n studies), in the careful choice of sites to observe, individuals to talk to, and documents or other text-analogues to study, and in the procedural systematicity brought about through the various categories for accessing and analyzing data. The dramatistic categories suggest where space-related data and their meanings might be accessed, and there are three processes for doing so; the four nonverbal categories suggest the kinds of communicative processes through which built spaces communicate meanings. In both phases, a context-specific comparative analysis of similarity and difference is central. Although the distinction between methods of accessing data and methods for analyzing them is analytically neat, in practice, analytic categories inform the ways one looks at built spaces, including the kinds of data one looks for.

    In studying built spaces—where the data are the bricks and mortar, so to speak—analysis proceeds by "translating" the visual data into words and verbal categories (e.g., size and scale, stone and glass, blue and green, steps and stories). Even photographs or sketches that are used to portray the spaces do not stand alone: Analysis is mediated by a descriptive narrative that turns visual data into words. Analysis, then, is already one step removed from immediate experience: The experience of space and its

---

[4]The other two analytic categories commonly used in studying nonverbal communication are paralanguage (the sound of the voice) and tactile behavior, or rules for touching, which, as Weitz (1974, p. 203) implies, is one end of the proxemics continuum. Many of the elements subsumed under these categories have also been treated as nonreactive (or unobtrusive) "measures" (Webb, D. T. Campbell, Schwartz, Sechrest, & Grove, 1966/1981). One should proceed with caution, however, in drawing too heavily on the notion of nonreactivity in accessing meaning. Webb and his coauthors were heavily invested in controlling research processes that would "contaminate" the data being accessed, including the impact of the researcher's person—hence, "nonreactivity." From an interpretive perspective, however, so-called "interviewer effects" or "response biases" are accepted as given, following from the third presupposition. Influenced by phenomenological humanism, many interpretive interviewers would argue that it would be unethical *not* to bring themselves into the engagement, quite aside from the impossibility of not doing so, in their view (see, e.g., Holstein & Gubrium, 1995, for an argument in favor of interviewer "reactivity").

meanings is initially one of bodily sensations evoked by visual and spatial elements; initial firsthand sensemaking and interpretation are responses to these, rather than to the words that come later. As Scheflen (1966/1974) notes (in the second epigraph), the research focus is not on measurement as a source of trustworthiness, but rather on descriptions of a sufficient level of detail that they can support inferences (what he terms "abstractions") and enable the researcher to reproduce the reasoning process by which she derived those inferences.

What made the Centers' design distinctiveness stand out was the sharp contrast of their design vocabulary with other buildings serving similar purposes, other public buildings, and local residences. The clearest answer to the question, How do physical artifacts mean? may be, through relationships of similarity and difference to their surroundings. Rafaeli and Pratt (1993) found similar processes at play in their analysis of dress, focusing on its contextual homogeneity and conspicuousness. These comparative elements become occasions for inquiry; the central analytic question is, The same or different with respect to what? Appropriate analytic comparisons may not become evident until one has dwelled with one's data for some time—in the Community Center case, drawing on metaphor analysis in combination with space analysis and finding appropriate comparisons in corner grocery stores and public libraries (Yanow, 2000); and the comparative case(s) may then suggest new ways of seeing, new data to access, and new questions to explore.

It is in this sense, too, that interpretive research is not "rigorous": It is constantly iterative and responsive, even while it is unfolding. Researchers need to be able to respond "in the moment"—in this, interpretive research is like theatrical improv (Yanow, 2001)—to whatever is being done by others with whom they are interacting or to whatever is being said by others they are interviewing. It is accepted practice to redesign an interpretive study while one is in the midst of carrying it out: Because it is so difficult to stipulate ahead of time what will happen in the field, there are far many more feedback loops internal to interpretive research design than there are, say, in experimental design (see Yanow, 2000). But interpretive research is no less systematic for this flexibility.

Space and other artifactual analysis may comprise its own focus or be part of a broader societal study. In the Community Center example, passive, reactive, or proactive engagement by local residents with the Centers' design elements and/or interior spaces (i.e., whether noting them while passing by en route to another destination or through actual physical entry) occasioned a nonverbal interaction between the values built in to those spaces—values of a particular socioeconomic class and its cultural practices, and hence societal status—and their own. Although local residents were, by and large, of a different (lower) class and status, they nonetheless read agency designers' intended meanings in the Center buildings, and responded to them. Data from other, nonspatial areas of the organization (written documents and conversational interviews) supported this argument (Yanow, 1996).

Presupposing that we do live in a world of potentially multiple meanings, and possibly conflicting ones at that, underscores the necessity of exploring design elements from the perspective of each research-relevant audience or group of "readers." It is crucial not to assume uniformity of meaning, that founders' or designers' (architects', CEOs') intended meanings are those that are read in the built spaces by other members of the organization, or that researchers' own personal responses to the space or other artifact are shared by organizational members (see chap. 4 by Elsbach, and chap. 1 by Vilnai-Yavetz & Rafaeli, this volume, for discussions of these points from other perspectives). Different stakeholder groups—different "interpretive communities," "discourse communities," "communities of meaning"—may interpret artifacts differently. These groups may fall along occupational or professional lines, in "communities" of practitioners (Orr, 1992); they may develop along geographic or consociational lines or axes of spatial proximity (an executive and her secretary, e.g.), such that their locational viewpoint creates a community of shared meaning, despite the fact that members conduct disparate practices; or some other organization-relevant or extraorganizational element may occasion shared interpretive perspectives.

This is especially critical when there are differences of power and/or authority between designers and those for whom they design, on the one hand, and workers or clients for whom the design is intended. As M. Edelman (1964) noted, a space that seeks to convey or reinforce such status distinctions "focuses constant attention upon . . . difference . . . ," creating in the participant a "heightened sensitivity" to "connotations . . . [and] authority" (p. 96). This is often the case with government agencies, such as social welfare, automobile licensing, and "justice" offices (jails, courthouses, police departments), as well as in some manufacturing plants or other settings that bring management and labor together in a single space. In addition, in assessing users' experiences of built spaces with respect to the intended meanings of designers and/or their clients, the researcher needs to know whether a building or space was designed for the organization using it or for some other occupant and purpose and retrofitted or taken over for "reuse" by that organization. The research question and setting might also call for attending to the distinction between those who use the built space and those who observe it from a distance, whether near (as passers-by) or far.

Lastly, the language I have used here may seem, at times, either to suggest that buildings speak for themselves or to attribute to them the meanings intended by their "authors" (founders, executives, architects) alone. I have written, for example, "buildings convey," when what I mean is, "the buildings comprise elements that their designers intended to use to convey" or "users and passersby interpret these spatial elements to mean. . . ." I have shorthanded my language to avoid a certain cumbersomeness, but I do not intend to suggest that meaning resides in the artifact. Meanings are what we read in design elements, whether "we" are architects or critics or researchers with a more schooled awareness of such processes or organization-relevant publics with more tacitly known understanding. Settings address a wider audience than that immediately present to observe the acts therein contained, as M. Edelman (1964, p. 100) pointed out, and spatial meanings may well be communicated differently to those who pass through and engage the artifacts and to those who only look upon them. In the end, the interpretation is important not only for its own sake, but, as others have also noted (e.g., Schön & Rein, 1994; Schmidt, forthcoming), for the fact that interpretive schemas typically lead to action along those lines.

4

Perceptual Biases and Misinterpretation of Artifacts

Kimberly D. Elsbach
University of California, Davis

In this chapter, I look at differences between the way physical artifacts are perceived by observers and the way they are intended to be perceived by their displayers. I focus on artifacts that are displayed and observed in corporate office settings which allows me to draw upon recent empirical research and to comment on one of the most common organizational contexts in which physical identity markers are observed (Elsbach, 2004).

In the following sections, I define physical identity markers and review research suggesting that such markers exist and are readily perceived in corporate office settings. I then propose that such markers may be interpreted differently by displayers and observers. I develop a framework, grounded in work on person perception and attribution that describes how and why physical identity markers are associated with such identity misinterpretations. I then illustrate some of these misinterpretations with data from an exploratory study of the interpretation of physical identity markers in corporate office environments. I conclude with a discussion of the theoretical and practical implications of my framework and findings.

Defining Physical Identity Markers

I define physical identity markers as material artifacts that cue and/or affirm a person's social and/or personal identities (Elsbach, 2004). In this definition, *social identities* refer to a person's central, distinctive, and enduring self-definitions based on affiliations with social groups or organizations (e.g., a university professor, a New York Giants fan), whereas *personal identities* refer to a person's self-definitions based on personal ideals and attributes (e.g., an optimist, a lover of Bach; Ashforth & Mael, 1989). Both personal and social identities are defined by the categorizations to which individuals perceive they belong (Brewer, 1991; Elsbach & Kramer, 1996; Frank, 1985). Typically, these identity categorizations define individuals in terms of either status (e.g., relative rank, such as "top-management") or distinctiveness (e.g., relative uniqueness, such as "engineer"; Brewer, 1991; Elsbach & Kramer, 1996; Frank, 1985). That is, personal identity categorizations may say something about how one is distinct and how one ranks compared to other ingroup members, while social identity categorizations may say something about how one's group is distinct and how one's group ranks compared to other groups (Brickson, 2000). As Brewer, Manzi, and Shaw (1993) noted regarding social categorizations:

> Social status and distinctiveness are independent group characteristics, both of which can influence the value of in-group membership and the probability [of group identification]. (p. 89)

Though most social psychological and organizational research has focused on the behaviors of individuals as markers of personal and social identities, recent research has begun to recognize the important role that physical artifacts may play in defining such identities (Dittmar, 1992). Based on this work, I argue that personal and social identity categorizations may be signaled and observed vis-à-vis physical artifacts. As Dittmar (1992) puts it:

> [Material] possessions can symbolize an individual's unique personal qualities, values and attributes, and they can be a symbolic record of personal history and relationships (self-expressive symbols). But material possessions also locate people in social-material terms: they signify the social groups we belong to, social position, and relative wealth and status (categorical symbols). Personal attributes and social locations are integral aspects of identity, as seen by both self and others. Thus, material possessions are important means of constructing, maintaining and expressing both personal and social identity. (p. 380)

In corporate office settings, physical identity markers might include items such as dress, business cards, office furniture, personal mementos, awards, diplomas, artwork, books, calendars, and equipment. Physical identity markers need not be visible to the general public to be identity affirming for an individual. For example, a professor may sport a hidden tattoo as an affirmation of his or her social identity as a "maverick" or "rebel" in a conservative profession. In the same manner, physical markers may be perceived by observers in ways that are unintended by the wearer. For example, a non-sports-oriented person may display a calendar depicting outdoor sports because it was given as a gift by a coworker. Yet, this calendar may be perceived by others as an indication that the displayer should be defined by the social identity of "typical macho male" who affiliates with sports groups and sports fans.

Physical Markers and Identity Perceptions in Corporate Offices

Three areas of research have focused on how physical markers might be perceived as symbols of the social and personal identities of people working in corporate offices: environmental psychology, organizational identity, and impression management. First, research in the area of *environmental psychology* (E. Sundstrom & Altman, 1989) has examined symbolic effects of office design and furnishings (Ornstein, 1989; E. Sundstrom & M. G. Sundstrom, 1986). A review of this research (E. Sundstrom, Bell, Busby, & Asmus, 1996) suggests that physical markers in corporate settings may signal and affirm an employee's identity by defining his or her status and distinctiveness categorizations.

For example, an office's size and location, number of windows, and quality of furnishings are commonly used as indicators of its occupant's organizational rank, prestige, and status (Sundstrom, Town, D. Brown, Forman & McGee, 1982). Although such physical status markers may have little real effect on day-to-day performance, researchers have found that perceived inequities in status markers (i.e., status markers that are incongruent with one's rank) evoke both strong emotional reactions from employees and calls for changes in markers to more appropriate levels (F. I. Steele, 1973). In one study, for example, Greenberg (1988) found that employees, who were placed in temporary offices that were viewed as either higher or lower status than appropriate, adjusted their performance to be in line with their new office (i.e., those in lower status offices lowered their performance, whereas those in higher status offices increased their performance). Appropriate physical status markers appear so important that, even when organizations attempt to remove status markers (e.g., by assigning everyone the same type of workspace regardless of rank), employees have been shown to improvise means of determining status vis-à-vis physical markers (e.g., by supporting unspoken rules about the number of personal artifacts allowed to different levels of management; Elsbach, 2003b; Zenardelli, 1967).

Similarly, research on territorial features of physical environments (I. Altman, 1975) suggests that personalization of one's office through decor and mementos may be a means of establishing personal boundaries that further establish an office worker's status. This type of boundary management is important to "maintain an optimum of accessibility vs. inaccessibility" signals (E. Sundstrom & I. Altman, 1989, p. 180), which are central to perceptions of status.

Finally, office personalization helps workers to signal and affirm distinctiveness categorizations related to individual interests and hobbies. For example, research has shown that workers are willing to forgo more practical privacy features (closeable doors or windows) for items that signal distinctiveness like personally chosen photos and plants (Biner, Butler, Lovegrove, & Burns, 1993).

Second, research in the area of *organizational identity* has examined organizational dress and its effects on corporate workers' perceptions and affirmations of identity (Pratt & Rafaeli, 1997; Rafaeli & Pratt, 1993). A growing amount of this work suggests that individuals may use physical markers in the development of social identities and identifications with their organizations (Ibarra, 1999; Pratt & Rafaeli, 1997).

In this vein, recent research on the symbolic effects of dress by medical professionals (Pratt & Rafaeli, 1997) and administrative assistants (Rafaeli et al., 1997) suggests that choices in clothing and accessories provide employees with a salient means of affirming and expressing their professional roles and identities. For example, in one study, Rafaeli et al. found that dress markers used by female administrative staff at a U.S. business school helped many of these office employees to affirm and signal their functional and hierarchical roles and identities. As one administrative employee noted:

> The other two people in my position who sit out front here, we all pretty much dress similarly—a bit more than casual but not quite business attire. The three admissions counselors always dress in suits and that's just because they are more or less at the supervisory level. . . . I think that if I dress casually, people get the idea that they should feel comfortable to come into the office. Whereas, people up in the placement office, even the receptionists, always wear suits. But up there they deal more with the corporate world than we do. (Rafaeli et al., 1997, p. 19)

In this manner, appropriate organizational dress helped these office employees feel like they fit their work roles and provided them with added confidence and psychological comfort in carrying out those roles.

Finally, psychological and organizational research on *impression management* (Schlenker, 1980) and *first impressions* (King & Pate, 2002) has examined the role of physical markers such as dress, decor, and material wealth on initial and lasting impressions of individuals who display such markers. This research suggests that first impressions of individuals are strongly influenced by easily observable attributes that are seen early on in an encounter. Such attributes include physical attractiveness (Cash et al., 1977), race (Hart & Morry, 1997), voice quality (Berry et al., 1994), manner of dress (Temple & Loewen, 1993), and first names (Steele & Smithwick, 1989), as well as a variety of physical artifacts, decor, and furnishings (Christopher & Schlenker, 2000; Greenberg, 1988; Laumann & House, 1969). Further, research on social cognition suggests that these first impressions tend to be enduring and resistant to change, in part, because they guide and bias all subsequent information processing regarding a target person's attributes. That is, if a first impression suggests that person is highly competitive, observations of subsequent behaviors will be interpreted in ways that support this initial impression, and information that is inconsistent with this initial impression will be discounted, ignored, or not sought out (S. Fiske & S. Taylor, 1991).

More recent research has linked office decor, in particular, to perceptions of individuals' social and personal identities (Dittmar, 1992; Elsbach, 2003b, 2004). This research has suggested that office decor is commonly viewed as an indicator of identity, and that observers may make attributions about displayers' social status and distinctiveness on the basis of a few, salient artifacts displayed in the office of a co-worker.

A FRAMEWORK OF PHYSICAL IDENTITY MARKER (MIS)-INTERPRETATION

Together, the aforementioned work from environmental psychology, organizational identity, impression management, and first-impression research suggests that physical artifacts may be used by corporate employees to signal and affirm their identities at work. Furthermore, this work suggests that displayers typically and routinely portray themselves in desired ways through their choice of physical markers. That is, this work has focused on the successful use of physical markers to display desired identities.

At the same time, however, researchers of social judgment processes (Devine, 1989; S. T. Fiske & Neuberg, 1990; Gilbert, 1989) continue to find evidence that observers are biased in interpersonal perceptions, especially those based on salient and visible cues such as physical markers. In particular, research in the areas of person perception and attribution suggest that observers' judgments of physical markers are likely to be incongruent with the interpretations intended by the displayers. Furthermore, this work suggests that the very characteristics of physical markers that make them useful as signals of their displayers' identities (i.e., the fact that they are salient, relatively permanent, and observable independent of their displayer) contribute to the specific perceptual biases and misinterpretations enacted by observers.

In the following sections, I develop a framework that defines the relationships between: (a) unique characteristics of physical identity markers, (b) observers' perceptual biases that may come into play when assessing physical identity markers of others, (c) displayers' perceptual biases that may come into play when assessing own markers, and (d) potential differences between observers' and displayers' perceptions of the same identity markers. In this manner, this framework describes how identity markers may be misinterpreted by observers.

1. Unique Characteristics of Physical Identity Markers

Physical identity markers are distinct, in three important ways, from more commonly researched behavioral identity markers (e.g., claims of identity, identity-consistent acts, or identity-affirming accounts of acts Elsbach, 2004). First, unlike behavioral markers, which are tightly linked to their displayers, physical markers routinely *exist independent of the displayer* (i.e., a worker's office may be observed even if he or she is absent). Consequently, physical identity markers are likely to be viewed and assessed in situations where the displayer is not present to explain them. Such markers may even be the first information an observer receives about a person (i.e., one may view a coworker's workspace before meeting its inhabitant).

Second, with the exception of dress, most physical identity markers in corporate settings are *relatively permanent* (i.e., they remain in place in an office over long periods of time). As a result of their permanence, choice and display of physical markers may be interpreted as a deliberate act, rather than a quirky one-time act, or temporary lapse of judgment, and may be repeatedly viewed, and reinforced over time as a strong indicator of a stable personality or identity (S. Fiske & S. Taylor, 1991). This contrasts with behavioral markers, which occur at one point in time, and are thus only temporarily observable.

Third, compared to many behavioral markers, physical markers are more likely to be *highly salient* due to their large size, prominent location, novelty, and contrast with surroundings. Cognitive social psychologists have argued that something is salient if it is conspicuous and draws our attention (S. Fiske & S. Taylor, 1991). Furthermore, they have noted that salience may be caused by a number of features, including being novel (e.g., being the only one of a kind), being figural (e.g., bright, moving), being unusual or unexpected, or dominating the visual field (S. Fiske & S. Taylor, 1991). In this manner, office furniture may be salient because it is large and may be seen from a distance, causing it to dominate the visual field and stand out from the surrounding environment. In addition, office decor may be placed prominently so that office visitors are likely to see it (or may have no choice, but to look at it) when they are in a coworker's office. Finally, office decor that is unusual or visually interesting may attract observers' attention merely because it contrasts with most office surroundings.

Of course, behavioral markers that are highly unusual (e.g., a manager making a presentation that sharply criticizes his organization's accepted wisdom) may be just as salient as many physical markers. Yet, I would argue that such salient behavioral markers may be less easily and less commonly used because of the emotional costs that accompany their use. That is, in the case of behavior, researchers have found that social salience is an uncomfortable experience because of the scrutiny that accompanies it (Ickes, 1984; S. E. Taylor, 1981). Such scrutiny has been shown to make salient actors anxious and impair their ability to interact effectively (Lord & Saenz, 1985). By contrast, it seems likely that the display of salient physical artifacts may be less uncomfortable, because those artifacts are less closely tied to the displayer, leading attention to be directed toward the artifact versus the person (S. Fiske & S. Taylor, 1991).

2. Physical Identity Markers and Bias in Observers' Interpretations

Although the above characteristics of physical identity markers make them useful for interpreting identity in organizations, these characteristics also increase the likelihood that physical identity markers will be the subject of cognitively-biased interpretations. In particular, cognitive psychology research suggests that the salience, permanence, and independence of physical identity markers are likely to lead observers to attend to physical artifacts more than other identity markers, to view them in terms of group identity stereotypes, and to use them to make assessments of status (vs. distinctiveness). These biases are explained by research on attribution, person perception, and categorization.

Interpersonal Attribution Biases. Research on the management of social identity suggests that attributional biases, including the fundamental attribution error and actor/observer effect, are likely to occur when observers assess others' identities (Lepore & R. Brown, 1999; Locke & Walker, 1999). A review of research on these attributional biases suggests that these biases may be especially likely when attributions are based on salient, independently observed, and relatively permanent physical identity markers. For example, social cognition researchers have documented the common occurrence of the fundamental attribution error (Ross, 1977), in which observable behaviors are attributed to the person displaying them, rather than situational factors that may produce them. Researchers have suggested that one explanation for the fundamental attribution error is that "what is dominant when one observes another person is that person behaving: the person moves, talks, and engages in other actions that attract attention" (S. Fiske & S. Taylor, 1991, p. 67). By contrast, they suggest that "background factors, social context, roles, or situational pressures that may have given rise to the behavior, are, by contrast, relatively pallid and dull and unlikely to be noticed in comparison to the dynamic behavior of the actor" (S. Fiske & S. Taylor, 1991, p. 67). As a result, visually prominent and salient physical markers may be interpreted as symbols of their displayer's identity.

Closely related to the fundamental attribution error is the actor/observer effect (S. E. Jones & Nisbett, 1972). This effect involves the tendency to perceive others' behaviors as the result of dispositional traits or core identities, while viewing one's own behaviors as the result of situational factors. The actor/observer effect can be explained, at least in part, by the salience of one's own motives versus others' motives. Because one literally cannot "see" one's own behaviors but can see others' behaviors, the latter are more salient. If these behaviors involve the consistent display of physical artifacts, which may be viewed repeatedly, observers may be especially likely to interpret them as symbols of the displayer's identity.

In the decades since these ideas of attribution error and observer bias were introduced, there has been an enormous amount of research that has confirmed their basic tenets and refined understanding of their application (for a review, see Macrae & Bodenhausen, 2000). In general, this research suggests that behaviors are most likely to be attributed to internal traits (e.g., identity affirmations) if they are viewed as specific to the individual (i.e., they are not commonly displayed by all persons) and are enacted consistently over time and across circumstances (i.e., they can't be explained as one-time responses to particular environmental conditions; S. Fiske & S. Taylor, 1991). If we extend these findings about the attributions based on behavior to attributions based on the display of physical markers, these findings suggest that visually salient aspects of an office work environment (i.e., large furniture, prominently displayed photos, unusual artwork) may be interpreted by observers as identity markers (i.e., as intentional signals of the displayer's identity), regardless of their intended use by displayers. Such identity interpretations are also likely to be biased in terms of the dimensions of the artifact that are attended to (see Vilnai-Yavetz & Rafaeli chap. 1, this volume). Thus, Vilnai-Yavetz and Rafaeli note that, depending on the context, observers are likely to attend to only one or two of the three dimensions that define artifacts (i.e., instrumentality, aesthetic value, and symbolism).

Person Perception Biases. Work on person perception (Waibel & Wicklund, 1994) suggests that evaluators may use physical markers, in lieu of more reliable performance indicators (such as assessment of completed tasks), when assessing the attributes or skills of another. Findings of this research suggest that observers rely on physical markers to judge the attributes of others because such markers are (a) visually salient (e.g., it's much easier to see dress than to see "personality") and (b) may be observed in the absence of their displayer (e.g., clothing may be observed in photographs of the displayer, or office furnishings may be observed prior to meeting an office's occupant).

For example, Waibel and Wicklund (1994) found that non-expert judges routinely relied on visible physical markers such as clothing, physical fitness, and hair style (to the neglect of actual task performance) to judge skill level of artists, athletes, and politicians. Furthermore, Wicklund, Braun, and Waibel (1994) found that evaluators who felt uncertain of their own competence (e.g., their business acumen) relied most heavily on such physical markers (e.g., one's automobile, professional clothing, and home furnishings) to judge the competence of others. Wicklund et al. (1994) suggest that such perceptual biases are the result of innate human tendencies to quickly stereotype others through the assessment of easily available cues:

> Underlying this attention to the performer [and his/her visible physical markers] is an earlier-instilled tendency to depend on person characteristics when one does not understand the details of performance. An accompaniment of this dependency on person descriptors is the desire to have an unambiguous portrait, or stereotype, of the performer at one's fingertips. (p. 439)

These findings suggest that degree of competence or skill (i.e., status categorizations) are commonly assessed through physical markers. Such status categorizations may be important to observers because they help them understand their relative standing in comparison with others. As a result, recent research suggests that observers may actively attempt to view physical markers prior to meeting their displayer as a means of determining their relative rank and appropriate behavior in future interactions (Elsbach, 2004a). That is, observers use the fact that they can observe physical markers independent of their displayers to help them assess and maintain status categorizations and hierarchies (Jost & Banaji, 1994). As Elsbach (2004) notes:

> Interpreting the status of a co-worker through office decor may be a priority in situations in which an observer does not know that occupant, but is motivated to maintain status hierarchies. For example, if an employee anticipates meeting a new co-worker, and is worried about maintaining norms related

to rank, the employee may look into the co-worker's office to gain some clues about his or her status. (p. 34)

Categorization Biases.   In addition to being motivated to seek out physical status markers, as suggested earlier, observers may focus on physical status markers as indicators of identity because they are easy to identify and categorize. That is, physical markers of status appear to be widely-known and agreed upon (see Fiol & O'Connor, chap. 13, this volume). In support of this notion, Dittmar (1992) found that observers' evaluations of material wealth (a type of status) could be best explained by a "dominant representations" theory, which suggests that most people, regardless of their own wealth status, make similar attributions of wealth based on observable material possessions. This outcome may result, in part, from the ubiquitous nature of symbols of material wealth (i.e., they are displayed in movies and on television, and may be encountered in retail stores, restaurants, and hotels). Furthermore, the gradations of status are relatively few (e.g., in terms of socioeconomic status, we rely on only three dominant categories: lower-class, middle-class, and upper-class), making them easy to remember and allowing for quick sorting of individual category members. Such links between material artifacts and status perceptions (e.g., quality of furnishings or size of office are linked to managerial status in corporate offices) are so widely agreed upon that organizations may focus on the symbolic value of physical artifacts, to the disregard of their practical value (see Vilnai-Yavetz & Rafaeli, chap. 1, this volume). In this manner, Vilnai-Yavetz, Rafaeli, and Schneider-Yaacov (2004) found that, despite their need for greater space due to their handling of large amounts of paperwork, lower level secretaries in one organization were given smaller offices than their higher level counterparts as a means of symbolizing their relatively low status in the organization.

3.   Physical Identity Markers and Displayers' Bias in Interpretation

The same types of biases that affect observers are likely to affect displayers of physical identity markers. Yet, research suggests that these biases would result in different preferences concerning attention and categorization of such markers for displayers compared to observers. I describe these effects next.

Interpersonal Perception and Attribution Biases.   The actor/observer effect would suggest that, in contrast to observers, displayers are much less likely to view their own physical markers as salient, unusual, and intentionally displayed (and, thus, are less likely to expect observers to view them as identity markers). Displayers of salient physical markers may not perceive them as especially salient or intend them to mark a distinctive identity because they know why they are displayed (e.g., a provocative toy was a gift from a friend), and because they don't appear prominent from their vantage point (e.g., artwork that appears "unusual" to observers may seem "normal" to a person who has much of it in his or her home).

In addition, displayers may be much less likely to view their own displays of artifacts as highly distinctive because they are biased by the false consensus effect (Kassin, 1979). This bias involves the tendency for individuals to see their own behavior as typical (i.e., to assume that under the same circumstances, others would behave in the same way). For example, an office worker who displays a diploma from a top-notch university might assume that everyone who has completed a university degree would want to display a diploma. This displayer may be making this assumption based on easily accessible memories, which typically include those that support existing beliefs (Marks & Miller, 1987). Furthermore, the displayer may resolve ambiguous details (i.e., the fact that displaying a diploma from Podunk U. may, in fact, be seen as a negative, not a positive) in a way that supports his or her chosen course of action (people don't really read the diploma, they just see that there is a diploma). Finally, because observers' reactions to these markers may take place when the displayer is not present (e.g., coworkers may notice office decor when you're not there or not paying attention), the displayer may have little information that contradicts his or her perceptions.

Because of their tendency to view their own behavior as typical and desirable, displayers may also be less aware of violations of norms about status displays. In general, people view public affirmation of distinctiveness categorizations as much more acceptable than the affirmation of status categorizations (Elsbach, 2004). For example, researchers have found that tactics for enhancing status in real-life organizations are more effective when they are subtle and normative (e.g., working hard, displaying knowledge, obtaining an education) than when they are more overt and antisocial (e.g., derogating others, boasting, using deception and self-promotion; Kyl-Heku & Buss, 1996). Despite these norms, displayers may violate them because they don't perceive their displays of status symbols (e.g., awards, diplomas, ostentatious furniture) as unusual or unacceptable.

Categorization Preferences.   Displayers are also likely to differ from observers in terms of their preferences for using physical markers as signals of distinctiveness (vs. status) categorizations. Specifically, displayers are likely to see physical markers as central to their marking of distinctiveness categorizations, whereas they perceive that status categorizations may be affirmed through both physical and behavioral markers. In this vein, Elsbach (2003b) found that occupants of corporate offices that moved to a hoteling arrangement (in which there were no permanently assigned offices, and the display of physical markers was severely limited) were more concerned about their loss of distinctiveness than their loss of status. Elsbach suggests that status was more resilient in the face of marker loss because status could be affirmed through social interactions and behaviors (e.g., high-status people command deference, are seated at the head of the table, and are given authority in decision making), whereas distinctiveness was often displayed only through physical markers (e.g., parenthood could be displayed through family photos, but not through other day-to-day interactions with colleagues).

4. Potential Differences Between Observers' and Displayers' Interpretations of Physical Identity Markers

If we look at the likely perceptual biases of both observers and displayers, there appear to be several potential differences between these two groups' interpretations of physical identity markers. First, observers' biases toward salient artifacts as identity markers compared to displayers' tendency to view both salient and nonsalient artifacts as identity markers, suggests that large, unusual, or prominently displayed physical artifacts will be overweighed as symbols of identity by observers versus displayers (i.e., *observers will be more likely than displayers to interpret on large, unusual, or prominently displayed artifacts as identity markers*). Second, these biases for observers and displayers suggest that permanent and repeatedly observable office artifacts, versus less permanent dress markers, will be overweighed as symbols of identity by observers compared to displayers (i.e., *observers will be more likely than displayers to interpret office artifacts as stronger identity markers than dress*). Third, observers' biases toward finding early cues of status through status symbol artifacts compared to displayers' tendency to perceive their own displays of status symbols as normative, suggests that physical artifacts that are stereotypically viewed as status markers will be overweighed as symbols of identity by observers compared to displayers (i.e., *observers will be more likely than displayers to interpret stereotypical status artifacts as identity markers*). Fourth, because (a) displayers are likely to view physical markers as most important to signaling distinctiveness versus status (i.e., because distinctiveness may be difficult to signal through behavior, whereas status can be easily signaled through social interactions), while (b) observers may more readily identify and categorize status markers versus distinctiveness markers (because there are typically only a few status categories, whereas there are many distinctiveness categories), *displayers are more likely to interpret any physical markers as indicators of distinctive identity categorizations, while observers are more likely to interpret any physical markers as indicators of status identity categorizations*.

Summary and Framework

Together, the aforementioned work suggests that an important means to understanding identity interpretation in organizations is to better understand social judgment vis-à-vis physical markers. In particular, it seems important to understand how judgmental biases may influence interpretations of such markers because such biases may lead to discrepancies between observers and displayers perceptions of identity markers. In turn, identifying and predicting these discrepancies in identity perceptions is important because such differences commonly act as the impetus for identity management (Elsbach, 2003a) and identity change (see Cappetta & Gioia, chap. 11, this volume) by organizations and their members. Based on the preceding review, I offer a framework defining some of the potential cognitive reasons for differences between displayers' and observers' interpretations of physical identity markers in corporate office settings.

PHYSICAL IDENTITY MARKER INTERPRETATION IN CORPORATE OFFICES: AN EXPLORATORY STUDY AND ILLUSTRATION

To begin to explore the relationships suggested in Fig. 4.1, I conducted an exploratory study with 85 full-time managers who worked in corporate office environments in Northern California. This study was intended to provide information about the types of different physical markers used to display and interpret identity in corporate settings, as well as to provide information about the types of differences that may arise between observers' and displayers' interpretations of physical identity markers. As such, it serves mainly as an illustration of the possible forms of identity misinterpretation in corporate settings, rather than as a rigorous test of my model.

Methods. The study used an open-ended questionnaire to gather data. Using this questionnaire, I asked 48 full-time managers who worked in corporate office environments to describe their own use of physical identity markers (defined as physical artifacts, like office decor, office layout, and dress). For each marker I asked them to provide a description of the marker, what that marker said about their identity, what they perceived to be the benefits (if any) of displaying that marker, and what they perceived to be the costs (if any) of displaying that marker. With a similar group of 37 participants, I asked the same types of questions, but requested that, instead of talking about their own marking, they discuss the use of identity markers by others in their work setting (i.e., describe the

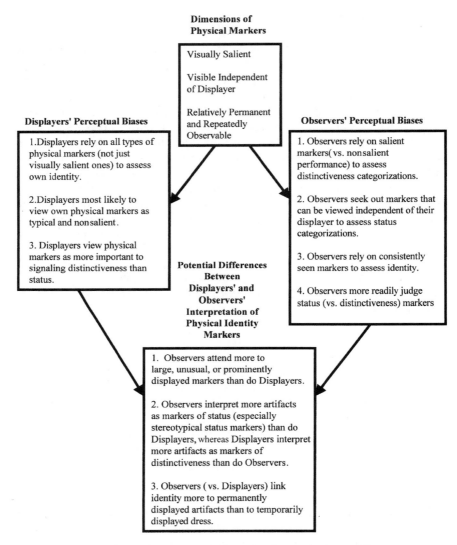

FIG. 4.1.   Relating dimensions of physical makers and perceptual biases to interpretations of physical identity markers.

physical identity markers you've seen others display at work, what do you think they say about the displayer's identity, what are the costs and/ or benefits of displaying such markers at work).

Because this questionnaire design required respondents to identify several specific types of artifacts that they used, it helped us to see not only the range of different types of artifacts respondents viewed as indicators of identity, but also their own perception of different categories of markers (i.e., by listing several specific types of markers and what each type said about identity, respondents provided information about their own grouping of artifacts into discrete categories). Participants identified 129 displayed markers and 125 observed markers. Using their categorizations as a starting point, the author and a second coder grouped the markers into categories based on the physical properties of the marker and its purpose in identity marking (as defined by the respondents). We completed this grouping for displayers and observers separately, and then compared across the two groups for differences. We found that most categories of markers (with a few exceptions) were identified by both observers and displayers. We then identified the identity categorizations associated with each type of marker for both observers and displayers. Based on our literature review, we looked for evidence that markers were used for either status categorizations or distinctiveness categorizations. We defined status markers as those that were used to indicate level of ability, achievement, or prestige (both positive and negative). Interestingly, we found that both observers and displayers were attuned to the potential negative status categorizations that might have been linked to specific markers. We defined distinctiveness markers as those that were used to indicate a distinctive and differentiating skill, ability, interest, background, or set of ideals. We discussed all evidence until we concurred on their categorizations.

Findings. Table 4.1 displays the 10 categories of identity markers indicated by participants. The percentage of displayers and observers indicating each type of marker is also displayed. Table 4.2 displays the perceived identity categorizations (indicated as either status or distinctiveness) associated with each of these markers for displayers and observers.

These tables reveal several interesting findings that relate to general corporate use of physical identity markers and the interpretation of markers. First, employees in corporate settings appeared to display and recognize a variety of physical identity markers—ranging from dress, business accessories, and office decor, to the display of personally created artwork, work-related products, and ideological messages—as cues of personal and social identities. Second, although there appeared to be many unambiguous markers, perceived similarly by both displayers and observers (e.g., family photos, casual dress, and funny artifacts), many markers were perceived differently by observers versus displayers (e.g., awards, formal dress, ideological artifacts). These differences included both discrepancies in the forms of categorizations indicated by each marker (i.e., status vs. distinctiveness categorizations), as well as discrepancies in the particular types of status or distinctiveness categorizations attached to each marker (e.g., professional vs. unprofessional). Finally, many intentionally displayed markers went

TABLE 4.1
Types of Physical Identity Markers*

Office Decor	Examples	Percentage of Displayers Identifying	Percentage of Observers Identifying
Family Photos	school photos of kids, wedding photos	20	11
Hobby Artifacts	posters of skiing, calendars of dogs, photos of fishing trips	16	18
Fun Artifacts	toys, bobble-head dolls, cartoons, silly photos	13	25
Formal Dress	dark-colored suits, white shirts, plain ties, conservative shoes	18	5
Informal Dress	casual pants, open-collar shirts, bright colors and patterns	9	3
Awards & Diplomas	trophies, university diplomas, training program certificates	7	20
Professional Products	product prototypes, industrial tools, professional books	7	8
Ideological Artifacts	religious posters and artifacts, social movement stickers/buttons	5	6
Provocative Artifacts	provocative artwork, controversial ideals/slogans, bright or neon colors, creepy posters/artwork	0	24
High-Conformity Artifacts	very plain and simple office, only standard-issue calendars and furniture, little or no adornment	3	0

Note. Data are based on coding of questionnaire responses and noting participants' own differentiation of artifacts.

unnoticed by observers (e.g., conservative, conforming dress and hair-styles), whereas many observed identity markers were unintended by displayers (e.g., highly salient and noticeable makeup and jewelry). These last two findings support the general notion that observers and displayers of identity markers are likely to interpret these markers in divergent ways.

In terms of my framework of identity interpretations, the evidence in Tables 4.1 and 4.2 provides support for its predictions. First, in looking at the *types of artifacts* that observers versus displayers were likely to notice in Table 4.1 (i.e., the percentage of observers vs. displayers who identified specific artifacts as identity markers), it becomes clear that observers focused their attention on artifacts that are likely to be salient due to large size, novelty, or contrast (e.g., hobby artifacts, fun artifacts, awards, and provocative artifacts), whereas displayers were more likely to attend to artifacts that were lower in salience due to their small size, commonness, and conformity to expectations (e.g., family photos, formal dress). In fact, whereas some of the most commonly cited artifacts by observers were sa-

TABLE 4.2
Interpretation of Physical Identity Markers

| | DISPLAYERS' INTERPRETATIONS | | OBSERVERS' INTERPRETATIONS | |
| | Identity Categorizations | | Identity Categorizations | |
MARKER	Status	Distinctiveness	Status	Distinctiveness
Family Photos		- Family oriented - Have outside life		- Family oriented - Says not always work focused
Hobby Artifacts		- Unconventional	- Unprofessional	- Approachable - Expert
Fun Artifacts Artifacts	- Unprofessional	- Unconventional - Humorous	- Unprofessional	- Self-aggrandizing - Show-off
Formal dress	- Professional - Leader - High status	- Unapproachable - Confident	- High Status	- Friendly - Snobbish
Informal dress	- Unprofessional	- Busy - True engineer - Approachable	- Unprofessional	- Easygoing
Awards, diplomas	- High status - Successful	- Hardworking - Competent	- Competent - Pathetic plea for recognition - Snobbish	
Professional products		- Skilled	- Expert	
Ideological arti-facts		- Noble - Value-driven		- Values profession - One dimensional - Zealot, radical - Idealistic - Activist
Provocative Arti-facts			- Unprofessional - Not a player	- Confident - Insecure
High-conformity Artifacts		- Conservative - Predictable - Cautious		- Distinctive

lient and flashy artifacts (provocative artwork, controversial artifacts), these items were completely missed by displayers (no displayers mentioned these types of provocative artifacts when describing their own identity markers). Although this effect might be due in part to social expectations (i.e., it's not socially acceptable to use flashy or provocative items to affirm an identity), it seems reasonable that these types of items would at least be mentioned, but not referred to as flashy (e.g., "I've got a poster of a nude photograph up"). Together, these findings suggest that observers are likely to interpret visually salient physical artifacts as identity markers, regardless of their displayers' intent.

Second, in looking at the *identity categorizations* that were suggested by specific types of physical markers, it appears that observers were more likely than displayers to interpret physical markers as indicators of status categorizations. As shown in Table 4.2, observers noted seven different types of markers that were indicators of status, whereas displayers only noted four types. Furthermore, as shown in Table 4.1, observers were three times as likely as displayers to interpret stereotypical status markers, such as awards and diplomas, as identity markers than were displayers (i.e., 20% of observers made these categorizations, while only 7% of observers did), and as shown in Table 4.2, observers classified all of these stereotypical status markers as indicators of status categorizations, whereas displayers were equally likely to classify them as indicators of status or distinctiveness. In addition, a number of observers viewed these stereotypical status symbols as indicators of low (vs. high) status.

Findings do not, however, provide strong support for the prediction that displayers would be more likely to focus on the distinctiveness dimensions of physical markers than would observers. The only cases in which this appears to hold are with a couple of markers that may be viewed as stereotypical distinctiveness markers (i.e., family photos and hobby artifacts). With regard to family photos, Table 4.1 shows that twice as many displayers interpreted these were identity markers as did observers (20% of displayers vs. 11% of observers). In the case of hobby artifacts, the percentage of observers versus displayers interpreting these artifacts as identity markers was equivalent (16% for displayers and 18% for observers), but displayers identified these markers as indicators of distinctiveness only, whereas observers noted that hobby artifacts could be markers of both distinctiveness and status.

Third, in looking at differences in observers' versus displayers' attention to *relatively permanent artifacts versus relatively temporary dress markers*, it appears that displayers were more likely than observers to interpret dress as an identity marker. For both informal and formal dress, Table 4.1 indicates that displayers were about three times more likely than observers to interpret these markers as indicators of identity. Furthermore, Table

4.2 indicates that displayers appeared to interpret dress as more distinctive than did observers (i.e., displayers identified more distinctive categories indicated by dress than did observers). For example, some displayers said that informal dress was a clear indicator of being categorized as a "true engineer." By contrast, observers mentioned no functional categorizations linked to dress. This difference in permanent versus temporary marker observation by displayers versus observers suggests that permanent markers are more salient to observers, while temporary dress markers that are, literally, attached to their displayer are quite salient to displayers.

DISCUSSION

Research on identity and perception suggests that people make judgments about a person's character within the first minute of meeting them (Elsbach & Kramer, 2003). Furthermore, research on social cognition suggests that information about a person that is salient and visible is more likely to be noticed and cognitively processed than harder to find information (S. Fiske & S. Taylor, 1991). Together, these findings support the notion that physical appearance plays a critical role in the formation and management of first—and lasting—perceptions. In corporate settings, this means that dress and office decor constitute the front lines of perception formation.

Findings from the present research extends these notions by suggesting that the identities of people working in offices are judged by the physical artifacts that they wear and work near, regardless of their intended use as identity markers. In particular, the framework of physical identity marker interpretation offered in this chapter suggests that differences in perceptual biases affecting observers versus displayers may lead to discrepancies in perceptions of such markers. These findings have implications for theories of social identity and social cognition, as well as for the management of office arrangement and corporate dress guidelines.

Theoretical Implications

The finding that vantage point (i.e., being a displayer vs. observer) affects the type of cognitive processing used to assess physical identity markers provides support and extension to recent models of social cognition that integrate theories of perception and attribution with theories of social identity. As noted earlier, theorists have suggested that social identity categorizations may be prone to errors similar to those found in social cognition research, including the errors of perception and attribution that lead to false stereotypes and prejudice (Lepore & R. Brown, 1999; Locke & Walker, 1999).

The current framework expands upon these notions by suggesting that identity categorizations that rely on physical artifacts may be especially prone to attributional and perceptual biases that lead to differences between displayers' and observers' interpretations of the same identity markers. In particular, it appears that visually salient aspects of an office work environment (i.e., unusual or provocative artifacts, and repeatedly observable artifacts) as well as stereotypical status symbols (e.g., awards and diplomas) are commonly interpreted as identity markers (i.e., as intentional signals of the displayer's identity), regardless of their intended use. In addition, more types of physical artifacts are perceived by observers (vs. displayers) as indicating status categorizations (e.g., unprofessional, high status).

This framework also supports and extends recent theories suggesting that the unique dimensions of physical markers may play specific roles in how they are interpreted (Macrae & Bodenhausen, 2000). Elsbach (2004), for example, found that office artifacts that were viewed prior to meeting their displayer were most likely to be interpreted as status markers, whereas artifacts that were viewed after meeting their displayer were most commonly viewed as distinctiveness markers. Current findings suggest that such tendencies are more likely to occur for observations of other peoples' markers, than for observations of one's own markers. Elsbach also found that because physical markers could be viewed repeatedly, observers were likely to use them as symbols of consistency in identity, rather than change. Again, current findings suggest that such tendencies would be more likely for observations of others' markers than for observations of one's own markers.

There are, however, limitations to the current set of findings. In particular, the current data focus on individual artifacts that observers and displayers recalled as indicators of identity. Yet, research on physical artifacts and perception suggest that attention to such individual artifacts may be preceded by attention to an overall pattern of markers, or general schema of the office decor. In this vein, Burns and Caughey (1992) found that the most common categories used to describe first impressions of set of restaurant interiors were "holistic" impressions (e.g., has a warm vs. cold atmosphere, or modern vs. traditional style), versus specific impressions about artifacts (e.g., types of tables, chairs, or artwork). Because I did not ask observers or displayers to comment on the impressions they got from the entire office, but rather to comment on specific artifacts they used or observed, I cannot comment on their perceptions of an overall gestalt or schema of the offices and their inhabitants. Yet, because this research also focused on offices that were observed repeatedly over time, it seems that such initial impressions probably influenced the responses provided by participants, and that participants' comments about the meaning of specific items could be expected to be consistent with their initial holistic impressions of the office. Future work should look at such overall patterns of markers more directly.

Practical Implications

Because physical identity markers are so readily observable and salient, and because individuals appear to commonly misinterpret them in making identity categorizations, the management of physical surroundings and dress in organizations may be important beyond issues of comfort and practical use. Organizational managers may be faced with the tough question of whether or not to regulate office dress and decor to ensure that employees' identities fit with their desired corporate roles. This may be especially important in alternative office environments (such as nondedicated offices, or drop-in centers), which severely limit employees' ability to display identity markers (Elsbach, 2001). Office decorating and dress guidelines could conceivably affect whether employees view each other as "accessible, team players" versus "unapproachable" or "intimidating."

Even more concerning is the fact that uncensored personalization of office dress and decor may lead to a situation in which certain individuals are shunned from projects and promotions because they are incorrectly identified as "nonmanagerial." The unjustified, negative consequences of racial profiling (i.e., negative or even criminal attributions based solely on one's race; Meeks, 2000) may also plague those who, perhaps unwittingly, display "unmanagerial" identity markers (e.g., dress or office decor inconsistent with a company's norms for managers).

On the positive side, it appears that with experience (or training), employees may come to understand the prototypes of managerial dress and decor in their organization. Although it may seem unpalatable to some to alter their physical identity markers to ensure positive reviews, most employees can be trained to at least understand the "rules of the game." Employees' willingness to play by those rules is another issue.

II

ARTIFACTS AND KNOWLEDGE

What can we learn from artifacts? What role do they play in the transference of knowledge within organizations and across knowledge communities? How does the material world enable organizations to exist? The section highlights the powerful role that artifacts play in the retention, creation, and dissemination of knowledge. *N. Anand* (chap. 5) illustrates how office door cartoons participate in the autoproduction of organizational culture. *Paul Carlile* (chap. 6) then focuses on the characteristics and role of boundary objects. *Anne Cunliffe* and *John Shotter* (chap. 7) continue the conversation on knowledge by noting how linguistic artifacts—such as words, stories, and metaphors—help illuminate distinctions between "knowing" and "knowledge."

5

Cartoon Displays as Autoproduction of Organizational Culture

N. Anand
London Business School

In this study I ask a simple question: Why do organizational members display cartoons on their office doors? In seeking the answer, I explore how organizational members manipulate artifacts within their organization. Schein (1990) defines artifacts as "everything from the physical layout, the dress code, the manner in which people address each other, the smell and feel of the place, its emotional intensity, and other phenomena, to the more permanent archival manifestations such as company records, products, statements of philosophy, and annual reports" (p. 111). Cartoons displayed on office doors fit the description. My research site was a medium-size private university in the southern United Sates. I recorded and interpreted the cartoons displayed on doors of faculty members in various departments of the university in order to make sense of how artifacts are implicated in constructing the culture of an organization (cf. M. O. Jones, 1996). Naturally, I also examine the role of humor—albeit the specific form of visual humor conveyed by cartoons—within the organization.

AUTOPRODUCTION OF CULTURE

Early sociological theories of how culture is produced emphasized the mirroring of the symbiotic relationship between a singular social system and its coherent overarching culture. This formulation was embraced equally by functionalists who believed that a set of monolithic abstract values determines the shape of social structure (e.g., Benedict, 1934), as well as Marxists who assert that those who control the means of wealth production shape culture to fit their own interests (e.g., Adorno & Horkheimer, 1972). More recent theories take the view that culture and social structure are somewhat loosely coupled. The production of culture perspective, for example, was explicitly developed to better understand contexts in which cultural symbols are consciously created for sale (Griswold, 1994; Peterson & Anand, 2004). The production perspective has been adapted to informal situations in which individuals and groups "receive" or "consume" symbolic products and in the process create collective meanings and identities for themselves. Where Adorno and Horkheimer might have viewed the consumption of artifacts as an unreflexive response to the hegemonic seduction of the popular-culture industry, recent studies focus on how different kinds of people such as punks, adolescents, and cross-dressers (see Gelder & Thornton, 1997) actively fabricate their own identity by incorporating mass media symbols. The cooptation of mass-produced cultural artifacts to signal distinctive identity has been termed the "autoproduction of culture" (Peterson & Anand, 2004).

Cartoon displays on office doors are a good exemplar of the autoproduction of culture. In this study, all cartoons displayed were cut out or photocopied from published sources and can therefore be regarded as purposefully created artifacts (Gagliardi, 1990). In this sense, one can understand this type of artifact as if it were an intelligibly assembled symbol with a view to uncovering underlying themes, meanings behind metaphors used, and reasons for choice of certain cartoons rather than others (Hatch, 1993; see also Schultz, Hatch, & Ciccolella, chap. 8, this volume). People manipulate artifacts, to paraphrase Geertz (1973), in order to "say something about something." I rely primarily on an interpretive approach (see Yanow, chap. 3, this volume) to grasp the meaning that is conveyed by the autoproduction of visual humor through cartoon displays. I also take a cue from structure-functionalists such as Radcliffe-Brown (1965) to explore the characteristics of individuals likely to engage in this form of artifact manipulation.

DATA AND METHODS

As I went about collecting the data, it became clear that an appropriate unit of analysis would be the office door cartoon display that could be clearly identified with a single person. Office door cartoon displays fulfill the criteria that define artifacts because they (a) exist independent of the displayer, (b) are relatively permanent, and (c) are visually salient and distinguishable from their surroundings (M. C. Suchman, 2003; see also Elsbach, chap. 4, this volume).

Office door displays seem to be what Durkheim (1965) terms "individual totems" (p. 190): They are not given to, but are acquired by, the person displaying them. To illustrate, on the door of one faculty member in the anthropology department, I found four *Far Side* cartoons. One showed a group of "natives" rushing to hide TVs and VCRs, as they see an individual approaching; one of them, a sentry, shouts, "Anthropologists! Anthropologists!" The other three cartoons are similarly on the theme of anthropology. This example shows up cartoon displays as a voluntary and intentional act of autoproduction on the part of a clearly identifiable actor.

I consulted the undergraduate and graduate bulletins of the university to obtain details of all departments and their locations. Of the 42 departments in the university (the Medical School was excluded because of problems of access), 24 had cartoons displayed in them. In this study I restricted my focus to faculty members who displayed cartoons. All data were collected within the duration of a week. I noted down the content of every cartoon. Table 5.1 lists the demographic details of cartoon displayers in my sample. Of the 666 faculty members in the 42 departments, 71 display cartoons on their door.

More than half the observed departments had at least one faculty member displaying cartoons. Although cartoon display as artifact is easily available to everyone, it is used only selectively. The data in Table 5.1 show that junior members of the organization are more likely to display cartoons: 17.1% of assistant professors display cartoons as opposed to 13.2% associate or 5.2% full professors. Analysis confirms that the difference is statistically significant ($F_{2, 665} = 9.69$, $p < .001$); a test of contrasts shows that assistant professors are more likely to display cartoons when compared to associate ($p < .01$) or full professors ($p < .01$). A greater proportion of female members of the organization (14.5%) display cartoons relative to males (9.5%).

In order to better understand the contexts of the cartoon displays, I left a questionnaire in the mailbox of each displayer that asked for responses

TABLE 5.1
Displayers of Cartoons

	Total	*Displayers*
Academic departments	41	24 (58.5%)
Rank		
Full Professors	306	16 (5.2%)
Associate Professors	173	23 (13.2%)
Assistant Professors	187	32 (17.1%)
Total	666	71 (10.6%)
Gender		
Male	495	47 (9.5%)
Female	171	24 (14.0%)
Total	666	71 (10.6%)

to questions such as: What cartoon strips do you like, and what makes a cartoon good enough to be displayed on your door? The objective was to obtain displayers' views of why they affix cartoons to their doors and to corroborate my own interpretation of the same. Forty-four individuals (62%) responded to the questionnaire and some of their responses are reported later in the chapter. With a few other respondents, I was able to conduct an impromptu interview about their cartoon display when I was caught in the act of collecting data.

Interpretation Protocol

At first glance, cartoons appear to contain very little verbal information. White space predominates most cartoon panels. But as I discovered in the process of data collection, this feature of a cartoon is extremely deceptive. To wit, it took me about 25 minutes and two sheets of letter-size notepaper to write down the contents of a nine-panel *Calvin and Hobbes* strip, along with field notes on what meaning it might convey in view of where it was displayed and by whom. Cartoons are dense with text and meaning and hence are therefore efficient referential and condensation symbols. Referential symbols (M. J. Edelman, 1964) are economical ways of referring to objective elements in objects or situations: Different people identify the elements in the same way. In addition to packing verbal information, cartoons can also pack emotions and affect. This enables cartoons to serve as condensation symbols. Condensation symbols "condense into one symbolic event, sign, or act patriotic pride, anxieties, remembrances of past glories or humiliations, promises of future greatness: some one of these or all of them" (M. J. Edelman, 1964, p. 6).

After noting down the contents of the cartoons that were displayed, I read through all of them and began to look for common underlying themes. I used the concept of "genre" to identify recognizable patterns to interpret the meaning conveyed by the totality of cartoon displays. The genre concept has been applied to recognized forms of communication characterized by structural, linguistic, or substantive conventions (Yates & Orlikowski, 1992). Though I understand that artifacts are inherently polysemic, I relied on the hermeneutic rule of seeking thematic unity (cf. Kets de Vries & Miller, 1987) by trying to categorize each cartoon into a single cogent genre.

I found that four genres emerged from my data (see Table 5.2). The first genre, labeled *communion,* evokes the conventions of the academic profession. The content of cartoons coded into this category suggests that humor is used primarily as a form social control by expressing approval or disapproval of certain types of behavior, expressing group sentiments, and developing and perpetuating stereotypes (Stephenson, 1951). The second

TABLE 5.2
Genres Evoked in Cartoon Displays

Genre	Number of Cartoons	Number of Displayers
Communion		
Structures a shared meaning system by celebrating the conventions of the academic profession—use of subculture-specific language, role distance, and satirizing expected roles	123 (46.6%)	52 (73%)
Crusade		
Reveals various social conflicts that the displayer is implicated in—hierarchical, gendered, and collegial	62 (23.5%)	29 (41%)
Persona		
Makes a reference to an aspect of the displayer's identity as a social being—e.g., parent, spouse, animal lover, etc.	22 (8.4%)	15 (21%)
Relief		
Provides comic relief	57 (21.5%)	21 (30%)
Total	264	71

genre, labeled *crusade,* makes a reference to the displayer's experience of various covert or hidden forms of social conflict within the organization. The third genre, which I call *persona,* evokes some aspect of the identity of displayer. As Freud (1960) noted, much of humor is self-referential, and this point is underscored by the account provided by one of the displayers in response to my question: "What makes a cartoon good enough" to be displayed? "I don't think I have ever put a cartoon on the door just because it was—to me—funny. It is usually a just a . . . representation of my being." Finally, the fourth genre in my data is *comic relief.* Cartoons coded into this genre serve as a release from restraints or controls, be they physiological, psychological, or social (Koller, 1983). I inferred these genres from the entire universe of cartoons display, so it is important to note that individual displayers may be associated with more than one genre. In the following section I explain the four genres in greater detail.

GENRES OF MEANING IN CARTOON DISPLAYS

Communion

Cartoon displays enable communion by invoking references to the conventions of the academic trade, mocking the stereotypes of professionals and students engaged in the occupation, and reflecting on the social distinction created by education. By using specialized vocabulary within the context of a shared meaning system, communication devices such as texts celebrate the social system they are situated in, thereby providing a sense of ritual communion (Carey, 1989). One respondent's criterion for a "good enough cartoon" on my survey was: "Makes those who read it feel part of a group—the *in group* who *gets it*." Communion is the most popular genre in the data (see Table 5.2), in terms of both the numbers of cartoons coded into this category (123 out of 264 or 46.5%), as well as the number of displayers evoking this genre (52 out of 71 or 73%). The choice of cultural goods (such as cartoons, e.g.) within a community helps structure a socially constructed meaning system through the articulation of explicit or tacit rules governing the consumption and exhibition of such goods (Douglas & Isherwood, 1979). Displayers indicate that the primary criterion that makes a cartoon good enough to be displayed is its relevance to their research or teaching interests (see Table 5.3). Consider this *Scarce Side* cartoon displayed by an economist:

Man [down on his knees with a ring, to seated woman]: Julie, there comes a time in every man's life when the expected marginal benefit of continued

TABLE 5.3
Survey of Responses by Cartoon Displayers,
Number (Percentage) Mentioning

Media sources for cartoons	
1. Local newspaper	23 (52%)
2. *The New Yorker*	9 (21%)
Favorite cartoon strips	
1. *The Far Side*	27 (61%)
Single-panel cartoon by Gary Larsen frequently featuring weird animals	
2. *Calvin and Hobbes*	19 (43%)
Multiple-panel cartoon by Bill Watterson featuring a young schoolboy and a stuffed tiger that comes alive in boy's imagination	
3. *Doonesbury*	16 (36%)
Multiple-panel cartoon by Garry Trudeau lampooning contemporary political events	
4. *New Yorker* cartoons	7 (16%)
Single-panel cartoons by various contributors	
5. *Peanuts*	6 (14%)
Multiple-panel cartoons by Charles Schultz featuring lovable loser Charlie Brown, his pet beagle Snoopy, and their friends	
What makes a cartoon good enough *to be displayed on my door*	
1. Is relevant to, or connected with, my research or teaching	29 (66%)
2. Is funny, laughable, interesting, humorous, or tasteful	20 (45%)
3. Is ironic, sarcastic, cynical, paradoxical, obscure, or bizarre	11 (25%)
4. Makes an intellectual point; conveys truth; provides solutions	7 (16%)
5. Is consistent with my sense of self, my views, or my politics	6 (14%)

Note. 44 respondents. All questionnaire items were open-ended.

marital search is equal to the expected marginal cost of the search. Julie, that time has come, will you marry me?

A fruitful consumption of this text can occur only within the context of a meaning system that renders its contents intelligible. While engaging in the act of autoproduction, the displayer assumes that a person reading this text would possess the necessary apparatus (knowledge of expected, marginal, and search costs) required to interpret it.

Similarly, on a display in the Math Department, I found this cartoon celebrating the joys of using a specialized vocabulary (cartoon source unknown)[1]:

Topologist at picnic brings the lemonade in a Klien bottle!

The purely conceptual Klien bottle is the three-dimensional analogue of the two-dimensional Möbius strip. A Klien bottle is hypothesized to have only surface, and consequently cannot contain any fluid. The joke is lost on those who do not know what a Klien bottle is. The point of employing obscure "in jokes" of this sort in an act of autoproduction that can clearly be understood by a particular individuals but not others seems to reflect the joy of simultaneously including those who are part of that subculture by virtue of getting the joke and excluding those who don't get it (Hebdige, 1979).

Cartoons belonging to this genre also show faculty members' playing with *role distance:* that is, they use humor to self-consciously distance themselves from a role that they are expert at playing. While introducing the concept, Goffman (1961) noted that the most careless riders of merry-go-rounds were young children who felt least anxious about the experience and were showing off to younger children who had not quite gotten the hang of it. One faculty member, responding to the question "what makes a cartoon good enough to be displayed?" stated, "[The cartoon] has to be almost totally absurd, or pointedly satirical of academic seriousness." This *Calvin and Hobbes* episode, displayed on three doors, pokes fun at a core academic activity:

Calvin: I used to hate writing assignments but now I enjoy them.
Calvin: I realized that the purpose of writing is to inflate weak ideas, obscure pure reasoning, and inhibit curiosity.
Calvin: With a little bit of practice, writing can be an intimidating and impenetrable fog. Want to see my book report?

---

[1]I have tried to trace and identify the cartoon strip wherever possible, but where I have not been successful I state "source unknown."

Hobbes: "The dynamics of interesting monological imperatives in Dick
          and Jane in psychic transrelational gender modes."
Calvin: Academia, here I come!

Consider this *Far Side* cartoon panel displayed by a professor in the
English Department, a renowned scholar of the literature of the southern
United States, where comic text is used to draw out the ironic contrast between serious literature and "cow poetry" and to signal the displayer's
mastery over more serious forms of poetry:

Cow Poetry.

The distant hills [reads a cow in a classroom]
The distant hills call to me
Their rolling waves seduce my heart
Oh how I want to graze in their lush valleys
Oh how I want to run down their green slopes
Damn the electric fence!
Damn the electric fence!
Thank you.

'Cow Poetry.' The Far Side® by Gary Larson © 1990 by FarWorks, Inc. All
Rights Reserved. Used with permission.

Similarly, in the Business School, a *New Yorker* cartoon displayed by a
strategy professor elegantly mocks the concept of leadership:

[Leader of a pack of wolves howling at the moon]: "My question is: are we
making an impact?"

Cartoons that constitute the communion category also exemplify Radcliffe-Brown's (1965) concept of *joking relationship*: a special form of alli-
ance that is an alternative to a relationship of extreme mutual respect and
restraint such as might exist between teacher and student and is typically
used between groups that are in some way separated through an asym-
metry in terms of power and authority. Humor functions to smooth the interface between two interdependent yet potentially adversarial groups. A
good number of the cartoons reinforce or undermine the stereotype of un-
der- and overachieving students, as well as students' skepticism over the
value of education. An example from the Languages Department:

(*Calvin and Hobbes*)
Miss Wormwood: You have a question, Calvin?
Calvin: Yes! What assurance do I have that this education is ad-
                 equately preparing me for the 21st century?

Calvin:	Am I getting the skills I'll need to effectively compete in a tough, global economy? I want a high-paying job when I get out of here, I want opportunity.
Miss Wormwood:	In that case, young man, I suggest you start working harder. What you get out of school depends on what you put into it.
Calvin:	Oh?
Calvin:	In that case, forget it.

Suchman (2003) notes that artifacts merit study "because of what they reveal about the lives and times of their makers and users" (p. 98). The autoproduction of the communion genre of cartoon displays by faculty members reveals their underlying need to express significant aspects of their professional roles and pursuits, and they seem to accomplish this symbolic activity much in the same manner as has been shown with other social groups such as punks and heavy-metal fans (see Gelder & Thornton, 1997).

Crusade

Cartoons belonging to the crusade genre articulate various forms of social conflict. This genre is constituted by 62 out of 264 cartoons displayed (23.5%) and is used by 29 (41%) displayers. Whereas a cartoon evoking the communion genre emphasizes the cohesiveness and homogeneity of the academic culture, crusade cartoons stress its divisive potential. These two antagonistic genres reveal the polyphonic nature of humor in its capacity to convey both cohesion and conflict (Stephenson, 1951). I noted a variety of conflicts articulated by displayers: hierarchical (anxiety over status differences), collegial (anxiety over dependence on colleagues), and gendered (experienced by women).

A few comic texts displayed by junior faculty members articulate anxiety over professional achievement and voice self-doubt concerning their own competence. As an example of how a hierarchy is embedded in symbolic conflict in organizations, consider these two cartoons, both displayed by assistant professors:

[Dean seated in his office, addressing an assistant professor across the desk]: The barbarians are at the gate Framely, and you talk of tenure. (*The New Yorker*)

[One professor to another]: You already have an endowed chair? Well, I have an endowed parking space! (source unknown)

The following *Far Side* cartoon, displayed by a faculty member who is also the viola player in a virtuoso string quartet, symbolizes the potential for conflict among interdependent colleagues:

St. Peter [at Heaven's gate to a man at the head of a line]: Welcome to heaven
. . . Here's your harp [penciled in by the displayer: "violin, cello, etc."].

Fallen angel [at Hell's gate to a man at the head of a line]: Welcome to hell
. . . Here's your ~~accordion~~ [struck through, penciled in: "viola"].

'Accordion Player.' The Far Side® by Gary Larson © 1986 by FarWorks, Inc.
All Rights Reserved. Used with permission.

The predicament of the viola player is an interesting case of collegial interdependence. Most viola players begin by playing the violin, but later
move to the viola and, typically, do not receive as much acclaim as the first
violinist in the quartet; yet their reputation depends on the competence of
others in the quartet (Murnighan & Conlon, 1991). The predicament may
not be generalizable to this particular viola player, but the improvization on
the cartoon by the displayer is extremely suggestive and provides a great
example of autoproduction at work. The displayer has taken a ready-made
artifact, and with a few deft modifications, has coopted it to symbolize his
angst at being, so to speak, second string to violinists in the quartet.
As an example of how gender is implicated in covert conflict within
this organization, consider this *Peanuts* cartoon displayed by a female faculty member who is involved with the study of Christian religions:

[Marcie and her friend are sitting on bench during the lunch break. Along
comes a boy.]

Boy: Move over little girls, let a man sit down.
Boy: Girls take up too much room. Girls are always in the way.
Marcie: Miriam was Moses's sister in Chapter 12 of the book of numbers.
          She asks, "Has the Lord spoken only through Moses?"

This cartoon, apart from connoting the field of research of its displayer,
also forcefully articulates the gender conflict that is usually suppressed in
organizations (Martin, 1990). Here humor has been used as a form of resistance (Collinson, 1988) related to both gender identity and the social organization of work within academia. Comic texts are also used to give expression to the strife experienced by subaltern groups (such as women) in
redefining images of themselves as competent professionals. One professor, who lists her research interest as "women's fiction, canon process
in literature, feminism, writing (nonfiction genres such as journalism, au-
tobiography)," and who defines a good enough cartoon as one that is
"usually political (about women's issues) and ironic" used the following
Doonesbury cartoon:

Mike: I'm sorry Nicole, I didn't mean to stare at you but you've . . .

Nicole:	Changed, yes. I know I'm not the slick hardbody you recall.
Nicole:	I finally got fed up, Mike. Fed up with all the obsessive behavior, the bingeing and purging, everything I did to pursue the male ideal of beauty.
Mike:	Wow!
Mike:	Still, wasn't it worth it? When you think of it?
Nicole:	You're still evolving, Mike, aren't you?

In this case, the displayer has indulged in the autoproduction of an artifact in order to question the existing state of affairs and to invite others to contemplate how it could be changed. As Schultz, Hatch, and Ciccolella (chap. 8, this volume) observe, in addition to reinforcing organizational values, artifacts are frequently used as symbolic wherewithal in attempts mobilize and motivate people to anticipate an alternative future.

Persona

Cartoons coded into the category of *persona* (see Table 5.2) make a direct reference to a public, or well-known, attribute of the displayer. Twenty-two cartoons (8.4%) coded into the persona genre make references to either the name of displayer, their gender, his or her social roles as parent, spouse, or animal lover, or their favorite pastime. Fifteen displayers (21%) used this genre.

In order understand the humor contained in the cartoons belonging to the persona genre, it is necessary for the observer to invoke some aspect of the identity of the displayer. To illustrate: A faculty member who has no small reputation as an amateur juggler displays a cartoon about jugglers, thereby making a reference to his alter ego as a juggler. Some cartoons were easily coded into this category because of the author's background knowledge about the displayer. Other interpretations were corroborated through questionnaire responses, where the respondent acknowledged the appropriation of public texts for personal voice by making explicit the link between the cartoon displayed and their own persona. For instance, one faculty member who displayed cartoons about cats wrote that a good enough cartoon was one that "I have to find funny personally. Often they reflect my own personal interests . . . cats."

As an example of this category, consider this *Tiger* episode displayed by a faculty member whose first name is Grace:

Tiger:	We were wondering, Julian. You get top grades, play the violin, chess, collect stamps. How do you do all these things?
Julian:	With *grace*.
Tiger:	No wonder, some girl helps him!

Within this genre, I also find instances of cartoons that make a reference to the gender of the displayer. For example, a male philosopher displayed this cartoon:

[Moses on the Mount, addressing himself to God]: Now let's get this straight—Do you want us to cut the ends of our dick off?

Grasping the humor conveyed by cartoons constituting the persona genre requires the observer to be aware of the manner in which the displayer's self is implicated in the cartoon display. The autoproduction of persona genre supports H. Markus and Wurf's (1987) idea of self concept as a "a multi-dimensional, multifaceted structure that is systematically implicated in all aspects of social information processing" (p. 301). Such individuals show a heightened sensitivity to self-relevant stimuli that helps them select self-relevant cartoon panels to use in their comic settings. As one displayer, responding to the questionnaire item relating to sources of cartoons, wrote: "I do not *look* for cartoons for my door—if I see something I use it."

Relief

For the 57 cartoons (21.5%) coded into the relief genre (see Table 5.3), I was not able to discern any direct reference (or connotation) to the displayer. So I have to conclude that the humor in such cartoons is denotative or literal. This *Rubes* cartoon displayed in the Faculty of Music is such an example:

[Two cannibals looking at a stew-pot]: Well, Teflon kettles are simply marvellous! We never have to worry about our guests sticking around after dinner!

This cartoon is relatively free of the milieu in which it is displayed (i.e., the academic community), and conveys its humor through the use of a pun. Perhaps these cartoons were displayed because of the comic relief provided. Twenty percent of my respondents define a good cartoon as one that is "funny," "laughable," "interesting," or "humorous" (see Table 5.3); and, 11% prefer a more acerbic form of wit, using adjectives such as "ironic," "bizarre," "sarcastic," or "cynical" as criteria for a good enough cartoon. The relief theory of humor (see Koller, 1983) holds that humor provides a release from restraints or controls, be they physiological, psychological, or social.

If we move beyond the individual level and speculate about more macrolevel effects of cartoon displays in the manner suggested by Kaghan and Lounsbury (chap. 14, this volume), we could say the autoproduction of the comic-relief genre of cartoons might help negotiate a pleasant, lighthearted, and somewhat welcoming ambiance in what is a very formal higher education institution with well-defined roles and expectations.

CONCLUSION

This study is a unique exploration of autoproduction—how people use mass-mediated artifacts to make personal and idiosyncratic statements about themselves and the social worlds that they are immersed in. However, in the autoproduced form, certain genres found in the mass-mediated world of cartoons are missing. In my data, for example, we find no action-adventure or romance genres of comics (e.g., *Superman, Batman, Modesty Blaise,* or *The Heart of Juliet Jones*) represented at all, not even to make an ironic or sarcastic comment. Instead, the cartoons used are, in some way, humorous. The genre of sexist cartoons popular in men's magazines (see Dines-Levy & Smith, 1988) is completely missing in the autoproduced form, as is any attempt at ethnic or racist humor.

About half of those who responded to my survey mentioned the local newspaper as the sources of their cartoons, and close to a fifth mentioned the *New Yorker* (see Table 5.3, top section). Displayers mention *The Far Side* and *Calvin and Hobbes* as their favorite sources (Table 5.3, middle section). There may be something about the content of cartoons in these two strips that lends itself to faculty members' concerns and allows the cartoon strips to be "borrowed" for autoproduction. The production of culture perspective suggests that users of cartoon displays are constrained in their choice of strips by organizational arrangements within the city that allows for the production and distribution of some cartoon strips but not others. Within such constraints, however, displayers were able to express a variety of intentions through the personal decoration of office space (cf. Scheiberg, 1990): They might refer to their research or teaching interest, state something funny or tasteful, point to something that is ironic or bizarre, make an intellectual point, or signal a point of view (Table 5.3, bottom section).

My data show that those indulging in the autoproduction of visual humor through cartoon displays tend to be junior and to a lesser extent female—subaltern rather than dominant members of an organization. This is in stark contrast to previous findings about the use of verbal humor that is more directly connected with power and dominance as well as active or subversive resistance (Collinson, 2002; Hatch, 1997a). Visual humor is altogether subtler. But such humor is also capable of baring fangs as some of my examples show. Perhaps the particular adaptability of visual humor lies in the fact that it can conceal malice yet allows the covert expression of aggression without the consequences associated with more overt behavior (Stephenson, 1951). Female faculty members seem to have the freedom to express contradictions among expectations of gender, professional, and hierarchical roles that they have to enact in a way that, for example, female employees at Land Rover do not (see Harquail, chap. 9, this volume).

I find that there are recognizable genres in which such artifacts are deployed: cartoons are used to signal communion, crusade, reveal an aspect of persona, or provide comic relief. These genres can be viewed as constituting the social conventions of the organization because "both shape and are shaped by individuals' communicative actions" (Yates & Orlikowski, 1992, p. 300). But conventions are equally defined by what is absent, prohibited, or taboo. As Fiol and O'Connor argue in chapter 13 of this volume, though members of an occupational group have a number of options they could pursue in terms artifacts that could be mobilized as appropriate symbolic vehicles, their ultimate choice of one or other iconic artifact reflects particular concerns about what can and cannot be legitimately expressed to the group's external constituents.

In this chapter I have focused almost exclusively on the symbolic aspects of cartoon displays as artifact. A limitation of my approach is that I ignore two other dimensions of artifact that need heeding in order to avoid what Vilnai-Yavetz and Rafaeli (chap. 1, this volume) call "artifact myopia." In some cases, a faculty member may have displayed cartoons not for the purpose of symbolic communication, but to share in the aesthetic pleasure of cartoons: inter alia, good craftsmanship, interesting use of color, excellent calligraphy, or an interesting resolution of creative tension of some sort.

In other cases, faculty members may use cartoons for instrumental or direct (rather than ambiguous or symbolic) communication. For example, a Business School professor responded to my question "what makes a cartoon good enough to be displayed on your door?" with this answer: "Criteria: (1) Paradoxical. (2) Describes a universal problem. (3) Gives possible solution." The sole *New Yorker* cartoon displayed on his door wonderfully encapsulates his three criteria:

[Executive talking over the telephone]: No, Thursday's out. How about never—is never good enough for you?

This can be interpreted as direct communication on the part of the professor to the effect that he is not interested in meeting students or holding office hours. Unfortunately, due to limitation of space and scope the aesthetic and instrumental aspects of cartoon displays are not adequately analyzed here.

In his seminal article on organizational culture, Schein (1990) observed that "the problem with artifacts is that they are palpable but hard to decipher accurately" (p. 111). In this chapter I have tried to make sense of a set of subtle but nevertheless essential and constitutive artifacts in an organization's culture. What seemed like a fool's errand when I began this study, I hope has turned out to be a fruitful, if somewhat quixotic, endeavor.

ACKNOWLEDGMENTS

I thank Thomas A. Gregor, Richard A. Peterson, Madan M. Pillutla, Mike Pratt, and Anat Rafaeli for comments on earlier versions. I am grateful to the London Business School for a research grant and to the Indian School of Business for providing a residency to help complete this chapter.

PERMISSIONS

I appreciate the permissions provided by Creators, Universal Press, and King Features syndicates to reproduce text from cartoons that I observed.

Calvin and Hobbes © by Bill Watterson. Distributed by Universal Press Syndicate.

Doonesbury © by Garry Trudeau. Distributed by Universal Press Syndicate.

6

Artifacts and Knowledge Negotiation Across Domains

Paul R. Carlile
School of Management, Boston University

OBJECTS AS ARTIFACTS

The material world, in one shape or form, always mediates human activity. People never act in a vacuum or some sort of hypothetical universe of doing but always with respect to arrangements, tools, and material objects (Engestrom, 1990). Even an idea generates value for the individual because it has material-objective force in terms of its consequences in the social world (Strauss, 1993). "Object[s]" write Bowker and Star (1999, p. 298), "include many things—stuff and things, tools, artifacts and techniques, and ideas, stories and memories—objects that are treated as consequential by a community members (Clarke & Fujimura, 1992)." This is sometimes hard to recognize because objects indeed have the power that they do because of the taken-for-granted state in which that exist in a given community. For example, in an academic setting such words as *assistant, associate,* and *full* are objects that have tremendous force in our social interactions because that have consequences on hiring, grant writing, student mentoring, and status. As we struggle to describe the importance of these words to those who have never been in an academic setting, we begin to recognize that they have the force that they do because of their accepted, but taken-for-granted state within our own community.

To understand how objects (artifacts) shape human activity in this chapter I examine organizations that design and build products. The focus of the chapter is on two things. The first is how objects shape or structure the knowledge of the various functional communities that are involved in producing new products (i.e., sales/marketing, design engineering, manufacturing engineering, and production). The objects used by actors within a specialized domain differentiate their knowledge in problematic ways from others, which results in boundaries that make collaboration across them difficult (Carlile, 2002). Second, despite this fact some objects actually help actors from different specialized communities (Lave & Wenger, 1991) to represent, translate, and even jointly transform the knowledge being used to define the product. These objects, what Leigh Star first described as boundary objects (Star, 1989; see also Carlile, 1997), help create a shared context between specialized communities because they help actors share their knowledge and assess the knowledge being used in other specialized communities (J. S. Brown & Duguid, 1991).

To resolve this apparent paradox, that some objects reinforce boundaries between functional domains whereas other objects actually help actors collaborate across the boundaries between functional domains, I outline the characteristics that allow a particular object to play the role of a boundary object. With all this done I then describe what I call a "relational" view, which focuses on the relationship between the actors involved and the boundary objects that they use. This relational view addresses both the *capacity* of the boundary objects to represent the differences and dependencies that are consequential (Carlile, 2004) between them, but also an actor's *ability* (Black, Carlile, & Repenning, 2004) to wield those boundary objects as they seek to represent and even negotiate the knowledge being used to define the product.

MATERIAL ARTIFACTS AND ORGANIZATIONS

The material world is a tangible one—a world of doing. It is a world that takes almost all of our time, but it is a world that is seldom focused on in the social sciences. It belongs to that bulky, but seldom examined category we call "taken for granted," or abstractly covered up by such concepts as technology, task, or even "the environment." But as in most anyone's work, and especially in the product development and manufacturing work being discussed here (Clark & Wheelright, 1995), the material world not only is the medium that shapes the knowledge that individuals use and value, but is also a collective outcome—that is, a social and contested process that produces a final product that can be sold to the customer for a profit.

Since the 1930s the field of anthropology has taken seriously the study of material artifacts in understanding human cultures (Malinowski, 1953; Reynolds, 1987). Besides the observational methods that give easy access to material artifacts, the most important reason why such attention was paid to artifacts was because they were so consequential in making sense of and describing non-Western cultures. In this effort a great deal of attention was paid to artifacts used in cooking, warfare, trade, and rituals. But beginning in the 1970s the new field of science and technology studies in sociology utilized a variety of historical and ethnographic methods that allowed one to explicitly focus on the material artifacts of science and invention to describe at a detailed level the historical evolution and social shaping of science and technology (T. Hughes, 1983; Latour, 1987; Pinch & Bjiker, 1984). In the field of organization studies, we don't begin to see a particular focus on material artifacts except indirectly by those taking a more situated view of technology starting in the 1980s (Barley, 1986; Orlikowski, 1992)—not surprisingly, this work was influenced by both anthropological methods and sociological studies of science and technology.

For the most part those coming from a social-psychological perspective in organization studies have not focused on material artifacts. However, this began to change in the 1980s with Ed Schein's cultural frameworks that emphasized an examination of artifacts as an initial means of understanding an organization's culture. This was followed in the 1990s by a series of scholars focusing on identity and some of the factors that determine belonging or not belonging to a given identity group (see, among others, Hatch, 1993; Pratt & Rafaeli, 1997). Empirically this work focused on such tangible artifacts as dress and other symbols of group identify or status.

Based on my own background in anthropological methods, the work that I started in the mid-1990s explicitly focused on the material objects used by actors in a given functional practice (Bourdieu, 1977) to bring some clarity to how knowledge is shaped differently in organizations and the boundaries or challenges that result (Carlile, 1997, 2002). In what follows, I review some of my work to outline the two fundamental questions laid out at the beginning of this chapter: How do objects structure knowledge in communities differently and how do objects facilitate collaboration across these communities.

THE POWER OF THE MATERIAL WORLD: OBJECTS AND THEIR ENDS

Product development organizations are in the business of designing and producing material artifacts—often at high volume, low variability (high quality), and low cost; and to do this well demands the specialization of knowledge across a variety of functional domains. To achieve such specialization actors in each functional domain create and use different objects and work with them toward different requirements or ends. For example, in sales, the focus is on the numbers (i.e., costing and volume numbers, specifications) and getting them "right"; in design, it is the prototype and hitting the required specification; in manufacturing, it is implementing a high-volume, high–cycle time process; and in production, it is getting good products delivered on time.

Figure 6.1 frames in a simple manner how the material world constrains and enables knowledge in a functional domain or practice. The three basic concepts contained in the graphic are objects/artifacts, problem-solving activities, and ends—three concepts that are interdependent as actors try to accomplish their work.

In a product development context individuals work with numbers, blueprints, faxes, parts, tools, products, and machines that individuals create to test and produce such products. "Ends" are outcomes that demonstrate success in creating, testing, and producing a product—a signed sales contract, a prototype parts order, an assembly process certification, or a high-quality part off the production line. The work itself is an ongoing series of problem-solving activities (Hipple & Tyre, 1996)—a process of moving an object from its initial state to a desired end state. This problem-solving process should be seen broadly, encompassing all of the know-how, techniques, and "trial and error" that it takes to move a material object toward a desired outcome.

The objects and ends of a functional domain are not separate from the problem-solving activities that occupy them. Furthermore, if the relations among artifacts, problem-solving activities, and their ends are dialectically constituted (Lave, 1988), then it is not possible to separate the means of problem solving from the artifacts and their ends. Take, for example, how a material artifact such as a design print is used differently by actors in different functional specialties. To sales, the print represents a one-dimensional object to be used in creating business and negotiating price. For a design engineer, it represents a singular, three-dimensional object

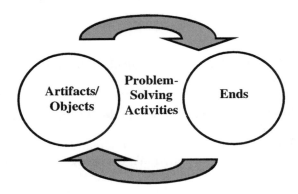

FIG. 6.1.   The material world: objects, ends, and problem-solving activities.

that expresses geometry, tolerances, and other key issues to ensure functionality. To a manufacturing engineer, the print represents the challenge of creating a high-volume process—"how do I make 2,000 of these a day"—requiring attention to the orientation and number of parts, corners, and material surfaces, and cycle time. To a production supervisor, it jogs memories of past bottlenecks, operator errors, and scrap problems that could be encountered. In each case, the print maybe the same, but the problem setting that an individual inhabits shapes what approach they take to the artifact (i.e., design print), what specification and numbers they look at, and what ends they are concerned about. In all of these cases, even though the artifact, the design print, is the same, the ends and the specialized knowledge used to reach those ends are very different.

Also, by focusing on the material world, we develop insight into the characteristics of knowledge that makes it so difficult to communicate or move across functional boundaries. So besides that tacit nature of knowledge (Nonaka, 1994; Polanyi, 1966), by focusing on the artifacts involved we observe that knowledge is localized around particular objects and ends, is embedded in a particular practice, and is invested in a given outcome. This is why, of course, knowledge may be seen as "at stake" (Carlile, 2002) in the sense that communities are reluctant to give up knowledge that has taken them a period of time to earn. Overall, a focus on objects and their ends provides a more concrete description of the situated and invested nature of knowledge than what has often proved illusive when less observational methods are used.

THE SHAPING OF KNOWLEDGE: FOCUSING ON OBJECTS AND THEIR ENDS

This section provides examples of how objects and ends structure actors' knowledge in different ways. I describe two functional domains: design work and manufacturing engineering work. This will provide a clear picture of how the material world faced by these two types of actors creates tensions between their knowledge and interests and generates barriers in their efforts collaborate across functional domains.

Objects and Ends: Structuring Knowledge in Design Work

X.T. Products was in the business of designing and producing a variety of performance and safety values for automotive fuel systems. At X.T. design engineers are handed the task of designing and building a prototype of the product that functions within the specifications defined by the customer. Specifications include overall dimensions, shape (the space the product will be going into), weight, materials, and quantity. Other specifications deal more with the actual mechanical function of the production, such as how efficiently it works (i.e., efficient use of energy), how effectively it does the work that it is designed to do (how well it seals on a surface, cools a room, etc.), and how well it deals with heat, vibration (noise), and overall wear and tear.

Design drawings are a fundamental artifact used in the work that design engineers do. The process of converting specifications into a product starts with a process of sketching, layout, and fine-tuning the dimensions and mechanical relationships on paper. Formal design drawings have to be generated, checked by another engineer to see if all of the dimensions stack[1] properly, and then sent back to the overseeing group of design engineers to identify problems and make recommendations. The goal of the design drawing is to work out all of the special and interdependent relationships so that prototype parts can be machined or ordered from suppliers as soon as possible. In the end, the success of a design engineer depends on their ability to make a physical prototype that can be tested to see if it works according to the required specification.

As I was told by the head design engineer at X.T., hitting "spec" is "science in the making. It is trial and error. It is a lot of work, blood, sweat, and late nights." The trial-and-error character of design work comes into dramatic play as prototype products are assembled for testing. For the design engineer, testing a design is an experience where 3 months of work can be negated with a pressure test that lasts for less than 30 seconds (just enough time to pressurize the valve) or a durability test that take several weeks to get results back. Most tests are often followed with other smaller, more specific tests to pinpoint the particular problem in order to make specific changes in an effort to fix the problem.

At X.T., to fix a problem identified in a test, new sealing materials were often tried, larger or smaller springs were tried, different kinds of plastics were tried (plastics with more buoyancy), or angles were modified. For example, the outcome of testing may alter the design of a part, add in an additional part, or increase the opening size in one chamber of the valve. To access these changes, new drawings have to be worked up and approved, and then new parts either machined or ordered from a supplier. For the design engineer, justifying changes to other engineers and negoti-

---

[1]To see if all of the dimensions "stack up" refers to adding up all of the smaller dimensions to see if they equal the larger dimensions on the outside. This is important because even if the smaller dimensions, say .25 inches, 1.5 inches, and, .75 inches, 1.25 inches, and .50 inches, and .25 inches, do not equal the overall dimension for the part, then the types of relationships (location of the center hole, depth of the inside shelf, and the . . .) could all be off, resulting in prototype parts that don't work, delayed testing results, and eventually a delayed design release.

ating approval from supervisors and customer representatives takes a lot of energy and time. Until the new prototype parts are available, the design process slows to a crawl.

Testing prototypes is the most concrete kind of problem solving that design engineers do. The test results are concrete outcomes of the material world. In many ways, the data from testing the product are as tangible as the product itself, and the success of any design engineering efforts come only after the test results come back positive. A prototype that "passes spec" is a combination of object and end that works—it is an outcome that a design engineer is going to "stand behind."

Objects and Ends: Structuring Knowledge in Manufacturing Engineering Work

In manufacturing engineering, you begin to experience the sheer volume of things—the number of parts, the number of operations, the number of nonconformities—the number of things that can go wrong. This is the world of manufacturing, where the law of large numbers rules. However, the additional challenge here is that each of these numbers has to be loaded, machined, sorted, assembled, and tested. This is where lies the distinction of a "product" engineer and a "process" engineer. A product engineer—a design engineer—worries about the product and its functionality. A process engineer—a manufacturing engineer—worries about the product too (its pieces and functionality), but the problem that he or she has to solve is to design and build "a high-volume process" that creates and assembles millions of parts in an efficient manner. When a manufacturing engineer talks about "process" they are concerned about several issues: how parts will be fed into the system, how parts will be properly oriented during an operation, the speed of each operation (cycle time), how bad parts will be detected, the wear and tear on machines, and how much the process will cost.

Trying to express concerns about orientation, tight corners, sharp edges, and small parts helps get at the differences between assembly prints and design prints—the difference between a manufacturing engineer and a design engineer. An assembly print provides a three-dimensional perspective that shows the interdependence between parts—the parts order, orientation, closeness to other parts, and so on. In a nutshell, one of the most advanced skills of any manufacturing engineer is to be able to look at a two-dimensional design print and put the parts together three-dimensionally in their head. Besides turning two-dimensional designs into three-dimensional perspectives, another difference is how manufacturing engineers look at a tolerance or dimension on a print (i.e., 0.8605 to 0.8606 or one ten-thousandth of an inch—1/10,000).

In building a high-volume process, the constant worry for a manufacturing engineer is variability, but variability comes with the territory of building products in high volumes. The more parts or operations that will occur, the more there is to go wrong. Variability comes in many different forms: (a) environment: humidity, light, dark, dirt, oil, and water; (b) machines: too little or too much pressure, electric fluctuations, test stand out of calibration, breakdowns in the welder or lathe, holding tolerances and flatness; (c) parts: poor fit in the fixture, nonuniformity in parts, misorientation, sticky parts, defects, vendor or print changes on parts; (d) operators: you have to assume the worst, so you can't assume you have a good operator—therefore, you have to verify everything.

For the design engineer, it is a number standing for a specified range— a representation. For the manufacturing engineer, the range is not just a representation, but introduces several practical problems that must be dealt with in order to hold that range at high volume or more descriptively, thousands of times a day: What other tolerances will impinge upon the ability to measure and hold this tolerance, how to hold the part, what kind of machining fixture to use, the order of the machining sequence, what type of tools (how course or fine the grinding wheel), and where to measure or gauge the part from (in relation to what, center hold, location holes, top of part), among others.

Given these issues of high volume and variability, the default for any manufacturing engineer is to "keep it simple, stupid"—the fewest parts and the fewest operations. But if simplicity is not possible, then a manufacturing engineer needs to be able to spend enough money to ensure that a "complex" product can be dealt with at high volume. Such was the case with a complex value such as the OVRV (a product); simplicity was not going to be an option. It was a first-time design with a very complicated functionality requirement. Mick Fry, the manufacturing engineer, kept trying his best to make suggestions to the design team to make it simpler, but that was a battle he was going to lose given the time frame and nature of the current design. Given the number of parts, complex calibration and testing required, volumes scheduled, and cycle time, Mick had solicited three bids from well-established automated assembly system producers. The bids to automate and achieve the kind of quality levels required ranged from $4.25 million to $3.75 million. The cost figure that Mick had been given to work with was $2.0 million. Mick's comment to Ken (head of sales) and any other manager present was that if it wasn't going to be kept simple, then he was going to have to spend nearly double the money to do it right. "Otherwise, this process will be a never-ending nightmare that we will try to tame, but in the end we'll have to live with."

Once a manufacturing process is implemented, it is both an artifact and an end. It is a tangible object in that is made up of various machines and operations, and handles various kind of parts. It is an end also in that it is the ongoing means of manufacturing a product, and so must be lived with and incrementally fined-tuned as best it can be. Unlike a complex product that may have 40 to 60 parts, a manufacturing process is an object that may have well over 10,000 parts. A manufacturing process is an object that is even more complex and harder to change once it is in production. A manufacturing engineer's greatest fear is having to live with or having a stake in a "process" that is plagued with problems. Bill Curl, the head of manufacturing engineering at X.T. Products, quickly pointed out to me how you can tell which engineers have to live with a bad process: "Paul, after you have been here a while, just listen to which manufacturing engineers are always being paged on the intercom to go up on the fourth floor [where most of the production equipment is located]. That is an engineer's [manufacturing] biggest nightmare."

RECOGNIZING AND RESOLVING THE PARADOX OF OBJECTS IN PRODUCT DEVELOPMENT

These examples make clear how the objects and ends of one's functional work structure knowledge differently. Furthermore, these differences create confliction between what is good for each community. Whereas a design engineering needs to build a one-of-a-kind prototype (product) that hits "spec," a manufacturing engineer needs to build a "process" that deals with all the variability of producing such a product 5,000 times a day. However, despite these obvious differences and the conflicts that surround them, I also observed that there were some objects that actors from differently communities used to jointly represent their knowledge, interpret differences (Dougherty, 1992), and negotiate the trade-offs required to resolve cross-functional problems. I first noticed this in situations where individuals from different functions who were sufficiently colocated could go next door and talk about a problem, easily bring a print or part to an ad hoc meeting or conversation, or walk up the stairs and view a machining process. In these cases conversations had a greater capacity in which to exchange concrete details and ideas, create shared problems and generate new agreements, and in the end solve many cross-boundary or cross-community problems. These objects operated as a tangible infrastructure (Star & Ruhleder, 1996) that made cross-functional conversations more concrete and less abstract. They helped represent the knowledge differences and their dependencies between the actors, and made the knowledge boundaries between function domains more visible and "workable." This provided a shared practice where both parties would engage their experiences and problem-solving skills to address these challenging problems that lie between communities.

In Star's (1989) study of heterogeneous problem solving in pharmaceutical research, she observed that in spite of the tremendous differences between scientists in various disciplines, they nevertheless were often very successful in cooperating to create "good science." Scientists were able to be successful through their use of what she called "boundary objects." Star defines boundary objects as "objects that are both plastic enough to adapt to local needs and constraints of the several parties employing them, yet robust enough to maintain a common identity across sites" (p. 42). Star's key observation was that "in heterogeneous problem-solving, it is a problem not in computation, but in representation" (p. 42). The problem, then, is not getting more information, but how one's knowledge or how the objects and ends of one's problem setting are represented to actors in other specialized domains. Star's description of boundary objects gave me a category that began to help me resolve the paradox that I was observing. Of course the question that remains is what are the characteristics that boundary objects have that objects within a community don't have? Before I address this important question, I introduce you to the different types of boundary objects that Star identified and that I used in my own observations.

Types of Boundary Objects in Product Development

To describe the variety of objects and how they were used I have adapted Star's (1989) four categories of boundary objects (repositories; forms and labels; ideal type or platonic object; terrain with coincident boundaries) in the following ways. First, *repositories* (i.e., cost databases, CAD/CAM databases, parts libraries) supply a common reference point of data, measures, or labels across functions that provide shared definitions and value for solving problems. Repositories function advantageously as shared resource from which different actors can pull when doing cross-domain work.

Second, *standardized form and methods* provide a shared format for solving problems across different functional settings. Forms come in a mutually understood structure and language (i.e., standards for reporting findings, problem-solving procedures [8-D Forms, D-FMEA, P-FMEA], engineering change forms, etc.) that make defining and categorizing differences and potential consequence more shareable and less problematic across different settings.

Third, *objects or models* are simple or complex representations that can be observed and then used across different functional settings. Objects or models (i.e., sketches, assembly drawings, parts, prototype assemblies, mock-ups, and simulations) depict or demonstrate the current or possible "form, fit, and function" relationships that define the differences and dependencies between actors.

Fourth, *maps of interdependencies* yield a snapshot of shared boundaries and dependencies that exist between functional settings with different objects and ends. Maps (i.e., Gantt charts, process maps, work flow matrices, etc.) help clarify the interdependencies between different cross-functional problem-solving efforts that share boundaries, resources, or other dependencies (i.e., test results, parts, deadlines).

Even though these four categories of boundary objects are pretty straightforward, the actual role that they play in product development organizations is indeed illusive. For example a design drawing can be useful in driving collaboration between a design and a manufacturing engineer, but when brought to be used with a representative from production who is unfamiliar with its use it can unintentionally be used to steamroll the production person's point of view—resulting in poor agreements and downstream delays. What this reminds us of is that the characteristics that allow them to work effectively are essential but difficult to maintain as circumstances change. To begin the conversation about the characteristics of objects that make them boundary objects it is first important to describe a story that illustrates these characteristics.

Developing Up-to-Date Assembly Drawings in the OVRV Design Review Phase

This story centers around the design review phase of a complex product called the OVRV and is a classic example of the conflicts that occur between design and manufacturing engineering. The OVRV was going to be a boon to X.T.'s future. The OVRV was a product that fit the Environmental Protection Agency (EPA) requirements of having nearly zero gasoline fume leakage from the filler neck of the gas tank (where the hose nozzle is inserted) and from the vapor recovery canister as well. X.T. had been in a race with two other, larger competitors to provide the first working prototype of this "on-board vapor recovery system" for a major automotive firm (Major Automotive). X.T. had been successful in that race and had not only passed Major Automotive's road tests, but had been the only company to even come close. Because of that success, the working prototype was enjoying considerable approval and it embodied X.T.'s future success in the highly competitive automotive marketplace.

As a story of boundary objects, it describes the role of the CAD system as a common repository of information that helps produce a variety of drawings (in this particular case, design and assembly drawings) to be used in cross-boundary settings. The critical characteristic this example illustrates is that both parties need to be able to represent their differences (preferences) and the dependencies or consequences between them in order to create better outcomes. In particular what we see is that when the assembly drawing doesn't reflect the current design the manufacturing engineer lacks the ability and the power to change the design according to what is important within his or her specialization.

Mick had been working on the OVRV project for about 3 months now. He had already been to three design review meetings, and was beginning to anticipate a lot of problems in trying to assemble and test a product with so many parts and critical sealing surfaces. As the soul representative from manufacturing engineering, he was beginning to get not only concerned, but frustrated with how things were going. Even if he wasn't worrying about the specifics in the back of his mind, he knew that the OVRV, with its 3,000,000-a-year volume, presented a completely different "beast" to be dealt with than previous products. And he was determined not to let the situation evolve into its worst-case scenario by having the design frozen the way it was at this point. Mick had already begun to make his case about moving to a four-subassembly design, but so far, he hadn't gotten any significant design changes approved. At this point, Mick's arguments only seemed to be inflaming the tempers of the other team members.

The current working prototype had been developed over a period of 3 years by the Advanced Development Team. They had faced a tremendous challenge in placing all of the EPA's requirements and the functional specifications of Major Automotive's engineers in a plastic canister about the size of short quart bottle. In brief, they had to put a lot of functionality (valves, sealing surfaces, springs, floats, and mechanics) in a very small space. This working prototype was successful not only according to the functional requirements, but also in terms of actually landing the business with Major Automotive and in placing X.T. in the driver's seat to grab the business of another major automotive company as well. Given the difficulties of the design requirements and the success of the working prototype, the current design had set a lot of things in stone. Practically and symbolically, changing aspects of the design to improve its manufacturability was going to be difficult—and besides that, Major Automotive wanted prototype parts to be delivered in less than 8 weeks. This all made for a relentless rush toward the current design.

X.T. had recently invested in a new CAD system, called PRO-E, and they now had the ability to not only design a product, but also do a lot of three-dimensional simulations and manufacturing modeling. The value of a CAD system is that it provides the possibility of a common repository of information (data points, coordinates, drawings, simulations, etc.) that can be utilized by different groups. Here, functional groups with different functional concerns can pull from a common database to make their points, build their arguments, and solve their problems. The problem was that X.T. hadn't been using PRO-E very long, and all of the experienced CAD operators had been pulled into design engineering in order to get the design finalized so prototype parts could be ordered. In essence, all of the PRO-E operators were doing drawings for design work and not for manufacturing. At the time when the OVRV project was first given to Mick and the manufacturing engineering group, they knew they needed the PRO-E tool to be up and running, especially on this product, which contained a lot of new manufacturing challenges to deal with (very high volume, large number of parts, multiple functions to test and verify). At Mick's and another departmental member's suggestion, the head of manufacturing engineering hired a PRO-E draftsman so they could utilize the collected data on the PRO-E system in a way that would demonstrate to the design team Mick's concerns.

One of the challenges that Mick had at previous meetings was that the assembly drawings that he would bring were essentially considered inaccurate because they were not up-to-date with the current refinements to the design. Because of this the designers had a hard time finding the assembly drawings useful. By the time the new PRO-E draftsman got up to speed and had begun to produce assembly drawings and three-dimensional manufacturing simulations that were easily updatable from ongoing design changes made by the design team, there were only 6 weeks left before Major Automotive's prototype parts deadline. In the next OVRV design and review meeting, Mick made the same points he had made before, but now with an up-to-date assembly drawing that reflected the current design. Even though Mick's arguments were no different from the ones he had made before (i.e., difficulties in assembly and testing that would occur), now that the assembly drawing reflected the specs, tolerances, and locations of critical sealing surfaces that were "at stake," they had a very different impact on the design engineers. This allowed Mick to describe in detail the assembly process that would be required to produce the current design and the high scrap rates that would result. On another copy of the assembly drawing, Mick roughed in the groups of parts that would allow for easily testable subassemblies, where they would be attached, and the approximate areas were design changes would be required to connect four "large" subassemblies. After this example was penciled in on the assembly drawing, vigorous discussion began about the benefits and drawbacks of changing the design. One of the drawbacks uncovered was that the current way of attaching parts (a high-velocity spin weld that melts plastic surfaces together) had always resulted in warping parts the size of these subassemblies. As the design engineer, Vaughn was now willing to change the design to accommodate subassemblies—but an alternative way of attaching them had to be found quickly.

Two days later at the next meeting a "snap-fit" design was proposed as a solution. A snap-fit approach had two advantages over the spin weld. First, the snap fit did not involve either a rapid spin weld of plastic parts or the warping and alignment problems that where common in large parts. Second, most of the snap-fit holes and their clips could be placed on the outside of the pump and should not degrade the current functionality of the value in a significant way. Over the following week, during two meetings and several informal conversations around the CAD system, the OVRV was redesigned with four independently testable subassemblies with snap-fit holes and clips providing the connection.

Analyzing the Story

Mick had proposed going to subassemblies in meetings before; what was different this time? In this case, the objects, or more specifically the assembly drawings used by the group in the design and review meeting were different. The assembly drawing that was not current did allow Mick to represent his concerns about assembly and testing in a way that was valid to the design engineers because it did not reflect the current design and concerns of the design engineer. It failed to be a useful tool in representing the differences and dependencies between them. With the up-to-date assembly drawing, however, both Mick and the design engineers were able to represent what was "at stake" for each of them. The assembly drawing also represented their dependencies and their consequences (e.g., how the current design makes "scrap rates" high for Mick or how going to subassemblies might undermine the OVRV's current functional capability). This allowed them to create a joint problem-solving space to develop trade-offs and eventually transform the design to accommodate a new approach (four subassemblies with snap-fit holes and clips).

By forcing explicitness about the specific details of assembling and testing the OVRV, Mick's up-to-date assembly drawing put his "assembly troubles" within the practical grasp of the design engineers. As a boundary object, the assembly drawing provided the practical infrastructure for cross-functional problem solving that led to concrete negotiations and ultimately changes in the design that accommodated four subassemblies. When we examine actors working across boundaries in product development, we see it more clearly as a process wherein each actor can competently represent their knowledge and participate in transforming—redefining and renegotiating the knowledge used to define the design of the OVRV.

THE CHARACTERISTICS THAT MAKE OBJECTS, BOUNDARY OBJECTS

What this example of the up-to-date assembly drawing illustrates is that not every object works as a boundary object. In a collection of more than 65 observations of the use of different boundary objects (i.e., drawings, prototypes, D-FMEA, process maps, etc.) in cross-functional settings, I identified three characteristics of an object that allow it to operate as a boundary object.

First, a boundary object *establishes a shared language for individuals to represent their knowledge.* In the case of Mick and Vaughn, the shareable quality of the assembly drawing as a representation is enhanced because both parties are familiar with it. For Vaughn, the assembly drawing represented critical tolerances and functional specifications. For Mick, the assembly drawing provided a three-dimensional representation of the orientation of parts and critical issues for assembly and testing. The design drawing was not an effective boundary object because what was "at stake" for both the design and manufacturing engineer could not be represented on it.

Second, an effective boundary object *provides a concrete means for individuals to specify and learn about their differences and dependencies—what is new—across a given boundary.* This allows individuals to specify what they know—what they worry about—as concretely as possible to the problem at hand. In the case of Vaughn, the up-to-date assembly drawing allowed him to specify his concerns about important specs and critical sealing surfaces. For Mick, it allowed him to specify the challenges of assembling and testing a complex product at high volume. To deal with a complex knowledge boundary the differences and dependencies between functions or groups must be specified, and the up-to-date assembly drawing identified the critical dependencies between the "functional spec" approach of the design engineers and Mick's concerns about assembly and testing.

Third, an effective boundary object *facilitates a process where individuals can transform the knowledge being used.* If there are negative consequences identified between actors then something must change; and so the actors involved must be able to alter, negotiate, or change the object or representation used (i.e., Mick's knowledge about assembly and testing problems before the updated assembly drawing). If an actor cannot transform the object being used, their knowledge will likely have limited impact on the problem at hand. In the case of Mick and Vaughn, dealing with the consequences identified required them to propose alternatives (i.e., subassemblies) and then alter the knowledge used to define the design (i.e., location of four subassemblies) and the particular manufacturing process developed (i.e., snap-fit holes). Individuals must be able to draw on, alter, or manipulate the content of a boundary object to apply what they know and transform the current knowledge being used to define the problem.

What should now be clear is that the content of a boundary object is no "magic bullet"; rather it is the process that it supports as actors use it to collaborate across boundaries. For example, an assembly drawing can be a boundary object with one set of actors, but can falter when another actor becomes involved who cannot use it to represent the knowledge that is important to them. By understanding the characteristics of boundary objects, we recognize the relational properties that allow an object to operate as a boundary object. These relational properties are defined by the *capacity* of the boundary object to represent the knowledge of consequences and the *ability* of the actors involved to use that object. This relation between boundary objects and actors is another reminder that power has a strong practical impact in working across boundary and collaborating.

When successful outcomes are desired, the capacity of the object to represent the differences and dependencies among actors and the relative ability among the actors to use that capacity has to be addressed. The reason why a boundary object ceases to be one when taken to another setting is that the boundary object can no longer represent what is now of consequence and/or the actors now involved can't adequately use or manipulate the boundary object. So whether the objects are prototypes or clothing or even more abstract cultural artifacts—if one actor has more ability to use or invoke those objects then they will have more power than the other actors involved. As we saw with Mick before the up-to-date assembly drawing, the opposite is also true because at a very practical level he did not have enough power to effectively collaborate with Vaughn to improve the design of the product.

IMPLICATIONS: BOUNDARY OBJECTS AND CHANGE (OR A LACK OF IT) IN ORGANIZATIONS

Although this discussion about boundary objects has focused on their use at a very practical level, the insights developed about their characteristics also apply to the more symbolic artifacts identified by many of the other authors in this book. We see in the case of Schultz, Hatch, and Ciccolella's (chap. 8, this volume) description of corporate branding how artifacts play a role in shaping and transforming the image of a company over time. Harquail's (chap. 9, this volume) focus on employees as branding artifacts raises interesting questions about individuals as boundary objects and how they are used by both the company and customers for each of their respective interests. This indeed raises troubling questions about the power or lack of power that a given actor has as they participate at a boundary with actors who have different interests. Cunliffe and Shotter's work (chap. 7, this volume) describes the importance of relationally responsive knowing for actors to be successful in linguistic interactions. This strikes at a cord similar to the importance of considering the relational properties of boundary objects (both capacity and ability) to fully understand how actors successfully use an object as a boundary object.

Indeed this is a reminder that not only do artifacts have power to shape our lives in organizations, but also that some actors in organizations often have more power in shaping outcomes than others. However, by making the role of artifacts less taken-for-granted and understanding the relational properties involved, all actors in organizations can potentially be more directed in the power that they have, that is, what they can do, to shape events and outcomes.

Linguistic Artifacts in Organizing and Managing

Ann L. Cunliffe
University of New Mexico

John Shotter
University of New Hampshire

> *Only in the stream of thought and life do words have meaning.*
> —Wittgenstein (1981, no. 173)

> *Perhaps what is inexpressible (what I find mysterious and am not able to express) is the background against which whatever I could express has its meaning.*
> —Wittgenstein (1980, p. 16)

> *For a large class of cases—though not for all—in which we employ the word "meaning" it can be defined thus: the meaning of a word is its use in the language.*
> —Wittgenstein (1953, no. 43)

Elsewhere we have discussed how managers create, in meetings with other organizational participants, meanings about the work that needs to go on within the organization (Shotter & Cunliffe, 2002). There, we took a social constructionist approach, which orients us toward the activities of organizing and managing as occurring, not in a world in which organization culture, collaborative action, identities, decisions, and so on, are all already-existing entities, but are always being constructed and reconstructed in dialogic exchanges between organizational members. This approach has relevance to the theme of the present book in the sense that the artifacts that can play a role in organizations include not only physical objects and behavioral manifestations, but also linguistic artifacts: words, stories, metaphors, and the like.

As Gergen (1985) suggests, "the world is understood [as] social artifacts, products of historically situated interchanges among people" (pp. 266–267). But linguistic artifacts are more than this; they consist also of conversational interchanges. Thus, dialogical exchanges are themselves linguistic artifacts, social activities that creatively bring into existence entities that, although they may be invisible and fleeting, can nonetheless play a real part in furthering an organizations' productive activities. Such exchanges may draw upon linguistic artifacts, not only on those situated historically and culturally in an organization's language community, but also on those created in the momentary use of language, in the momentary responsive interactions occurring in meetings when meanings emerge spontaneously as we speak and respond to others. This perspective has implications for how knowledge and meaning is created within and about organizations.

In particular, we suggest that organizational participants (in our examples, managers) can draw on and create more implicit forms of knowledge that can inform practice, but can do so only if they understand what they are doing in a self-reflexive, self-aware way. A way in which, so to speak, they know *what* they are doing in doing it (Cunliffe, 2002a). Here, we call this form of knowledge "knowing," because it is emergent in the moment of the meeting between a manager and those they must manage. As such, it is not usually noticed, and is often left unarticulated. However, as Mike, the vice president of a health care organization, makes clear, in the following excerpt from a research conversation with one of us (ALC), the distinction between knowing and knowledge is a distinction that does in fact make sense to him:

Mike: "Knowing is an ongoing process, it's more synthetic, contextual [than knowledge], what you're doing at the time, almost with that knowledge and the experience you're having at the time—almost the intersection of experience, environment, and knowledge becomes knowing."

Ann: "Something that's not graspable?"

Mike: "It happens in time; it affects your future knowing but it's not like knowledge in the sense that you can take it off the shelf. Knowing changes you—knowledge gives you more bricks to build your wall out of."

Ann: "It could change you on a moment-by-moment basis because it's something you react to?"

Mike: "Well, I was thinking in the way you know things in the future, it's kind of . . . I don't think knowing is something that happens and you forget it and it had no impact on the next event in your life. . . . it seems to me your very ability to know is continually being reformed by your experiences of knowing . . . in the process you are changing the shape of the vessel."

Ann: "Just going back to the point you made about delving into your experience . . . and sometimes that may not be totally conscious . . ."

Mike: "Oh, absolutely, I would say that there are the deep structures inside that in essence are knowing . . . that control even the fields that are open to you . . . a very base kind of knowing . . . they have the same impact as a conscious kind of knowing but you can't control them you can't process them, they're processing you."

Ann: "And it's like a preknowledge stage in a way?"

Mike: "There's probably a level of knowing as you're using it that is preknowledge, almost a precondition of being able to access knowledge, some process—a deeply embedded process that is like your heart beating; it's autonomic . . . like a mental autonomic system that probably works at a very fundamental level."

In other words, as Mike makes very clear in the preceding discussion, this form of knowing is fluid, grounded in our everyday experiences and interactions, something that we may not be aware of but that does nonetheless influence the way we see and act in the world.

Elsewhere, one of us (JS) has called this kind of situated knowing or understanding on which all our more explicit formulations are based, a practical knowing *from within,* or a "knowing of the third kind" (Shotter, 1993a, 1993b). This was to contrast it with Ryle's (1949) claim that there are only two basic kinds of knowledge: "knowing that," to do with knowing facts, and "knowing how," to do with knowing skills. What is quite special about this kind of knowing is that although the joint activities occurring in a meeting are unintended by any particular individuals, as living activities always "in development," they nonetheless have *intentionality;* that is, in their very nature they always "point to" or "gesture toward" something in the future beyond themselves. They posit a "world of meaning or reference," a world of "next steps," which makes its appearance even as the collective activity occurs. And it is this ephemeral world of meaning that functions as the shared, momentary context within which the sense of each action occurring within it can be understood. Here, we simply call it knowing. But this is why we see this kind of knowing as directly connected with the influence that can be exerted on us by unique, one-off linguistic artifacts created in (sometimes, quite informal) meetings, because it is only if this kind of implicit knowing is present among all the participants that they can be so influential. In fact, it usually *is* present to some extent in all such meetings (even those between authors and readers); if it wasn't, then we would be unable to use (in *deixis*) such words as *this* and *that,* to refer to not-now-present entities occurring earlier on in a conversation.

In the rest of the chapter, then, we try to bring the nature of this implicit kind of knowing or sensemaking occurring in our interactions, and the background role played by the momentary linguistic artifacts that can be created within it, out into the open, into rational purview, so to speak. We do this first by contrasting it with more traditional understandings of knowledge. We then link this form of knowing to the linguistic artifacts and dialogical practices used by managers in their daily interaction (Cunliffe, 2002b), and assess the practical implications of these activities in organizational cultures and processes.

RELOCATING THE LEGITIMACY OF KNOWLEDGE: FROM MEETING GENERAL SCIENTIFIC CRITERIA TO MEETING MERELY CONTEXTUAL OBLIGATIONS

The last 30 years have seen a number of fundamental challenges to the meaning and construction of knowledge (e.g., Chia, 1996; R. Cooper, 1990; Foucault, 1972; Gouldner, 1970; Heidegger, 1966; Lyotard, 1984). Within Organization Studies, debate has focused on how we can make management knowledge more applicable to practitioners, and on the perceived limitations of scientific knowledge for better understanding how we manage and work within organizations. In particular, a number of authors (Clifford & Marcus, 1986; Garfinkel, 1967; Shotter, 1993a) have suggested that in treating knowledge in a representational-referential manner, as required in scientifically based studies, that is, as an abstract, pure, structured representation of an outer reality, we have moved away from people's ordinary everyday activities and their own *local* understandings in terms of which *they* conduct them. This kind of knowledge, with its origins in the purely rational considerations of academic experts, often disregards the particular knowledge of local practitioners and cannot always be applied by people to their practices in meaningful ways (Argyris, 1982; Lave & Wenger, 1991; Schön, 1983). Indeed, representational knowledge can be imposed only externally, that is, by practitioners turning their responsive attention away from the details of momentary events and their situated practices, toward the application of preexisting abstract rules and general principles.

Paradoxically, this "official" conception of knowledge focuses on presenting both grand abstractions (supposed to be representative of all possible occurrences of an event) and grand simplicities (supposed to represent just the essential features of the event), for in theorizing about people's behavior, academics have abstracted generalized principles and models from specific interactions and events, and then attempted to extend these generalizations across all organizational settings. In this way, entwined and complex interactions with many unique and crucial details have been reduced to simple principles, which, once found, are then accepted as "right" and offered as generally applicable—an approach that, most unfortunately, diverts our attention away from the already existing relations between people and directs our attention to supposed ideas, plans, knowledge of rules, and so on, existing hidden inside the heads of individuals.

Toulmin (1982), however, in a discussion of the genealogy of the word *consciousness*, has noted that it has an original meaning in Roman law of people jointly knowing something along with others (*con* [with], and *scio/ scientia* [knowing]), as in participating with others in a conspiracy. He shows how many such terms have migrated inward and been redirected to refer to events in the individual, conceptual domain, rather than referring to concrete meanings, thoughts, and sensations out in the public domain— the domain we share with others. For example, *role, identity, personality*, and *organizational culture* are all generalized terms invented to explain individual behavior, ways of being, or shared activities. They require a conceptual, passive understanding of a decontextualized kind and often become linguistic artifacts with sedimented meaning and practice. Organizational members engaging in ongoing, day-to-day activities, intuitively or otherwise, recognize that there is a distinction between this decontextualized knowledge and their everyday practices (as Mike shows in the earlier conversation). Indeed, they rarely describe their organizational lives in such decontextualized terms. The excerpt from Vince, the president of a small manufacturing company, also shows this. He comments that the theoretical, ordered discourse of his MBA experience was not all that helpful in coping with the "need to survive" that encompassed his daily organizational experience. In his experience, the legitimacy of the knowledge he draws on is located not in its scientific veracity, but in *his* personal ability to meet, manage, and take advantage of quite particular but very uncertain contextual obligations. And to do this, he must be extremely knowledgeable about all the relevant details—his authority (his right to "author" the relevant linguistic artifacts in shaping the possible paths forward for all to follow) depends on it. If others have to remind him of small but crucial facts missed or forgotten, his managerial competence will be in question:

Ann: "Is that difficult . . . standing back?"

Vince: "Yes, it's difficult and I do feel insecure, and I'll tell you why—because the three guys that handle the operations here have grown up within the organization and I've spent some time personally with them, sharing things that I've learned [*at the university*], exposing them to management seminars and I've tried to do some development. We've done the Ropes Course, eight of us, the management team, which was a very positive experience. But it's one thing to come into an environment that's organized and you talk about theory and all that sort of stuff but it's another thing when all of a sudden you show up at the plant and you say 'Yeah, I'm going to go around talking to employees today,' and the next thing you know a machine is broken and customers call in and *boom* you're on this ma-

chine trying to get things up and running because of some key account, and you promised the parts for tomorrow and the air line
shuts down . . . that's reality!"

All the complexity that Vince describes, of knowing how to go on in our
everyday practical lives, is absent from the codified and conventionalized,
formal knowledge of organizational practices provided in academic
courses. But the trouble is, their complexity is not eliminated by applying
scientific, propositional forms of knowledge to them; instead, it is simply
rendered rationally invisible. Bewilderment results. Indeed, as Vince suggests, no matter what "thin simplifications" (J. C. Scott, 1998) we might
produce to give order to life's activities, chaos happens; and we must deal
with it in ways that are spontaneously responsive to its unique and crucial
details as they change and develop.

It is no use turning our attention away from the concrete particulars before us, to *think* about how best we might see them *as* fitting into a general
scheme or framework; we need help now, something that directs us toward picking out and relating relevant details both to each other and to
possible actions that we (and others) might take. And we need to give
voice to this in ways others can understand not just simply intellectually,
but also practically, that is, can make use of in their own actions. This was
reiterated by Howard, the sales manager in the same organization:

> We . . . have so many different products and _____ has such a va-
> riety of applications. . . . Sales forecasting is one of our biggest areas of un-
> certainty and is a recent activity; 4 years ago we didn't do this. The manage-
> ment of the [sales] reps, who are mainly commissioned, is difficult . . . just
> trying to get them to understand the variety of those applications . . . I go out
> and talk to people—I may be in a furniture plant one day, a car plant and
> jewelry place the next . . . . so trying to train the reps is very difficult . . . you
> can't be an expert in any one area because you can't afford to be. . . . We
> don't really go after specific markets, we go after some; for example I'm go-
> ing to a musical instruments show and while I'm there I'll call on a pneu-
> matic tube business.

Although there has been much discussion about how we, as academics,
can develop knowledge and techniques (such as sales forecasting) of
greater relevance to practitioners, we suggest that much of this discussion
has missed the point. Indeed, as Howard just stated, many linguistic artifacts that occupy prominent positions in management lore (e.g., sales forecasting), because of their unrelatedness to our spontaneously responsive
ways of acting in our daily affairs, can be completely dysfunctional. To re-
peat, instead of orienting our attention to otherwise unnoticed but important details in our circumstances to which we ought to respond, they di-

vert our attention away from them. By focusing our Western philosophies only on circumstances that present us as already intellectually well-developed adults, with problems for thought, we have tended to ignore this implicit knowing from-within-the-moment completely.

But how can a merely *felt sense* of what it *might* be fitting to do next be in any sense sharable, never mind justifiable? Yet clearly, organizational members do have this implicit background knowledge, an idea of how to be a competent member of their organization or community of practice, and just as Howard does, they make use of it on a daily basis.

Indeed, our implicit knowledge and actions are part of who we are, our identities, and so we often fail to notice the impact of our linguistic practices and the intricate cleverness of our responsive bodily activity in their execution. We would like, therefore, to turn next to the debate about the nature of knowledge, to suggest that is not just about epistemological priorities, but also about ontological commitments (Chia, 1996); that is, that it is not just about the way we theorize but also our ethical and political assumptions about the nature of reality and our ways of being in the world (Shotter, 1993b)—and hence, ultimately, related to issues of power. In other words, associated with this kind of knowing, along with the possibilities for understanding and agreement, are possibilities also for disagreement and contestation—its very openness and indeterminacy can give rise to many uncertainties and anxieties. Only if we can reflexively surface and articulate more explicitly how we create meaning between us will we be able to act and interact in more responsive and ethical ways.

KNOWLEDGE AND KNOWING: EPISTEMOLOGICAL, ETHICAL, AND ONTOLOGICAL IMPLICATIONS

> *Truth is not born nor is it to be found inside the head of an individual person, it is born* between people *collectively searching for truth, in the process of their dialogic interaction.*
>
> —Bakhtin (1984, p. 110)

Epistemological Implications. We began this chapter with an excerpt from a conversation with Mike, the vice president of a health care organization, responding to a question about knowing from one of us. In that excerpt he suggests that knowing is entwined with who you are, your identity, and that there are "deep structures inside" that "you can't process [because] they are processing you." We link Mike's comments to our argument by suggesting that these deep structures can in fact be interpreted as linguistic artifacts—words, stories, gestures, metaphors, and so on, that play through our conversations in a gestural manner to direct our attention and to influence our momentary responses and, thus, how we create meaning.

Indeed, as Wittgenstein (1980) puts it: "The origin and primitive form of the language game is a reaction; only from this can more complicated forms develop. Language—I want to say—is a refinement, 'in the beginning was the deed' " (p. 31). And, he suggests: "The primitive reaction may have been a glance or a gesture, but it may also have been a word" (1953, p. 218). "But what is the word 'primitive' meant to say here? Presumably that this sort of behavior is *pre-linguistic:* that a language-game is based *on it,* that it is the prototype of a way of thinking and not the result of thought" (1981, no. 541). In other words, without any deliberate awareness of allowing ourselves to be influenced, in being spontaneously responsive to expressive movements of others, we can find ourselves involved with them in creating, not only new language games, but also what goes along with them, namely, new ways of thinking—new ways uniquely suited to the circumstances in which they come into being.

Thus Mike's comments in this respect are revealing. As he suggests earlier, we are often unaware that we are influenced, or how such influence occurs—although we do assume we can influence others in this direct and spontaneous way. Indeed, what Mike goes on to say later bears on this in an important way. For he suggests that, by being reflective in so doing, we can come to engage with them in more responsive and ethical ways:

> How you come to that knowing, is in my case 49 years, 3 months, and 25 days. I think it's all that's gone into bringing you to the point where you are. So, part of it is how well you've acquired knowledge, part of it is the experiences you have had—experiential learning which is not knowledge bound, part of it is the values you bring to the situation, some of it is your own ability to be reflective in different situations . . . I don't know a snappy answer to that question of how does one know.

In his comments reported previously, and here, Mike highlights a number of issues: He distinguishes between knowledge and what he calls "experiential learning"; he highlights the importance of values, as well as the importance of being able to reflect on what is happening. From this, we can draw a distinction between what Mike sees as knowledge acquisition—an externally imposed system of abstract propositions—and a more *implicit knowing-from-within*, that is, what one only knows from understanding one's situation in a context along with others. His comment about the ability to be reflective can be associated with an ability to understand how we might create and construct explicit understandings from within already ongoing and shared, implicitly knowledgeable practices. This distinction is summarized in Table 7.1.

TABLE 7.1
The Constitutive Structure of Knowledge and Knowing

Knowledge	Knowing
Assumes a reality independent of knowledge.	Assumes realities constructed and known only relationally through linguistic and other expressions.
Understanding lies in a thinking, rational, reflecting self as an inner, hidden, cognitive process.	Understanding is a shared sense constructed in and among participants in relational activities.
Language is a means of *representing* reality and internal thoughts.	Language is central to the *constructing* or *construction* of social realities and of one's self or identity.
Knowledge is bounded in disciplines and categories.	Knowing is unbounded, fluid, intuitive, and often tacit.
The goal is progress through theory development, with the aim of gaining greater control over our surroundings.	The goal is a more informed practice through a reflexive awareness of the influences at work in processes of social construction.
Theory is transcendent of time, context, and knowers.	"Practical theory" is useful only in relation to the moment of construction, and is therefore context-bound.
Theory is concerned with the discovery and systematic explanation of patterns and events in a supposed "real" world.	"Practical theorizing" creates momentary descriptions to account for and to construct (or to articulate) our experience.
Legitimacy of knowledge is based on objective, generalizable, and accurate facts, provable within a framework.	Legitimacy of knowing is based on creating momentary possibilities for moving on that are rooted in our conversations and activities.
Written forms privileged.	Dialogue and speech privileged.
Linearity of cause and effect is privileged.	A multidimensionality, in which everything is interrelated, is privileged.
Concerned with the replication of knowledge and the ability of research methods to represent rules and regularities in reality accurately.	Concerned with the construction of a shared (or shareable) sense in which all participate, and that all acknowledge, at that moment, as providing them with an acceptable orientation.
Learning based on recall and the application of theory, acquired elsewhere, to one's practices.	Learning based in being reflexively aware of the processes at work in the dialogic construction of meanings with others, a learning that can be acquired in one's practices.

Ethical Commitments in Our Dialogic Interactions.

Rob: "I actually spend a fair amount of time just building relationships, talking to people, . . . building my credibility with those people, so that when I do come in and make a decision that goes against them, they feel good about it. They say, 'OK, he came and talked to me and

> understood where I was coming from; he chose the other way, but OK, we're going to move on and get this done.' "
>
> Mike: "I think the essential management skills—as I use the term, the management of people—reside on this continuum that has things about communication, your ability to communicate your ideas, to empathize with other people . . . you make meaning with them jointly . . . you present ideas that are powerful—but you can't do that unless people have faith in you."

We cannot separate talk and action from self, nor self from others, as Rob's and Mike's preceding comments, about credibility and faith, highlight. They are each extremely knowledgeable about their own inner "workings," about how they themselves must "orchestrate" with others the unfolding movement of their activities in relation to others: what precisely and concretely must be related to what and in what order. The kind of practical "authoring" required, if one is to make meanings jointly with others, must be respectful and ethically sensitive to *their* rights (and duties) in the shared circumstances.

Indeed, to the extent that I need you in order to be me, if my appearance in the human world as another person of worth depends on your responsiveness to my expressions, then strange though it may seem, ethical values are prior to, not a consequence of, our knowledge of the others around us. To appreciate this, consider those occasions when simply, we meet the eyes of another person, when we are struck just for a moment by their presence before us. If we dwell for a while on the character of such moments, one thing we find within them is a sense of being obligated to the other in some way, a way that we *must* play out according to the local (moral) requirements of our actual involvement with them. We become aware of such obligations if, for instance, we stare for too long at someone, or look away from them too quickly—either response seems to express disrespect and can occasion anger. Similarly, if in the course of our involvement with another person, they sense us as failing to respond to their expressions appropriately, they feel justified in complaining: "Hello," they say, knocking on our forehead, "anyone at home?" Thus, linguistic artifacts can be characterized not only by what is said, but by what is not said, the gestures, the responses, and the interplay of voices.

Hence, we suggest that "good" authorship takes place only in a realm of mutually, spontaneously responsive activity, in which possibilities are discussed and debated, and where the relevant "realities" are constituted, not as mine or yours, but as *ours*. Goffman (1967) explores how, if we are to sustain such a sense of a collective we between us, we find ourselves with certain "involvement obligations" in our joint affairs—obligations that, if we fail to honor them, can give rise to many different forms of "alienative misinvolvement" in our relations to others. We need not list them all here. Suffice it to say that, it is only if we honor such ethical obligations in our conversations with those around us, spontaneously, that we can each gain a sense of each other's unique "inner worlds," that is, where we each are coming from and/or going to. To put it in personal terms: Only if "you" respond to "me" spontaneously in a way sensitive to the *relations* between your actions and mine can "we" act together as a "collective we." If I sense you as not being sensitive in this spontaneous way, then I feel immediately offended in an ethical way—I feel that either you lack respect for "our" affairs, or you are being insincere in some way with me.

Thus, as Goffman (1967) puts it:

> [A participant] cannot act *in order* to satisfy these obligations, for such an effort would require him to shift his [*sic*] attention from the topic of the conversation to the problem of being spontaneously involved in it. Here, in a component of non-rational impulsiveness—not only tolerated but actually demanded—we find an important way in which the interactional order differs from other kinds of social order. (p. 115)

Indeed, it is only if we all allow our conversation to lead us, rather than any of us trying to lead it, that allows us to feel that a conversation can be truly *our* conversation. As Goffman goes on to point out:

> All encounters represent occasions when the individual can become spontaneously involved in the proceedings and derive from this a firm sense of reality. And this kind of feeling is not a trivial thing. . . . When an incident occurs and spontaneous involvement is threatened, then reality is threatened . . . [If] the illusion of reality will be shattered, the minute social system that is brought into being with each encounter will be disorganized, and the participants will feel unruled, unreal, and anomic. (p. 135)

Thus, as Rob noted earlier, it mattered that he had credibility, talked with people and understood their position. Or as Mike remarks about being able to present ideas that are powerful: "You can't do that unless people have faith in you"; that is, others must in fact trust their very being, their sense of self to you. And they must do this bodily, in a "living" way, spontaneously, without having first to work out how to respond to you. It is in this sense that an implicit ethics (and politics) is at work in all our interactions. It is also in this sense that our idea of knowing becomes crucial—for we need to understand how we relate with others, how we construct between us meanings, organizational realities, and a sense of self/others. This form of knowing requires a reflexive understanding of how our (spontaneous and/or conscious) use of linguistic artifacts influences these ways of relating, and the ethical and moral commitments associated with such relational activities.

Ontology I: The Dialogical in Relationally Responsive Interaction. In this section, we want to explore how it is possible to talk with some definiteness and precision (in our talk of possibilities) of what does not yet in fact exist. How it is possible to inquire into *possibilities not yet actualized,* to talk with conviction when one, clearly, does not yet know "what" one is talking about, that is, to "go on" without losing one's way.

Previously, we have gestured toward the special nature of peoples' jointly conducted activities and practices. In this section we would now like to focus directly on their special and in fact quite strange nature. For they do, we feel, constitute a third realm of activities *sui generis,* quite distinct from either *action* or *behavior,* the two other major spheres of study in social theory. They cannot be studied in terms of individual people's *reasons* for their actions are, within this kind of activity, in spontaneous response to things occurring around them. Nor can we explain such activity in merely *causal* terms, as it exhibits knowledge and understanding in its performance. But more than this, unlike the other two kinds of knowledge, it is also knowledge of a *moral* kind, for it depends on the *judgments of others* as to whether its use and expression is actually fitting in a situation or not—one cannot just use it or express it on one's own, wholly within one's own terms.

Such responsive relations are uniquely related to, and situated in, the concrete particularities of their surroundings. A number of other features are crucial to their nature: Because we cannot not be spontaneously responsive to some extent to events occurring around us, everything we do is a complex mixture or "orchestration" of influences issuing from ourselves and from others; thus the dialogical activities that take place between us are neither wholly within nor wholly out of our control. But because they work to create a "world," a world that seems to exert its own requirements on us, they can easily be experienced as issuing from a "third agency" (neither from ourselves nor the others) that creates its own (ethical) demands and requirements to which both we and the others feel *answerable.*

In saying this, we are following Bakhtin (1986), who notes that:

> All real and integral understanding is actively responsive, and constitutes nothing other than the initial preparatory stage of a response (in whatever form it may be actualized). And the speaker himself is oriented toward such an actively responsive understanding. He does not expect passive understanding that, so to speak, only duplicates his own idea in someone else's mind. (p. 69)

And he continues:

Each dialogue takes place as if against a background of the responsive understanding of an invisibly present third party who stands above all the participants in the dialogue (partners). . . . The aforementioned third party is not any mystical or metaphysical being . . . he is a constitutive aspect of the whole utterance, who, under deeper analysis, can be revealed in it. (pp. 126–127)

This is crucial. Everything of importance for us in our social and organizational lives together, occurs *from within* such complex, ongoing, living relations as these. From within them, we express, negotiate, and contest our selves, our relation to others, and our position in the larger flow of social activity in which we are rooted and have our being.

To illustrate something of the complexity of what is involved here, we would like to turn to further comments made by managers in a study of what might be called the everyday discourse of managers managing (Cunliffe, 2001). Lisa, a project manager in a large, high-tech organization, draws our attention to the ceaseless flow of relationally responsive, bodily activity, and to the way in which it matters to us in our lives:

The other thing I came across recently was—we ran into a manager who just got really got bent out of shape about the space standards, really outraged and started making a big stink about it. My initial reaction was to say, "I haven't managed him or haven't given him information; I should have done something differently." And after spending a weekend beating myself up about it, I came in Monday morning. . . . I briefed my boss, who went to his boss who is also on the Exec Committee and was in the meeting where they agreed to the space standards. And he basically said to that guy, "Look, if you want to make exceptions, that's fine, but you are going to have to go to your peers and tell them what you're doing" and that cleared things up. . . . We haven't been communicating effectively so that's why people do not buy into the complexity of the problem and the project. So people do not understand, when they kick up a fuss for a week, what the cost is. . . . The personnel manager . . . her reaction was—it's not about the space standards, it's about how he's been feeling—not well taken care of.

As can be seen in this example, relationally responsive action is in fact a complex mixture of many different kinds of influences. Influences from our body senses, our own and others' responses, are all mixed together in the ongoing process of constructing meaning. Each unique, complex, indivisible unity in which we are involved with the others and othernesses around us, puts us into responsive contact with our surroundings, and just as our utterances are interwoven into the world around us, so the world is interwoven into our utterances. What Lisa and her colleagues produce between them is a very complex mixture of contestable and not wholly reconcilable influences.

To summarize, it is in our living contact with others that we create meaning, understanding, and a sense of space with depth to it—a depth in terms of how we are placed in relation to the possibilities for movement within our surroundings.[1] And this sense of depth is often an implicit knowing, taken for granted and unarticulated as we live our lives together without quite realizing the social, ethical, and political nature of the "space" around us. Indeed, because no one is individually responsible for them, the socially constructed nature of the space of possibilities open to us at any one moment remains unnoticed in the background of lives together. This is what is so special about our dynamic, unfolding relationally responsive activities: Opportunities and possibilities for action emerge continually. In our attempts to make sense of our lived experience, fleeting, one-off, unique, unrepeatable "once-occurrent events of Being" (Bakhtin, 1993, p. 2) occur that can make a difference to our lives (Bateson, 1972). If we take a reflexive stance, we not only may notice these events and understandings as they occur, but can draw the attention of others to their occurrence and their possibilities.

Ontology II: Life Within the Third Realm.   Bakhtin (1981, 1984, 1986) and Wittgenstein (1953) both emphasize, then, in their own different ways, that as living, embodied beings we are always already embedded in an intricate flow of complexly intertwined relationally responsive activities—a third realm. And, as soon as a second living human being responds to the activities of a first, then what the second does cannot be accounted as wholly their own activity—for the second acts in a way that is partly shaped by the first (in which the first's acts were responsive also). This is where all the strangeness of the dialogical begins. Indeed, straightaway we can say that, if meaning and action emerges in our moment-by-moment, back-and-forth responsive activity, then we cease to be wholly responsible for our own actions in such a space. Furthermore, because it arises in people's spontaneous, mutually responsive reactions to each other, the "realities" or "spaces" constructed in such joint activities are experienced as having their own (ethical) demands and requirements that

---

[1]This is where Bateson's (1972) notion of "double description," and of "differences that make a difference," is of great relevance. For it is, of course, in binocular vision that our sense of depth has its origins. It arises out of the two slightly different views from the two eyes being, not merged into a blurred two-dimensional, averaged view of our surroundings, but from them being used (in the optic chiasma) in very precise ways, as we move our two eyes to fixate and find a clear focus, on features of our surroundings, both near to us and distant from us in terms of the movements *possible* for us relation to them. We can thus find a useful metaphor here, for the way in which different, quite distinct voices can contribute from their own different positions, both toward the "depth" and toward the "dialogical truth" they can construct between them (Shotter, 2003).

control us (as Mike said in the interchange at the beginning of the chapter), not we "it." It is because we never act wholly alone, but always act within a context shared with others, that the language communities within which we live and work, their history, culture, and their linguistic artifacts, can have a major impact on our utterances and our understandings. Our relationally responsive activities are thus *inherently* situated. Hence, a person's utterances must always presuppose, "not only the existence of the language system he is using, but also the existence of preceding utterances—his own and others" (Bakhtin, 1986, p. 69).

As Bakhtin (1981) remarks:

> Within the arena of almost every utterance an intense interaction and struggle between one's own and another's word is being waged, a process in which they oppose or dialogically interanimate one another. The utterance so conceived is a considerably more complex and dynamic organism that it appears when construed simply as a thing that articulates the intention of a single person uttering it. (pp. 354–355)

We see an example of this in the following, where Rob, a program manager, talks about how organizational problems are vague, amorphous, and open to construction and negotiation:

Rob: "It's very rare that things need to get resolved today."

Ann: "So the problems you deal with are different to those you dealt with in manufacturing?"

Rob: "Problems are at a much higher level of abstraction; nothing is designed, nothing is given, everything is what you decide it is. If you ask somebody, 'What is this product going to do?'—'Well I don't know, you tell me.' 'When is it going to be finished?' 'Well I don't know—you tell me.' 'How much is it going to cost?' 'Well I don't know—you tell me.'"

This makes it very difficult for us to characterize the nature of our face-to-face, conversationally conducted meetings in terms of any preexisting, structured, or proposition-based forms. Indeed, the defining feature of activities in what we have called this third realm of activity is precisely its lack of any final specificity, and its *openness to being further by those (and only those) involved in it.*

As has been noted before, organizational realities are created by organizational members as they try to make sense of what is happening, both as it occurs and in retrospect (Shotter, 1993a; Weick, 1969/1979, 1995). Managers and other organizational members construct organizational experiences, problems, environmental demands, and constraints, as they select and bring shared features into the realm of dialogue and action. These features do not exist as an already-formed reality, but are constructed between people in their everyday interaction as if "participating in a conspiracy" (Toulmin, 1982, p.). Our social experience has neither a fully orderly nor a fully disorderly structure, is neither completely stable nor easily changed, and has neither a fully subjective nor fully objective character. So if much of this is based on an implicit knowing, how can we develop skilled and knowledgeable practices relevant to our own local surroundings and language communities? We suggest that organizational members need to understand the intersubjective and embodied nature of their interactions, the responsive impact of their words, and how they jointly construct meaning and possibilities for action. This requires them to recognize and articulate the type of knowing we outline herein. Knowledgeable practices also require self-reflexivity—questioning assumptions and practices, ways of being, the ways in which we relate with others, and the influence of linguistic artifacts on shared and contested meaning. By doing so, we can engage with others in ethical and responsive ways. In the following section, we explore what this means for organizing and managing.

KNOWING, DIALOGUE, AND LINGUISTIC ARTIFACTS: IMPLICATIONS FOR ORGANIZING AND MANAGING

A number of implications emerge from relationally responsive and knowing perspectives for the way we view organizations and managers. Typically, from a representational-referential perspective, organizations are viewed as already-existing structures, systems, and procedures, and managers are effective if they plan, organize, and coordinate activities and are able to apply management techniques to practice. From a relationally responsive perspective, organizations are seen as relational landscapes continually shifting from the implicit to the explicit as organizational participants articulate between them a shareable formulation of their organization's crucial features. Organization culture can be reframed as the form of organizational discourse or discourses used by organizational members: the types of conversations that occur and the linguistic artifacts embedded within. The following statements were made by managers from the same organization:

> I come in in the morning now and I'm a skeptic. I say, "OK, first tell me about all the casualties."

> It's such a shotgun approach.

> Boom! Something happens.

> It's hard because you have three or four things thrown at you.

They all illustrate how the linguistic artifacts, mostly images and meta-phors, used by the managers can reflect a shared organizational discourse. They seem to draw on an underlying image of a battlefield. Indeed, lin-guistic features such as "casualties," "shotgun approaches," and "boom" can orient ways of talking and likely responses, can construct shared meanings and possible actions. It is through the way specific linguistic ar-tifacts are used in relationally responsive interaction that the third realm emerges—in this example, an image of an organizational culture charac-terized by chaos into which organizational members act and assume ex-ists independently as an uncontrollable situation.

If we accept this perspective, the skills required by managers are not purely technical but also linguistic, involving an ability to create conversa-tions in which such shared articulations occur and possibilities explored. Managing becomes an everyday dialogical activity in which managers and other organizational members socially construct their sense of self and their ways of relating with others in their everyday dialogical prac-tices. This is the view of a manager as a "practical author" (Cunliffe, 2001; Shotter, 1993a; Shotter & Cunliffe, 2002) in which managers continually make sense of and construct their organizational realities in their every-day interaction. However, managing not only is responsive, embodied, and dialogical sensemaking, but is also an ontological project—managers negotiate a sense of self and ways of being in their daily interactions. This negotiation can be ongoing, fragmented, and contestable; consider, for ex-ample, the following statement by Lisa:

> One of my biases is that issues of diversity are very personal and that unless you confront them in a personal way, organizations just aren't going to get anywhere. It's about how do I get Lisa to fit into this White, male-oriented organization because there is going to come a point at which I say, "No, I'm not going to give up who I am to do that."

We therefore need to focus on the singular events and conversations within which we construct practical accounts of our actions, identities, and relationships with others, and that may guide our future action. If we focus on the form of knowing outlined here, then we begin to think more reflexively about how we construct our realities and selves through dia-logue and linguistic artifacts. We begin to recognize the constructed and dialogical nature of reality, to think more critically about ourselves, our actions, the types of conversations we engage in, the language we use, and how to carry out reflective conversations in which (to some degree) shared constructions of organizational experience allow possibilities for action to emerge. We can see this happening in the following excerpt from a manager's journal (Jim, an MBA student):

I see my team projects in the context of a war or a battle. The enemy is the deadline and we have to fight hard and with dramatic fervor to achieve our goal successfully. Any weakness in the team could be fatal for my team and me. In war, such an exposed weakness could allow the enemy to strike us down. If any one soldier fails to perform his or her specific function, then the whole unit may be put at risk. That's my philosophy—if someone else does not do what they should and you have to do it for them, do it in the manner you would have done it yourself. This metaphor has two major implications for the way I act in teams: first, I am goal-driven, and second, I do what it takes to win without thinking about the impact on others. As a result of reading about group and communication process and discussing the so-cially-constructed nature of reality, I have begun to reflect on my own as-sumptions and actions and their impact on others. I have begun to see teams as relationally-responsive interactions (Shotter, 1993a) in which we need to think not about war, but building a team in which conflict and differences are accepted and dealt with in a constructive way.

By becoming more self-reflexive, we begin to think (as Jim does) about how we, with others, construct realities and identities and to create new readings of our experience. In doing so, we can work toward more lin-guistically expressible and reflexive accounts. Such self-reflexive and self-developing practices may involve noticing certain ways of talking, draw-ing attention to striking moments, responses, and feelings created by words and gestures. As Wittgenstein (1953) states: "It is, rather, of the es-sence of our investigation that we do not seek to learn anything *new* by it. We want to *understand* something that is already in plain view. For *this* is what we seem in some sense not to understand" (no. 89). His interest is in moving us in some way, of changing our relationship to our surround-ings, changing our sensibilities: the things we notice and are sensitive to, the things we seek and desire, and so on. And to do this, we need to seek the same kind of direct, unproblematic, spontaneous, continually chang-ing, embodied seeing (and acting) within which all our everyday forms of life are grounded—in other words, a special reflexive practice within our everyday practices (Cunliffe, 2002b).

CONCLUSIONS

What is most difficult here is to put this indefiniteness, correctly and unfalsi-fied, into words.
—Wittgenstein (1953, p. 227)

We have focused, then, on the responsive orders in which, at any one mo-ment, we can be embedded, and how, as we come to feel at home within them, we can learn how to answer to the distinctive calls they exert on us without any need for external aids in moving around inside the worlds they present to us. We have shown how these calls issue from momentary, linguistic artifacts we construct between us, while often remaining quite unaware of our part in their construction. If we are to become familiar with this third realm of spontaneously responsive mutual activity, this realm of joint or dialogically structured activity, we must acquire various ways of knowing that allow us to move around, to go on, more easily within it. Thus, we can (but not easily) learn how to see the world of human social practices in depth, but to do so we must learn to embody some new ways of looking—a *relationally responsive* knowing or *participatory* knowledge—as we participate intimately with others and othernesses around us. In doing so, we dialogically unfold between us intricately intertwined relationships of many, uniquely different kinds. This requires, as both Shotter (1984) and Spinosa, Flores, and Dreyfus (1997) term it, the acquisition of new "ontological skills"—that is, one must learn not just how *to be* a city manager, a company director, or a regional planner, by acquiring certain sensibilities and attunements, one must also come to know one's way around sustained realities or organizational experiences. To do this we must learn how to see what is around us in depth, as offering us a space of possibilities for our actions. Such a sense emerges for us only from within our dialogic relations with the others around us. As organizational participants we need to be sensitive to linguistic artifacts, and refine our collaborative dialogic relations—especially the practical, unique moments that allow us to relate to each other and our surroundings and move on.

III

ARTIFACTS, BRANDS, AND IDENTITY

How do artifacts become brands? How do artifacts shape and reflect "who we are" as individuals, organizations, and professions? How do organizations attempt to change employees and other stakeholders through artifacts? The various chapters in Part III illustrate the powerful role of artifacts in constructing, maintaining, and deconstructing identities of individuals and collectives. *Majken Schultz, Mary Jo Hatch,* and *Francesco Ciccolella* (chap. 8) use the example of the LEGO Company to examine how artifacts facilitate a shift from product to corporate branding. *CV Harquail* (chap. 9) continues the conversation about brands by examining how organizations attempt to transform employees into "living brands" via "employee branding." *Yehuda Baruch* (chap. 10) focuses on the critical first-impression messages conveyed through organizational logos. *Rossella Cappetta* and *Denny Gioia* (chap. 11) conclude Part III by integrating the role of sensemaking and sensegiving in maintaining organizational identity and image in the fashion industry.

8

Brand Life in Symbols and Artifacts: The LEGO Company

Majken Schultz
Copenhagen Business School

Mary Jo Hatch
University of Virginia

Francesco Ciccolella

Brand Life in Symbols and Artifacts

Branding is an area of management that was born of symbols and artifacts. In most cases artifacts such as logos and names have been designed to symbolize the company in ways that transfer management's intended meanings or desired associations to external stakeholders. But as companies move toward corporate branding, they start to recognize that the brand plays an important symbolic role within the company as well. In this chapter we examine how brands live in the artifacts and symbols of the LEGO Company. By elaborating the corporate-branding model developed by Hatch and Schultz (2001), we show a variety of ways in which the company used its core artifacts—the brick and the formal statement of company values—and their associated meanings to implement their new corporate-brand strategy and integrate it with their stakeholder relationship building activities. We focus in particular on how employees make use of symbols and artifacts provided by LEGO management to transform the culture of the company.

How Brands Live in Symbols and Artifacts

Branding is an area of management that was born of symbols and artifacts. From the burning of ownership marks into the hides of cows in the Wild West, to the contemporary love affair with designer labels, brands are associated with artifacts that producers and consumers alike use to symbolically express their identity.

Most people associate brands with distinctive names, colors, icons, and shapes, whether it is Coke's sinuous bottle, the Wells Fargo stagecoach, or the distinctive four letters of the LEGO or SONY name. However, in its symbolic role, the brand operates considerably beyond the narrow confines of this artifactual existence. In the field of marketing, brands have been approached in one of two ways. The approach that dominates the corporate-identity field concerns design, wherein strategists, marketers, graphic artists, and communicators conspire to create a brand to suit corporate or strategic purposes and deliver its desired meaning to the customer (Olins, 1989, 2000). This approach focuses on artifacts expressing the organization's self-image via name, logo, tagline, and color. The second approach emphasizes how brand artifacts are used by consumers in the expression of their individuality and in the construction of emotional relationships to their brands of choice (Fournier, 1998). Most often, these artifacts are found among product brands, for example, my favorite 501, special café latte, or Harley motorbike. Both approaches have produced prescriptions for companies regarding how to market themselves toward different external stakeholders.

However, numerous brand scholars (e.g., Aaker & Joachimstahler, 2002; Balmer & Greyser, 2003; Hatch & Schultz, 2003; Olins, 2003; Schultz & Hatch, 2003) claim that we are witnessing a shift from product branding to corporate branding; that is, companies are increasingly seeking to brand themselves as organizations based in the distinctive features of their identity, organizational heritage, or unique central idea. Thus, corporate branding implies that one set of corporate artifacts unites all company activities across different business areas making it clear to all stakeholders (external as well as internal) that the company stands behind all its products and services (e.g., NOKIA Connecting People in each of its product brands). In order to create a credible corporate brand, companies must engage in self-reflection. They must consider how all stakeholder relations contribute to their brand building, realizing that a corporate brand cannot be constructed through innovative design, creative marketing, and great products alone, but must reside in the company's identity and what it stands for. To be trustworthy it must live up to its promises (see, e.g., Olins', 2003, analysis of airlines and financial services not living up to promises of the brand).

The reasons for the shift to corporate branding range from the economic efficiency gained by global awareness and more focused marketing and communication efforts, to the need for employees to identify with their company and the pressure from stakeholders for more corporate transparency (e.g., Fombrun & Van Riel, 2003). To move away from product branding corporate branding must move from being a communication/marketing-driven activity toward being a strategic framework for managing the organization, where all corporate functions express the distinct identity of the brand. Thus, corporate branding highlights the important role employees play when branding on the inside of a company becomes more visible and strategically important than branding on the outside (Ind, 2001; Schultz & De Chernatony, 2002).

Issues like credibility and relevance of the brand rest heavily on the shoulders of employees, whose cultural behavior supports the company's claims to brand uniqueness. That is why we see more and more companies engaged in making the brand understandable, relevant, and engaging to their employees through a host of different internal activities such as employee communication campaigns, company intranet Web sites, corporate merchandise, and staged events that are often conceived as "Living the Brand" or "Being the Brand" (Ind, 2001). Company artifacts are used in the context of these activities as communication tools designed to make the brand coherent, recognizable, and exciting to employees who are then expected to transfer their knowledge and enthusiasm to other stakeholders.

In this chapter we go beyond the use of artifacts as communication tools to explore how employees use artifacts associated with branding and in the process change their symbolic meaning in effect using them to construct new artifacts. We base our argument on the importance of artifacts for all elements of the corporate brand and claim that brands live by the organization's ability to engage in the ongoing construction of new artifacts that change the meaning of artifacts already in place.

The conceptual framework for examining this constructive role of artifacts in relation to corporate brands is found in the corporate-branding model proposed by Hatch and Schultz (2001, 2003; Schultz & Hatch, 2003). It is further elaborated here with the inclusion of the concept of identity, which allows us to explore the tensions between tangible and intangible/abstract artifacts. We base empirical illustrations on our longitudinal involvement with the LEGO Company (see Endnote 1 describing our involvement with the LEGO Company), which is a company rich with heritage artifacts and a long tradition for conceptualizing the construction of artifacts. The first part of the chapter shows how artifacts are embedded in all dimensions of corporate branding, whereas the second provides illustrations of how artifacts have been used by employees in the construction of the LEGO corporate brand. We particularly focus on the relationship between the two core artifacts—the ubiquitous LEGO brick, and the formal statement of company values—as this poses a major challenge to implementing the company's new corporate-brand strategy and to building stakeholder relations.

ARTIFACTS IN CORPORATE BRANDING

Corporate branding implies that the whole organization serves as the foundation for brand positioning and entails the organization making specific choices such as constructing organizational process and executing activities in ways that are distinct to the organization when it is compared with its competitors or with mainstream trends. Accordingly, the values, beliefs, and aesthetic sensitivity held by organizational members become key elements in differentiation strategies, as the company itself moves center stage in the branding effort. In defining successful corporate branding, Hatch and Schultz (2001) emphasized how corporate branding resides in the alignment of strategic vision, organizational culture, and stakeholder images, which they defined as:

- Strategic vision: the central idea behind the company that embodies and expresses *top management's* aspiration for what the company will achieve in the future.
- Organizational culture: the internal values, beliefs, and basic assumptions that embody the heritage of the company and manifests in the ways *employees* feel about the company they are working for.
- Stakeholder images: views of the organization developed by its *external stakeholders;* the outside world's overall impression of the company including the views of customers, shareholders, the media, the general public, and so on.

Together the key elements of corporate branding just defined underpin Hatch and Schultz's (2001, 2003) model. To enhance or maintain corporate-brand alignment, Hatch and Schultz argued that companies must pay attention to all three elements of corporate branding simultaneously, focusing not on consistency between claims made about them, but on alignment or resonance between the elements themselves and thus on the feelings and thoughts they invoke when contact is made with them.

Based on our previous and continuing work on the relationships between corporate branding and organizational identity, we believe it is possible to add identity as a conceptual anchor for expressions of who the organization is and what it stands for (Hatch & Schultz, 2000, 2002). Contrary to strategic vision, which embodies future aspirations for the company, identity is composed of claims regarding who the company is as an organization—now and often based in heritage—which is increasingly explicitly expressed in many companies through abstract artifacts, such as organizational values or core beliefs (Whetten, 2003). In practice, however, there may be little difference between vision and identity, as identity claims sometimes express desired future identity rather than describe actual organizational behavior, just as the vision–mission–values rhetorics in companies are often intertwined. Whereas identity is a privileged claim of self among organizational members, images reside among multiple (other) stakeholders engaged in different interpretations and applications of corporate artifacts and this leaves a multiplicity of images as sources for the continuous development—or fragmentation—of the brand.

Organizational culture, in contrast, refers to a single organization and emerges from the taken-for-granted assumptions and tacit webs of meaning that lie behind everyday employee behavior. It is through the behavior that is influenced by cultural assumptions that numerous cultural forms, such as rites and rituals, symbols, values, myths, stories, and so on, are manifested (Hatch, 1993; Martin, 1992; Schein, 1992; Schultz, 1994). In this regard organizational culture serves as a contextual reference for collective reflections of who we are as an organization. The concept of culture also includes espoused values. Espoused values are similar to identity claims in that they focus on the definition of an organizational self rather than on its being; for example, espoused values often involve formal codes of conduct for organizational behavior. Thus, adding identity as the fourth element of corporate branding extends the Hatch and Schultz model of corporate branding (see Fig. 8.1)[3]:

- Identity: occurs at the juncture between vision, culture, and image and underpins the corporate brand; partly the effect of comparison with others and partly of organizational self-insight; often expressed as claims about organizational values, central ideas, or core beliefs.

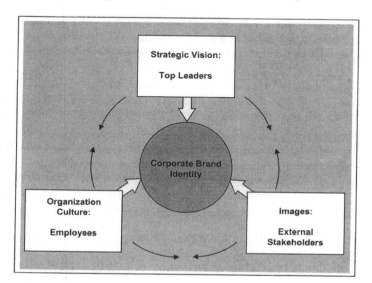

FIG. 8.1. The elements of corporate branding. Adapted from Hatch and Schultz (2001).

On the basis of this elaboration of the model, the corporate brand becomes a symbolic representation of the organization's identity that is expressed through numerous artifacts. In the remainder of this section, we explain how each element of the elaborated Hatch and Schultz model engages different kinds of artifacts and their associated meanings and offer illustrations from the history of the LEGO Company.

Organizational Culture Artifacts

As pointed out by scholars of organizational culture, artifacts are the most tangible aspects of culture. Edgar Schein (1992) defined artifacts as the visible, tangible, and audible results of cultural activities grounded in values and basic assumptions. Gagliardi (1990) later emphasized the physicality of artifacts stating that they maintain "the *natural* innocence of the physical world, despite the fact that they are inherently *artificial*" (p. vi). He argues that the construction of artifacts involves manifestations of specific perceptions and "sensory skills" in the organization, where aesthetic experience and sensitivity among organizational members imply a judgment of taste influencing the physical construction of artifacts and their relations with our senses (feel, touch, see, etc.). These sensory skills link the role of the organization as a pure "economic machine" (i.e., the material production of goods) to its role as a "symbol generating machine" (Deleuze & Guttari, 1984, p. 1). It is this connection that explains why artifacts must be analyzed beyond their primary (economic, practical, or instrumental) function to include examination of their symbolic function and its relationship to the primary function.

As demonstrated by symbolic-interpretive researchers, the distinction between symbols and artifacts is important in that all symbols are artifacts, whereas not all artifacts are symbols (A. Cohen, 1976; Hatch, 1993; Morgan, Frost, & Pondy, 1983). Though artifacts represent pure instrumental and tangible devices in organizations (e.g., a coffee mug), using artifacts-as-symbols "call[s] for the association of certain conscious or unconscious ideas in order for them to be endowed with their full meaning and significance" (Pondy et al., 1983, p. 5). Thus, artifacts are turned into symbols by organizational members when they are associated with specific meanings; for example, the coffee mug reminds organizational members that everybody is expected to make their own coffee. As suggested by Hatch, "artifacts must be translated into symbols if they are to be apprehended as culturally significant objects, events or discourses" (p. 670). Until artifacts are symbolically linked to particular meanings they do not connect with the wider system of meanings that constitutes the culture. This implies that the same artifact can carry multiple meanings. This symbolic ambiguity is one of the intrinsic qualities of symbols: "Symbols are objects, acts, relationships or linguistic formations that stand ambiguously for a multiplicity of meanings, evoke emotions and impel men to action" (A. Cohen, 1976, p. 23).

At the LEGO Company the most distinct cultural artifacts are found among the play materials the company produces (see Fig. 8.2). Although the brick was developed by the LEGO Company in 1949 and is responsible for LEGO's global success (to the extent that each inhabitant on the planet on average owns 52 LEGO bricks), the company was not founded as a manufacturer of bricks, but as a producer of play materials based in a profound set of company values.

The studded, multicolored, plastic binding brick (since 1958), and later, the minifigure (since 1978) have been the core tangible artifact within the LEGO culture in terms of both material production (e.g., LEGO products and product extensions) and generation of cultural symbols (e.g., organization members' self-expressions using the brick universe; internal communication material using the brick shape and primary colors; heritage company visuals filled with brick references). Some users refer to the bricks and minifigures as "LEGOS" thereby linking them to a key symbol of the company—its name. For decades the bricks were produced in only primary colors and a limited number of shapes and sizes. The first radical change to the brick occurred in 1962 when wheels were introduced; gear wheels and technical plates with holes were added in 1977, whereas the small gearstick was introduced as late as 1985, illustrating that each step in the transformation of LEGO core artifacts has been a long and careful process within the company (see *The Ultimate LEGO Book*, 1999). During this process the brick has been reinterpreted and transformed many times over, by asking, for example, questions like the following: What are the appropriate play values? What does construction mean? Where do we draw the boundary around the LEGO brick? (color, shape, applications). The brick is also used by employees in many different cultural manifestations, such as the playful use of bowls of bricks located in meeting rooms, the display of elaborate sculptures made from bricks in factory buildings, the design of the London office using the studded shapes and primary colors of the brick to create LEGO-themed workspaces, and the small individual brick constructions found in most offices.

Strategic Vision Artifacts

Although the notion of artifacts has rarely been used in the literature related to strategic vision (cf. Gagliardi, 1990), symbols have played a role in the corporate-identity area, where artifacts such as logo, slogans, and colors are presented as symbolic carriers of the strategic vision of the company and as deliberate statements of what the company aspires to stand

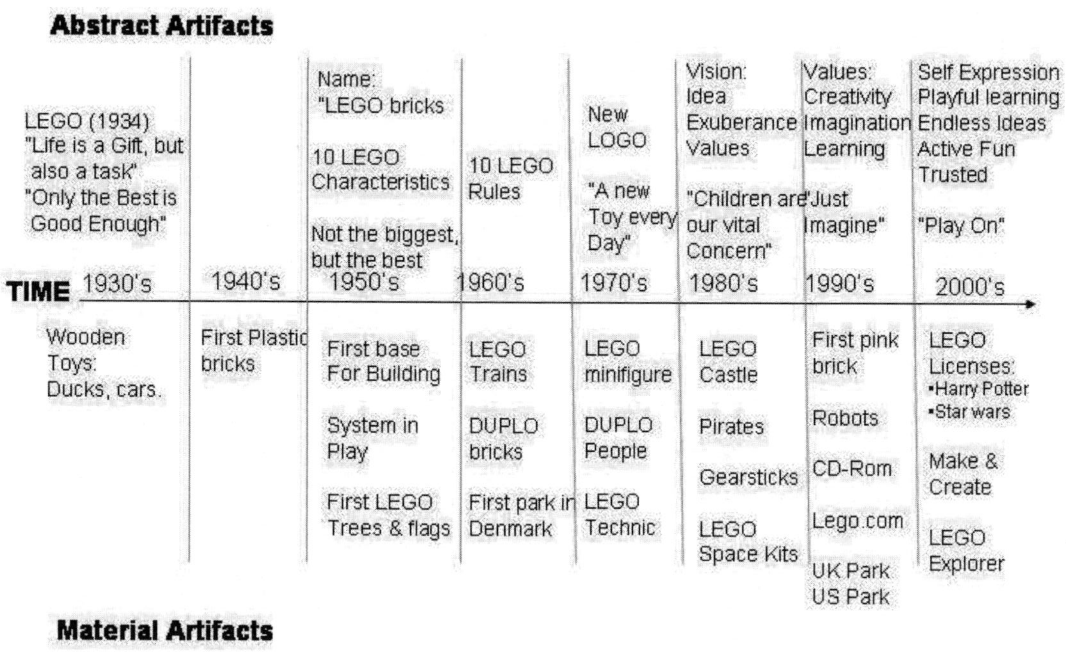

Abstract Artifacts

	1930's	1940's	1950's	1960's	1970's	1980's	1990's	2000's
Abstract Artifacts	LEGO (1934) "Life is a Gift, but also a task" "Only the Best is Good Enough"		Name: "LEGO bricks" — 10 LEGO Characteristics — Not the biggest, but the best	10 LEGO Rules	New LOGO — "A new Toy every Day"	Vision: Idea Exuberance Values — "Children are our vital Concern"	Values: Creativity Imagination Learning — "Just Imagine"	Self Expression Playful learning Endless Ideas Active Fun Trusted — "Play On!"
TIME	1930's	1940's	1950's	1960's	1970's	1980's	1990's	2000's
Material Artifacts	Wooden Toys: Ducks, cars.	First Plastic bricks	First base For Building — System in Play — First LEGO Trees & flags	LEGO Trains — DUPLO bricks — First park in Denmark	LEGO minifigure — DUPLO People — LEGO Technic	LEGO Castle — Pirates — Gearsticks — LEGO Space Kits	First pink brick — Robots — CD-Rom — Lego.com — UK Park US Park	LEGO Licenses: •Harry Potter •Star wars — Make & Create — LEGO Explorer

Material Artifacts

FIG. 8.2. Historical development of core artifacts in LEGO Company. Sources: *The Ultimate LEGO Book* (1999) and www.lego.com.

for (Balmer & Greyser, 2003; Olins, 2003). Furthermore, in their visioning processes, companies increasingly turn to physical (e.g., drawings, collages) or audible (e.g., stories, fairytales) artifacts that enable them to imagine what Collins and Porras (1994) labeled Big Hairy Audacious Goals. In order for these artifacts to work as symbols for a corporate brand, internal and external stakeholders must associate them with top management's vision.

As suggested by Firth (1973) symbols can play an instrumental role as tools for expression, communication, knowledge, and control of artifacts. In relation to corporate branding this implies that symbols can serve as devices for expression, communication, and control of strategic vision, as seen in vision and mission statements and the various ways companies make these statements tangible and operational, for example, corporate cards, posters, and art. By turning vision artifacts into powerful organizational symbols, top management licenses organizational members to engage in the construction of cultural artifacts by giving them a specific purpose and direction that may stimulate the creation of new artifacts or change the symbolic meaning of existing ones (Firth, 1973). The limitations of top management's use of artifacts for cultural control have been documented by students of organizational culture (e.g., Kunda, 1992; Martin, 1992), whereas others have pointed at the managerial challenge in balancing the multiplicity of unpredictable and shifting images associated with global-brand artifacts (Aaker & Joachimstahler, 2000; Schultz & Hatch, 2003).

As stated earlier, the most noticeable artifact used by the LEGO Company to represent its aspirations is its formal statement of strategic intent, which also includes a statement of corporate beliefs and mission. These aspirations have provided strategic direction since the founding of the company in 1932 and have been handed down through three generations of owners, albeit elaborated and redefined from time to time (*The Ultimate LEGO Book*, 1999). The current strategic intent of the company sets the long-term ambition: *to become the world's strongest brand among families with children.*

It is supported by mission and core beliefs, which were defined in 1978 by the third-generation family owner and express the kind of company LEGO aspires to be. The mission statement reads: *To nurture the child in each of us.* Corporate beliefs include: *Children are our role models. They are curious, creative, and imaginative.*

Other examples of artifacts related to strategic vision have also been passed down through the generations, from the first corporate slogan, "The best is never good enough," and the company name based in the Danish phrase *Leg Godt* (meaning Play Well), to the new slogan "Play On." The contemporary expression of vision includes the highly visible yellow-red-black logo typeface (in use since 1973), and the Idea House. Idea House, located in the corporate headquarters in Billund, Denmark, is a tangible expression of all the play experiences offered by the LEGO corporate brand. It consists of an open space dominated by statements of the company's beliefs and values that includes core beliefs and mission statement painted on the walls in primary colors with banners hanging from the ceiling showing the LEGO values in the colors and shapes of the brand. The other part of the house is divided into separate spaces showing the types of bricks and brick constructions that belong to a specific play experience. There is a room showing what you can do with free construction of LEGO materials, a display of robotics and tech products (e.g., the Mindstorms robotics), and a room where all the different LEGO thematic universes are on display (e.g., Harry Potter, Star Wars, Knights' Kingdom). Thus, the Idea House is an elaborate presentation of the core artifacts of the LEGO brand that is used to symbolize the richness of the brand vision and show the multiple tangible manifestations of the brand code to employees and special guests visiting the House.

Artifacts: Stakeholder Images

Students of brands and consumer behavior have long commented on the use of brand artifacts by consumers to express their individuality (e.g., the logo-emblazoned T-shirt). Consumer research has shown how brand artifacts operate as vehicles for the transfer of meaning from the brand to the consumer and how strong artifacts become woven into the identities of consumers by creating emotional and self-expressive benefits (Aaker, 1996). Others have pointed at how artifacts contribute to building lasting relations between brands and consumers (Fournier, 1998). The perceptions and utilization of artifacts by consumers can be related to material products (e.g., coffee as demonstrated by Fournier); represent a whole lifestyle or set of activities symbolized by a distinct company logo (e.g., Harley Davidson); or serve as seals of approval, trust, style, and so on, depending on the perceived distinctiveness of the brand identity (Armani means understated style; IBM means trusted service; SONY means quality). In some cases consumers join brand communities (Muniz & O'Guinn, 2001), where brand artifacts provide the starting point for joint developments of the meanings of the brand. Brand communities can be either initiated by the company or orchestrated by consumers themselves. Recently, instances of consumer adaptations and transformation of brand artifacts have exploded on Internet sites such as Ad-busters (www. adbusters.org) and Behind-the-Label (www.behindthelabel.org). Whether brand artifacts are embraced, transformed, or criticized, they act as iconic symbols of the brand in the construction of stakeholder images, often traveling across time and space.

For the LEGO Company the artifacts most readily embraced by consumers are the material products themselves (bricks turned into all kinds of play experiences) supported by the company logo, which has served as a seal of trust and approval in the company's long-standing war against copycat competitors. In some markets the brand has become so strongly associated with the generic plastic artifacts that consumers have lost sight of the specific values offered by the LEGO brand in relation to children's development. This has made it easier for competitors to imitate the LEGO bricks and engage in price competition, such as Mega-Blocks in the U.S. market. In other parts of the world, most notably Germany and Scandinavia, LEGO Company is much more highly associated by consumers with values enhancing children's learning and development, making the LEGO brand about much more than bricks and thus acts to protect the brand from copycat competition.

In line with the development of brand communities, the LEGO Company has sought to engage consumers directly in events, such as the First LEGO League, where children compete in the construction of their own artifacts (LEGO robots). LEGO artifacts have also been adapted by consumers on their own terms, most significantly at the Web site www.lugnet.com, where LEGO fans all over the world exchange ideas, experiences, and opinions related to LEGO products (e.g., Brick Feast in the United States; Antorini, 2003).

Identity Artifacts

As noted in our distinction between culture and identity, identity comprises the collective definitions of the organizational self—most often stated as perceptions or claims that constitute what is most core, distinctive, and sometimes enduring about "we" as an organization (Gioia, Schultz, & Corley, 2000; Hatch & Schultz, 2003; Whetten, 2003). Furthermore, Whetten has argued that identity claims have to be institutionalized in order to work as the organizational "constitution" and serve as a source of internal and external legitimacy. Thus, as stated by Hatch and Schultz (2000), identity is more explicit, instrumental, and narrative than culture, which implies that artifacts expressing identity are often found among the orchestrated, deliberate attempts to define the organization—or in our case the identity for the corporate brand. Identity artifacts overlap with vision, as when logo, name, symbols, and house style are taken to be the most tangible expressions of identity. However, identity claims are increasingly stated as more abstract artifacts, such as company values, corporate stories, autobiographies, and other kinds of corporate narratives, where organizations not only define who they are, but also tell how these self-definitions have evolved through organizational history (see Czarniawska, 1997).

Since its origin, the LEGO Company has been concerned with values. It has always defined itself as a value-driven company. Early on these values focused on defining the play experience offered by the LEGO Company; for example, the "LEGO characteristics" served the company since the 1970s in the capacity of instrumental and aesthetic guidelines for the construction of play related artifacts:

Unlimited play possibilities
For girls, for boys
Enthusiasm for all ages
Play all year round
Stimulating and absorbing play
Endless hours of play
Imagination, creativity, development
Each new product multiplies the play value
Always topical
Leading safety and quality

In the late 1970s the company added identity claims for the company to its list of characteristics, although it has given these claims different narrative forms along the way. As part of the new corporate-brand strategy, in 2001 the classic values of the company were restated and interpreted in ways to make them more distinctive in relation to its competitors' positioning:

Creativity means Self Expression
Imagination means Endless Ideas
Learning means Playful Learning
Fun means Active Fun
Quality means Trusted

These values or identity claims were then given distinct visual expressions and were displayed on everything from posters to mouse pads used by the LEGO Company employees (see Fig. 8.3).

ARTIFACTS IN THE LEGO CORPORATE BRAND

As shown in the aforementioned examples of artifacts of the LEGO Company culture, the brick has been a dominant tangible artifact since early in LEGO's history. However, the abstract company values related to corpo-

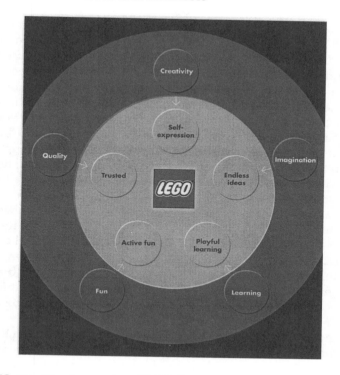

FIG. 8.3. Visual expression of LEGO Company values. Copyright © 2004 The Lego Group. Company logo reprinted by permission.

rate vision and identity have been part of the company since its origin and they preceded and in some ways directed the incremental development of the brick (LEGO started out with the construction of wooden toys). Although the specific symbolic meanings of all LEGO's artifacts have changed over time and varied between different global markets, they are all relevant to the elements that Hatch and Schultz argued underpin the corporate brand—vision, culture, images—as well as to identity, which we are claiming here also constitutes the foundation for the brand.

Toward Corporate-Brand Strategy

The function of and interrelations between the core artifacts of LEGO culture are being transformed by LEGO's newly defined strategy of becoming brand driven—or rather to regain and strengthen the global position of the LEGO company name and the core construction idea, which have been neglected and sometimes lost in the pursuit of numerous individual product lines, subbrands, and volatile licensing agreements (e.g.,

Star Wars, Harry Potter). In general, the shift to corporate branding at the LEGO Company has been implemented by top management through their emphasis on company values both as an articulation of what the LEGO brand stands for compared with other play experiences, and in providing opportunities for development of new products and services outside the traditional realm of the brick. In contrast to more abstract artifacts, such as value claims, the brick represented—and still does—the well-known, award-winning tangible artifacts of the LEGO brand to many of its stakeholders. The point of departure in the development of the brand thus resided in the original artifact—the brick—and its multiple extensions, which have been nurtured by the LEGO culture throughout its history. The move to corporate branding, however, changed the focus from the tangible artifact to the *ideas* behind the artifact, which are being stated as company values, beliefs, and the mission of the LEGO Company as a brand as opposed to principles for the material construction of bricks (e.g., the LEGO Characteristics). Thus, the company sought to revitalize its visionary past as a value-driven company with a strong dedication to quality and play values, as highlighted by the founder in his motto, "Only the best is good enough," rather than invent a new set of company ideas.

We argue that the ability to balance the relationship between these different artifacts and their symbolic meaning was one of the core challenges in the creation of a successful corporate brand—and still is. In terms of Hatch and Schultz's corporate-branding model and our extension of it here, this includes the relations between vision, identity, and culture, awaiting the reactions from stakeholder images once the strategy has been executed. These relations are illustrated in Fig. 8.4.

As shown in Fig. 8.4, top management initiated the branding process in an attempt to sharpen and revitalize the value-driven heritage of the LEGO Company as a leading provider of play materials dedicated to a construction idea that combines imagination, creativity, and learning (see Item 1 in Fig. 8.4). Once the reflections on the foundation for the LEGO corporate brand were expressed as a set of identity claims (see Item 2 in Fig. 8.4), these new abstract artifacts had to become meaningful to organization members by being embedded in the organization culture. Thus, the five brand values were intended to guide the construction of new tangible artifacts to be offered to external stakeholders awaiting their feedback and the impact on the overall LEGO company image (see Item 3 in Fig. 8.4). However, the embedding and interpretation processes of abstract artifacts into the LEGO culture used tangible artifacts, rooted in the culture, in order to connect with the tacit understandings and the heritage of the company (see Item 4 in Fig. 8.4). As a next step these new artifacts were offered to stakeholders (see Item 5 in Fig. 8.4), whose response will then influence

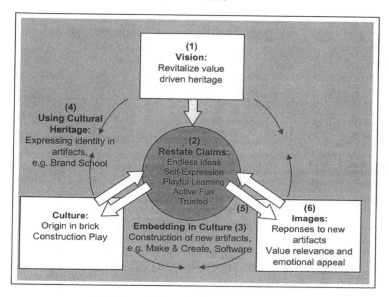

FIG. 8.4. Artifacts in the corporate brand.

the brand image and feed into the further development of the corporate brand (Item 6 in Fig. 8.4).

One successful example of this process was the construction of LEGO Make & Create, which represented a new revitalization of the original freestyle LEGO brick sets, but used small technological twists, resource books, and so on, to expand the brick experience. It has a strong foundation in the LEGO identity and was rapidly taken up within the organizational culture where it revitalized the scope of classic LEGO artifacts; last, but not least, it has been very well received among consumers. Thus, the relations between abstract and tangible artifacts generated the construction of new tangible artifacts based in a stronger perception of the LEGO brand identity and a sharpening of the aesthetic sensitivity among employees of what makes artifacts unique to LEGO (e.g., stronger use of color, odd and wild expressions, appealing to children's own imagination).

The Constructive Role of Artifacts

The additional examples demonstrate different ways in which artifacts were used and reinterpreted by employees during the shift to corporate branding illustrating various processes in our extension of the Hatch and Schultz corporate-branding model (Items 3 and 4 of Fig. 8.4 in particular). Both of our examples focus on artifacts in the relations between identity and culture, but driven by vision in the sense that the revitalization of vision was translated and communicated by top management to employees using the redefinition of identity claims as a central device. The role of stakeholder images and the relations between abstract and tangible artifacts differ between the two examples, one referring to shifts in the perception of artifacts among the employees developing LEGO Software products for consumers, the other referring to the development in the LEGO Brand School, where employees are being exposed to the redefined identity of the LEGO brand.

LEGO Interactive. LEGO Interactive (now a part of LEGO Virtual) illustrates how artifacts based in the cultural heritage have originated, transformed, and spurred the construction of new artifacts within the organizational culture. LEGO Interactive was a recent business division based in the UK dedicated to the development of interactive games (e.g., PlayStation, CD-ROM Games, GameBoy, X-Box, etc.) that add an interactive dimension to the LEGO play experience. This new business area was in many ways radically different from play material in terms of competition, speed, and play themes, which meant that new people with new skills and experiences were hired to create this important extension of the LEGO brand. In their initial development of LEGO Games, employees took "the brick literally" and transferred the brick and the LEGO minifigure directly from their tangible forms to a digital display (see Endnote 2). This direct transfer of artifacts was expressed in several ways; for example, games would include three-dimensional brick-building play experiences, the digital minifigure would be an exact copy of the tangible figure, a simple construction element would dominate game development, the CD-holder of the games would have a studded frame, and the communication material would be decorated with bricks. These artifacts were all developed within a "square" and brick-driven conception of constructivism, which dominated the organizational culture of LEGO Interactive at its inception. In their own explanation, the reasons were both that the company itself was keen to ensure the application of the recognizable "brick universe" to this new extension of the brand and the fact that most employees were new recruits from outside of Denmark, whose image of LEGO Company resided in the brick rather than a deeper understanding of the LEGO values.

However, these brick-based perceptions of LEGO games were challenged by both the strategic vision enhancing brand recognition and the abstract artifacts stating the values behind the LEGO brand (identity), and finally also by reactions from consumers (stakeholder images), which did not engage in the brick universe only. Gradually, employees were beginning to develop a more abstract understanding of how new artifacts of the LEGO play experience could be constructed in closer alignment with the LEGO values, as the identity became embedded in the organizational culture.

Here, employees started to ask questions such as: What is a LEGO story and how does it unfold? What are the special constructive features in the game experience? How can children express themselves through games? As a first step the minifigure was given a prominent role in the games, as a lead character was needed for children to form a relationship to the game experience. Later on, the shapes and expressions of the minifigure were changed—less square and more human—in order to provide stronger personality and more variation. The next steps involved using the LEGO values as criteria in the material construction of new products (i.e., new, more flexible and endless games; exploration of active fun; development of new construction features). This enabled employees to move forward in the development of a LEGO Game experience in ways that were engaging and unique to consumers and thus—ultimately—to stakeholder images.

Thus, employees took the artifact of identity claims literally as briefs for new-product development projects (e.g., the value for active fun inspired new LEGO games such as LEGO Island), implying that the abstract value as artifact became symbolized as a license to create a new generation of LEGO game products and enrich the LEGO culture. The new creativity may stimulate a new level of cultural understanding about what product development is possible based in the LEGO values that may lead to an expansion of the range of artifacts in the future.

LEGO Brand School. The goal of the LEGO Brand School was to introduce the vision to organizational members and redefine the LEGO brand identity. The Brand School was founded in 2002 and consisted of 1- to 3-day workshops facilitated by a team of internal coaches supported by top-management talks. So far LEGO Brand School has involved 1,500 participants. The first round of Brand Schools focused on generating increased awareness of company values and brand strategy by communicating and debating the abstract artifacts of the LEGO brand (mission, beliefs, value statements). As it turned out, people had difficulties making these abstract artifacts relevant to their ongoing work and connecting them to the LEGO everyday behavior. These experiences influenced the second round, which was more concerned with "living the brand" by creating role models among LEGO managers for how the LEGO brand values should be enacted on an everyday basis. When developing the second Brand School, the responsible people teamed up with LEGO Learning Institute, which is a network dedicated to understanding children's learning and play. This generated new ideas about how cultural knowledge of playful learning can contribute to the interpretation process of LEGO Company values along with creating stronger consumer understanding. Thus, in their own explanation, the renewal of the Brand School was based on the ambition to combine a deeper understanding of the core beliefs of the company, stating that

"Children are our role models," with a stronger insights into the unique capabilities and mind-set of children. Thus, learning from how children engage in playful learning and creative self-expressions, the Brand School sought to facilitate similar processes among the participants in their involvement with both abstract and tangible artifacts. This ambition inspired the construction of a range of new artifacts with strong symbolic meanings, such as exercises and working methods, wherein abstract values were turned into tangible artifacts by the Brand School participants. In this process the use of the brick as the core artifact rooted in the culture was particularly important, and spurred several creative applications of the brick, as the participants were invited to create their own expressions of the brand, for example, playing with giant bricks made of soft material and engaging in self-expressive building exercises such as building company values and discussing their symbolic meanings with others afterward. The Brand School also constructed other new material artifacts, which took on new symbolic meanings; for example, a "value gallery," which is a game where pictures are used to help the participants articulate their associations with company values.

In this case, the Brand School invited participants to use tangible material artifacts deeply embedded in the LEGO culture (the brick) to interpret abstract value artifacts and transform them into new tangible artifacts that were used by the participants in their own symbolic play to express their interpretations of the LEGO identity and reflect about their own roles in the future development of the company. This interpretation process was facilitated by the use of material artifacts of the LEGO culture, which in turn were twisted and used to produce new artifacts (e.g., exercises and gallery) that express identity claims in new ways by embedding them in behavior and products that are recognized by employees. Thus, as they engage in the construction of new artifacts with symbolic meanings, the LEGO Brand School takes advantage of the interplay between abstract and material artifacts, using the tangibility of the brick to facilitate and expand employee interpretations of the company vision.

ARTIFACTS IN A BRAND-DRIVEN COMPANY

In this chapter we showed how artifacts as collective accomplishments in organizations are relevant to all elements of a corporate brand and argued that the interpretation and construction of artifacts by all employees are becoming extremely important in the shift from product branding to corporate branding. We have focused on the relations between artifacts that express organizational culture and identity, because the dynamic relationship between the abstract identity artifacts and the cultural material artifacts embedded in organizational practices were crucial to the brand-building process within the LEGO Company.

Although it is well-known that top managers use artifacts as tools to communicate company vision and identity claims to stakeholders, it is less obvious that artifacts play powerful roles in reinforcing the integration of a company's values. On the one hand abstract artifacts are devices for embedding identity claims in organizational culture. This results in the construction of a new range of tangible artifacts. On the other hand, cultural artifacts (e.g., the brick) from the organizational history are used to express identity claims and facilitate the understanding and relevance of identity claims to organizational members. Artifacts, thus, may serve a dual function both in maintaining the current culture (i.e., artifacts as carriers of memory: who we are and where are we coming from) and in anticipating a new identity (i.e., artifacts as carriers of a project and of strategic intent, where we want to go, what we want to stand for). In a dynamic way the "perfect artifact" within a brand-driven company should always be able to disintegrate one order of perception by restructuring a new one, making the brand "contemporary" for stakeholders while maintaining its relevance and recognizability. This is particularly important for a "heritage company" such as the LEGO Company where artifacts are central manifestations of past legacy. Thus, when artifacts are used by organizational members to make sense of who they are and what they are doing, they generate new symbolic meaning as well as reinforce old ideas. In this sense, artifacts become the tangible and abstract material used by organizational members to connect with their external stakeholders' images, their cultural heritage, and their aspirational future.

ACKNOWLEDGMENTS

In the writing of this chapter we offer special thanks to Iben Eiby Johannesen for help in describing the LEGO Brand School and to the team from LEGO Interactive for sharing their experiences.

ENDNOTES

1. The empirical case study of the LEGO Company is based in three different roles. The first author has been an external affiliated professor on a consultancy basis since the end of 1999 and has particularly been involved in the formulation and implementation of the new corporate-brand strategy. The role of the second author has been to act as a sounding board and to help the first author articulate and conceptualize the tacit understandings developed as part of the participant-observation process. The third author has been a key player in the formulation and implementation of the new corpo-

rate-brand strategy, having first the responsibility of the new Global Brand Function and later Corporate Development until the end of 2003. Ciccolella is no longer with LEGO Company. This function included among others brand development, market intelligence, and human resource management. Thus, the findings presented in this chapter are the result of a mutual knowledge-building process, where insights are elaborated and more deeply understood in a continuous dialogue between outsiders and former insiders from the LEGO Company.

2. These reflections emerged during two full-day workshops with the present LEGO Interactive team and their manager, who were founding LEGO Software during fall 2002, in order to discuss and implement the new corporate-brand strategy in the LEGO Software area. Two of the authors were present during those seminars.

3. Figure 8.1 is based on the Corporate Brand Tool-Kit (Hatch & Schultz, 2001), but in this chapter we extend the Tool-Kit by adding identity to the corporate brand and offer a different visual illustration.

Employees as Animate Artifacts: Employee Branding by "Wearing the Brand"

Celia V. Harquail
University of Virginia

Fueled by and fueling a larger cultural trend toward consumerist notions of social relationships is a hot management fad: celebrating the power of brands and recommending marketing concepts and branding practices as tools for general organizational management. An initial wave of advice on expanding branding as a marketing tool (e.g., Pine & Gilmore, 1999) is now giving way to arguments for organizations themselves to become brands. Under the rubric of "Living the Brand" (Ind, 2001; Pringle & Gordon, 2001), these arguments go beyond advising organizations on how to create brands to recommending that organizations apply branding practices to themselves (S. M. Davis & Dunn, 2002).

By presenting branding practices as tools for general management, marketing rhetoric is largely appropriating long-standing knowledge about organizational socialization and culture, repositioning it, and re-naming it organizational branding. What's new here is the way that marketing rhetoric is being used to reposition the desirable relationships between an organization, its products, and its members (Hackley, 2003). Marketing rhetoric tells managers to "treat employees as customers" by "selling" the organization to its employees and treating employees' evaluation of their organization as a kind of "customer satisfaction" (Cardy, 2001). Living-the-brand advocates go even further, recommending that employees themselves become part and parcel of the organization's product and the customers' experience of the brand. Employees throughout the organization should be involved in branding, so as to "enhance the sale" and "make the brand come alive" (Mitchell, 2002, p. 99) for the consumer. Arguments for treating employees as part of the branded product are implemented through *employee branding,* and find their most visible expression in the practice of "wearing the brand."

Employee branding attempts to link employees' everyday work behavior to a larger *raison d'etre* of the organization: the organization's brands. Through the extension of these branding practices into the organization, particularly having employees wear clothing associated with the brand, and through the subsequent incursion of the brand into individuals' personal behaviors, these employee-branding initiatives promise to engage individuals more fully, while appropriating more of their personal selves. Thus, at the same time that these programs align employee behavior and bring the entire organization into the circle of enthusiasm and creativity that enables brand stewardship (S. M. Davis & Dunn, 2002; Ind, 2001), they also encourage organizations to treat their employees as artifacts of their organization's products, an approach that has far-reaching effects on employees as well as the organization. In this chapter I discuss employee branding and the specific practice of wearing the brand to consider how these programs might subvert conventional organization–employee and product–employee relationships, turning employees into artifacts of the brand.

BRANDING AND THE EMPLOYEE

Branding is the practice of taking something more or less generic (be it a product, service, or experience) and making it distinctive, by associating the product with real and imagined qualities that marketers hope will help a customer prefer that brand over others. The brand itself is the social construction that links a material product with a set of beliefs about the product's tangible and intangible attributes. Brands help differentiate a product from similar or competitive others on three dimensions: performance, imagery, and consumer insight (Keller, Sternthal, & Tybout, 2002). Brand performance associations distinguish the product in terms of its functional benefits (e.g., it cleans thoroughly). Brand imagery associations create a sense of the kind of person who uses the product and the circumstances that the product creates for the user, evoking the "romance" of a brand. Finally, consumer insight associations show how the brand can resolve the consumers' own problems better than similar brands. Together, these associations create the functional, symbolic, and emotional aspects of the brand.

Brands themselves are organizational artifacts (see Schultz, Hatch, & Ciccolella and Cappetta & Gioia, chaps. 8 & 11, respectively, this volume), and they are important sensemaking tools within the organization as well as for the consumer. For the consumer, a brand is an artifact that helps answer the question of why a product, service, or experience is preferable to others. For members of the organization, the brand helps to answer the question, what do we want to communicate about this product that describes it to consumers, differentiates it from similar products, and leads consumers to prefer this product over competitive others? What managers understand about and desire for the brand's meaning also helps them make decisions about the physical product itself. In these ways, brands are sensemaking tools that help organization members create, evaluate, and deliver the tangible and intangible promises represented by their organization's products.

Directed at organizations themselves, "internal branding" advocates a system of socialization and communication practices intended to inspire employees to deliver on a brand's promise, by leading employees to internalize brand values and by instilling brand values in key internal organizational processes (Dell et al., 2001). Employee branding focuses on the employees' role in creating and maintaining the brand attributes associated with the organization's products. The action implied by the label employee branding is meant literally, because these programs are intended to impress brand attributes onto the work behavior of employees, who are then expected to infuse brand attributes throughout their work (Ind, 2001; Mitchell, 2002) through "on-brand behaviors." On-brand behaviors are those that enact, demonstrate, and maintain the brand's attributes. Employee-branding practices encourage employees to think about the brand more consciously and actively consider the brand's interests as they make decisions. To encourage employees to associate the brand and its attributes as closely as possible to their selves, employee-branding advocates recommend orienting the organization's culture toward the brand so that every expression of the organization, from common organizational artifacts such as decor, equipment, publications, and uniforms to underlying organizational values, manifests the brand's values and attributes. The goal of employee branding is to create employees and a work environment where every decision and every behavior enacts and displays the specific attributes of the brand. Because branding advocates want employees to internalize the brand's values, however, they seem to hope that employees will come to believe that they share the attributes of the brand and to define themselves as one with the brand. Thus, "by weaving the brand messages into employee's everyday experiences, managers can ensure that on brand behavior becomes instinctive" (Mitchell, 2002, p. 1010). The intent of employee-branding programs is, ultimately, to change the ways that employees think and behave so that their thoughts and behaviors always prioritize the brand's interests.

Conventional brand education programs designed to help employees keep the brand in mind have focused on teaching employees about the brand. These programs assume that the more employees know about a brand, the more effective the employees can be at translating the brand's desired attributes into marketing and product development decisions. These programs work through cognitive mechanisms that maintain a separation between the employee and the brand: The brand is the object of the employees' efforts. In contrast, employee-branding advocates describe employee branding as a process for tightening the relationship between the brand and the employees by associating the brand and its attributes with the employees themselves. Employee-branding programs assume that the more the employees can act like the brand, the more they can execute on-brand behavior. Employee branding asks employees to assume the role of the brand's representative at all times, regardless of their role or function within the organization. Advocates promise that employee branding will increase the frequency and intensity with which employees evoke the brand's values in everyday work practices. They argue further that stronger employee branding will lead to increased positive feelings toward the organization, interest in organizational successes, and uniformity both in employees' understanding of the brand and in their approaches to delivering on the brand promise (Mitchell, 2002). Perhaps the greatest promise is that branded employees will prioritize the brand automatically and uncritically and to always put the brand's interest first.

PRACTICES AND FORMS OF EMPLOYEE BRANDING

Employee-branding programs recommend that managers redeploy practices that reinforce the norms and values of the organization itself—practices such as socialization (e.g., training and communication), organizational decor, the distribution of organizational artifacts, and controlling employee appearance—and use these practices instead to educate and reinforce beliefs about the brand. Perhaps the most common form of employee branding is training programs where all employees are taught the basics of branding and marketing principles and instructed on the attributes to be associated with their specific brand. For example, as part of Bath & Body Works' new employee orientation, new employees receive training on the concept of branding, on the retail brands that compete with the Bath & Body Works brand, and on the specific attributes of the brand that the organization promotes. Every organization member, from hourly workers who pack and ship stock to the firm's accounting professionals who manage the firm's capital, participates in this brand orientation. Employees are expected to know all about their company's brand and to display the brand's attributes and promote the brand's interests through on-brand behaviors in their everyday work, even when their jobs have little or nothing to do with marketing.

In addition to training programs, employees are branded through a variety of organizational communication practices. For example, internal corporate press and new-product launches are designed not simply to inform or educate employees but also to persuade them and influence their behavior (Ind, 2001; Mitchell, 2002; Pringle & Gordon, 2001). In addition, communication practices that were previously directed only at outside constituencies—such as brand advertising and public relations (PR) campaigns—explicitly are being redesigned to target employees as well as outsiders. Not content to depend on whatever indirect effects these communication practices may have on employees (Elsbach & Glynn, 1996), organizations see their advertising and PR efforts as tools to influence employees and encourage on-brand behavior (Mitchell, 2002). As a result, Wal-Mart's television advertising, featuring the greeter welcoming customers as they come into the store, is as much about demonstrating what attributes the employees are expected to display in their own behavior as it is about promoting Wal-Mart's brand to the general public.

Indirectly but still explicitly, employees are branded by organizational decor that reflects the brand, such as brand-consonant aesthetic schemes (e.g., color palettes, furniture styles), corporate art, and three-dimensional product displays designed for retail environments. Organizations also distribute to employees brand-related artifacts such as copies of print advertising, product prototypes, promotional materials like key chains, mugs, and decorative accessories (see Elsbach, chap. 4, this volume), and clothing emblazoned with the brand's logo that symbolize and communicate desired brand associations. These artifacts are intended for use outside and inside the work environment, to surround the employee with reminders that reinforce the desired associations between the product and its attributes, and the brand and the employee.

EMPLOYEE BRANDING BY CONTROLLING EMPLOYEES' APPEARANCE

Somewhat less common and becoming more popular are employee-branding techniques that work by controlling employees' appearance, through programs that advocate "wearing the brand." Wearing the brand requires employees to dress themselves for work in ways that symbolize the brand and the brand's attributes. By mixing their own personal work wardrobe with organizationally specified brand-expressive clothing— clothing that by its style, type, and functionality, as well as its emotional and "romantic" associations, symbolizes the brand to the wearer—employees use their own physical appearance to communicate the brand's attributes to the internal organizational audience.

At first glance, employee-branding practices that control employees' appearance looks like a simple extension of a common practice of clothing retailers. Clothing retailers often require that their salespeople wear items that the company sells (Merrick, 2003), so that salespeople model and demonstrate for customers the fashions for sale (Cappetta & Gioia, chap. 11, this volume). For example, The Gap requires retail store employees to wear Gap-brand clothing or clothing similar to it. Salespeople's appearance may also be controlled so that they project or even personify to the consumer the image of the brand's ideal customer. The dress code of clothing retailer Abercrombie & Fitch (A&F) refers to employees as "Brand Representatives," whose defined duties include "looking great in A&F-style clothes" and "projecting the A&F brand with enthusiasm and energy" (Greenhouse, 2003; Merrick, 2003). Potentially more nefarious is the practice of controlling salespeoples' appearance by selecting them on criteria such as their physical attractiveness, ethnicity, age, and perceived social class. A&F is currently being sued by former employees who contend that they were denied retail sales jobs because their appearance did not reflect the White, Anglo-Saxon, frat-boy image of A&F's brand.

More recently, policies for controlling employees' physical appearance have been adopted for employee branding. Instead of focusing on influencing the consumer, wearing the brand is intended to influence the thoughts and behaviors of employees themselves. Rather than being a superficial requirement intended to influence only the employees' surface appearance, wearing the brand is directed more deeply at the individuals' beliefs about the brand, their relationship with the brand, and the link between the brand and their own behaviors. Controlling appearance through dress is potentially an effective way to influence individual's behavior, because of the ways that dress reflects, influences, and helps to construct individuals' social selves (F. Davis, 1991; Entwistle, 2000). By formally and informally expecting employees to express the brand through their physical appearance, especially by asking employees to dress in ways that symbolize the brand's attributes, organizations strive to link brand attributes to their employees' sense of self.

Wearing the brand is supposed to make the brand's values and message consistently salient for employees. As employees put on brand-expressive dress, they become conscious of whether and how they individually are representing what the brand stands for. When employees wearing the brand interact with others inside the organization, their own and their colleagues' brand-expressive dress triggers them to keep the brand and its attributes in mind. Thinking "as the brand," these employees may be more creative when considering how the brand ought to be represented in different situations (Pringle & Gordon, 2001). Because every organization member can or should be able to find ways to wear the brand, members throughout the organization can express the brand through their appearance, reinforcing and maintaining the salience of brand attributes. Employees wear the brand for themselves, for each other, and for the brand itself.

LIVING THE BRAND AT LAND ROVER NA

To some, wearing the brand may seem silly, whereas to others it may seem banal. But employees of one corporation, Land Rover NA, found the practice to be very effective at keeping their minds and their behaviors on brand. Land Rover NA, the marketing, sales, and retailing management division of the larger Land Rover Corporation, actively practiced wearing the brand from its formation in 1985 with 10 employees until about 1998, when it employed 170. As the former chief executive officer Charlie Hughes tells it, managers at Land Rover NA were focused on the overall goal of living the brand, of finding ways to make the brand come alive and feel alive to the employees, so that their everyday work could be focused on and infused with a deep understanding of the brand's attributes and of its meaning to customers (Moore & Harquail, 2003). Their living-the-brand program included training on the mechanical aspects of the vehicle, training in off-road driving techniques to understand the performance of the vehicles, and workshops to discuss the Land Rover brand heritage and how it could be communicated to North American consumers. During their first week working together, the 10 Land Rover NA executives decided to dress like the brand as an exercise to get in touch with their brand and to generate an esprit de corps.

Land Rover was positioned as a lifestyle brand, in which the product's basic functional proposition is augmented with a set of values that connects with and adds meaning to the lifestyles of particular consumer groups. Lifestyle-branded products come with idealized social situations attached to them and are heavy on brand imagery. As Hughes explained, "Land Rover customers are buying a piece of hardware—but they are really buying a dream" (Moore & Harquail, 2003, p. 4). To dramatize, the Land Rover brand lifestyle and imagery suggests that Land Rovers are driven by quasi-British, upper-crust men with adventurous spirits who enjoy bird hunting, going to the country lodge or on a big game hunt in Africa, and the thrill of driving through rough, wild countryside that no European man has explored before.

Living the brand at Land Rover was boosted by an unplanned outcome of promotional events directed at Land Rover customers. Early in the reintroduction of the brand to North America, Land Rover held customer driving workshops and off-roading events to generate excitement around the brand's performance and imagery associations. For each of these promotional events, Land Rover NA created some unique clothing and accessory items, which it called Land Rover "gear." At first, Land Rover gave customers T-shirts, key chains, baseball caps, and other logo wear. Shortly thereafter, managers decided to make the merchandise more unique and brand specific. They began distributing Wellington boots, Barbour jackets, hunting vests, shooting caps, and other Anglophilic outdoorsy items. The gear was so popular that customers asked to purchase it outright. The company began to produce the gear to sell at retail, hired a designer to create it, and issued spring and fall gear catalogs. All this time, employees at the Land Rover NA headquarters were wearing gear that they collected while working at the promotional events themselves, mixing it in along with more conventional workday clothing intended to express the brand's attributes. The consumer-gear program and the wearing-the-brand initiative ultimately converged, when Land Rover NA employees were instructed to purchase gear from the catalog (at a significant discount) and to mix this gear into their work wardrobes so that they could wear the brand at work. On any given workday, employees' appearance would reflect the Land Rover brand through a mixture of Land Rover gear, accessories, and brand-expressive clothing items from their personal wardrobes. Land Rover NA executives believed that employees enjoyed wearing the brand. As Hughes said, "I think we created magic . . . We created a team that everyone wanted to belong to" (Moore & Harquail, 2003, p. 7). But behind the magic, being part of the brand team also required a lot of work.

THE WORK OF WEARING THE BRAND

One could argue that wearing the brand is merely an entertaining example of organizational dress, the patterns of clothing and artifacts that employees wear at work that are achieved through implicit dress norms or explicit dress codes (Rafaeli & Pratt, 1993). Organizational dress is intended to facilitate employees' work within and for the organization (Rafaeli et al., 1997; Rafaeli & Pratt, 1993) because dress can help employees engage and execute their roles and establish role-appropriate emotional states and relationships with others (Rafaeli et al., 1997). Organizations themselves, through organizational dress, influence what information employees can communicate about themselves, their organizations, and their role at work by controlling each employee's visual self-presentation.

Though all forms of organizational dress require physical and cognitive work (Rafaeli et al., 1997), the work of wearing the brand is comparatively complex. Wearing the brand demands that employees think regularly about the brand, about how to translate the brand and its attributes into clothing-borne symbols, and about how to present themselves as artifacts of the brand. Wearing the brand is a unique twist on organizational dress because this psychologically complex work facilitates a subtle yet profound shift in the status of employees—from being creators of the brand to being the brand's subjects.

On the surface, the process of wearing the brand appears relatively straightforward: Employees dress for work in combinations of their own clothing and items judged to symbolize various attributes of the brand, so that the employees' finished appearance represents the brand. Examined more closely, wearing the brand involves a lot of work by employees. It requires employees to invest themselves in learning about the brand, and pushes them to take the role of the brand, to consistently communicate brand attributes to others in social interactions, and to attach brand attributes to the individual's self.

Wearing the brand is the outcome of several effortful activities, including acquiring branded clothing that fits, acquiring branded accessories, paying for and maintaining a wardrobe, and choosing clothing each day. Each morning, the process of getting dressed for work activates the individual's brand schema and the individual's symbolic judgment, as he or she tries to assemble an outfit that expresses the brand. With the choice of each brand-relevant or personal clothing item, as with the assembly of the overall outfits, employees must assess whether any brand attributes are reflected, which brand attributes are reflected, whether they have achieved a coordinated look, and whether they are branded "enough."

Whereas some employees might be able to reduce wearing the brand to an automatic, mechanical process (e.g., select trousers from pile A, shirt from pile B, vest or sweater from pile C), for others, wearing the brand each day requires more concentration. People may make routine clothing combinations on some days and unique combinations on other days as they respond to seasonal changes or one-time situations. In addition, individuals need to incorporate all these elements into outfits in which they feel reasonably comfortable, both physically and psychologically. Thus, wearing the brand challenges employees to express the brand's attributes while reflecting some of their physical need, preferences, and personal style.

Dressing each day to wear the brand asks employees to transfer meaning from the brand to themselves by creating a symbolic value chain. The value chain begins at work, where a set of brand imagery and consumer insight associations are symbolically attached to a functional product to create the brand. Next, employees must transfer meaning from the brand idea into individual clothing items, into the daily outfits they assemble for themselves, and onto their bodies. Then, employees take the symbolic product—their own branded appearance—back into the workplace, where they are expected to reflect, consider, and enact in their behavior the attributes that their branded outfits and selves symbolize. Each morning, getting dressed to wear the brand requires employees to put their more abstract, intangible understanding of the brand into some kind of tangible symbolic expression and then to be that symbolic expression themselves, all day long.

Each time employees dress to wear the brand and when they add branded and individual items to their wardrobes, they reinforce and elaborate on their ability to translate the brand's essence into the symbolism of clothing. Wearing the brand requires employees to learn or even create the associations between clothing attributes (color, cut, functionality) and brand attributes. Day in and day out, they have to consider what the brand attributes are, how they might be reflected, and how they could be aggregated, through a set of dress symbols. As they observe other employees also wearing the brand, they may imitate the tactics of employees who wear the brand with a certain panache, thus expanding their repertoire of wearing the brand. Employees also receive feedback from other employees that confirms, disconfirms, and or otherwise educates them on how well they have symbolized the brand through their dress. At Land Rover NA, employees commented on each other's brand dress, especially when a person found an item of apparel that expressed the brand well (e.g., a rugged corduroy shirt from Land's End Outfitters) but was not from the gear catalog, or when an individual showed up with an antique or otherwise rare artifact (e.g., a belt from the first "off road rodeo"). They complimented each other not only on particular items that reflected the brand but also on outfits that seemed to convey the brand effectively. Through their own experimentation, through observing others, and through responding to feedback on their efforts to wear the brand, individual employees develop insight into the brand and how it can be expressed symbolically. Wearing the brand gives an employee personal daily practice at "operationalizing the brand" (S. M. Davis & Dunn, 2002, p. 227), by expressing the brand's conceptual attributes through combinations of material symbols.

THE INTENDED EFFECTS OF WEARING THE BRAND ON EMPLOYEES' SENSE OF SELF

Learning how to associate dress attributes with brand attributes and performing this work daily influences not only how employees conceptualize the brand but also how employees conceptualize themselves. The same general process that marketers use to brand products—constantly associating symbolic attributes with the physical product so that consumers psychologically transfer the attributes to the product—is applied to employees through wearing the brand. Just as consumers use rituals of possession and personal grooming to transfer the social meanings of advertised goods to themselves (McCracken, 1988) employees transfer their knowledge of the brand into their clothing as a means for transferring brand knowledge into their behaviors and cognitions, and then transfer brand attributes into their self-concepts. Transferring brand attributes into self-attributes through dress employs several mechanisms, including identity claiming and identity negotiation, role performance, basic processes of attitude change, and self-consistency pressures. All of these mechanisms share a basic process: that of continually associating the individual with the brand's attributes, so that the individual comes to think of him or herself as actually possessing those attributes.

Individuals intentionally associate themselves with a variety of attributes and groups to indicate who they are, through behaviors known as identity claiming. Identity claiming is an impression-management process in which individuals present themselves privately and socially as having the identities and attributes that they desire to possess (Bartel & Dutton, 2001; Harquail, 2003; Snow & Anderson, 1987). Clothing is a common tool for claiming identity attributes for the simple reason that the proximity of a symbol to an individual's body is used by the self and others to approximate the importance to the individual of the meaning attached to the symbol (Entwistle, 2000; Thatcher, Doucet, & Tuncel, 2001). Because dress is highly visible and is closely attached to our bodily selves, it quickly assumes "the quality of a metaphor" for an individual's identity (Belk, 1988; F. Davis, 1991). Because individuals' self-conceptions are constructed and negotiated in social interaction (e.g., Cooley, 1902) as they respond to the reactions of others to their self-presentations and maintain and modify their private self-concepts in response to these reactions (Swann, 1987), wearing the brand may engender a cycle of social interaction that may lead employees to internalize the brand's attributes.

When a person wears the brand, others may perceive the person's clothing as making an effort to communicate who that person is, and so employees wearing the brand may be interpreted by others as claiming the brand's attributes as their own. Whether the association between displayed attributes and the individual is intended for self-definition or for some other motive such as "operationalizing the brand," the public association of attributes and individual through the symbolism of clothing sets in motion the social negotiation of identity. Whether the employees intend it, others in their social environment will read their branded behaviors and symbols as identity claims and respond accordingly. If employees are treated by others as though they have the brand's attributes, they may conclude that they do indeed have these attributes.

Wearing the brand may also influence employees' self-concepts through the general influence of dress on role taking and the influence of role taking on the self-concept. Because new roles require new skills, behaviors, attitudes, and patterns of interactions, they may produce fundamental changes in an individual's self-definitions (Ibarra, 1999). Dress helps employees execute their organizational roles by helping them enter one role and shed others, by helping to establish emotional states that facilitate role performance, and by helping them relate effectively to others by influencing their relationships within the organization (Rafaeli et al., 1997). More than regular organizational dress, wearing the brand cues a very specific role: that of "being" the brand. Employees can "be" the brand by seeing the world from the brand's frame of reference and by acting "as" and "for" the brand, as though they were playing the role of the brand. Playing the role of the brand involves making salient an employee's cognitive schemas about what the brand is and how it should be expressed. These brand schemas may then influence an employee's frame of reference so that he or she interprets situations and establishes priorities and goals consonant with the attributes and interests of the brand. In addition, branded dress may maintain the salience of the brand's attributes, perhaps even making them as or more salient than other attributes in the individual's self concept. Although employees may be playing the role of the brand and pretending to have the brand's attributes, over time this role playing may lead employees to believe that these attributes are not just performances but are, instead, their own authentic attributes (Ibarra, 1999).

Employees wearing the brand may also be influenced by basic processes of attribute change as a result of being part of a branded group. Kelman (1958) outlined three ways that individuals accept group influence and come to display the values and attributes of a group: (a) compliance or exchange, (b) identification or affiliation, and (c) internalization or value congruence. Compliance occurs when individuals display group values and attributes simply to avoid punishment or gain rewards. Identification occurs when individuals adopt group values and attributes that they respect (or don't disagree with), without accepting them as their own. Internalization occurs when an individual already holds values and attributes that are the same as or congruent with those of the group.

For individuals who do not possess the same attributes as the brand, displaying brand attributes for compliance and identification may lead individuals over time to internalize these attributes as their own. Because individuals strive to maintain consistency between their behaviors and their self-beliefs (Gecas, 1982; C. M. Steele, 1988), employees who wear the brand may seek to think of themselves as being the way that they present themselves at work. Though we often think of self-beliefs as leading to behaviors, behaviors also lead to self-beliefs. Consistently dressing oneself in the brand's attributes and demonstrating these attributes through one's behavior may lead an employee to internalize these attributes and adopt them as self-defining. Thus even after they take off their work clothes employees may discover that they are still—behaviorally and cognitively—branded.

Wearing the brand is a prosaic yet comparatively extreme example of a workplace practice that derives its power from constraining, directing, and disciplining the individual's sense of self while at work (Clegg, 1994; Collinson, 2003; Trethewey, 1999; Willmott, 1993). Because wearing the brand controls an employee's self-presentation at work, it is a form of "identity regulation" (Alvesson & Willmott, 2002) that encourages individuals to present themselves as valuable objects in the eyes of their authority while subordinating their own subjectivity in the process (Ashforth & Mael, 1998). Wearing the brand regulates identity by controlling the amount of an individual's appearance that is left to his or her discretion and by controlling the content of what the individual can display. If clothing and other personal artifacts serve to extend the self metaphorically (Belk, 1988; J. B. Cohen, 1989), wearing the brand may lead to the subordination of the individual's authentic and autonomous self by shrinking the psychic space in which they can experience their individuality.

Individuals whose physical appearance, demographic group, psychographic profile, social identities, and personalities overlap with a particular brand and its attributes will be less constricted in their self-presentation than will individuals whose appearance, social roles, and personalities clash with their role as a brand artifact. For example, a tall, northern European White man wearing the brand at Land Rover will experience less identity regulation than a short Korean man because his physical appearance is more consonant with the brand's identity.

The match between the attributes the brand represents and the attributes the employees actually have will also affect the identity regulation they experience. Whether or not the employees personally hold the brand's values they must appear as though they do. Displaying the attributes of a specific brand may be more of a burden for some types or classes of employees than for others. For example, female mangers at Land Rover needed to reconcile gender expectations, professional role expectations, and brand expectations while figuring out how to display the masculine attributes of the brand. Managing any conflict between the attributes of a brand and ones personal attributes or social roles might also be emotionally difficult (Ashforth & Humphrey, 1993; Rafaeli & Sutton, 1987). Self-presentations that can be justified as self-representative are more likely to feel comfortable and to be internalized more easily than self-presentations that contradict self-beliefs and social expectations (Schlenker & Trudeau, 1990). Employees who feel pressured by the organization to present themselves in a way that is at odds with their self-definition may react negatively (Covaleski, Dirsmith, Heian, & Samuel, 1998), perhaps alienating themselves from the brand's attributes. In addition, individuals who are generally apathetic about dress may be less affected than those who regularly use dress to express their individuality

(Shim & Bickle, 1994). Given the infinite number of combinatorial options in creating an outfit and the symbolic ambiguity inherent in clothing (F. Davis, 1991), wearing the brand may still leave room for individuals to resist conforming their self-expression completely. But employees who resist or who remain unskilled at wearing the brand may appear to be "not branded enough," calling into question their more global ability to express the brand's values as well as their commitment to the brand.

COMPLICATIONS FOR EMPLOYEES' SENSE OF SELF SPECIFIC TO WEARING BRANDS

All of the complications and concerns mentioned previously could be raised, to one degree or another, with any form of organizational dress. Yet controlling employee appearance to serve the brand is uniquely problematic because of three qualities inherent in commercial brands. First, brands are not real. Both the consumers who buy them and the employees who craft them understand that brands are fictions that combine truth and fantasy. Second, brands and their attributes are created by marketers to elicit consumers' desire. The attributes of a brand are chosen and manipulated to fit what marketers believe that consumers should want; the needs or particular talents of employees and organizations have little or no bearing on the attributes that are attached to the brand. Third, the attributes of a brand are tethered to the product very tenuously. Beyond the material, functional attributes of a product, every other attribute comprising a brand is ephemeral, and so what the brand means—its social signification—is inherently unstable. What a brand means or stands for is always at the mercy of the marketplace. Brands mutate in response to shifts in the socially constructed meanings of comparison brands, to changes in fashion, and to changes in consumers' tastes. The unique problems of wearing the brand boil down to these: (a) employees are asked to present themselves as something they know is at least partially fictitious, (b) employees are asked to present themselves as part of the product, designed to please customers, and (c) employees are asked to transform themselves to fit an image that is itself unstable.

Consider first what it means for branded employees that brands are fictions. Marketers strive to create a symbolic, partly fictional meaning for their brand that will entice consumers into a relationship where the branded product helps consumers construct their identities socially and fulfill themselves emotionally (Elliott & Wattanasuwan, 1998; Herman, 2002). Using "compensatory symbolism" (Solomon, 1983) and "symbolic consumption" (Elliott & Wattanasuwan, 1998) consumers use branded products to fill the gap between an idealized set of behaviors and attributes that they desire and their own ability to enact these behaviors or have these attributes in real life (Helman & de Chernatony, 1999). When consumers construct their sense of self by associating themselves with brands they usually find for themselves a comfortable balance between authenticity and fiction. However, compensatory symbolism can go too far when, instead of being fulfilled, consumers pour themselves into brands and let brands become their identity. They become all about surface appearance, lose their core sense of self (Quart, 2003), and lose their sense of personal authenticity.

Moreover, when one's association of self with brand is enforced rather than voluntary, compensatory symbolism and symbolic consumption have different effects. Employees wearing the brand have little or no authority over the brand or attributes with which they must associate themselves, and they are unable to control the balance between authenticity and fiction because they do not control how branded they need to appear. Yet regardless of whether the relationship between the brand's attributes and the employees' attributes is improbable or inauthentic, the employees' individual identities are still shaped and perhaps even distorted when they must present themselves socially as the brand. Employees who are not and cannot plausibly "be" the brand are still required to associate their selves with the brand in ways that create for them, however briefly and intrapersonally, the experience that they are what they cannot be. This kind of emptied out relationship can threaten the authenticity of their relationships with other employees and with the organization itself (Tracy, 2000). Even worse, this relationship with the brand may threaten employees' sense of personal authenticity.

Second, consider that employees wearing the brand are being directed to present themselves as part of the product. When a Land Rover executive explained that "wearing the brand gives people working in that company permission to be just like the products" (Moore & Harquail, 2003, p. 7), he implied that being like the product is something employees should desire. But if employees are treated like products, as interchangeable commodities distinguished primarily by their degree of branded-ness, employees are no longer unique individuals with valuable skills and experience. In addition, the more employees are like products, the more they risk "becoming characters for commerce" (Tracy, 2000, p. 90) who are required to present whatever public face will please the customer. When employees have to anticipate the needs of customers, even when they never interact with these customers, the customers become yet another boss.

Finally, consider that if the meaning or social significance of a brand is unstable, so then is the standard against which the branded employees must perform. Branded employees must be willing and able to change their self-presentations whenever marketing experts want to adjust or evolve the brand, and branded employees must buttress their self-presentations against the vagaries of market trends and consumer preferences. For example, if employees get any pleasure out of presenting themselves and their brand as hip, then they stand to lose something when and not if consumers' changing tastes make their brand and the employees themselves "uncool." If employees are effectively branded, so that brand attributes and their meanings are deeply embedded in employees' self-presentation and work behavior, employees might find it hard to exchange old attributes for new ones or protect their self-esteem when attributes that were once desirable fall out of public favor.

COMPLICATIONS OF EMPLOYEE BRANDING FOR THE ORGANIZATION–EMPLOYEE RELATIONSHIP

In addition to the unintended effects of wearing the brand on the employees' sense of self and on the relationship between the employee and the brand, employee-branding practices may also complicate the relationship between the employee and the organization. Potential complications stem from (a) the breakdown of internal–external organizational boundaries, (b) any lack of overlap between the between the meaning of the brand and the core values of the organization, and (c) the distortion of the power dynamics between the organization, the brand and the employees.

The Breakdown of Internal–External Boundaries. One organizational complication of employee branding stems from the breakdown of the organization's internal and external boundaries. Previously, organizations were encouraged to keep their internal functioning separate from their external relations (Hatch & Schultz, 1997), so employees were rarely cultivated as consumers. The emerging practice of employee branding treats employees (organizational insiders) as consumers (organizational outsiders), even though employees and consumers may have different interests and different perceptions. Insiders and outsiders have access to different information about organizations and apply different values and goals in interpreting this information (Dutton, Dukerich, & Harquail, 1994). Employees who experience the organization from the inside while being targeted as consumers by communications that construct the fiction of the brand may be more sensitive to the degree of consistency between the practices of the organization projecting the brand and the image of the brand that is promoted. For example, can a facial cleanser produced by an organization that exploits child labor be environmentally friendly? Branded employees may also be more sensitive to the consistency between the brand's advertised attributes and the processes through which the actual product is created or manufactured. Can an automobile built in Detroit by AFL-CIO workers actually "be" the handcrafted, finely tuned machine transport of the British upper class? When employees see a disjunction between the attributes of the brand that they are supposed to represent, the attributes of the processes creating the branded product, and the attributes of the organization they are part of, they may question the authenticity of the brand, the authenticity of the organization, and their own personal integrity.

The Overlap Between Brand Attributes and Organizational Values. The relationship between the values of an organization itself and the attributes of the brand it constructs may pose an important obstacle to operationalizing recommendations of employee branding. A fundamental assumption of employee-branding programs is that the set of attributes that compose the brand are consonant with, if not the same as, the values and attributes that compose the organization's identity. Under this assumption, programs that reinforce the brand serve to reinforce the organization. But embedded in the relationship between the brand attributes and the organization's attributes is the question of brand structure, or how the organization's name is related to the major brand(s), subbrands, various business units, geographic areas, and channel descriptors. Functionally, there may not be an effective correspondence between the brand structures (how brands are related) and organizational structures (how units are organized). Thus, the alignment of brands with employees and brand groups with work groups may lead to situations where employees in the same work group dress as different brands, or vice versa. Moreover, some functional groups may find the brand consonant with their strategy, whereas other functional groups find the brand associations to be a hindrance.

When the corporation is the brand, and when the corporation's name represents all the products and services that the organization provides, this problem is supposedly simplified. Yet even in its simplest case, where a single brand "name" represents both the company and the consumer brand, "coherence is not guaranteed" (Cappetta & Gioia, chap. 11, this volume). If there are important differences between the attributes of the organization and the attributes of the consumer brand, especially if these sets of attributes conflict, employees may find it difficult to adopt the consumer-oriented brand beliefs and transfer them into the workplace. At the purely visual level, would having employees dress like the brand make the workplace look less like a workplace and more like a theme park? At a deeper level, what might happen if employees of companies like Playboy Inc. were directed to reflect the consumer brand's attributes and values in their everyday workplace behavior? Employee branding asks employees to attach themselves to the brand, and when the brand is unlike the organizations' values, this may set up tensions that are difficult for employees and organizations to negotiate.

The Distortion of Power Relationships Between the Organization, the Brand, and Employees.   Another possible complication stems from the repositioning of the target of the organization's branding efforts and the change in power relationships that this suggests. In conventional product-branding practices, the brand is the creation of the organization and its employees; it is their intentional social construction. In employee-branding practices, the employees and the organization become the creations of the brand. Like a science project gone awry, employee-branding initiatives subvert the power relationship between the creator and what is created. When the brand becomes more important than the organization itself, managers may make decisions that benefit the brand yet damage the organization. For example, the $30 million a year that Nike pays to a celebrity athlete to endorse a sneaker might be better spent as performance incentives for low-level employees within the organization itself. Employee branding makes the employees and the organization instruments of the brand and subject to the brand's power and interests.

The practice of wearing the brand may also affect the organization's identity in ways that marketers have failed to consider. When organizations institute the practice of wearing the brand, they may trigger the replacement of organizational identity with brand identity. The dominant dress attributes across an organization are believed to convey the central, distinctive, and enduring values of the organization (Rafaeli & Pratt, 1993) and to express the organization's identity (Cappetta & Gioia, chap. 11, this volume). By instantiating, reminding, and reinforcing brand values by making them ubiquitous, visible, and constant through dress, wearing the brand makes brand attributes available to be construed by employees as the central, distinctive, and enduring attributes of organizational identity (Harquail & King, 2003). Because advocates of living the brand assume that organizational and brand values are consonant, this is precisely the outcome they seek. But whereas both brand identities and organizational identities are sets of beliefs about central, distinctive, and continuous attributes, brand and organizational identities differ in a subtle yet profound way. Brands are beliefs invented about a product to make a product more desirable, to sell it, and to make a profit. In contrast, organizational identities emerge from members' collective values and help to provide the organization and its members with a deeper, broader reason for being. Certainly, many organizations exist to sell products, but for most organizations, this is not their sole source of meaning or purpose. To supplant the collective, organic meaning of organizational identity with a commercial fiction such as a brand is to diminish what is possible for employees and organizations to achieve and places commercialism and even cynicism at the organization's heart.

Implications

So what are we to make of employee-branding practices, especially programs like wearing the brand that work by manipulating employees' self-presentation and self-expression? Are these branding programs as harmless and simple to execute as their advocates would make them seem? As with so many programs intended to transform employees' relationships to work, employee branding in general and wearing the brand specifically are compelling ideas that, if managed thoughtfully, may indeed bring about behaviors that managers desire. It is hard to argue with the basic premise of these programs: Employees who understand the brand and keep the brand in mind will be better at delivering on the brand promise throughout the organization and to the consumer. Certainly, the positive experience with wearing the brand that Land Rover executives report suggests that wearing the brand can focus an organization and might even be fun. Given the purported benefits of these programs and recognizing the ways that employee branding may constrain individuals' authentic self-expression at work, perhaps the more important issues are not whether to brand employees but, instead, how much branding is necessary, what branding processes are most appropriate, and at what point the benefits of employee branding become outweighed by the costs to employees and organizations.

Employee-branding programs offer organizational scholars some intriguing avenues for exploring the specifics of complex relationships among the organization, the organization's products, and the organization's employees, and for evaluating the effects of these relationships at the individual, collective, and organizational levels. For example, can asking employees to develop a relationship with a brand by presenting themselves as expressions, symbols, or artifacts of the brand lead them to become overly attached to the brand and to its current attributes? Would this reinforce internal complacency and overconfidence and prevent employees and organizations from attending to external risks and opportunities? Organization scholars could consider how using beliefs about a product originally intended to influence external consumers can and should influence internal organizational processes, especially when these beliefs are known to be fictions.

As a unique twist on organizational dress, the dynamics of wearing the brand demonstrate how basic processes of organizational dress can be complicated when dress expectations prioritize interests outside instead of within the organization. Exploring wearing the brand and similar programs may give us new appreciation for the ways that employees access, personalize, and employ personally manipulable symbols to serve their needs and the needs of the organization. More broadly, observing how individual employees' selves are used to sell product beliefs to themselves and each other should raise our awareness about the power dynamics involved in making employees instruments of the organization's brand. Finally, with regard to the broader incursion of marketing rhetoric into organizational analyses, we should look closely and critically at the applicability of marketing rhetoric to larger questions of organizational leadership. Organizational scholars and managers alike need to judge whether newly hyped perspectives are really new or merely repackaged, and whether the management advice they generate facilitates or subtly manipulates the relationships between employees and organizations. As they say in marketing, *caveat emptor*.

10

On Logos, Business Cards:
The Case of UK Universities

Yehuda Baruch
University of East Anglia

Meeting a person in a business context, a typical introductory activity (or a ritual to be completed upon adjourning the meeting) will be an exchange of business cards. Typically, the most prominent and distinctive feature of a business card is the organizational logo. Upon receiving a letter from a company representative, printed on their official letterhead paper, a prominent and distinctive visual feature of the letter would be the organizational logo on the letterhead. Browsing the Internet, looking at web pages of organizations, a logo will be positioned in a central, focal point, as if to set the tone of the "virtual place."

The common denominator for these scenarios is the prominence of the organizational logo, and its crucial role in forming the first impression the organization will make upon you. The cliché that you have no second opportunity to make a first impression is highly valid in this case. Thus organizations should devote considerable attention to their logo and the way it represents them. The same is true of a variety of organizational artifacts. In this chapter I present the case of the role of artifacts in the UK academic system, as well as their use in business cards.

LOGO

What is the logo? A logo (or at least, a good logo) is a symbolized manifestation of the organization. It is part of the identity, a representation of organizational spirit, and at the practical level, a marketing tool for the organization and its members. The word *logo* is derived from the Greek for "word" or "speech." Logos are symbolic, graphic artifacts aiming to produce a certain image of an organization, to convey a message, and when designed and presented they are expected to create certain impressions of that organization. They manifest the public face of the organization, and can be a powerful window through which an organization can represent itself. The logo's role is not restricted to external perception of the organization. It also serves as a vehicle to help build both a self-image and group identity of the group members. It can be a quintessential conveyor of the group distinctiveness of the organizational members. Thus one duality for the logo is the distinction between its role within the organization compared with its role that is external to the organization.

Another duality in the nature of logos is that they are designed to appeal both to logic and to an unconscious perspective. The study of symbolism depends to a large extent on the concept of the unconscious (Gabriel, 1999). Symbols actively elicit an internal experience of meaning: Dandridge (1993) argues that whereas signs "help a person to denote and comprehend knowledge of external world objectively," symbols "go further as they help to translate an unconscious or intuitively known internal world of feeling into the comprehendible terms of our visible reality" (p. 71). People use both logical interpretation and their unconscious in decoding and underpinning the meaning of logos. Applying social identity theory to organizational contexts may mean that where individuals define themselves in terms of the organization in which they are members, such identifications can operate as cognitive frameworks, and this is where symbols such as the logo have a significant role in shaping and manifesting such identification. Organizational identification has perceptual, attitudinal, and behavior consequences that are congruent with the identity. Such identification makes it likely that employees will think, feel, and act in the interests of the organization (Dutton et al., 1994; Tyler, 1999). In the case of organizational symbolism, the logo is part of a collective of symbols and artifacts that help to generate an organizational identity. However, whereas some symbols mostly address the realm of logic (such as organizational name—see Glynn & Abzug, 2002; see also Glynn & Marquis, chap. 12, this volume), the logo aims at a latent level of both logic and unconscious. These two dimensions are applicable also to the way the external environment perceives the organization via its logo.

Close attention to the aesthetic and the design is of great appeal and attraction for customers (Heskett, 1980), and this should also be applied for the symbols associated with the organization, including the logo. Moreover, a logo should readily evoke the same intended meaning across different people (D. Cohen, 1986; Durgee & Stuart, 1987; Kropp, French, & Hillard, 1990). Schmitt and Simonson (1997) indicated that smart organizations have gained a competitive advantage through aesthetics, in particular when marketing the organization as a whole, which is exactly what logos are created for, bearing in mind that this is their external role.

What's in the logo? The logo, like many other cultural symbols, may derive an extraordinary power, a phenomenon that is hard to explain (van Buskirk & McGrath, 1999). The logo or emblem represents the entity with which people may feel strong identification. The role that a flag plays for a country may be comparable to the one that the logo represents for an organization. Whereas many have died fighting for their country flag, such a level of commitment would not be expect within an organization. Indeed, Gabriel (2000) stated that "some symbols, such as flags, words and emblems stand for particular ideas in a conscious and explicit way" (p. 92). On a totally different, commercial perspective, the big M represents for most not only McDonald's as a restaurant but all of what McDonald's the corporation represents and stands for (Ritzer, 1996). Similarly, the trademark Coca Cola is the force that generates much of the sales for this drink (apparently 'Coca Cola' is the second most well-known word worldwide after the symbolic word *OK*).

From a marketing point of view, the word *logo* refers to the graphic designs that organizations use to identify themselves or their products (Bennett, 1995). However, marketing literature contains no systematic research on the effect of design on consumer evaluation of logos (P. W. Henderson & Cote, 1998), ignoring the inside role of the logo for its members. From a research point of view, the study of logos is usually covered by the marketing discipline, and is mostly commercially oriented. Nevertheless, logos should also be studied as organizational symbolic artifacts, not merely as marketing tools. This chapter examines logos from a wider organizational studies perspective, which generally suffers from a dearth of research (see Sproull, 1981, for an exception).

What Makes a Logo Unique?   The logo is part of the wider system that organizations utilize for their impression management. As such, the logo is just a component or one of the "ingredients" of a comprehensive system that is generated to represent the organization and its image. The development of self-image for organizations may resemble the formation of self-image for individuals, which is a complex and multifaceted process (Litterer, 1973). This development is an important organizational aspect, affecting both strategy and practical management, and is vividly visible in the academic context (Gioia & Thomas, 1996). This is where the logo and its role are unique. The uniqueness of the logo is concerned with its visibility, representation, and the issue of the first-impression impact. Logos are recognizable, reiterate familiarity with the organization, and elicit consensually held meaning in the "market" (D. Cohen, 1986; Robertson, 1989). Thus for the general public, as well as for the organization's members, the logo instantly corresponds with the organization, its image, and even its ethos. The logo, as for many other organizational artifacts, has both symbolic and aesthetic qualities (Vilnai-Yavetz & Rafaeli, chap. 1, this volume), but unlike other artifacts (e.g., dress or architecture of buildings), the logo is *the* symbolic element of the organization, or at least is designed to be one.

The following case is a vivid example of the important and relevant role the business card (with the logo as its main feature) plays in self-identity construction: People may have several organizational identities, and some work for or represent more that one organization. A colleague of mine is a university professor, and also serves as an editor of an academic journal. When he meets colleagues at conferences he is expected, as part of the etiquette, to exchange business cards. Which one will he produce—the university or the journal business card? The answer is concerned with both the issue of impression management and organizational identity. In this specific case, his employing university does not have the reputation for being one of the best in the country, but the journal has a very good academic standing, so it's no wonder he will likely pull out the journal's business card, emblazoned with its distinctive logo.

A Word of Caution.   There are certain limitations that should be borne in mind when dealing with logos. The logo comprises only a small part (albeit important) of the whole image of the organization. Moreover, the interpretation of a logo, in particular as it "speaks" to the unconscious, depends on the interpretation by the receiver. This, as Rafaeli and Worline (2000) noted, differs as much as people differ in their interpretations of symbols. Also, unlike most organizational artifacts that are developed and controlled by the organization and/or its members, a unique feature of the logo is that the actual design is usually done by media professionals who are not from within the organization; such external designers might miss the idea or concept behind the organization and the way it wishes to be perceived by the external environment. When a logo is proven unfit or problematic it can be changed. Such a change can be a one-off, major change or a subtle, continuous series of updating. However, like changing the name of the organization, changing the logo requires a considerable investment in terms of brand-name repositioning.

SYMBOLS AND ORGANIZATIONAL CULTURE

Pettigrew (1979) introduced the notion of organizational culture into the study of organizations. The culture of the organization dwells in people's minds, and comprises one of the most influential factors in creating successful organizations (Peters & Waterman, 1982). Nevertheless, culture is not easy to evaluate or measure (Sheridan, 1992). Part of organizational culture is its identity. Organizational identity is a relatively young field of study, brought in to the management literature by Albert and Whetten (1985). The role of organizational identity as a relevant concept in understanding organizational phenomena is important, for example, when organizations go through mergers (Millward & Kyriakidou, 2004). Weick (1969/1979) has argued that it is employees who enact organizations and make them real, but the external environment too makes sense of the organization. Either way, both internal and external perceptions of logos form part of the wholeness of an organization and its identity. Although symbolic representation of organizational identity is of significant importance, there is a shortage of writing on the role of organizational symbols (for an exception, see Stern, 1988).

Within the three-level classification of organizational symbols suggested by Czarniawska-Joerges and Joerges (1990)—labels, metaphors, and platitudes—logos are closest to labels, though they do not necessarily include verbal expression. If an image is shared (as is the case with logos), the artifact logo helps to link present with past and provides a compelling image that maintains a sense of identity. Along the same lines, Jung (1964, cited in Dandridge, 1983) describes symbolizing as helping to translate the world within us into a visible reality. When bestowed on newcomers, it makes them true members of the organizational community (Weick, 2001), and later it helps in developing the bond between the organization and its members (Pratt & Rafaeli, 2001).

Symbols are one ingredient of culture (Schein, 1985). In particular, Gabriel (1999) argues that symbols form a prominent role in basic culture development for the study of organization, building on ethnography. Symbols can be seen as the building blocks of culture, embedding multiple meaning, and energizing action, as suggested by Pondy et al. (1983). As argued earlier, the logo usually serves as an organizational symbol, many times forming the first impression of the organization.

To clarify the distinction and association between symbols and artifacts as separate constructs and the relevance of these constructs to logos and business cards, it would be useful to relate to Vilnai-Yavetz and Rafaeli's framework (chap. 1, this volume), which regards instrumentality, symbolism, and aesthetics as the three dimensions of any artifact. Indeed, the logo and the business card represent much more than their physical matter. They are instrumental in conveying organizational nature, culture, values, and status. They represent a symbolism of the organization, and they are, by their nature, a manifestation of the aesthetic visualization of the organization.

Comparing Schein's (1985) framework with the one suggested by Hatch (1993), as prospective frameworks to understand the role of artifacts in shaping culture, it is interesting to note that Hatch's framework allows for dynamism in the relationship between the components of culture, and thus perhaps fits better for the purpose of cultural analysis (see Fig. 10.1). The distinction between symbols and artifacts is not simple, though. Logos are in fact symbolic artifacts. It seems that Hatch has identified artifacts as physical objects that have not yet been infused with extra meaning or value. Thus, logos could be positioned in either one of two places: (a) if a logo is specifically designed with one message in mind (e.g., merely to identify a school by its name), then it is an artifact; (b) if it has additional meanings to it (e.g., further characterizing the institution), then it has moved to the symbolic realm.

Hofstede (1991) tells us that organizations are programming the mind of newcomers. Introducing the logo and other symbols helps in making this process a success. It also helps enact a shared reality and sensemaking of the organization to internal members and to the external environment (Morgan, 1997; Weick, 2001). The logo, symbols, and style of organizations are part of what makes them develop and maintain distinct identities (Scherer, 2003). These perspectives focus on the internal rather the external role of the logo.

The role of design is important in logos. The aesthetic dimension is fundamental to understanding symbols, and adds to its power (Gagliardi, 1990; see also Strati, chap. 2, this volume). Sometimes the aesthetic element of the logo or business card may even conceal the imperfections of the organization or its process (Strati & Guillet de Monthoux, 2002), especially if they come to represent different social realities (Yanow, chap. 3, this volume). The logo can manifest the core idea that brings the organization together. For example, NetEducation (2003), a higher education institution, indicates how the organizational logo represents its mission state-

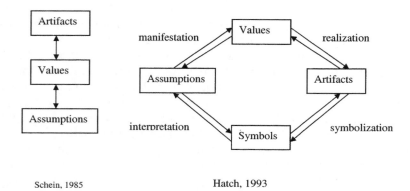

Schein, 1985   Hatch, 1993

FIG. 10.1.   A comparison of frameworks. From Hatch (1993). Copyright 1993. Adapted by permission.

ment: As claimed in their promotion material, the essence of the logo (see Fig. 10.2) is its dynamic and expanding shape:

> The shape expresses the core of modern education that uses technology in several nuanced ways. As its appearance, the NetEducation Centre itself is an ever expanding community which reaches the information networks of the world. Its dynamics is controlled and systematic within a calm entity. The shapes are soft and human emphasizing humanity in the world of modern technology. The expanding shape reminds of ripples that proceed on the surface. This motion is parallel to the principle of life-long learning.

The logo also implies a spatial dimension of infinite networks in a world that is becoming a global village. On a more individual level the logo can be seen as a stylized fingerprint, as an imprint of a very personal nature.

As manifested in Fig. 10.2, the logo is expected to symbolize the organization in a graphical manner. It needs to be distinct from others, but represent a certain type of organization (in this case, universities). The logo is expected to display the nature, notion, and even the underlying ideas, vision, and direction of the organization.

Heskett (2002) praises the efficiency in design, comparing the past with today's design of symbols, which tend to be less explicit. This efficiency is reflected in many logo designs. As explained later in this chapter, the new 1992 universities in the UK held it as crucial to be explicit and reemphasize the label "university" in their logo. Such a trend is clearly manifested in logos of products with a long history (an interesting example is the development of the logo for the whiskey Johnny Walker: within a century it transformed from an explicit figure of a person walking with his boots on,

FIG. 10.2. The NetEducation logo. Copyright 2003. Reprinted by permission.

holding a whip in his hand, into, in later logos, a few curved lines symbolizing the same figure).

Apart from the marketing and identity issues, logos are also a legal asset and can become a legal issue for organizations (see also Glynn & Marquis, chap. 12, this volume). Names and logos are highly important, and there is a wide body of legislation that has dealt with the protection of brands via names and logo (Schmitt & Simonson, 1997). New organizations or organizations that change their nature might try to build on established brands when they modify or revise their name and logo. Brands add value to companies and products, as they satisfy social and psychological needs (de Chernatony & McDonald, 1998). As is demonstrated later, this is exactly what happened when UK polytechnics were transformed into universities in 1992, and tried to choose names that resembled those of established universities (opting sometimes for names that were considered too similar, raising legal confrontations).

Logos in Practice

Before newcomers to the organization will have a chance to learn about more in-depth substantial issues, such as organizational identity or culture, they will be presented with the organization's letterhead, business card, and so on, all carrying the logo of the organization. Thus the logo is one of various representations that enable both the organization's internal and external environments to perceive and evaluate the organization. The logo presents, maintains, and reinforces an image of the organization. It is not clear, yet, how the logo, being an organizational artifact, helps individuals and collectives "make sense" of the organization. Next I examine the role of logo as an artifact that is a fundamental ingredient/component of organizational culture (e.g., Hatch, 1993; Schein, 1985), while acknowledging the logo as an individual artifact (e.g., Sproull, 1981).

THE IMPORTANCE AND RELEVANCE
OF ARTIFACTS IN ORGANIZATIONS

The organizational logo plays a critical role in organizational life. Two important perspectives are the people management issue and the issue of marketing or public relations. Internally, the logo is there for employees, operating as a source of immediate contextualized information that inevitably plays a role in how other information is processed. Externally, it represents the organization to the wider environment, being part of the ongoing marketing campaign for recognition as well as for increasing the brand visibility and promoting it (Belch & Belch, 2001; de Chernatony & McDonald, 1998).

For a junior employee, the entitlement to a business card or to the right to use formal organizational letterhead represents progress and recognition of responsibility and appreciation on behalf of the organization. Such an entitlement can be seen as part of the *rite of passage* for new members of the organization (Trice & Beyer, 1984). A PhD candidate at a U.S. university was recently heard at the Academy of Management meeting, mumbling with mixed emotion, humbleness, and frustration that "We, PhD candidates at &&&, are not considered to be worthy of having our own university's business cards."

Of course this is just one of many elements; with the advent of new technologies new types of symbolic artifacts are emerging. For example, technological devices such as cell phones and laptops are serving as new types of status markers, alongside the traditional ones, such as company cars (Owens & Sutton, 2002).

As Rafaeli and Pratt indicated in the introduction to this volume, cultural symbols—logos being one of them—often serve as "shorthand" reminders of an organization's history. In addition, they can play a central role in how organizational members and other constituents come to know and understand their organizations. They can initiate such sensemaking, or may be the targets of visionary leaders' attempts to use artifacts to shape members' perceptions.

LOGOS AS REFLECTIVE ARTIFACTS—THE CASE OF UK UNIVERSITIES

Like most organizations, universities have a variety of artifacts, among which one may count the logo, architecture (e.g., building style), and dress code. The case introduced in this chapter presents and analyzes the utilization of logos in the UK academia, and in particular shows how a subtle (and sometimes not so subtle) distinction may be made between different types of UK universities.

The main direction of analysis focuses on a comparative illustration of the three major types of universities in the UK: old, new (1960s), and 1992 (Former polytechnic). The old includes universities such as Cambridge, St. Andrews, Manchester, and London. They have a long history, and have set the tone and reputation of British education for generations (in particular Oxford and Cambridge). The new universities emerged as a natural response to the increased demand for higher education. Many of them were established in the 1960s, when the UK establishment realized the need for widening the tertiary educational cover. Among them one can find Exeter, Keele, Loughborough, UEA, York, and Warwick. The third group of UK universities emerged from polytechnics that were given a university status in 1992, when the government decided to allow them to become (or title themselves as) universities. Middlesex, University of Central Lancaster, Manchester Metropolitan, Oxford Brookes, and South Bank are examples of this group.

In the rest of the chapter I analyze how these universities differ in terms of their logos, their symbolic nature, and their organizational representation. I look at how these are utilized to make sense of the organizations. Some intriguing questions or cases can be developed along the following lines:

- Can a distinction be made among the logos according to the type of university?
- Why do logos within each of these groups of universities resemble each other?

University Logos

Each university, like any other established organization, has a specific, unique name, accompanied by a distinctive logo, which aims to represent it to the wider public and environment. Sometimes the meaning of the logo needs to be explained (see example in Fig. 10.3) and it is probable that in some cases, too high a level of resources is required to absorb the message. A 'resource matching perspective' (Meyers-Levy & Peracchio, 1995) means that an optimal level of stimuli will have the advantage of enabling people to adequately process a stimulus can be reached. As the time people devote to screening a logo is limited (say, when they browse the net, receive a business card, or company letter) the logo need not to be too complex or too simplistic.

UPE logo

The UPE logo was introduced as a new visual symbol that would support, and represent, our transformation process. The logo is used on all marketing material as well as stationery, signage and other corporate identity material... Abstract symbolism has been used in the design of the logo. The twin uprights represent the University itself. Although loosely related to the Main Building, the most visible feature of the UPE campus, they are open and free flowing rather than rigid and closed. They symbolise the upward thrust of intellectual and personal development. The curved blue band represents UPE's location at the sea; the green, the land and our nature reserve; and the sun, a bright future.

FIG. 10.3. Logo meaning. From http://www.upe.ac.za/aboutpe/general/crest.asp. Reprinted by permission.

THE CASE OF UK UNIVERSITIES: A COMPARATIVE
MANIFESTATION OF DIFFERENCE

As mentioned earlier, the universities in the UK can be roughly divided into three major categories: Old, new (1960s), and 1992. The old are those established in the distant past, with traditions of high-quality academic work and fit for the upper echelons of society. Though there have been efforts to change this notion in recent years, such as encouraging of students of working-class background to attend old universities, it is not yet clear whether the change is mere lip service to political correctness, or if it is a deeper one. The new universities were established (or gained university status) in the 1960s. And the 1992 universities comprise some 50 former polytechnics that were apparently transformed in 1992 into having university status. Some indeed worked toward changing their identity and culture into a university one; others continue to carry the legacy of teaching institutions.

Using the Yanow (chap. 3, this volume) approach to interpretive approach in studying artifacts, a random sample of university logos is presented in the following subsections to demonstrate the difference in the nature and notion of the institutions, relating to their status.

Old Institutions. See Fig. 10.4 for some examples.

FIG. 10.4. Logos of some old UK universities. Reprinted by permission.

Reflecting on the common denominator, clearly the most prominent element in each of these logos is the ancient emblem. Though only some present the full name, all have a distinguished design, representing ancient symbols of wisdom, knowledge, books, or a motto written in Latin. This is mostly a medieval style. A typical color combination includes some three colors.

The 1960s. During the 1960s, the UK government realized that a substantial increase in the number of universities would be required to keep up with the high demand for a more qualified workforce, and to maintain a competitive edge over other countries. Many universities were established. Figure 10.5 displays the logos of some of them.

Reflecting on the common denominator, one notices simplicity, "modern" letters, and sometimes the whole logo is composed only of letters, the university name, or its abbreviations. This is in line with the trend of pattern for including the organizational name in the logo as pointed out by Glynn and Abzug (2002). The name may appear in full, supporting Olins' (1989) corporate identity theme of the importance of the name as part of the identity bond that individuals build with their organization (Glynn & Abzug, 2002). The style represents fairly modern 20th-century principles. Coloring is simpler, with the typical shape including a single color, two at the most.

The 1992 Universities. In 1992, the UK government enabled a large number of polytechnics to reposition and rename themselves a "university," with the hope that these institutions would indeed be transformed into "real" universities by managing a repositioning process in self-marketing (Belch & Belch, 2001). One of the first things many former polytechnics had to do was to change their name (and subsequently either amend an old logo or design a new one). Was this meant to follow the metaphor of pouring new wine into old bottles? What type of logos have these new universities chosen? Figure 10.6 presents a sample of these logos.

FIG. 10.5. Logos of some 1960s universities. Note that Brunel University is a conversion of a former college, thus the 'traditional' element of the logo. Reprinted by permission.

FIG. 10.6. Some logo examples of 1992 universities. Reprinted by permission.

Reflecting on the common denominator, one notices a clear attempt to reflect the fact that it is a university—almost all made sure that the word *university* appears in the logo. Many added distinctive modern style symbols. In general they were trying to imitate the 1960s logo style rather than the old university ones as a role model.

According to Schmitt and Simonson (1997), there were some legal battles over brand protection. Having the chance and option to choose a new name and new logo designed to reflect their new identity, many schools names resembling those of the traditional university in the same geographical area, in some cases provoking some legal issues over name ownership. Former polytechnics have tried to build on established brands of traditional universities when changing their name and logo, and in many cases, added further identification to make sure there is a clear distinction between them and the local established university (e.g., Nottingham Trent University, to distinguish from Nottingham University; Sheffield Hallam University, to distinguish from Sheffield University;

University of Central Lancaster, to distinguish from University of Lancaster; and Leeds Metropolitan and Manchester Metropolitan University, to distinguish from Leeds/Manchester University).

The context for understanding this is legal: The basic legislation suggests that organizations cannot use certain identity elements (including colors, names, symbols, etc.) already in use by another organization "if such use would likely to cause confusion or mistakes in the marketplace . . . or if such a use would misrepresent their products or services" (Schmitt & Simonson, 1997, p. 217). This was indeed the argument in the legal battle between UEA (University of East Anglia) and Anglia Polytechnic, ending with the latter using the name APU—Anglia Polytechnic University (the only one of the 1992 polytechnics that kept the label polytechnic in its name).

Meaning—The Message Conveyed

It seems that there is a high level of resemblance of the symbolic logos within the three groups, which support Sevon's argument of whether identity is distinctive or whether organizational identities are institutionally determined via processes of imitation (Sevon, 1996, in Hatch & Schultz, 2000). Indeed, university logos try first to generate the idea of university (thus the clear resemblance), and only then to find an individual distinction for the specific university.

What can be learned for each group in terms of (a) the message, (b) what it is reflecting on, and (c) how can it be interpreted, both positively and negatively?

For the Old Universities.   The message is: we are the privileged, for the privileged. We are the provider of wisdom. We are rooted in ancient time, are well tested, and have a tradition of creating new knowledge and providing for its dissemination.

Reflecting on tradition, excellence, elitism, and style, a positive interpretation might relate to the notion of selecting and nourishing future leaders, scholars, and the next generation's elite. A negative interpretation reveals snobbery and the old boys' network. The conflicting interpretations may be due to differences between internal and external perceptions.

For the 1960s Universities.   The message is that they represent a new, fresh wave, are innovative, and can do as well as the old. The future will bring competition on level ground. Reflecting on the real need for more universities and a strong need for new perspectives and relationship to the current world, a positive interpretation might relate to the following notions: modern, inevitable development, and competing as equals. Some of the 1960s universities, in fact, went steadily along this route, overtaking many of the old universities in both research and teaching excellence (York and Warwick are fine examples of such achievements). Negative interpretations range from, on the one hand, advocates of the old university system saying, for instance, "well, wait a 100 or 500 years before you think you are a 'real' university"; on the other hand, what was innovative in the 1960s may not be so in 1990, 2000, 2010. The choice of style in shaping the logo is subject to fashion—and it is interesting to see how, at about the same period, the founders of SONY in Japan chose to use a combination of letters as a trademark, forming the actual logo from the name (Morita, 1987). This very same concept was applied by UEA, incidentally even using similar types of fonts.

For the New Universities. Having the label university in the name is part of the building of an image and reputation (Fombrum & Shanley, 1990), so, yes, the message is "we too are a university." Reflecting on political ambitions and wish for growth, complying with a governmental vision, and fulfilling self-prescribed high aims, a positive interpretation might relate to the notion of yes, it is possible—and some have indeed made a real effort to transform themselves from teaching-only institutions into learned, knowledge-creating universities. A negative interpretation might be: But whatever you do you are still a "former poly"; and again, a clear distinction may be made between internal versus external perceptions of what they have achieved.

Before moving to the discussion I wish to emphasize that the differences in logos are accompanied by a wider distinction between the types of universities, most notably the level of performance of research and teaching (more so for the former), and certainly of the overall culture. Some of the differences are reflected in other artifacts too, such as architecture: Old universities are mostly located in buildings dated back to medieval times, which have unique "character" and distinct features; 1960s universities typically use the most advanced concepts of the time, thus the label "red brick" universities; and typical 1992 universities are set in large, school-type, simple, functional buildings, which are usually dull, gray, unimaginative, and purpose-built. Even the geographical location can serve as an indicator: Many of the old universities are located in city centers, the 1960s universities were typically built on the outskirts of midsize cities, and the 1992 ones are likely to be situated in inner cities.

Thus, although in this chapter I limited myself to the issue of logos and business cards, I wish to acknowledge the wider perspective and components of the case in hand.

DISCUSSION

The case of UK universities' logos reveals the importance and relevance of logos in general. Like other organizational artifacts, they form part of an identity-creating system (Albert & Whetten, 1985; Olins, 1989; Scherer, 2003). They contribute to the development of the bond between the organization and its members (Pratt & Rafaeli, 2001) and represent the organization to the wider external environment (Cappetta & Gioia, chap. 11, this volume).

The same questions that Glynn and Marquis (chap. 12, this volume) ask in their chapter—"Do individuals have preferences about how closely artifacts match the institutional environment, and do such preferences affect individuals' perception of organizational legitimacy?—can be asked about the logo. The rebranding of 1992 universities in the UK included renaming and new logo designs, aimed specifically at changing the nature and perception of those former polytechnics into institutions worthy of the title university. However, sometimes the design of the logo was aimed at concealing the true nature of the organization—university in this case—with certain imperfections, in line with Strati and Guillet de Monthoux's (2002) argument (see also Strati, chap. 2, this volume).

A mere change of name will not be sufficient to generate such a wide, comprehensive change, and needs to be accompanied by further changes. In fact, in many cases, the name will provide no further way to distinguish between organizations of similar nature, where the logo can provide such differentiation: For instance, the name UL Bank will provoke the same feeling for people as the name LU Bank, be they organizational members or the general public. The logo, which carries certain rich figurative information, may say more about these institutions. Similarly, for a person not familiar with the UK academic environment, the names University of Bagnor, University of Keele, University of Humberside, might mean the same: but their logos will be distinct, and may provide the additional input of their nature (old, new, and former polytechnic, respectively).

Nevertheless, a change that is limited to an artifact level might be insufficient, and as both Schein (1985) and Hatch (1993) agree, symbols are just one element of a culture. To change the nature of an organization, much more than a mere change of name and logo is required. The question that may come to mind is: What would be easier—to change the culture of an existing organization or to create a new culture by building a new organization from scratch? It may be too early to say, but judging from the inevitable comparison, the 1960s "wave" meant creating and establishing universities from the ground up, with a university culture (and competition on an equal footing with the traditional establishment). The theme was "creating something new out of nothing." This was clearly a success story, and just a few decades later it is difficult to distinguish between most of the old and the 1960s institutions in many aspects, such as research and teaching quality, leading to a fair mix in a variety of UK "league tables" (though a handful of old universities, in particular Oxbridge, are clearly in a league of their own).

As for the 1992 universities, these had to change from a culture of strictly teaching institutions into research-led institutions. A transformation was required, but the theme was different: as stated previously, "creating something new out of something old." There was no equal ground for a fair competition. Lecturers were required to carry on with high teaching loads *and* to conduct research with insufficient research training, finance, and so on, and thus to compete from a disadvantaged starting point. Despite being branded universities, a decade later, even the best of the 1992s universities are generally lagging behind the worst of the established ones in terms of assessment of research quality. Some extreme cases of this are, on the positive side Oxford Brookes, which managed to establish a viable research culture albeit at a low starting point, and on the negative side, Thames Valley University, which "managed" to come in typically at the bottom of most league tables. A more special case is that of University of Derby, who, with a good teaching tradition, managed to positively exploit their new status to expand overseas, becoming a worldwide leading institution (for teaching, mostly in management) with several subsidiary business schools outside the UK.

Further Perspectives

How does the symbolism reflect or represent these three tiers of the university system? First, it is clear that the three layers of status inherited in the system are reflected and reinforced by a number of artifacts, most notably the logo. Unlike the case of fashion, where the use of symbolic artifacts is probably the most crucial element in constructing both identity and image (Cappetta & Gioia, chap. 11, this volume), in the academic system the symbolic artifacts are used to reinforce a message, rather than embody it. Nevertheless, like the case of the fashion industry, there is a somewhat clear pecking order in the academic system.

Conclusions

The analysis of the nature of logos is revealing. Nevertheless, one should remember that logos are just one artifact in the full picture of an organization's symbols, artifacts, and overall culture, which is composed of elements of culture that are "in varying degrees interdependent, and there is convergence in the way they relate to the functional problems of integration, control, and commitment" (Pettigrew, 1979, p. 576). According to Schein's (1985) analysis of cultural levels, artifacts are the "shallower" level. Nevertheless, they are a crucial part of the organization, and deserve more than the little attention they have received so far in the literature (Gagliardi, 1990). That said, a certain realism should be incorporated into any such evaluation. Logos and other symbols are important, and need to accompany organizational changes, but they stay only within the level of symbols. If they do not represent the real nature of the organization, their impact will be limited.

Final Note

In this chapter I explored and analyzed logos as organizational symbolic artifacts. The literature dealing with such artifacts, and in particular with that of the logo (and other visual representations of organizations), is sparse. Moreover, it is spread around a variety of disciplines: management (especially within the subdisciplines of organizational culture, impression management, and marketing), psychology, sociology, anthropology, and the media (from the aesthetics and art perspectives). Perhaps this is the reason why there is not yet a single comprehensive and coherent framework that deals with organizational symbolic artifacts in a just way.

The case of the UK university system manifests the relevance and significance of symbolic organizational artifacts. In particular, the logo is an organizational symbol that is relevant to our understanding of their role, and is significant at several layers. These layers are the conscious versus the unconscious, the individual versus the organizational and society level, internal versus external perspectives, the theoretical versus the practical, and the differing time dimensions. All these were discussed in the literature review and were reflected in the visual data presented in this chapter.

The way artifacts such as logos, architecture, dress code, and other boundary-spanning features work for organizations deserves further and in-depth investigation in management and organizational studies. I hope that future work will expand on both theory development and the practical implications of the role of symbolic artifacts in organizations.

Fine Fashion: Using Symbolic Artifacts, Sensemaking, and Sensegiving to Construct Identity and Image

Rossella Cappetta
Bocconi University, Milan, Italy
and SDA Bocconi Graduate School of Management

Dennis A. Gioia
Penn State University

> *At times the ugliest and most disagreeable things are in fashion almost as if fashion itself wants to demonstrate its power in having us wear all that is most detestable; its nonchalance in proposing in one instance the useful, in a second the absurd and yet in a third that which is totally indifferent in terms of practicality and esthetic, thus demonstrating its complete carelessness of the objective norms of life and returning to other motivations, that is, to typically social ones.*
>
> —Simmel (1895)

Fine fashion is an industry *defined* by its artifacts, that is, its clothing, accessories, shops, and so on. It is also an industry that lives and dies by its artifacts—via the images and meanings those artifacts convey. Fine fashion artifacts are pervasive, obvious, and important to both internal and external audiences. Their raison d'etre is a curious one, however: to produce exclusive products that buyers use mainly as a way of making a statement about their personal identities, social status, and aspirations. Yet, it is the purely symbolic purpose of these artifacts that opens a window allowing academic insight into the broader role of artifacts in organizations.

Perhaps most interestingly, it is primarily through their artifacts that the firms in this industry develop, sustain, and change their *organizational* identities (i.e., "who they are as an organization") and communicate those identities to different constituents through image-based "sensegiving" processes. Given the theme of this volume, there is no more definitive industry to study to derive insights about the relationship between artifact, image, identity, and sensemaking and sensegiving processes than the fashion industry. Our purpose in this chapter is to examine the projection of organizational and brand image, by means of products and other firm artifacts, to gain insight into the relationships involving sensemaking and sensegiving processes and the construction, maintenance, and change of organizational identity.

Artifacts as symbols have crucial expressive and instrumental roles to play in organizational sensemaking and sensegiving. Meanings given to organizational artifacts shape both internal and external images of the organization, which, in turn, affect the sensemaking and sensegiving processes that influence organizational identity and the maintenance or subsequent revision of the artifacts that represent that identity. Effectively managed, organizational artifacts should contribute to the creation of a virtuous circle between organizational/brand image and organizational identity over time.

In general, the organizational literature has tended to downplay the significance of artifacts in identity, image, sensemaking, and sensegiving (Dutton et al., 1994, excepted). One of the reasons is that Schein (1984), in explicating organizational culture, identified three levels at which culture might be understood: (a) the surface or artifactual level, (b) the deeper level of values, and (c) the deepest level of taken-for-granted, ground assumptions. This typology tacitly implies that artifacts are the most superficial of the ingredients for understanding culture (and its nomological net, which includes identity). As useful as Schein's typology might be, it disguises the significance of artifacts. We argue that artifacts *matter*. They not only act at an obvious surface level, but are less obvious, though essential conduits for understanding the deeper processes that affect identity and image.

Gucci is a perfect exemplar. Bright, expansive, and empty white walls of the headquarters contrast with the luxuriant black leather armchairs and black moquettes. Similarly, the big doors of Gucci's stores, their striking black furniture, the chic nonchalance of the salespeople inside, and the highlights on only a few products in the large windows show modernity, style, elegance, power, and solidity. All these features announce "Gucci" in such a clear and definitive way that Gucci's flagship store at Via Montenapoleone 5 in Milan does not even need to place the name Gucci on the entrance. Even the headquarters office has but a very small and understated sign on the door of Via Montenapoleone 12 in Milan. Gucci's Director of Corporate Communication noted that:

> As the commercial success of the Gucci brand is strengthened, the stores' design is incorporating innovative materials. While staying true to the brand's inherent style, the new stores, designed by Tom Ford and William Sofield, offer a new interpretation of contemporary urban elegance . . . the dark-veined

wood contrasts with modern counters and bronze chandeliers. New features are being introduced, such as leather armchairs trimmed with metal hinges, corduroy divans or ivory or chocolate colored crocodile-skin banquettes.[1]

Artifacts are so transparently obvious in the fine fashion industry that we hope to draw insights that go beyond this industry to develop concepts that apply to other industries where the role of artifacts is likely to be more latent. Overall, we treat the fashion industry as a revealing context for understanding some organizational processes usually hidden in less image-focused industries. Our observations derive from an ongoing research project involving some of the most visible names the fashion industry, including Versace, Bottega Veneta, Ferragamo, Gucci, and Louis Vuitton, among others.

THE FINE FASHION INDUSTRY CONTEXT

Despite the common view of fashion as a somewhat superficial industry, it has been the subject of long-standing study in the sociological literature (Barthes, 1983; Descamps, 1979; Eco, 1976; Simmel, 1895; Veblen, 1899/1979). Recently, however, fashion also has become an interesting phenomenon in the organization and management literature (e.g., Djelic & Ainamo, 1999; Richardson, 1996). The industry's products have been viewed mainly as conduits for the expression of social identity (Blumer, 1969b; Breward, 2003; F. Davis, 1992), as well as organizational identity (Cappetta, Perrone, & Ponti, 2003). The apparent message conveyed at the organizational level is: "We are a firm (we are an industry) that is distinctive and exclusive. Our products convey to the people who buy them that *they* are distinctive and exclusive." It is important to note that this is an industry where image is (almost) everything. Image governs virtually all activities.

There is a notable pecking order among fashion industry firms. At the highest level is "haute couture" ("high fashion"), which produces custom, one-off designs. Next, is prêt-à-porter[2] ("ready to wear"), which produces fashion products that the average person would still think of as quite expensive, but that nonetheless can be bought off the shelf. Even within the fine fashion segment, there is a pecking order: high (e.g., Armani, Dior,

---

[1]From "Gucci: Openings in Major Fashion" published in the PPR group's intranet Web site for the media community.

[2]Prêt-à-porter originated at the end of 1960s as "democratization" of haute couture. It broke with the past: Garments needed to reach wider audience tastes; furthermore, the role of the designers went from simple executor of clients' whims to interpreter of collective tastes and influencer of public opinion. In the meantime, tailor-made or sartorial fabrication transformed into enlarged industrial manufacture (F. Davis, 1992).

Gucci, Louis Vuitton, which stage the "runway" fashion shows in Milan, Paris, London, and New York and are frequently quoted in the important trade magazines), middle (e.g., Calvin Klein and MaxMara), and low (e.g., Zara, Gap, Benetton). Our focus in this chapter is on the high end of prêt-à-porter or what we term the "fine fashion" industry.

Perhaps the key role in defining fine fashion boundaries is held by the fashion arbiters, who are able to declare which players are in and which are out within this specific segment. The most notable of these arbiters are the fashion magazines and their editors (Breward, 2003). The status of these magazines has been continuously strengthened by the growing importance of stylish photography and by the emphasis on the idea of fashion as art (Jobling & Crowley, 1996). The fashion press has served to emphasize the symbolic value and to de-emphasize the materiality of fine fashion products. One magazine, in particular, has contributed to the transformation of fine fashion from a simple manufacturing to a cultural industry, _Vogue_ (Breward, 2003).

As a cultural industry, fine fashion firms and arbiters have increasingly stressed the aesthetic and symbolic qualities of the products at the expense of their instrumentality. Does anyone really _need_ a Hermes "Birkin" bag for $5,000 or a Bottega Veneta "alligator skin" bag for $20,000? The answer differs for different types of "needs." It might be informative, for instance, to note that the waiting list for the Birkin bag exceeds 3 years. An instrumental need might be satisfied for $50, but the symbolic need cannot (cf. Barthes, 1967; Bourdieu, 1984b). Fashion products create a symbolic language to be used to distinguish oneself from others: less instrumentality implies more distinctiveness (Barthes, 1970/1972, 1970/1982; Bourdieu, 1984a; Simmel, 1904/1957).

Historically, then, the fashion industry has been almost entirely symbol driven. Curiously, turning a profit was not central to its early existence. The industry is rooted in "cults of personality"—almost all these firms were inextricably tied to their genius founders (e.g., Giorgio Armani, Coco Chanel, Christian Dior, Cristobal Balenciaga, Gianni Versace, etc.). Yves Saint Laurent, for instance, is a recognized genius, whose firm was an economic disaster prior to its acquisition by Gucci. The context now has shifted, however. Economic factors have become as important as symbolic factors, which has led to an integration of the expressive symbolic factors and the economically instrumental factors in the design and delivery of artifactual products.[3] Fulfilling both expressive and instrumental

---

[3]There is a fine line that is important not to cross, however. If a fine fashion firm is _too_ successful economically (so that many people own their products), their great success negatively affects the perception of distinction of the firm and its products. Thus, economic success can undermine distinctiveness—the key to success in this industry. We term this phenomenon the "paradox of success" in the fine fashion industry.

criteria depends on "style," an aesthetic choice a fashion company makes regarding the individual pieces of its whole collection (including clothing and accessories), their main features (e.g., cut, color, fabric, length), and how they are combined (Cappetta & Cillo, 2001).

Over time, a fashion company and its brand should be characterized by a recognizable "semifixed" style with historical continuity. Each specific collection, however, is influenced by "temporary" styles that affect the whole industry for short periods. Some styles become a fashion *trend*—a style toward which companies converge in a specific period (Cappetta & Cillo, 2001). Style is expressed in artifacts. Most obviously, it is expressed by the company's products, but also is expressed by store layout, advertising, the "look" of the models, and the testimonials chosen to present the products. Therefore, all company artifacts should contribute to defining a coherent company style. The social dimension of artifactual "style" is crucial in identifying leaders and followers in this industry and in understanding sensemaking and sensegiving processes and their link with identity and image.

COMPARISON AND CONTRAST OF ARGENTO INC. AND BIANCO INC.

As a basis for illuminating some of the relationships among artifacts as symbols, identity, and image, and the processes of making and giving sense, we first present a comparison and contrast between two Italian fine fashion houses.

Bianco Inc. Bianco (a pseudonym) is a family-owned company that was quite successful in past, but in recent years has suffered a decline in the distinctiveness of its style and in its image and reputation. Corporate headquarters is located in an old palace decorated by gorgeous frescos, 18th-century furniture, and damask curtains, looking not at all like offices (few computers and no papers). On each floor there is a formally dressed valet, yet the palace is often empty, except during show periods. In the palace are the family members' offices, the showroom, and the creative-design department. The founder bought the place because "he loved the lines of it, the force of it." Today the founder's family says that "we base the designers here and the history influences their spirit of creativity. . . . The history permeates us." The operational offices are in a modern, undistinguished building outside the city and are integrated with a production plant and a warehouse. Most of the employees work in this more mundane atmosphere.

Employees are well aware of the story of the brand and the legends linked to the founder and his family, yet they do not seem to know the products well, nor the seasonal "collection" designs. Knowledge of the company style is not reinforced by any specific artifacts and the employees do not receive company products free, although they can buy items from previous collections at a discount. Few do so, however. Even the employees who work in the palace feel that "it is a magnificent building, but it doesn't say anything about the company style." Furthermore, products are not visible in either the headquarters or operational offices; catalogs or fashion magazines are not visible in either office.

Bianco's is not a univocally defined style; it represents a "classic" and "comfortable" elegance. It does not have a specific, printed logo and does not have a unique label—for the accessories there are three different labels (the same brand name in different character and size), the oldest and the most "out of fashion" label is the one for the most exclusive and expensive line. For all these reasons, employees express only a vague, general idea of the product as "comfortable but old-fashioned, suitable for old people." They are not able to articulate a company style, nor describe the main features of the products with the exception of a few historical (out-of-production) pieces.

A similar sense pertains to the salespeople. They do not dress in a company style: They instead wear a black standard uniform that is not part of the seasonal collection. Similarly, they work in stores that do not have a specific, corporate style. The stores are relaxing, generic places in which functionality is a central element: beige moquettes to try on shoes, comfortable chairs to sit on, easy-to-reach shelves for the products. Furthermore, the salespeople receive very few instructions and guidelines from the home office, even though almost half the stores are company operated. As consequence, the correct products often are not highlighted (e.g., in many stores seasonal product displays are not in the choice positions; instead, that is where the "classic" pieces generally are).

Like the employees, customers also know Bianco's name and history, but have trouble distinguishing Bianco's products. Perhaps worse, they do not recognize the quality of the products (i.e., customers do not know that Bianco's top line is handmade) and consequently are not able to justify the price, because they tend to compare Bianco's products with lower quality fashion houses. Similarly, customers do not distinguish Bianco's stores. Like the employees, their knowledge of Bianco's style is not reinforced by symbolic artifacts: There are few reviews in the magazines, very few catalogs (available only in the stores, not mailed to prime customers), and little advertising. It is apparent that Bianco does not systematically project its image, because its customers are unable to specify a distinctive style. It is not able to give a sense of itself as a company through its salespeople, probably because it has not given a sense of itself to its own employees. The key people in the company (all members of the founder's family) adhere to the founder's approach and the identity he instilled years ago. They have not been able to renew the company style, which is the core element for a fashion company's identity. The entrenched elements of the old identity are the exclusive "property" of the founder's family. Although the company currently finds itself in a turbulent environment that demands an image and identity shift, it has not been able to move from a family identity to a company identity.

The style, therefore, has become old, indistinct, and out of fashion; their image in the marketplace has become old, generic, and out of fashion; and the corporate identity has become old, exclusively linked to the founder's family, and negatively affected by the image. As result of this situation, in the last 5 years there has been a serious turnover problem (close to the 60% in some periods) and difficulty in recruiting new people, both designers and managers. It is eminently clear that people in this industry want to work in a company with a distinctive brand image that is consistent with their own identity. They no longer want to work for Bianco because Bianco's image has fallen. For these reasons, in 2000 a project to define a new brand image began. Projecting a new brand image is the first step toward changing organizational identity because a fashion company's identity is based on branding a style. As result of this project Bianco formulated a new brand image and took some actions to instill the new brand image in customer perceptions, including:

- A strong investment for a new advertising campaign beginning in 2002.
- Restyling of some important stores and the construction of new stores in 2002.
- Recruiting a new designer and extending the woman's wear collection from 2003.

As a result of these actions, Bianco's image seems to be improving. The new stores are well received by customers and fashion editors, product photos in magazines have increased, and magazine reviews after the shows are more numerous. After less than 2 years, it seems that new, "right" collections, an expert photographer with a famous model, two well-organized social events with celebrities and fashion arbiters, and the inauguration of an annual exhibition have been enough for Bianco to tell a new story. More generally, it seems that in this symbol-intensive industry managing a few critical artifacts has positively affected brand image and corporate image. Has it affected organizational identity?

Employees, like customers, see the new advertising campaign with the new products, as well as the new stores with a clearer, more coherent style and brand message. At the same time, Bianco's employees recognize that this new style does not represent "how Bianco is, but rather how it wants to be." They note that "inside, the company is not really changed, that it is more of a "make-over operation." To try to effect an identity change, the HR people attempted a half-hearted redefinition of organizational identity using the projected brand image as a base. At first, they tried to translate each brand image component ("timeless elegance," "craftsmanship," "functionality") into employee/company identity elements ("excellence," "passion," "integrity"). Then, they reworked aspects of the reward systems, attempting to link them to these new identity elements. Unfortunately, employee responses do not appear positive. There is general skepticism that "it's all image, all for customers" and that "nothing really has changed for the employees, even if the stores are becoming more beautiful." By concentrating on the customers and fashion arbiters, Bianco's top managers overlooked giving sense to their employees. They did not create new stories to augment the founder's legends, nor did they project artifacts internally to give the sense of renewal to the members of the organization. For the fashion industry, it is necessary to start with projected the brand image, but it is necessary also to connect quickly with personal and organizational identity. For Bianco, acting on brand image and organizational identity separately has been markedly unsuccessful. In a fashion company organizational identity is a critical element, but it must be "in style"; it must be "fashionable"; it cannot diverge too far from the image. Otherwise, it becomes difficult to manage the discrepancy (i.e., when *identity < image*).

Argento Inc. Argento (another pseudonym) is a very successful company; today its brand is one of the most well known and regarded. Argento's style is strongly defined, recognizable, and represented by a famous logo. This "Argento style" was developed about 10 years ago after a period of deep renewal within the company. Today the style is reflected by each piece of the seasonal collections and by the company stores themselves. The store windows are defined by fashion experts as "edgy," expressing "how they stay on the cutting edge of the fashion business." The windows are centered and the spotlights are all pointed to a select few pieces. Behind the windows and a grand door, the store spaces are very large with thematic, luxurious, and exclusive furniture. On the walls and ceiling are many mirrors and translucent surfaces with dramatically reflecting lights for both night and day. Impeccably (and thematically) dressed salespeople keep a respectful distance, but clearly make themselves available to help and to answer questions; they wear a black, structured ensemble that is a company seasonal piece.

The company headquarters is close to the original plant, in a modern building designed by the company artistic director. He designed not only the collections theme, but the stores, layout, and furniture as well (with the support of a famous interior designer). The headquarters building is a large, bright-white contemporary building. Behind a 10+-foot door are very large and high spaces. On one side the receptionists are dressed in company black seasonal suits; on the desk are the two most popular products from the seasonal collection, some fashion magazines, and the Argento catalog. On the other side, the lucent white walls are empty and a tropical plant and three black leather armchairs stand out. In front of the main door there is a big steel elevator moving in a transparent space for four floors. The symbolism communicates power, modernity, richness, and elegance, which are the distinctive characteristics of Argento's style.

Argento's style has defined a dominant trend now followed by many other companies. Employees know the relevance and the influence of "their" style; out of the office they can see "signs" of their company: many people using Argento's dress and accessories; many advertisements in the streets and in magazines; many celebrities on TV or in movies using or talking about Argento's products; many magazine articles featuring Argento's pieces. The employees express pride and feel privileged to work for the company. They are well-informed about their products and are able to easily distinguish them from competitors' products. "Fashion sensitivity" is suffused at all levels: The top managers attend more to style than in other industries (e.g., the HR director is able to describe their collections and he buys several pieces each season). The top managers always wear the company's best suits (generally, a black seasonal suit in fine materials). Close to the offices there is a company mall in which the employee can buy Argento's products at a discount. All employees use it.

Ten years ago Argento's leaders engaged in a strong identity/image (re)construction process. In the beginning they identified the new style, changing their original style in a radical way, but maintaining and reproposing its famous logo, its famous shapes, and its special materials. This crucial sensemaking process was prompted by a period of crisis, so the identity/image renovation was necessary to save the brand, the company, and its history and heritage. It was a major challenge. Immediately after the style identification (and before obtaining a clear market response), they created this style and simultaneously launched an identity transformation. The new organizational identity was characterized by a strong work ethic, entrepreneurship, speediness, and modernity. They hired new, skilled top managers, building what one financial analyst called "the best management team in the fashion industry." At the same time, they were able to project a compelling image toward fashion arbiters, other fashion houses, and customers, as well as a coherent image toward both creative and operational employees. "Giving sense" to external stakeholders involved:

- Heavy investment in visible advertising (capturing the first three to four pages of *Vogue, Marie Claire,* and *Elle* simultaneously), as well as in events, exhibitions, and shows.

- Heavy investment to restyle all the company stores and open new stores. In some cities they literally "bought a street, the best street" and opened "flagship" stores.

Attempts to give sense to employees involved other actions:

- Systematic internal communication about the products and the company (with detailed reports on revenues, costs, number of opened stores, etc.).
- Restyling of the company headquarters (layout and furniture).
- Developing specific selection and training programs.
- A new system of evaluation and compensation (linked to competencies).

The attempts to give sense to external stakeholders, however, also acted indirectly on the internal stakeholders. In Argento's case, the ability to encompass all the different stakeholders in this sensegiving process and the coherent use of multiple symbolic artifacts have been a key element in their success. In this way, the brand image moved together with the organizational image and, consequently, also with the organizational identity. Multiple artifacts were employed in influencing both the external and internal constituents and used a language that was coherent to all parties.

An important lesson from these contrasting examples is this: If you build a story that attends only your brand image (how your products are perceived by your customers) but not your identity (how your employees perceive who they are as an organization), then you will need at least two stories: one story to tell your customers and the other to tell your employees—and coherence will be difficult to achieve. Instead, a single story for both constituents improves the likelihood of coherence. Argento's top managers were able to build a single story, regarding not only product style but also lifestyle and, in the case of employees, a work-life lifestyle. The strength of this story is that it is for different stakeholders and different times. It is a story of self-confidence, modernity, power, need to excel, and to be exclusive that resonates with customers, celebrities, fashion arbiters, investors, and employees alike. Furthermore, Argento was able to project a coherent set of artifacts to support the storytelling as a way of "making sense" for themselves and "giving sense" to internal and external stakeholders. In this way, Argento accomplished convergent sensegiving and sensemaking that defined the fashion trends by simultaneously persuading fashion arbiters, customers, and other companies—a feat never achieved by Bianco.

Figure 11.1 depicts the various artifacts employed in the numerous cycles of sensemaking and sensegiving in the fine fashion industry.

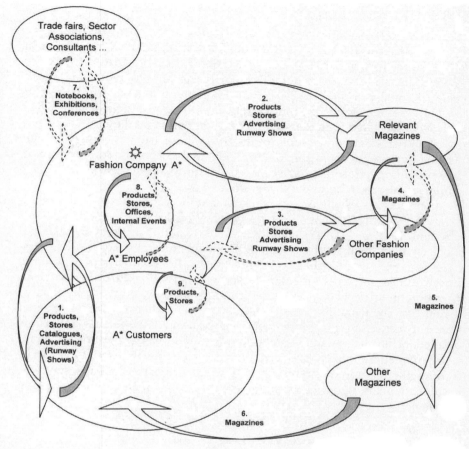

A* = our point of view

✿ = Internal sensemaking, to make sense of new external stimuli or of new internal ones

1 = Sensegiving process towards customers

2 = Sensegiving process towards relevant magazines

3 = Sensegiving process towards other fashion companies

4 = Sensegiving process towards other fashion companies supported by relevant magazines

5 = Sensegiving process towards other magazines supported by relevant magazines

6 = Sensegiving process towards customers supported by other magazines

7 = Sensegiving process towards consultants, show coordinator

8 = Sensegiving process towards employees

9 = Sensegiving process towards customers mediated by employees

■ = Main artifacts

FIG. 11.1.   Sensemaking and sensegiving processes in fine fashion industry.

ARTIFACTS AND THE FINE FASHION INDUSTRY

Artifacts have been the subject of some study in the organizational litera-ture (Gagliardi, 1990; Pratt & Rafaeli, 1997; Rafaeli & Vilnai-Yavetz, 2004a; Rafaeli & Worline, 2000). As Gagliardi noted, however, artifacts have re-ceived little attention compared with their relevance to understanding or-ganizational workings. In particular, little attention has been devoted to what we might term "defining artifacts"—those products or features so closely associated with the identity of a company that they affect the way that all perceivers make sense of the firm. These artifacts convey specific meanings about its raison d'etre, such that corporate communication (sensegiving) efforts are focused to an extraordinary degree on the "ideal" interpretations to be given these artifacts.

Artifacts are usually taken as residing at the surface level of an organi-zation's culture (i.e., as "visible organizational structure and process," Schein, 1991, p. 251). Trice and Beyer (1984) define artifacts as "material objects manufactured by people to facilitate culturally expressive activi-ties" (p. 655). For Gagliardi (1990) artifacts are "pathways of action and constitute a concrete element in the social structure" (p. 16). Most of the at-tention on artifacts has converged (understandably) on the "physicality" element. The usual focus on materiality can, however, mask the broader role of artifacts in conveying deep meanings and as powerful symbols. As noted, artifacts as symbols can assume different values and meanings for different audiences. Symbolic value is a perceived value and, thus, can be differentiated for different perceivers. All artifacts can have symbolic value, depending on the meaning assigned to them (see Vilnai-Yavetz & Rafaeli, chap. 1, this volume).

The Range and Relevance of Artifacts

The organizational literature has focused mainly on the obvious artifacts (dress, physical layout, furnishings, etc.). Yet, many rites and ceremonials can be construed as artifacts (Trice & Beyer, 1984). In the fine fashion indus-try, the seasonal shows might be seen as ceremonials, but they are better viewed as artifacts in light of their image-projecting character. Similarly, some special events, in which famous people wear a fashion house's dresses and are photographed for the fashion magazines, are also artifacts. Logos are especially critical artifacts. As Baruch points out in chapter 10 of this volume, the logo is a symbolic, graphic artifact aiming to convey a mes-sage and to produce identification. This is especially true in fine fashion where the logo (e.g., the LV logo on the Luis Vuitton Monogram line, the double-F logo on the Fendi "baguette" bag) is a sign with a dual function: to identify an elite and to distinguish it from others (Bourdieu, 1984a).

Fine fashion employees are themselves animate artifacts and not only because they "wear the brand": Employee-branding programs "are intended to impress brand attitudes onto the work behavior of employees, who are then expected to infuse brand attributes throughout their work" (Harquail, chap. 9, this volume). This is evident for salespeople in a fashion store: They must communicate company style, not only with their clothing, but also with their interpersonal style. As we noted earlier, the chic nonchalance of Gucci's salespeople in their Montenapoleone store is a clear expression of Gucci style; the salespeople even share physical characteristics (tall, beautiful, with modern haircuts, etc.).

Thus, a wide range of organizational features (not only physical objects) can be construed as artifacts, and such artifacts can influence both internal and external constituents (see Schultz, Hatch, & Ciccolella, chap. 8, this volume). Of more import, perhaps, is the idea that *patterns* of artifacts can be integrated together to produce a unified impression, as in Argento's case, to benefit of the organization (see Pratt & Rafaeli, 2001).

The Functions and Effects of Artifacts

Artifacts have more functions (see Vilnai-Yavetz & Rafaeli, chap. 1, this volume) and greater influence than usually assumed. M. J. Edelman (1964), writing with an orientation toward political theory, argued that symbols are associated with the "expressive" elements of politics and that substantive actions were associated with the "instrumental" elements. Gioia and Chittipeddi (1991), however, demonstrated the simultaneously expressive and instrumental roles of symbols during strategic change. Relatedly, Strati (1992) argued that artifacts have not only "aesthetic," but also "functional" dimensions. Because artifacts are usually granted only an expressive symbolic role, we want to highlight their instrumental role. We can note that "artifact as instrument" works at two levels. At the first level, like Strati, we maintain that artifacts can be "things" with literal meanings and clear instrumental functions. Obvious examples are professional dress that functions not only as dress, but also as "recognition" markers (Pratt & Rafaeli, 1997; Rafaeli & Pratt, 1993) and office furnishings that serve practical functions (D. E. Campbell, 1979; T. R. V. Davis, 1984; Strati, 1992). In Yves Saint Laurent stores, the dressing rooms have clear instrumental functions, but these dressing rooms, with their suffused lights, plush armchairs, dark silk dressing gowns, free water and soft drinks, also harbor symbolic functions beyond being merely places to try on new clothes. They convey exclusivity (via precious metals), distinction (armchairs instead of simple chairs), and indulgence for customers (i.e., soft lights are perfect for hiding imperfections).

Artifacts as "symbolic givers-of-meaning" thus have an undeniable instrumentality. "Symbol as sensegiver" serves as a major means of projecting image, so artifacts can have both instrumental and expressive functions in sensemaking and sensegiving.

Artifacts and Image

Clearly, fashion is an industry where image matters above all else. Image governs virtually all activities and is transmitted predominantly via artifacts. Fashion artifacts are numerous and different. Table 11.1 summarizes some of the artifactual features of the fine fashion industry, all of which act at personal, organizational, and industry levels.

IDENTITY, IMAGE, AND FINE FASHION

Put simply, organizational identity is the collective sense of "who we are as an organization" (Albert & Whetten, 1985). Identity is usually conceptualized as comprising features that are central, have continuity over time, and help to distinguish the organization from others in an industry (Albert & Whetten, 1985; Gioia et al., 2000). Image, on the other hand, often is conceptualized in two different ways, depending on perspective. From an insider perspective, image can be viewed as "how organization members think outsiders see the organization" (which is why this form of image is sometimes labeled as "construed external image"—see Dutton et al., 1994). From an outsider perspective, image concerns how outsiders actually perceive the organization in either the short term ("transient image"—Gioia et al., 2000) or the long term ("reputation"—Fombrun, 1996).

As noted, artifacts are the main means by which firms project their images (especially their brand images) to their stakeholders so that those stakeholders perceive the firm in the ways the organization's leaders desire. Brand image, then, is an outsider perception, so for the sake of clarity we refer to *perceived brand image*. Ultimately, these images, especially if they are discrepant with identity beliefs, serve as an impetus for altering identity (Gioia et al., 2000). A strong perceived brand image is of extraordinary importance for "high symbolic intensity" firms like those in the fine fashion segment. *Projected brand image* might then be viewed as the set of desired associations projected by the organization. Perceived brand image might or might not coincide with projected brand image. Discrepancies foster changes in one or the other. Projected brand image is affected by *organizational* identity ("who we are as organization"), in that the values underlying organizational identity are usually intended to be represented in the projected brand image.

Organizational identity questions loom very large in the fashion industry, mainly because the major fashion houses started life as a "cults of per-

TABLE 11.1
Artifacts in Fine Fashion

Fine Fashion Artifacts

Logos:
- Brand logos printed on the clothing and accessories.
- Logos as shape of some products (handbags, wallet, keychain, etc.).

Fashion products
- Seasonal products sold in the stores (especially those representing the whole seasonal collection, and those used in advertising campaigns and in window dressing).
- Classic, not seasonal, products sold in the stores.
- Vintage or in-waiting list products shown in the stores.
- Products shown in famous museums or in the company museum.
- Products shown in the headquarters offices.
- Products given or sold (at a special price) to the employees.
- Products the employees are obliged or strongly encouraged to wear while at work.

Fashion product representations
- Videos: seasonal shows, designers' interviews, top managers' interviews; company history, selection of movies with company products, celebrities interviewed with company products.
- Photos: advertising campaigns, magazine photos, photos by famous photographers, photos as decor for stores, exhibitions, and offices.

Supports of fashion product representations
- Catalogs produced to present the new collection, shown in the headquarters and in the stores, given to the company guests, and sent to all the important customers.
- Style notebooks and textile notebooks, produced by sector associations and trade fairs to present the previsions on the seasonal trends, the colors, and the fabrics.
- Fashion press (with a special mention for *Vogue*[a]) sold to the potential customers, used for the advertising campaign, reviewed by the company's press office, shown in the headquarter halls and offices, or put in a frame when they dedicate a cover page or a major article to the company products.
- Employees infusing brand attributes throughout their work.

Company layout and furnishing
- Store location, layout, dimension, and furniture (colors, style, materials).
- Headquarters location, layout, and furniture (colors, style, materials).

[a]*Vogue*, launched in the United States in the 1892, "capitalized on design innovation introduced in the production of European art magazines at the turn of the century, repackaging the fashion magazine as a desirable object in its own right, an harmonious and authoritative style guide that functioned as a bible for the fashion-conscious" (Breward, 2003, p. 123). For more than a century *Vogue* used well-known photographers. From the 1930s to the 1970s painters such as Dali, Cocteau, De Chirico, and Botero made regular contributions. The magazine production has "dematerialized" the fashion product; stylistic photography, in particular, has shifted the emphasis from the description of products to the creation of symbols.

sonality." That is, they all were created by a visionary founder. In recent years, however, many fashion firms have had to reinvent their identities. As they grew, or as a new chief designer with a different style achieved fame, the question became: "Who are we, if we are not Gianni Versace or Salvatore Ferragamo or Yves Saint Laurent?" Not all the companies have been able to resolve this question. Some have (Dior, Chanel, Louis Vuitton); others have had more difficulty (Yves Saint Laurent after acquisition by the Gucci Group). The challenge is not easy: to remain known for a distinct company style, while modifying the style itself. Obviously, the products fashion firms produce, as well as the presentations of their shops and their sales employees constitute a key (artifactual) element of their identity. That means that the designers in these companies constantly focus on making products that will be distinctive, attractive, and successful; all these features sustain their identity.

Brand image is intentionally projected to produce a positive impression for outsiders. A great brand image serves as a surrogate for a host of other elements. If the brand is desirable, everything else falls into place. Yet, brand image can change over relatively short periods of time in the volatile fashion industry. Because of the close links among brand image and organizational identity and image, a changing brand image implies a potential change in both organizational identity and image (Gioia et al., 2000). The constant movement of fashion style makes the brand, and consequently the organizational identity in this industry a more "mutable" concept compared with other industries. Therefore, we suggest that in "high symbolic intensity" industries, strongly represented by their artifacts (like fashion), organizational identity will be characterized by a relatively high degree of dynamism.

To delve a bit deeper into this process, construed external image (the way insiders think outsiders view the organization) is crucial, because that image is constantly compared to organizational identity. If that comparison generates a discrepancy, it can affect identity. When this discrepancy is unfavorable (*identity > image*), it will tend to generate attempts to more strongly communicate the organization's sense of identity via projection of stronger brand images through advertising and key company artifacts. For example, to improve the previously weak image of Bottega Veneta, after the Gucci Group's acquisition, the firm worked not just on advertising but on identifying a few, crucial "symbolic products" and on their coherence with the image of luxury they wanted to project.

A different discrepancy is produced, however, when projected brand image is seen as better than identity (*identity < image*). When efforts to project desired images succeed, it is possible to seem better than organization members know themselves to be. The image is recognized as false (as in Bianco). This second discrepancy cannot be resolved by working on transient impressions regarding the brand. It requires deeper work on organizational identity. A prevalent view in fine fashion is that so long as buyers buy and arbiters include us in the elite circle, identity is safe. Recently, however, because of the increasing size of fashion companies, the professionalization of their management, internationalization, and public stock offerings, internal stakeholders have become more important. Simply having a positive brand image is not enough to guarantee a positive organizational identity. A discrepancy between a poor identity and a good external image becomes problematic.

Artifacts facilitate awareness of an image/identity discrepancy, but at the same time they facilitate the resolution of this discrepancy. In fact, artifacts can be seen as both the means and the ends of sensegiving and sensemaking activities intended to enhance the identity or image of these image-driven organizations. When image is worse than identity, artifacts can work as image projecting vehicles enacting a sensegiving mainly directed at the external stakeholders. When identity is better than image, artifacts can work as identity influencing vehicles enacting a sensemaking mainly directed at the internal stakeholders.

SENSEMAKING AND SENSEGIVING VIA FINE FASHION

Sensemaking has to do, quite literally, with the ways that organization members make sense of their experience. The process involves the reciprocal interaction of information seeking, meaning making, and action (Thomas, Clark, & Gioia, 1993). Sensegiving has to do with the ways that (usually) members of the top levels of organizations attempt to influence the sensemaking processes of their stakeholders and constituents. Fine fashion firms must first project their artifacts and symbols to potentially critical audiences, then observe what happens in response, before deciding what to say or do next to try to sway perceptions in a desired direction. Ideally, the meanings given to organizational artifacts positively influence both internal and external images of the organization. These images, in turn, affect sensemaking and sensegiving processes that can either affirm or question organizational identity, and influence whether the artifacts that represent that identity should be maintained or changed. Artifacts, then, by either design or default, become image projecting (and identity influencing) vehicles. In industries attuned to their power, artifacts must, as noted, fulfill the simultaneous missions of conveying coherent images that can address the sometimes differing desires of differing audiences.

Employee responses to a firm's own fashion artifacts are critical. There are many triggers for internal sensemaking (e.g., critical commentary or indifference from arbiters like *Vogue,* fewer runway invitations, customer complaints about style). In the extreme these provoke executives of the firm to reexamine identity. One response might be to associate the firm with the next lower class in the pecking order of firms (not an attractive option). Another is to figure out new fashion tactics that will lead customers and arbiters to validate a position among desirable peer firms. In the best case, sensegiving entails convincing many perception brokers (via product hook, advertising, and creation of buzz) that the firm is producing a "trend" that defines the dominant style for one or more seasons.

This is *the* goal, the "rainmaker" style, that generates bandwagon effects because *"our* style is *the* style." The major fashion players have a strategic sensemaking goal—to "change the conversation" (the dominant style) in their own image. For instance, in the early 1990s Prada chose the rigid "minimalism" style that anticipated strong social desires, which allowed them to dictate a style, and facilitated their aesthetic transformation for the next decade. The strong symbolic and financial success made Prada, first, a reference point and then a key player in the industry, all of which positively affected its identity.

Style artifacts, then, can be judged according the responses they produce (Ornstein, 1986; Rafaeli & Vilnai-Yavetz, 2004a; Strati, 1999). Artifacts affect the sensemaking of many stakeholders, producing desired responses from customers (buying), arbiters (kudos), and employees (commitment). Sensegiving via artifacts is by no means an easy process. As Fig. 11.1 shows, a fashion firm must orchestrate many different sensegiving processes, using the right artifacts in the right sequence—all in the service of enhancing image and identity. At least one season before, the firm must start to work on fashion editors and trendsetters, persuading them that its style is "the coming style" by sending advance products to celebrities and fashion editors. Then, the firm has to persuade arbiters—via magazines, pseudo-events (Boorstin, 1961), and so on—that other fashion houses are imitating its style, supporting the sense that they have created a dominant design. Then, the company gives the sense of the season's style to the customers with runway shows, new products, flagship store alterations, and advertising. At this same time, it also has to give sense to the employees, who make sense via the magazines and advertising, like any customer, but also by means of dedicated artifacts: internal communications, company events, and so forth.

Overall, by analyzing fine fashion firms we gain insight into the complex roles of symbolic artifacts. Artifacts are "meaning creators" working to produce meanings that both express and affect image and identity. At the same time artifacts are "meaning givers" working to maintain or revise internal and external organizational images across a constellation of stakeholders.

CONVERGENCES AND EXTENSIONS

Fine fashion is an industry that depends on its "defining artifacts." A look at the fashion industry opens a window on the broad role that artifacts are likely to play in other industries, as well. Perhaps most interestingly, we see that it is not only through the expression of core values by founders and executives, but also through their artifacts, that the firms in this industry develop, sustain, and change their organizational identities and communicate those identities to different constituents through image-based "sensegiving" processes. These image projections, and their stakeholders' responses to them, in turn, affect the identities and subsequent artifacts produced by these image projecting firms. Put differently, fashion artifacts are revealed as both the means and the ends of sensegiving and sensemaking activities intended to enhance the identity and image of image-driven firms.

Artifacts as Symbols. In the fine fashion industry, as in many industries where the product is closely associated with the firm, artifacts are functional symbols. For that reason, developing systematic, thematic coherence around these artifacts is crucial in creating (and especially in maintaining) brand image, as well as organizational identity, image, and reputation. Effectively managed, organizational artifacts contribute to the creation of virtuous circles in the interrelationships of identity and image over time: stronger brand image → stronger internal and external organizational images → stronger organizational identity, and so on, in mutually enhancing cycles.

M. J. Edelman (1964) once argued that acts could be either expressive ("symbolic," in his usage) or instrumental (substantive). The fashion industry is based almost entirely on images that serve *both* symbolic and substantive roles, however. Images are the *stuff* of this industry. Yet, we might note what we term the "paradox of instrumentality": Fine fashion products are intentionally designed to be aesthetic, expressive objects and *not* to be instrumental objects for consumers. Yet, they are extraordinarily instrumental in conveying meaning to the various stakeholders of the fashion houses and the fashion industry itself. In symbol-intensive industries, therefore, there is a very fine line between image and substance. The fashion industry's artifacts blur that line, a phenomenon that allows insight into not only the social construction of style and fashion, but also the social construction of substantive reality, more generally.

Image as Identity. A lay view would typically assume that identity drives image. Our analysis can actually imply the opposite possibility, however, because over relatively short time periods, identity can depend on image. In an industry in which image (style) changes so quickly and firms survive or suffer on the basis of their artifactual images, both brand image and organizational image have significant influence on organizational identity. Ill-considered use of important artifacts can, therefore, produce a debilitating discrepancy between image and identity with serious consequences for both.

Given that there are dominant industry trends, it is important that a given company perform a fine balancing act—by being distinctive in its designs, but also consistent with overall fashion trends. This need for synchronized similarity and difference is analogous to that noted by Erickson (1950) in discussing individual identity. He noted that people first try to identify or associate themselves with a certain desirable group and then try to distinguish themselves within that group. This observation applies especially well at the organizational level within the fine fashion field. "Argento" and "Bianco" want to be seen as members of the top class of prêt-à-porter fashion, but also to distinguish themselves from each other within this realm. In this industry, they can do so only via their artifacts (including products, store layouts, advertising design, and even their animate artifacts, their salespeople). Firms like "Argento" that have a strong and clear identity as an input to their strategy, action, and products have a competitive advantage over firms like "Bianco" that do not have a clear understanding of who they are.

Sensegiving as a Sensemaking Imperative.   Firms communicate via symbolic artifacts to varied audiences, each of whom might be looking for something different (i.e., customers are looking for something different than employees or competitors). Hence, firms have yet another balancing act to perform: making the message multivocally coherent and yet tailored to each audience—a very complicated act of corporate communication and image projection. Successful sensegiving strives to create the virtuous circle, enacting processes that lead to attention from the external arbiters of success, as well as the attraction and retention of the best talent in the industry.

CONCLUSION

Symbols and artifacts need to be considered in light of the identity elements they convey, the images they are intended to evoke, and the sensegiving they are designed to effect among multiple constituents. As a consequence of our analysis, artifacts are revealed as multilevel vehicles for sensemaking and sensegiving. They are influential at the individual, organizational, and industry levels. Artifacts in both physical and symbolic forms *have* meaning and *create* meaning for people, firms, and industries.

Overall, we have examined an industry that is peripheral in most people's consciousness to analyze the central role of artifacts in sensemaking, sensegiving, and the construction and maintenance of brand image, as well as organizational identity, image, and reputation. In the fashion industry, such artifacts obviously play central roles in organizational life, but the fashion industry experience suggests a similar, if more latent and less obvious role, in any other industry that is infused with potent symbolic artifacts.

IV

ARTIFACTS AND LEGITIMACY

How do artifacts relate to institutions and professions? What are their roles in maintaining and undermining the legitimacy of organizations? The fourth and final part of our book argues that artifacts establish not only identity, but also legitimacy and trust. *Mary Ann Glynn* and *Christopher Marquis* (chap. 12) report on organizational names, and how they affect perceptions of organizations and organizational legitimacy. *Marlene Fiol* and *Ed O'Connor* (chap. 13) consider the broader question of how and why artifacts evoke and maintain legitimacy, focusing on key artifacts as visible traces of the establishment and subsequent decline of legitimacy in the U.S. medical profession. *William Kaghan* and *Michael Lounsbury* (chap. 14) conclude this part by suggesting that artifacts can be used in creating a "collective mind" that connects the institutional environment, collective practices, and organizational action.

Fred's Bank: How Institutional Norms and Individual Preferences Legitimate Organizational Names

Mary Ann Glynn
Emory University

Christopher Marquis
Harvard Business School

> *You have to have a command of the English language or you're just nowhere. I mean like . . . say you get out of college or whatever . . . you're gonna go into business, you're gonna open a bank just for an example. You've got to give it the right name. It's gotta be something big and strong like "Security First Trust and Federal Reserve." And you have to name a bank that because nobody's gonna put their money in "Fred's Bank." "Hi, I'm Fred, I have a bank. You got $1,500? . . . ahhh, I'll put it here . . . in my white suit."*
>
> —Steve Martin (Philosophy)

Steve Martin's comedic stand-up cited in the opening extract alerts us to how organizational names can serve as wellsprings of legitimacy. Martin's insights resonate with the core tenet of institutional theory, that is, that isomorphism legitimates. As institutionalists have demonstrated, organizations whose names, symbols, and artifacts conform to prevailing normative practices tend to be seen as more comprehensible and thus more legitimate (Glynn & Abzug, 2002). As Martin suggests, "Security First Trust and Federal Reserve" connotes credibility, but "Fred's Bank" arouses such suspicion that "nobody's gonna put their money in [there]." Thus, the names by which we christen organizations serve both as touchstones for legitimacy (Glynn & Abzug, 2002) and as cues that guide individuals' perceptions about an institution, thereby functioning like other organizational artifacts (Pratt & Rafaeli, 2001).

In this chapter, we empirically investigate how institutional norms and individual differences interact to affect individuals' perceptions of, and preferences for, organizational names. Broadly speaking, we take up the question of how symbolic isomorphism, the institutional conformity that confers legitimacy, may be affected by differences in individual preferences. We explore how individual differences in the receptivity to institutional isomorphism affect their understanding and choices of names. Our core research questions are: Do individuals have preferences about how closely organizational artifacts should match their institutional environment? And, do such preferences affect individuals' perceptions of, and preferences for, organizational names?

That the legitimacy conferred by institutionalization in organizational artifacts, such as names, may be subject to individual variations is suggested by Rafaeli and Worline (2000) in their statement that "people's interpretations of symbols may differ" (p. 74). We investigate whether there are variations in individuals' understandings of, and preferences for, certain organizational symbols over others with regard to the artifacts' visible social fitness. Artifacts have a very emotional character that relates individuals to institutions (e.g., Pratt & Rafaeli, 2001; Rafaeli & Vilnai-Yavetz, 2003), arousing latent processes of sensemaking and interpretation by the individuals who apperceive them. Perhaps for some individuals, in some neighborhoods, Fred's Bank is appealing; one might imagine it to be the name of a local loan shark (who substitutes for "Security First Trust and Federal Reserve") or a nickname that signifies the generosity of a favorite uncle (Fred). Thus, names may resonate with personal meanings above and beyond those derived from the institutional environment.

A useful illustration of these dynamics is provided by the baby names chosen by parents. Such children's names are "one of the rare measures of collective taste" (Orenstein, 2003, p. 28). As in other matters of style, institutionalized trends create a sort of "fashion quotient" that breeds names that are considered traditional or classic; however, "names generally rise and fall independent of larger cultural or historical events" (Lieberson, quoted in Orenstein, 2003, p. 28). Thus, as much as names may reflect cultural trends and fashion trajectories (Lieberson, Dumais, & Baumann, 2000), they may also reflect a need to make a personal statement (citing Sartran, in Orenstein, 2003) or be distinctive, to differentiate one's child from others. Thus, we see symbols, such as names, as subject to a dual set of influences, one driving toward conformity, and the legitimacy it confers, and the other, toward distinctiveness, and the uniqueness it confers. We examine both sets of influences for their effects on individuals' perceptions of organizational names.

Our research contributes to the literatures that focus on organizational artifacts as important markers of organizational identity as well as that focusing on institutional dynamics. To the former, we build on theories that have delineated how organizational artifacts symbolize organizational culture and meaning (Rafaeli & Worline, 2000) and relate individuals emotionally and cognitively to the organization (e.g., Pratt & Rafaeli, 2001; Rafaeli & Vilnai-Yavetz, 2003). Furthermore, we expand this perspective to locate artifacts within the broader cultural and institutional environment that gives them meaning. To do this, we focus on the symbolic realm of organizational names.

Taking Pratt and Rafaeli's (2001) notion of "symbols as language" seriously, we examine the case when symbol *is* language, that is, the organization's name. And, complementing studies that assess individuals' reactions to artifacts, we assess how individuals understand artifacts in the context of institutional norms that locate organizations within that normative environment through naming practices. Essentially, we bring these perspectives on artifacts to the macrolevel institutional environment, as a source of meaning to which individuals respond.

As well, we seek to contribute to institutional theory. Suchman (1995b) clearly indicates that "legitimacy is a *perception* or *assumption* in that it represents a reaction of observers to the organization as they see it; thus, legitimacy is possessed objectively, yet created subjectively" (p. 574). And yet, institutional theory has tended to overlook the subjective and social constructionist role of individual perception in legitimating organizations. We extend the reach of institutionalism to the microlevel, by examining individual variations in responsiveness to symbolic isomorphism (Glynn & Abzug, 2002). Institutionalists seem to have assumed that individuals universally perceive conformity as legitimating; we investigate this generalization by examining how individuals with different beliefs and preferences about the value of symbolic conformity react to different names. We ask: Do individuals vary in their preference for institutional conformity in symbolic artifacts, and does such variance affect their perceptions of organizations?

We explore these questions in a survey designed to assess how institutional norms and individual differences affect individuals' comprehension of, and choices about, naming organizations. We begin by theorizing names as artifacts and develop hypotheses about the influences of institutional and individual factors on individuals' perceptions of, and preferences for, organizational names. Our findings speak to how organizational artifacts are embedded in both institutional realms of meaning but also subject to individual differences in naming preferences. Thus, we locate the study of artifacts at both macro- and micro-levels of meaning. We start by exploring how organizational names function as artifacts.

THEORIZING ORGANIZATIONAL NAMES AS ARTIFACTS

We focus on names as important organizational artifacts because they signify categories of meaning (Brown, 1958), sorting organizations into equivalent and nonequivalent sets, for example, "Security First Trust and Federal Reserve" versus "Fred's Bank." In encountering an organization for the first time, we ask: What kind of organization is this? We answer by interpreting the cultural artifact—the organization's name—that is before us, and sorting it into the appropriate category (e.g., legitimate banks or illegitimate banks).

Organizational symbols and artifacts cue meanings, helping the perceiver to socially construct the nature of the organization as well as his or her relationship to it (Pratt & Rafaeli, 2001). The primary linguistic conduit for this is labeling or naming. Names are organizational claims about an organization's identity that locate an organization in institutional space, as a member of an organizational field (a bank, e.g.), and cue its distinctiveness for quality, service, or products (e.g., strength and security) (Glynn & Abzug, 1998). Thus, names serve as organizational artifacts that classify organizations into fields and distinctively mark an organization's identity attributes, such as quality and service. As one organization proclaims, "Best Chairs Inc: Our name says it all," explaining that "At Best Chairs, Inc., we combine the BEST Quality chairs, with the BEST Prices. Pride and dedication are evident in everything we make" (www.bestchairs.com). We examine these two features of names as artifacts: first, their institutional embeddedness, and second, their service as markers of organizational identity attributes.

Organizational Names as Institutional Artifacts

Organizational names, like other organizational symbols, are subject to isomorphic pressures at the field level (Glynn & Abzug, 2002). Such institutional pressures can affect the names that organizations choose; for instance: "I just took Coca-Cola as a name similar to other advertising names . . ." (Frank Robinson, circa 1900, from The World of Coca-Cola).

Institutional theories suggest that language plays a critical role in shaping organizational symbols (Hirsch, 1986; Meyer & Rowan, 1977). Meyer and Rowan emphasized the importance of organizational language in creating categories of meaning. The institutional environment, consisting of the social, political, legal, competitive, market, and other forces that embed firm behavior, offers a portfolio of linguistic practices that are often *theorized* by relevant and authoritative actors (Strang & Meyer, 1994). This process of theorizing provides explanations and accounts to support specific institutionalized behaviors, routines, and symbols, which are themselves legitimate. Isomorphism with the symbols authorized by the institutional environment secures legitimacy and comprehensibility for the organization (Glynn & Abzug, 2002).

An institutional perspective on organizational names alerts us to how the institutional context shapes naming practices and their understanding. As Mohr (1998) points out, cultural meanings are built out of structures of differentiation; patterns of relationships define and link various organizational elements. Names identify organizations, voicing their claim on a specific region of institutional space; for instance, a name like First National Bank is a firm's claim of membership in the category of banks or the field of the banking industry. By choosing names that are symbolically isomorphic, that is, names that conform to the constitutive rules that define an organizational field or industry (Glynn & Abzug, 2002), organizations locate themselves within institutional contexts that lend them comprehensibility and legitimacy.

Legitimacy, defined by M. C. Suchman (1995b), is "a generalized perception or assumption that the actions of an entity are desirable, proper, or appropriate within some socially constructed system of norms, values, beliefs and definitions" (p. 574). The extent to which conformity is clear and transparent should render organizations legitimate. And, in turn, legitimacy yields organizations that are "more meaningful, more predictable, and more *trust*worthy" (M. C. Suchman, 1995b, p. 575), signaling that it's just the kind of place where you'd feel comfortable putting your money (or Steve Martin's!).

Organizations that seek legitimacy through institutional conformity adopt artifacts and names that signal social fitness (Glynn & Abzug, 2002). Firms embed cues in their names so that an audience can easily apperceive their cultural appropriateness, typically by advertising their membership in institutional fields. Thus, names tend to conform to industry naming practices and patterns (Glynn & Abzug, 2002); in turn, such conformity should be easily readable by an interested audience. M. C. Suchman (1995b) argues that "not all explanations are equally viable: To provide legitimacy, an account must mesh both with larger belief systems *and* with the experienced reality of the audience's daily life" (p. 582). Thus, organizations' claims on legitimacy will succeed to the extent that audience members can access such cultural accounts *and* believe that those cultural accounts signify legitimacy.

Following this logic, we propose that organizational attempts at cultural alignment with sanctioned institutionalized practices will succeed

in garnering legitimacy to the extent that individuals believe those accounts to be important. In other words, individuals who believe that
names like "Security First Trust and Federal Reserve" signal trustworthiness will find such a name more comprehensible and more legitimate.
Conversely, individuals who do not associate legitimacy with institutional conformity will, instead, disregard cues that suggest institutional
conformity. Conceptualizing organizational names as institutional artifacts, we hypothesize the following.

Hypothesis 1 (H1).   Individuals' beliefs about the function of organizational names will influence their accuracy in assessing a firm's institutional identity.

- *Hypothesis 1a (H1a):* Individuals who believe that an organization's
  name functions as a legitimating artifact by its conformity to institutional norms will be more attentive to connotations embedded in the
  firm's name and thus be more accurate in assessing the firm's institutional identity.
- *Hypothesis 1b (H1b):* Individuals who believe that an organization's
  name functions as a marker of a firm's distinctive identity will be less
  attentive to institutional connotations embedded in the name and
  thus be less accurate in assessing a firm's institutional identity.

Organizational Names and Perceived Identity

Viewing names as institutional artifacts stops short of fully capturing how
meaning is embedded in organizational monikers. Apart from institutionally derived connotations, names are clearly subject to variations in individuals' perceptions. As Humpty Dumpty happily explains to Alice in
Wonderland:

> "... But tell me your name and your business."
> "My name is Alice, but . . ."
> "It's a stupid name enough!" Humpty Dumpty interrupted impatiently.
> "What does it mean?"
> "Must a name mean something?" Alice asked doubtfully.
> "Of course it must," Humpty Dumpty said with a short laugh. "My name
> means the shape I am—and a good, handsome shape it is, too. With a name
> like yours, you might be any shape, almost." (Lewis Carroll, *Through the
> Looking Glass*)

Although names can locate organizations in institutional realms of
meaning, they can also imbue it with other identifying attributes, signal-

ing, for instance, the firm's quality, price, or service (Glynn & Abzug, 1998) or a nursing unit's cultural assumptions (Rafaeli & Worline, 2000). With a name like *Best Chairs,* an organization clearly marks its quality orientation. By contrast, the furniture store moniker, *Innovations,* might, as Humpty Dumpty says, "be any shape, almost." Ambiguous names tend to be less useful as identifiers or organizational markers.

With their names, then, organizations can symbolize or codify images, meanings, and qualities that are important aspects of their identity, or those organizational attributes that are central, distinctive, and enduring (Albert & Whetten, 1985). Language embodies patterns of meaning that define organizational realities (Morgan, Frost, & Pondy, 1983), imbuing an organization with qualities it may see as desirable and defining of its identity. Such words cue broader sets of meanings that encourage valuations in that direction. For instance, *Best Chairs* implies the quality that individuals may expect; we argue some individuals may value such quality signals more than others. March and Simon (1958) observed that "the world tends to be perceived by the organizational members in terms of the particular concepts that are reflected in the organization's vocabulary" (p. 165). By invoking words that mark an organization's attributes, organizational names evoke standards of evaluation in audience members who are attuned to receiving such signals. This argument is consistent with what Putnam and Fairhurst (2001) term "cognitive linguistics," which asserts that "meanings . . . reside within language users" (p. 118).

We view organizational artifacts, and names more specifically, as signals that are drawn from the common cultural vocabulary that members of a society (or organizational community) share. However, we argue that the recognition of those signals will vary depending on individuals' receptivity to those cultural accounts. We hypothesize that individuals have preferences for certain kinds of names over others. And, although such preferences can vary in a number of important ways, we focus on two that are relevant to the institutional nature of names: The first is individual preferences for more creative or unusual names (such as "Fred's Bank") and the other, individuals' preferences for institutionalized or legitimate organizational labels (such as "Security First Trust and Federal Reserve"). Individuals who prefer more creative names will make name choices consistent with their preferences. The way such preferences affect name choices is evident in the case of baby names: Some parents seek to individuate, giving their child an uncommon name (Lieberson & Bell, 1992), but others signal conventionality, by using popular and common standards, naming boys "Michael" and girls "Kate" (or some slight variation on each of these).

We anticipate that individual preferences for creative or conventional names will affect individuals' preferences for certain types of organizational names. Individuals with creative preferences will tend toward less conventional, traditional, and more uncommon, unusual, or nonstandard (deviant) names. Conversely, other individuals with different preferences will tend toward more normative organizational names, that is, those that fit with institutionalized patterns of nomenclature. Thus, we hypothesize the following.

Hypothesis 2 (H2). Individuals will differ in their preferences for symbolic isomorphism in names and this will influence their choices for new organizational names.

- *Hypothesis 2a (H2a):* Individuals who believe that an organization's name should be isomorphic with the organizational field will choose new organizational names that conform to institutionalized practices.
- *Hypothesis 2b (H2b):* Individuals who believe that an organization's name need not be isomorphic will choose new organizational names that do not conform to institutionalized practices but rather, are uncommon, creative, or unusual.

METHODS

Survey. The survey data used in this chapter are part of a larger study of organizational names reported by Glynn and Abzug (2002). The survey had four main sections. Section 1 focused on comprehensibility of names and assessed how respondents were able to *accurately* assess the industry of a number of relatively unknown companies. Section 2 asked participants their *preference* for a name that would be best for attracting customers for five types of firms: dry cleaning, banking, meat processing, plastics manufacturing, and a pizzeria. Section 3 asked participants to rank-order which of seven characteristics of names are most important. These included names reflecting products/services' specificity, traditions, creativity, the founder, geography, competitive advantages, or abbreviation. Section 4 asked respondents for agreement (using a 5-point Likert scale) on 17 questions about individuals' preferences regarding the purpose or effectiveness of organizational names (e.g., "A firm's name should describe specifically what the firm does," "People think highly of a firm because of its name"). A final section captured demographic data about the respondents.

Sample. Because we were interested in understanding variations in perceptions, we surveyed two different types of respondents who had very different organizational and educational backgrounds. One subset of respondents (n = 516) had significant business experience; all were students who were enrolled in Master of Business Administration (MBA) programs. The second subset consisted of respondents who had little or no exposure to business organizations; these were college undergraduates from a sorority ($n = 41$) and adults who were active in the arts ($n = 55$). The resulting total sample of 612 had the following characteristics: 38% female, with an average age of 27.6 ($SD = 5.7$), 5.1 years of work experience, and 51% with bachelor's degrees. See Glynn and Abzug (2002, pp. 274–275) for further details about the sample.

Measures: Dependent Variables. Because our hypotheses concern how respondents interpret names, we created two binary dependent variables reflecting respondents' *accuracy* in assessing the industry membership from names and respondents' *preferences* for deviant names. We use binary measures for these variables because this allows us to collapse responses for a number of questions into one measure (e.g., respondents got all the questions right, or selected one of a number of names).

Accuracy was measured using Section 1 of the survey, where respondents were asked to categorize relatively unknown companies according to industry. We used only firms whose names included an industry root that provided a clue to the correct industry choice: Alagasco (oil and gas), Contel (telecommunications) and Lifetime (medical/health). Responses were coded a "1" if they were able to accurately assess all three of these names and "0" otherwise.

Preference was measured using Section 2 of the survey. We coded a "1" if the respondents selected any of the least popular name choices, and "0" otherwise. For each of the names of firms in Section 2, there was generally an agreement on what would be the "best" name (e.g., Tony's Pizza was selected by 58% of respondents as the best name for a pizzeria), and there was also an agreement on what would be the least desirable name. Table 12.1 reports the modal and least frequent name choices for each new organization.

The statistics in Table 12.1 show clear differences in choice patterns. Names that were chosen most frequently we termed modal name choices. These were chosen by 40% to 58% of the respondents. Conversely, names that were chosen least frequently were also easily identifiable. These most infrequent name choices were selected by no more than 7% of respondents. For example, only 7% of respondents indicated a preference for a meat-processing company being named "The Meating Place" and only 0.4% had a preference for a pizzeria being named "First National Pizzeria." We see these name choices as indicating a preference for more creative, unorthodox, or deviant names.

Independent Variables. Because we hypothesized that the latent interests and characteristics of respondents would influence the perceptions of names (H1 and H2), as our independent variables we used data from

TABLE 12.1
Modal and Infrequent Name Choices for New Organizations
(Questionnaire Section 2)

New Type of Organization	Modal Name Choice	Standard Deviation	Most Infrequent Choice (% Chosen)
Dry Cleaning Store	Park Ave. Cleaners 53%	1.2	Abe Lincoln's Laundry 2%
Bank (in Atlanta)	BancAtlanta 53%	1.0	Tony's Bank 1.3%
Meat Processing Company	Quality Meats 40%	1.7	The Meating Place 7%
Plastics Manufacturing Company	XL Plastics 45%	1.0	XLT 5%
Pizza	Tony's Pizza 58%	1.1	First National Pizzeria 0.4%

Note. $N = 612$.

Sections 3 and 4 of the survey indexing the significance of name attributes to respondents. From responses to Section 3, we created two binary variables that indicated whether respondents' first or second choices for names were *creative* or *conforming*. Using the scale items in Section 4, we conducted exploratory factor analysis (principal components factors, varimax rotation) and were able to identify two significant factors, each with eigenvalues greater than two, and together accounting for 30% of the variance.

One, which we are calling *names as artifacts,* indicates the strength of respondents' beliefs that names reflect the organization's institutional context. This factor consists of the following five items: "A firm's name is important in establishing its reputation," "Clients and customers are attracted to a firm because of its name," "Choosing a new name for a firm is an important strategic business decision," "The name of a firm is a key part of its identity," and "A firm's name can give the business credibility and legitimacy."

The second factor, which we are calling *names as identity markers,* indicates the importance of names as reflecting key attributes of the firm, such as the quality of "goodness" of the firm. This factor is composed of two questions: "A firm can be no better than its name," and "A firm's name is indicative of its quality and service."

Control Variables. We included a number of controls regarding the demographic characteristics of our respondents, including: *gender, years of full-time work experience, level of education,* and whether they are enrolled in an *MBA program.* We also included in our analytical models a binary variable taken from Section 3. This indicated if respondents' first or second choice for name characteristic was the following: a name that *specifi*cally describes the product or service. We are controlling for this because this was the most popular choice for all respondents.

Analyses. Because both of our dependent variables were binary, we used logistic regression.

RESULTS

Correlations and descriptive statistics are presented in Table 12.2 and regression results testing hypotheses one and two are presented in Table 12.3.

For each of our two sets of analyses (predicting *accuracy* and predicting *preference*) we estimated (and present) four models. The first model for each set (Model 1 and Model 5) consists of only the control variables. These are presented primarily for informational purposes and to verify that the addition of the independent variables significantly increases the model fit.

The main models that we interpret are Model 3, which tests how individuals' beliefs about the functionality of names influences *accuracy* (H1a and H1b), and Model 6, which tests how individuals' *preference* for different types of names influences their choice of creative or deviant names (H2a and H2b). The other models presented are primarily for informational purposes and include the independent variables from the other set of analyses. These test how preferences for creativity or tradition influence accuracy (Model 2) and how beliefs in the functionality of names influence preference for deviant names (Model 7). Also included in Models 4 and 8 are full models with both sets of independent variables.

Hypotheses 1a and 1b, predicting how individuals' beliefs about how the functionality of organizational names influences their accuracy in assessing firms' institutional identity, found support (see Model 3). Individuals who believe that an organization's name functions as a legitimating artifact were more attentive to institutional connotations embedded in the firm's name, and individuals who believe that organizational names function as markers of a firm's distinctive quality were less attentive to institutional connotations.

Hypotheses 2a and 2b, predicting how individuals' preferences about symbolic isomorphism influence their choices for new organizational names, also found support (see Model 6). Individuals who believe that an organization's name should reflect industry norms will choose new organizational names that conform to institutionalized practices. Individ-

TABLE 12.2
Descriptive Statistics and Correlations for All Variables

	Mean	SD	1	2	3	4	5	6	7	8
1 Name as Artifact	3.45	.493								
2 Identity Marker	2.58	.836	.124**							
3 Preference: Specific	.646	.479	-.037	.016						
4 Preference: Creative	.517	.500	.059	-.053	-.231**					
5 Preference: Conforming	.221	.415	.052	.029	-.249**	-.149**				
6 Gender	.391	.509	.074	.030	.073	-.020	-.023			
7 Experience	5.12	4.49	.058	-.007	.014	-.051	.026	-.076		
8 Education	4.21	.868	.004	-.008	-.074	.015	.003	-.253**	.291**	
9 MBA	.848*	.359	.084	.021	-.074	.000	-.027	-.300**	.042	.579**

$*p \leq .05.$ $**p \leq .01.$

TABLE 12.3
Logistic Regression Results

Model	Individuals' Accuracy in Assessing Names (1 = All Correct)				Individual Preferences for Deviant Names (1 = Prefer at Least One Deviant Name)			
	1	2	3	4	5	6	7	8
Individuals' Beliefs about the functionality of names:								
H1a Names as Artifacts			0.366*	0.371*			0.404	0.480†
			(0.181)	(0.182)			(0.254)	(0.266)
H1b Names as Identity Markers			−0.241*	−0.241*			0.109	0.149
			(0.105)	(0.105)			(0.142)	(0.147)
Individuals' Preferences for:								
H2a Conforming Names		−0.006		−0.026		−1.819**		−1.888**
		(0.216)		(0.218)		(0.487)		(0.492)
H2b Creative Names		0.205		0.147		0.509*		0.502*
		(0.178)		(0.180)		(0.254)		(0.256)
Control Variables								
Preference for Specific Names	0.288	0.338†		0.329†	−0.246	−0.447†		−0.423
	(0.176)	(0.191)		(0.193)	(0.238)	(0.255)		(0.258)

(Continued)

TABLE 12.3
(Continued)

Model	Individual's Accuracy in Assessing Names (1 = All Correct)				Individual Preferences for Deviant Names (1 = Prefer at Least One Deviant Name)			
	1	2	3	4	5	6	7	8
Experience	0.028	0.03	0.026	0.026	-0.050	-0.053	-0.054	-0.06†
	(0.020)	(0.020)	(0.020)	(0.020)	(0.035)	(0.036)	(0.035)	(0.036)
Education	-0.007	0.004	0.006	0.013	0.017	0.017	0.069	0.078
	(0.129)	(0.129)	(0.130)	(0.130)	(0.174)	(0.174)	(0.176)	(0.177)
MBA	0.804*	0.818**	0.741*	0.764*	-0.132	-0.184	-0.165	-0.284
	(0.310)	(0.312)	(0.315)	(0.317)	(0.427)	(0.444)	(0.438)	(0.457)
Constant	-1.134*	-1.489**	-1.738*	-2.082*	-1.143†	-1.001	-3.152**	-3.183**
	(0.489)	(0.518)	(0.786)	(0.813)	(0.643)	(0.688)	(1.100)	(1.160)
LR χ^2	15.13*	16.54**	20.17**	23.74**	6.71	35.57**	8.62	39.15**
Δ LR (v. baseline models 1 and 5)	—	1.41	5.04*	8.61**	—	28.86**	1.91	32.54**
Observations	591	591	588	588	591	591	588	588

Note. Standard errors in parentheses, two-tailed tests.
†$p \leq .10$. *$p \leq .05$. **$p \leq .01$.

uals who believe that organizational names should be creative and unusual chose new organizational names that did not conform to institutionalized norms and practices.

Our control variables, with the exception of enrollment in an MBA program, did not provide any systematic or interesting patterns. Perhaps confirming the validity of our tests, being in an MBA program increased individuals' accuracy in assessing names, suggesting that an MBA education provides socialization experience into industry and organizational conventions.

DISCUSSION AND CONCLUSIONS

By taking a multilevel approach to organizational artifacts, incorporating both macrolevel institutional norms and microlevel individual differences, we sought to enrich existing approaches to studying symbols in organizational practices. Our work embeds artifacts in a blend of institutional forces and individual variation that help to explain why artifacts function as such potent carriers of meaning.

Our first hypothesis posited that individuals' beliefs about the function of organizational names would influence their perception of naming connotations and their accuracy in assessing firms' institutional identity; we found significant support for H1. More specifically, we found that individuals who believe that an organization's name functions as a legitimating artifact were more accurate in assessing the organization's institutional identity; in contrast, we found that individuals who believed that an organization's name functioned as an identity marker were less accurate in making this assessment.

To interpret these findings, we speculate that individuals' beliefs directed their attention to cues embedded in the organizational names. For those individuals believing a name to be an institutional artifact that locates the organization in a field of meaning, cues that connotated industry membership, for example, Alagasco (oil and gas), Contel (telecommunications) and Lifetime (medical/health), may have been more salient and thus more comprehensible. However, individuals believing that names served as distinctive identity markers, indicating a firm's particular attributes, such as quality (e.g., "Best Chairs"), may have directed their attention toward such cues and away from others that signaled institutional membership. Important to note in this study, the stimulus words did not embed such cues. Perhaps distracted from the institutional cues that were in the names, these individuals were less accurate in assessing the industry membership of firms. Clearly, future research might test our speculation by surveying individuals' responses to names that function as institutional artifacts and as identity markers. However, the support for Hypothesis 1 (as well as H1a and H1b) suggests that isomorphism matters but matters more to those individuals who hold beliefs consistent with an institutional perspective on artifacts.

Whereas the first set of hypotheses focused on accuracy cued by normative conformity, the second set of hypotheses turned to examining artifacts that were potentially deviant and nonconforming. Our second hypothesis posited that individuals' preferences about symbolic isomorphism would influence their choices for new organizational names; more specifically, individuals with preferences for normative naming patterns would choose names that conformed to institutionalized practice. By contrast, individuals with creative preferences would choose more deviant, unusual, or uncommon names. We found significant support for these hypotheses: In choosing names for new firms, individuals aligned their name choices with their name preferences.

Overall, the results offer implications for both the study of artifacts and the study of institutional dynamics. Our findings indicate that artifacts derive their meaning from both more macrolevel institutionalized fields of meaning and more microlevel individual variations. Artifacts have cultural moorings that reflect institutionalized values, norms, and practices, but they are also subjectively perceived by individuals in light of their personal beliefs about, and preferences for, artifact characteristics. As such, we extend current theories about artifacts that tend to focus meanings primarily at the organizational level (e.g., Pratt & Rafaeli, 1997; Rafaeli & Worline, 2000) or at the individual–organization interface (Pratt & Rafaeli, 2001). Broadening this view to the institutional level, we show how organizational artifacts can carry meanings to audiences who are not organizational members or employees. Borrowing from a cultural toolkit (Swidler, 1986) afforded by normative and institutionalized practices, individuals construct the meaning of artifacts so as to fit them to their personal belief systems and preferences.

Our findings extend institutional theory by revealing how audiences subjectively construct meanings, comprehend organizations, and sanction or legitimate institutions by apperceiving artifacts. We find that isomorphism, or organizational conformity to normative practices, does not mean the same thing to all people. People vary in their preferences for standardized, normative organizational symbols, and these preferences affect their choices in crafting and understanding organizational artifacts. We might speculate that it is organizational appellations such as "Fred's Bank" that appeal to individuals with more creative impulses. Conversely, it is individuals with preferences for normative names who would deposit their money in "Security First Trust and Federal Reserve."

To conclude, we find that both institutional and individual factors affect the construction of meaning for organizational artifacts. It is the ongoing process of institutionalization, and the valorization perhaps of the preferences of powerful or elite individuals, that eventually become the standards and traditions in symbolizing organizations. We have looked at one aspect of the process, asking people to judge and to choose organizational names; we leave it to future researchers to uncover other layers of meaning in organizational artifacts.

ACKNOWLEDGMENTS

We are indebted to Rikki Abzug for her inspiration and her involvement in the earlier research, as well as to Eric Newman for alerting us to the Steve Martin routine.

13

Stuff Matters: Artifacts, Social Identity, and Legitimacy in the U.S. Medical Profession

C. Marlene Fiol
Edward J. O'Connor
University of Colorado at Denver

> *Two years ago, as I was helping my sister move, I spotted the black bag in the back of her U-Haul truck—she was using it to carry her household tools. A flood of memories rushed through me. This was the bag that my dad, a physician in Paraguay, South America, had used from the 1940s until he retired. He was "el señor doctor" . . . and the black bag, strapped to the saddle of his horse, was a symbol of the respect he commanded. He and the bag traveled extensively throughout the countryside of Paraguay, seeking out leprosy patients, abandoned by friends and family and in desperate need of medical attention. The bag was his companion, providing the tools he needed, or simply sitting open, near the cot of a sick or dying patient.*
>
> *Today the black leather is cracked and peeling in places; the handle is well worn.*
>
> *I never thought a black bag could evoke such powerful memories.[1]*

Identity work is an interactive process that entails both "claiming" and "granting" behaviors (Bartel & Dutton, 2001). The acts that individuals engage in for the purpose of displaying their distinctiveness and status as members of a group are identity-claiming behaviors. External validation or legitimation of these social claims occurs through identity-granting behaviors. Artifactual displays are important symbolic resources that communicate claims of social identity (e.g., I feel like a physician when I wear

[1]In loving memory of our father, Dr. John R. Schmidt, 1911–2003.

the white coat) and/or the granting of legitimacy of those claims (e.g., TV shows portray white coats as positive status symbols).

On one hand, social-identity theorists have focused on how individuals claim central and distinctive attributes of a group by which to define themselves (Ashforth & Mael, 1989). This portrayal recognizes the dynamic nature of identification processes by which people gain a sense of belonging to a social group that is somehow distinct and different from others. Though identity is a categorization device for denoting both similarity and distinctiveness, identity theorists have tended to focus more on distinctiveness than on similarity. They have also largely failed to take into account the role of outsiders in granting legitimacy to the group's identity, thus underestimating the constraining effects of external forces on the creation and maintenance of social identities.

On the other hand, institutional theorists in a largely unrelated stream of research have described the external granting of legitimacy to a group's identity when its activities are aligned with generally acceptable societal norms (DiMaggio & Powell, 1991; Meyer & Rowan, 1977a). Even though legitimacy, like identity, is a categorization device for grouping what is similar and different, institutional theorists have tended to emphasize similarity over distinctiveness. They have also tended to focus on the stabilizing effects of institutional logics, and until recently have been largely silent about the processes by which actors may construct and reconstruct their social identities in ways that shift the underlying sources of their legitimacy. Institutional theorists have thus tended to underestimate the role of individuals in shaping the meaning contexts within which they operate.

This chapter focuses on the relationships between a group's internal social-identity claims and external legitimacy granting in the U.S. medical profession. We agree with W. R. Scott's (2001) recent assertion that the most informative studies are those that identify and trace the effects of legitimation and delegitimation processes across two or more levels, from individual actors to organizations and organizational fields (community of organizations with a common meaning system), and even to society's norms and values. We trace a dynamic and multilevel view of legitimacy-granting and identity-claiming processes, as reflected in the interweaving of the social realities of physicians, the medical profession, and U.S. society at large over the course of the 20th century.

The chapter addresses two related questions. First, what is the role of members' social identities in the establishment and maintenance of their legitimacy as a group? At the beginning of the 20th century, hospitals in the United States were religious and charitable institutions. Independent physicians tended not to work in the hospitals, but treated higher income patients in their homes. They enjoyed little or no professional legitimacy.

We trace the role of these actors' social-identity claims as they gained increasing legitimacy as a profession.

Second, what is the role of members' social identities when institutional logics change and the group's legitimacy begins to erode? Once conferred, legitimacy tends to be largely taken for granted, but institutional environments remain vulnerable to challenge (Goodrick, Meindl, & Flood, 1997). This has been the case in the medical profession during the latter part of the 20th century in the United States. The hard-won professional legitimacy of physicians has been in danger of slipping away as societal norms are shifting. We contrast the role of physicians' social-identity claims as they have attempted to reestablish their legitimacy as a profession with the role their identity claims played in the original establishment of legitimacy.

To begin to unpack these processes at multiple levels of analysis, we draw on several key artifacts that have been both reflective and constitutive of the changing social realities in U.S. health care: the black bag, the white coat, and the electronic medical record (EMR). Though on the surface, these three artifacts appear unrelated, they have been central players in the drama of the rise and fall of the legitimacy of the U.S. medical profession. After a brief review of the literatures on institutional legitimacy-granting and social-identity-claiming processes, we discuss the role of artifacts in both reflecting and enacting them.

Legitimacy, Identity, and Artifacts

To be legitimate as an organization or profession is to be understood well enough to be largely taken for granted (cognitive legitimacy) and to be accepted as appropriate and right (sociopolitical legitimacy) by external constituencies (Aldrich & Fiol, 1994). Legitimacy is conferred when actors are perceived by influential constituencies as being consistent or in alignment with a more or less shared definition of a social reality. Institutional theorists have described this shared social reality at varying levels of analysis, including single organizations, organizational fields (multiple organizations that operate from a common meaning system), and society at large (W. R. Scott, 2001).

Our examination of the processes by which legitimacy was initially constructed, maintained, and then eroded in the U.S. medical profession complements extant institutional theory by focusing on largely overlooked questions about the interrelationships among different levels of social reality. It contributes to the growing interest in the role of individual actors in shaping the sources of both social order and social change at the level of a collective.

We recognize that even a social constructionist view must begin with the assumption that actors cannot modify institutions directly, because institutions by definition represent social facts that are beyond the reach of individual actors (Goodrick & Salancik, 1996). However, individual actors may come together to form a collective with a set of identity features that rest on new sources of legitimacy, drawn from a new set of institutional logics, or from fragments of preexisting logics. Alternatively, individuals may relabel their collective identity to be more closely aligned with current institutional logics. Or they may change their individual memberships to groups perceived as being more legitimate. All of these represent ways that actors influence the sources of their legitimacy through the creation and re-creation of their collective identities.

Artifacts may play an important role in the movement from disparate individual identities to the emergence of a collective sense of self. William James (1890), who laid the foundations for modern conceptions of self, argued that our things are an important component of our sense of self. Belk (1988) referred to the self-plus-our-stuff as the "extended self" (p. 140). Collective conceptions of self emerge as individuals embrace similar artifacts to express their extended selves (Belk, 1988). The medical white coat, for example, became an identity marker that distinguished individual physicians from quacks; it also symbolized the emergence of a collective professional identity and expressed similarity and belonging in the group. A recent study showed that the top reason physicians gave for wearing a white coat was the distinctive status that it signified (Lynn & Bellini, 1999). The coats have also provided users (especially young users) with added confidence and psychological comfort in carrying out their professional roles (Barrett & Booth, 1994).

Artifacts may also serve as symbols of external legitimacy that lend an institutional quality to activities associated with them (W. R. Scott, 2001). Pratt and Rafaeli (1997), for example, described dress markers in the medical profession as indicating status, expertise, and professionalism to external constituencies. Until recently, the white coat has been the most common accessory in media depictions of the profession; the artifact has been practically synonymous with the profession itself (V. A. Jones, 1999). Conversely, artifacts may signal illegitimacy (e.g., the black bag of the early 1900s denoted voodooism).

To understand the emergence, re-creation, and decline of legitimacy in the U.S. medical profession, we must focus on the dynamics at the intersection of actors' claims of extended selves and external constituents' granting (or not) of legitimacy to those selves. This necessitates a cross-level perspective. Individuals' extended selves may converge (more or less intentionally) around a set of common artifacts, signaling the emergence of a social identity category (e.g., white coat signals medical profession). Members' social identities are then based on attributes of the social category as a whole that is perceived as distinctive, and category members perceive themselves as reflections of that distinctiveness. The distinctive status a group confers on its members (i.e., the perceived legitimacy and rank associated with it) is not perceived as an individual identity marker, but rather as a group attribute adopted by its members (Brewer et al., 1993). A social group gains legitimacy (or not) based on its adherence to socially accepted norms, and individuals experience the consequences of legitimacy or nonlegitimacy to the extent they self-categorize themselves as part of that group.

In sum, projections of extended selves and subsequent social-identity claims represent meaning-making and meaning-breaking processes that mediate between individual actors and external legitimation. When identity-claiming and legitimacy-granting processes are aligned, new meanings of "who we are" can swiftly emerge and take hold; when claiming and granting processes are misaligned, old meanings of "who we were" may just as swiftly be broken down. Understanding these processes provides insights into the dynamics of legitimation at multiple levels of analysis—how actors may positively influence the emergence of legitimacy or alternatively hasten the erosion of legitimacy through their identity-claiming behaviors. The various instrumental and symbolic meanings of the artifacts that both the users and external constituencies attribute to them represent a path by which to trace these dynamics over time, which we now turn to.

From "Black Bag" to "White Coat"

The lone-ranger physician in the United States at the end of the 19th century and into the beginning of the 20th century worked autonomously and was not considered a professional (Starr, 1982). Conditions were harsh, pay was low, and the work was not considered legitimate. Science had damaged the respectability of medicine by demonstrating that its cures were worthless, thus relegating much of medicine to the realm of quackery and healing cults (V. A. Jones, 1999). Whereas scientists were admired, physicians were generally distrusted.

The medical black bag was a tool that fit the role of physicians during this period. It contained everything needed for house visits, thereby supporting the autonomous nature of the work. So for physicians, the bag was instrumental, a necessary tool, as well as symbolic of autonomy and independence. For outside constituencies, the black bag symbolized evil-smelling and -tasting concoctions, of little value at best, and consisting of downright quackery and voodoo at worst (Gordon, 1950). Given this negative external image and a lack of external legitimation, it is not surprising that a strong collective identity among physicians during this time never emerged. Physicians continued to work as autonomous agents and the medical field remained fragmented.

In the early part of the 20th century, physicians turned to science, believing that the labs that were transforming communication and transportation could also provide breakthrough advances in curing disease. Over time, taking on a science-based identity allowed physicians to differentiate themselves from quacks and fakes, and held them up to be something special. In this way, the medical profession initially borrowed legitimacy by aligning itself with the preexisting institution of science. Medical historians depict this movement toward science as a conscious and deliberate process of identity alignment with a more acceptable set of societal norms (Preston, 1998; Starr, 1982).

At about the same time, seeking to visibly represent themselves as scientists, physicians adopted the scientific lab coat as their standard of dress (V. A. Jones, 1999). At first, justification for the white coat was purely instrumental. It was thought to prevent cross-contamination between physician and patient. The white coat very quickly became a strong status symbol for its users, a symbol of the authority of science (Van der Weyden, 2001). And the symbol of status and authority was readily accepted/diffused among external constituencies because it was aligned with a broader set of accepted institutional logics. The artifact quickly became embedded in the larger frame of scientific endeavors.

The emerging borrowed external legitimacy certainly had its source in the acceptable scientific discourse of the time, a discourse that physicians borrowed to re-create their own identity. However, it was significantly enhanced by the new artifact, the white coat, which quickly became a unifying symbol of a shared extended self. Physicians became a group of "we's," rather than a fragmented bunch of "I's" as a result of both the distinctiveness-enhancing self-categorization processes of insiders, and the emerging legitimacy conferred on them by outsiders. And the "we-ness" caused the newly adopted scientific beliefs to diffuse more rapidly than if actors had remained autonomous and highly dispersed (Zucker, 1988).

The black bag continued to serve as a tool for physicians until it was no longer useful—when the autonomous lone ranger no longer went forth alone to visit patients, but instead became part of a professional group that patients came to see by appointment. The negative symbolic image associated with the black bag shifted when physicians borrowed the social-identity category of scientist, and the legitimacy of the profession began to emerge. For a time, the bag coexisted as a symbol of the emerging field of medicine, along with white coats. It is interesting to note, however, that the black bag soon disappeared as the signifying icon of medicine, as the white coat—more clearly aligned with the scientific societal norms of the time—gained increasing symbolic dominance. Today medical black bags are to be found in antique stores, at garage sales, in the cobwebbed attics of doctors' homes (and in a sister's U-Haul, filled with a bunch of household tools!). They were abandoned both for lack of practical value in the new social reality and for the sake of appearing to be in alignment with science—a source of emerging legitimacy for a previously fragmented group.

ESTABLISHED LEGITIMACY: THE "WHITE COATS" RULE

As the century wore on, both the social identity of physicians and the legitimacy accorded them by outsiders strengthened until the near unassailable power of the profession became rulelike, and physicians' high status in society a given. Given the close alignment between the scientific beliefs underlying the institutional environment and the actors' social identity, establishing and maintaining the newfound legitimacy occurred almost automatically.

The white coat—like a portable pedestal—continued to set physicians above the crowd as individuals of great education and achievement (Preston, 1998). In fact, the white-coat symbol became so powerful that some medical historians refer to it as though it began to take on a life of its own. Rothman (2000), for example, described a medical student who, when she donned her fresh white coat on her first day of orientation at Harvard Medical School, assumed a complex new identity. And junior physicians were regularly advised that if they were lacking self-confidence, the white coat would help them grow into their role (Barrett & Booth, 1994). Preston provided a similar example of the power of the white-coat symbol for a physician fresh out of medical school. He had borrowed the money to pay the first month's office rent, and had bought the simplest and most inexpensive furniture he could find. Finally, he put on a clean white coat, and then he sat down and waited for patients. Even with an empty desk and a blank patient roster, the young doctor possessed the one symbol that affirmed his identity as a physician—his white coat. External constituencies, too, began to perceive the white coat as embodying the profession. As noted earlier, the white coat was long the most common artifact used by the media to depict physicians (V. A. Jones, 1999). All of these examples suggest that the artifact had become synonymous with the social reality it symbolized in the eyes of both users of the artifact and external legitimating audiences. It was simultaneously distinctive and consistent with broad trends, much like the fashion artifacts that Cappetta and Gioia discuss in chapter 11 of this volume.

Declining Legitimacy: The Battle of Competing Artifacts

Medicine's powers and prestige reached their zenith in the 1950s and 1960s, a period widely known as the Golden Age of Medicine (Hafferty & Light, 1995). Beginning in the late 1960s, a number of frame-breaking changes brought about sharp departures from the past in U.S. health care (Shortell, Morrison, & Friedman, 1990), beginning with the introduction of Medicare's prospective payment system, and including massive technological advances, growing numbers of uninsured persons, and the emergence of third-party payers. Costs skyrocketed and health care as usual could no longer either meet the needs of its communities or cope with the complexities of the modern-day field. As a result of these changes, the health care industry experienced tremendous changes in its institutional structure, incorporating new actors (e.g., large for-profit chains) and responding to a different set of rules (e.g., administrative logics of "suits" running large health care systems) (Scott, Ruef, Mendel, & Caronna, 2000).

At about the same time, radical changes were also transforming the broader societal values in the United States. With the Age of Aquarius in the late 1960s, old-fashioned formality got a bad name and egalitarianism surged. Beginning in the 1970s, the United States became increasingly pro-business and the consumer became king. The logic of the new administrative "suits" that permeated the health care world, in fact, closely mirrored the broader societal values. Health care organizations began to feel the need to justify their apparent business inefficiencies (Goodrick et al., 1997). They responded by trying to imitate the models and mentality of for-profit businesses. Voluntary hospitals began to redefine themselves as efficient and market-oriented, stressing their similarities to for-profit organizations. They adopted for-profit structural forms, systems, diversification patterns, expansionary activities, and corporate-type boards.

As a result of these changes that were in close alignment with widely held societal values, the power and legitimacy of administrative "suits" increased at the expense of physicians (Goodrick et al., 1997). As W. R. Scott (2001) noted, "entrenched power is, in the long run, helpless against the onslaught of opposing power allied with more persuasive ideas" (p. 60). Administrators brought with them a social identity rooted in the highly persuasive ideas of efficiency, technological superiority, and bottom-line productivity, thereby eroding physicians' professional authority. Though science continued to be valued, medicine began to be treated as a business, and definitions of effectiveness changed from meeting the needs of the local community to the bottom line.

Professional and bureaucratic principles represent largely incompatible logics (Bunderson, Lofstrom, & Van de Ven, 2000), so not surprisingly, conflict has ensued. Given the interdependent relationship between physicians and administrators, it is little wonder that the ongoing conflicts are a consistent theme in the annual MGMA Report on "Performance and Practices of Successful Medical Groups." And when health care leaders are asked to identify strategic concerns, antagonistic physician–administrator relations are consistently high on the list (O'Connor & Fiol, 2002). Sociologists and organizational theorists, too, have studied physicians and administrators and the conflicts their differences have engendered (Bacharach, Bamberger, & Conley, 1991; Bunderson et al., 2000).

At one level, the conflicts have been about administrative efficiency versus quality of care. However, we suggest that at a deeper level, the conflicts have to do with competing sources of social identity and external legitimacy. The practices that reflect legitimate institutions were clearly changing in the U.S. medical arena. External constituencies were increasingly conferring legitimacy to those health care organizations adopting the new science of integrated business systems. And health care as an integrated system—of which physicians were one part right along with the "suits"—was antithetical to physicians' social identity rooted in professional differentiation.

White coats, the artifacts once synonymous with the social reality of medical dominance, became less distinctive as other nonmedical groups began to adopt them (e.g., chiropractors, urgent-care centers, etc.). And where they still symbolized distinctiveness, they became an inappropriate status symbol in systems where integration was increasingly the aim. The coats themselves began to be the targets of society's attacks, rather than just the physicians who wore them. This is consistent with our argument that in the heyday of medicine, white coats took on a social reality of their own. That reality was at the core of the social identity of physicians, and it had come under threat. White coats began to be seen by those outside of the medical profession as a barrier to system integration, rather than as a symbol of physician power and trustworthiness. Objections were raised about their excessive formality (V. A. Jones, 1999). As early as 1987, a study published in the *Journal of the American Medical Association* found that many physicians were being advised to get rid of their white coats (Preston, 1998). The changes in society and in health care that turned physicians into health care providers and patients into clients, consumers, or customers were hinting at the extinction of the white-coated demigod (Van der Weyden, 2001).

Emergence of a Competing Artifact

Not only has the white coat been under attack as reflecting what is no longer an undisputed source of legitimacy, but a new class of artifact has emerged in the U.S. health care world of the end of the 20th century that both reflects and has helped construct the legitimacy of integrated health systems: the EMR. EMRs consist of a centralized, longitudinal approach to patient data, providing a single, comprehensive source of data for all involved in the health care delivery chain, from physicians to accountants. Proposed benefits include higher quality documentation, error minimization, less paper filing, fewer lost charts, and improved communication and integration of the various components of the health care delivery system (Mildon & T. Cohen, 2001). Despite its many proposed benefits, adoption of EMRs has been low (5% to 10%) and flat over the past decade (Loomis, Ries, Saywell, & Thakker, 2002). Physicians have been especially resistant to using such a system, with stated reasons ranging from poor functionality and performance of the system to lack of access and training (Hodge, 2002).

Like the white coat, the EMR artifact carries multiple layers of meaning. The instrumental layer of meaning may tell only a small part of the resistance story. In the discussion that follows, we suggest that physician resistance may stem from the new source of legitimacy the EMR reflects and has helped to create, more than from what it does or does not do in a functional sense.

EMRs and white coats, on the surface, would appear to have very little resemblance as functional artifacts. At a symbolic level, however, they appear to be contradictory symbols of a single dynamic of opposition and conflict. For external constituencies, the EMR signifies positive system-level integration. Its purpose is to seamlessly link all aspects of health care delivery, thereby symbolically creating a level playing field for all parties within an umbrella health care system. Such integration contradicts the professional differentiation that has been at the core of physicians' well-established social identity and that has been symbolized by the white coat. For many physicians, the EMR is a negative symbol because it negates their sense of distinctiveness, whereas for many outsiders the white coat is a negative symbol, seen as an attempt to uphold that status distinctiveness.

There is reason to believe that the tension between these two contradictory symbols will continue to grow, rather than resolve itself. People who perceive themselves as belonging to a distinctive subgroup experience threats to their distinctiveness when their group is categorized as belonging to a more general superordinate group (Hornsey & Hogg, 2002). Threat-rigidity theory (Staw, Sandelands, & Dutton, 1981) suggests that when threatened, actors will actually exhibit decreased behavior concerned with actively searching for new solutions, in this case a new source of identity. Instead of abandoning a symbol that has become a fatal flaw in the eyes of its constituencies, the medical profession has acted very much in line with what Staw and his colleagues would have predicted: They have redoubled their efforts to make the white coat live on. "White Coat Ceremonies" were first initiated in 1993 by the Gold Foundation of Columbia University College of Physicians and Surgeons. Only 5 years later, by 1998, 93 of the 142 accredited medical and osteopathic schools in the United States conducted this rite of passage (Van der Weyden, 2001), a ceremony typically performed for the incoming class at the beginning of each academic year.

The wide dissemination of this ritual suggests a groundswell in the preoccupation with a threatened identity. As Meyer and Rowan (1977a) noted long ago, rituals have the potential to influence social meanings through the ceremonial bestowal of worth and status. Geertz (1973) also suggested that rituals can provide symbolic models of the social world that participants can internalize as legitimate representations of reality. He described ritual participants as both creating and reflecting the social order in which they are embedded, thereby perpetuating traditions. Six components of the white-coat ceremonies reflect actors' intent to perpetuate and revitalize the professional identity as legitimate (Van der Weyden, 2001):

1. The presence of family and friends suggests a close value system.
2. The presence of dean and faculty reflects value systems of the medical schools.
3. The address by physician role models suggests perpetuity.
4. The personal robing signifies the medical community's belief in the student.
5. The ceremonies represent public and visible proclamations.
6. The ceremonies include celebratory receptions.

No amount of ritual is likely to bring back outdated sources of legitimacy if the social reality that is ritualized is not in alignment with broad societal values. Through the white-coat ceremonies, physicians are certainly reinforcing their own perceptions of legitimate reality (Geertz, 1973). But instead of serving as visible externalizations of that reality for outsiders, this form of ritual may only be exacerbating the disconnect between the medical profession and societal values in the late 20th century.

Figure 13.1 summarizes the path from individual physicians acting alone, to the emergence of a legitimate collective, and its subsequent decline. The arrows indicate the primary directions of influence among the factors we discussed, highlighting the fact that artifacts served as both drivers and reflections of the changing social realities. In the late 1800s, external categorizations were driven by societal views of doctors as "quacks," not to be confused with science. The black bag, which outsiders

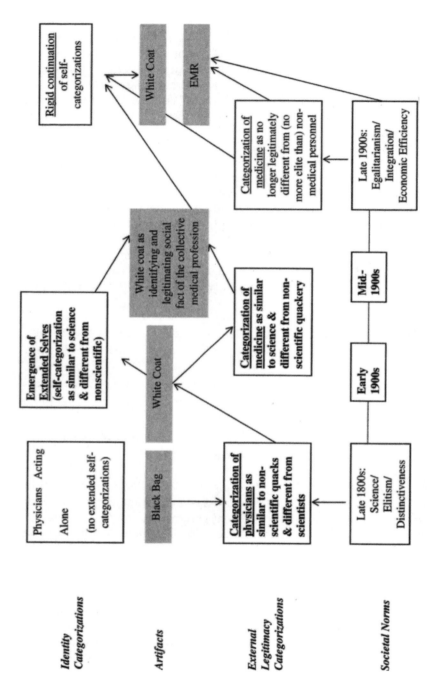

FIG. 13.1. Identity and legitimacy over time in U.S. health care. Arrows indicate the primary directions of influence among the factors depicted in the figure.

associated with a lack of valued scientific outcomes, reinforced this view, and the absence of self-extensions into a collective led to physicians exerting little collective influence to change it.

The stigma associated with the negative categorization of physicians appears to have been a key driver of the search for a positive icon—the white coat—around which physicians could rally, leading to the simultaneous emergence of extended self-categorization of physicians and the external legitimation of that emerging collective. The alignment of internal identity and external legitimacy categorizations led to the white coat attaining social-fact status by the mid-1900s.

Though science continued to be important, egalitarianism and economic efficiency characterized the changing societal norms in the late 1900s, and outsiders began to no longer associate the white coat with the results they most valued. The growing popularity of EMRs, a perceived source of integration leading to reasonably priced quality outcomes, reflects this shift in societal norms. Threatened by the potential loss of distinctiveness that EMRs imply, the medical profession has fought to keep alive the dying symbol of the white coat.

Figure 13.2 depicts the different meanings that external constituencies and internal actors have attributed to the two central artifacts in the late 1900s, the white coat and the EMR. It shows the single system of contradictory meanings that has enveloped the two apparently distinct artifacts. Whereas external constituencies are resisting white coats as negative symbols of undesirable status distinctiveness, physicians are resisting EMRs as contradictory negative symbols of their nondistinctiveness. And whereas external constituencies are granting legitimacy to EMRs as positive symbols of systemwide integration, physicians are clinging to their white coats as contradictory positive symbols of their professional differentiation.

The fact that the different artifacts appear to have become carriers of contradiction within a single meaning system gives each of them more symbolic power than they would have alone. That is, a battle over the appropriateness of white coats, alone, would likely be less entrenched than a battle where the white coat stands contrary to the EMR, and where each takes on meanings that are opposite the other. Such an interlocked system of meanings is likely to create a self-perpetuating downward cycle. Much like the self-energizing process that led to white coats assuming the status of social fact, the warfare between the competing artifacts (and the social realities they represent) is likely to continue to exacerbate the downward slide of physician legitimacy.

In line with our theoretical rationale, health care analysts predict that physicians are not likely to identify with the nonmedical staff of health care systems and that the "administrative suits" and the "white coats" will evolve in different directions (Hafferty & Light, 1995). The growing

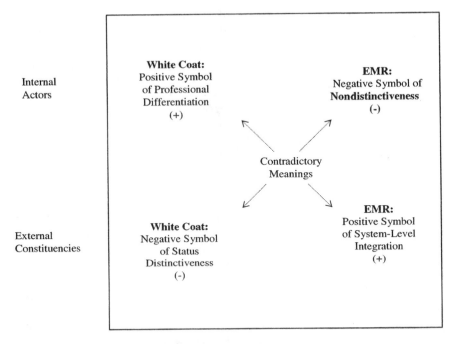

FIG. 13.2.   Competing artifacts within a single meaning system.

rift is similar to the fragmentation that Kaghan and Lounsbury refer to (chap. 14 in this volume) in their study of contracts and contracting that results from poor quality of "articulation work" across different communities of practice. The "suits" are likely to become the more dominant of the two for the same reason that the "white coats" ruled 50 years ago: They are ideologically closer to the broader societal institutional logics (though the logics may again be shifting). External signs appear to point to the continuously diminishing legitimacy of the medical profession. For example, candidates for medical school have been dropping steadily over the past decade. According to the American Academy of Family Practice Physicians' Web site (2003), there has been a 25.7% drop in medical-school applicants from 1996 to 2001.

We have argued that actors cannot confer legitimacy on themselves directly, thus granting relatively less sensemaking and sensegiving power to individual actors than others have suggested (e.g., Belk, 1988; see also Schultz, Hatch, & Ciccolella, chap. 8, this volume; Cappetta & Gioia, chap. 11, this volume). However, we have posed the argument that they can and do change the underlying sources of their legitimacy through their self-extensions and through processes of social identity categorizations and recategorizations. To follow this argument to its logical conclusion suggests that a way out of the self-destructive cycle of declining legitimacy may entail that physicians claim a social identity that is aligned with the new science of rationalization and integration, while still retaining some form of professional distinctiveness.

Though the purpose of this chapter has not been to attempt to solve the problems of physicians' declining legitimacy, our arguments suggest that finding a solution must entail an appreciation of the deep symbolic meanings of a few key artifacts competing for supremacy. On one hand, physicians are engaging in rituals to uphold an artifact that once signified their grandeur; rituals that will likely fail to hold meaning for outsiders unless they reflect the changing social order. On the other hand, health systems are losing millions of dollars in failed attempts to integrate physicians as part of large systems through the use of EMRs; the attempts will likely continue to fail unless they encompass physicians' deeply embedded need for distinctiveness. As Schultz et al. (chap. 8, this volume) state, the "perfect artifact" in the face of change is one that is able to maintain traditional foundations while appearing contemporary.

DISCUSSION AND CONCLUSIONS

Physicians in the United States in the late 1800s were autonomous actors with minimal collective identification with, and no external legitimacy as a profession. The black bag, a strong early symbol of both the independence of individual physicians and their negative external image, was relatively quickly and easily relinquished in the face of an emerging professional social identity that was in alignment with positive societal norms. The white coat became synonymous with the social identity of its users and the rapid legitimization of the medical profession.

Conformity with institutionalized norms and practices leads a group to ways of thinking and doing that are understood and seen as appropriate by outsiders, thereby providing external legitimacy. Conformity with a group's internalized norms and practices leads to ways of thinking and doing that are self-defining, thereby reinforcing group members' distinctive social identity. To the extent that external institutional norms and actors' social identities are consistent with one another, they reinforce each other. Actors' internal sense of "who we are" is strengthened by outsiders' validation and legitimization of that social identity and vice versa. And external legitimacy is more easily garnered when individuals identify with a group, rather than acting in isolation. So legitimacy is conferred to the focal group by societal outsiders and status and distinctiveness are perceived by insiders—a state of congruence enjoyed by the U.S. medical profession throughout much of the 20th century.

When social identities are aligned with institutional norms and expectations, the symbolic meanings of the artifacts that both reflect and help to create them become taken for granted as social facts. Their presence and use serve to reinforce continuing legitimacy, often without conscious intent of the users of the artifacts. Societal changes, however, have led to misalignments between broader societal norms and the well-ingrained social identities of medical professionals. If societal expectations change and actors' social identities remain embedded in old norms that are no longer legitimated, the meanings attributed to the old artifacts will become misaligned. Under these threatening conditions, actors are likely to become more intentional in their use of those artifacts, struggling to maintain legitimacy by holding onto old symbolic meanings.

It is interesting and perhaps useful to contrast the periods of non-legitimacy (late 1800s) and declining legitimacy (late 1900s). In both eras, the identity of physicians was misaligned with societal norms. And in both eras, external constituencies held the artifacts reflecting the physicians' identity as a negative symbol (black bag in the late 1800s, white coat in the late 1900s). Why was the black bag (as compared to the white coat of the 20th century) relatively easily relinquished in favor of an artifact more closely aligned with societal values? Regarding its relative instrumental value, the white coat holds little more functional value in the late 20th century than the black bag did earlier in the century. Regarding its symbolic value, however, the two differ markedly. Though the black bag surely symbolized important aspects of the autonomous physicians' individual identity, it held little social-identity value for insiders, given the lack of a collective profession with which to identify. The white coat, in contrast, quickly gained social-fact status for both actors and observers, and became a familiar icon of physicians' social identity as well as external legitimacy. In this latter instance, then, physicians' social identities are strongly tied into old symbolic meanings of the artifacts, leading to conflict and resistance.

The role of artifacts in the legitimacy path we have traced in this chapter raises interesting questions about who owns an artifact that symbolizes an extended self. Physicians borrowed the white coat from another group. Is it theirs? Nonmedical personnel increasingly perceive the coat as an inappropriate and even illegitimate artifact. To what extent do they control its destiny? We suggest that any group can own an artifact and use it as an extension of self; but a group does not own the meanings that others attach to it. As we noted earlier, this view accords less power to actors to intentionally manipulate the meaning of their artifacts than others have assumed (e.g., Belk, 1988).

We draw four conclusions from our journey in this chapter. The most obvious is that stuff surely does matter, and in ways that go well beyond its instrumental value. As W. R. Scott (2001) aptly noted, "the symbolic freight of some objects can outweigh their material essence" (p. 82). Tracing physicians' artifactual identity markers over the past century reveals the power of artifacts as both facilitators of and barriers to social change. Second, stuff matters most when it attains social-fact status, in effect becoming the social reality it symbolizes. Again, the social-fact status of artifacts can either accelerate social change (the white coats early on) or make users blind to social change (white coats later on). Third, stuff that symbolizes and represents a group's social identity appears to be far more powerful than is stuff that reflects individual identities. There is power in the numbers that see themselves reflected in their stuff. And finally, different stuff that is functionally distinct and unrelated may take on symbolic meanings that lock each other in a battle within the same meaning system.

This final point leads to a practical implication of our modeling of the two competing artifacts. It is only through an appreciation of the social meanings of the artifacts that a way out of such a battle becomes possible. Rather than continuing to hold onto their old stuff with old meanings (through activities such as the white-coat ceremonies), it may be time for actors to explore new stuff as an opening for new symbolic meanings to emerge that are in alignment with societal expectations, while still providing a basis for a distinctive social identity. One such possibility, for example, might consist of physicians taking advantage of the very capabilities that drive the EMR in order to electronically enhance the clinical aspects of care that only they as medical professionals can fully understand. Through such new meaning making, they may once again align a distinctive sense of self with the legitimated newest science.

14

Artifacts, Articulation Work and Institutional Residue

William N. Kaghan
Touro University International

Michael Lounsbury
Cornell University

Traditionally, sociologists and anthropologists have been concerned with the role artifacts play in maintaining social order (e.g., Durkheim, 1965; Geertz, 1973). For instance, consumption of different kinds of goods can symbolize membership in a particular class or status group, thereby reproducing societal stratification (Bourdieu, 1984a; Veblen, 1979). In a similar fashion, organizational researchers have begun to explore the role of artifacts in establishing and maintaining organizational order (e.g., Gagliardi, 1990; Pratt & Rafaeli, 1997). They have been particularly interested in how artifacts affect the sensemaking activities of various organizational stakeholders and how managers can better appreciate and manage these meanings (Cappetta & Gioia, chap. 11, this volume; Harquail, chap. 9, this volume; Schultz & Hatch, chap. 8, this volume). While it is clear that artifacts certainly do play a role as symbols in maintaining social and organizational order, these studies tend to downplay other aspects of artifacts (e.g., instrumental or aesthetic) that have important effects on social and organizational action (Rafaeli & Vilnai-Yavetz, forthcoming). More particularly for our purposes, most studies have conceptualized and studied artifacts in a relatively static way and elided a broader understanding of how artifacts are produced and come to circulate in the world (Becker, 1982; Latour, 1987).

In this chapter, we focus attention on the relationship between institutionalized understandings about the way in which artifacts should be constructed and used and the articulation work (Fujimura, 1996; Strauss,

1988) done by knowledgeable actors to embed these institutionalized understandings in concrete artifacts that are well adapted to a particular line of action (Blumer, 1969b; Strauss, 1993). Artifacts, like actors, are caught up in broad institutional processes that provide stability and predictability over time and space (Hughes, 1971; March & Olsen, 1989; Scott, 2001). As a result, artifacts are imbued with an institutional residue that shapes how artifacts are constructed, used, and understood. However, we emphasize that in the process of constructing and using artifacts, actors often do more then merely uphold or reproduce institutionalized understandings. They also extend, modify, adapt and sometimes directly challenge these understandings. In turn, these local modifications are often fed back into the broader institutional field, sometimes leading to editing of existing templates and changes in broader institutional beliefs (Barley & Tolbert, 1997; Becker, 1982; Edelman, 1992; Feldman & Pentland, 2003; Fiol & O'Connor, chap. 13, this volume; Lounsbury & Rao, 2004).

To study how artifacts are penetrated with institutional residues and how these residual elements are used in everyday activities, we propose a practice-centered framework to guide research. Practice-centered analyses aim to provide a bridge between institutional and sensemaking perspectives by focusing on patterns of collective action carried on by organizations, groups and individuals involved in enacting those patterns (Kaghan & Bowker, 2001; Kaghan & Phillips, 1998; Lounsbury & Kaghan, 2001; Lounsbury & Ventresca, 2003). To illustrate how the study of artifacts can simultaneously inform the study of institutions and the study of sensemaking activities, we examine formal written contracts as one particular category of artifact. We explore the role that formal written contracts play in providing structures within which on-going exchange relationships can proceed sensibly over time. Drawing on the case of technology transfer managers and technology transfer contracts, we illustrate the articulation work required to imbue artifacts with institutional residues that allow these artifacts to be interpreted and used in conventional ways.

A Practice-Centered Framework for the Study of Artifacts

While there are a great variety of studies and orientations that coexist under the heading of practice-centered approaches (e.g., Bourdieu, 1977; Douglas, 1986; Giddens, 1984; March & Olsen, 1989; Mohr, 1998; Strauss, 1993), they are generally united by their shared emphasis that the microdynamics of social interaction and the broad institutional context in which this interaction occurs are connected through the application and interpretation of particular sets of practices within particular sociotechnical structures (Barley & Tolbert, 1991; Lounsbury & Kaghan, 2001; Lounsbury & Ventresca, 2003). The patterns of interaction within and between organizations are guided and made sensible through the application of particular sets of practices in the context of complex sociotechnical systems and the reflection of knowledgeable actors on the results of these applications. Organizational practices provide the mechanisms through which institutionalized collective cognitive structures (collective mind) and large-scale technological structures (systems of artifacts) are routinely reproduced and new collective cognitive structures and large-scale technological structures emerge over time (see Fig. 14.1).

As shown in Fig. 14.1, we have borrowed the concepts of sociotechnical systems and collective mind to enrich our practice-centered framework. The concept of sociotechnical systems was pioneered by organizational researchers with an interest in technology and organizations (Barley, 1990; Bechky, 2003; Emery & Trist, 1965; Orlikowski, 2000; Orlikowski & Barley, 2001; Perrow, 1984) and, in a somewhat different way, by researchers in the Sociology of Science and Technology (e.g., Kaghan & Bowker, 2001;

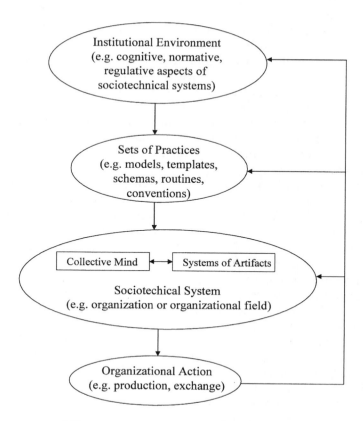

FIG. 14.1.   Practices, organizations, and artifacts.

Kling, 2000; Latour, 1996; Vaughan, 1996). In the sociotechnical systems view, organizations and organizational fields are modeled as interdependent social and technical systems that are interconnected in complex ways. The social system is composed of knowledgeable human actors connected in some sort of social structure. The technical system is composed of artifacts connected into a system that is both functional and meaningful. Importantly, artifacts are seen as having both instrumental and symbolic aspects. When the focus of a study is on the instrumental aspects of an artifact, the artifact is viewed as a tool. When the focus of a study is on the symbolic aspects of an artifact, the artifact is viewed as an ornament. When viewed this way, practice-centered approaches can be generalized to apply not only to the study of social structure and social interaction narrowly construed but also to the structure of relationships and patterns of interaction within a complex and interdependent system of interconnected actors and artifacts.

The concept of collective mind has been developed by researchers in the sensemaking approach to organizational cognition (Crowston & Kammerer, 1998; Weick & Roberts, 1993) to account for the fact that knowledgeable actors who are members of a community not only make subjective sense of the world around them but also attend to the network of knowledgeable actors and artifacts in which they are embedded. For the most part, actors do not invent responses to events *de novo* but apply or improvise on sets of conventional or routine practices. When the practices of the different actors in a community are well-aligned, achieving collective goals is facilitated. When the orientations of actors in a community are well-integrated over time, a sustainable state of collective mind can be maintained.

Organizations and organizational fields are composed of functional specialists who tied to each other and to a system of artifacts in complex and ever-evolving ways. We view these functional specialists as belonging to distinct occupations or, alternately, communities of practice (Brown & Daguid, 2000; Wenger, 1999). Figure 14.2 emphasizes that organizations and organizational fields are built by linking members of different communities of practice into sensible and effective patterns of interaction. Distinct communities of practice are characterized both by a distinct set of skills applicable to their particular functional specialty and an orientation or disposition to action and the place of the activities in the larger systems of work in which they are involved (Becker, 1982; Bourdieu, 1977; Lave, 1988).

Our framework suggests three particular areas for investigated in relation to organizational artifacts. First, as noted above, practice-centered approaches emphasize that organizational activities (in which artifacts are implicated) are encumbered with a number of occupationally important understandings and governed by a number of occupationally important

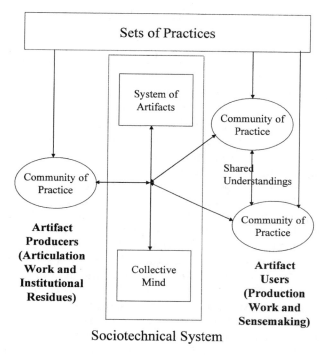

FIG. 14.2.   Practices, articulation work, and sensemaking.

conventions about the way work will, or should be, conducted (Biggart & Beamish, 2003). How these institutional residues are interpreted varies among different individuals, different occupations, and different organizations. These differing interpretations often lead to misunderstandings and disputes that need to be resolved in some fashion if collective mind and collective goals are to be achieved. Thus, practice-centered approaches focus on the details of how the form and significance of organizational artifacts help (or fail) to moderate on-going misunderstandings and disputes and facilitate interaction.

Second, unlike many economic and even sociological and behavioral approaches that analytically separate social and technical systems, practice-centered approaches focus on uncovering the often hidden interdependence of social and technical systems that drives both the construction and use of artifacts. That is, practice-oriented approaches emphasize that artifacts operate simultaneously in both the social and material world. The construction and use of artifacts can have important consequences not just for relations between people but also for the relations between artifacts and the relations between people and artifacts. For example, an automobile is an artifact. The symbolic aspect of the ownership of a particular automobile (e.g., a Corvette or a Porsche) may affect the status of the owner and affect the relations between the owner and various other people. However, the owner normally also drives the automobile. As soon as the owner enters the automobile and starts the engine, he or she is transformed into a driver with a particular relationship both to the artifact and other drivers. Finally, the production and use of a particular automobile has an effect on the production and use of other artifacts whether those artifacts such as automobiles, alternative forms of transportation such as buses or trains, or the physical infrastructure (e.g., roads, traffic lights, service stations) in which automobiles operate.

Finally, as artifacts "objectively" become institutionalized over time, these same artifacts are treated "subjectively" as conventional elements in patterns of interaction. As artifacts become institutionalized, generic forms are developed and behaviors toward those artifacts become routinized. Generic forms provide models that guide the construction and use of artifacts in particular situations. Routinized behaviors reflect the "common-sense" understandings about the meaning and use of artifacts in particular sorts of situations or lines of action. Practice-oriented approaches emphasize that as these generic forms and routine behaviors develop, specialized occupational groups of experts emerge who take responsibility for the proper use and interpretation of these model forms (Abbott, 1988; Strauss et al., 1964). Specific occupational practices and orientations develop around the proper interpretation of model artifacts and the proper way to construct concrete artifacts. In particular, though there may be only one or two direct producers of a concrete artifact, a great many more people are implicated in the construction of an artifact. Thus, as shown in Fig. 14.2, the relations between producers and users of an artifact become an important focus of research.

A Practice-Centered View of Formal Written Contracts

In this and the next section, we explore a particular sort of organizational artifact, formal written contracts, from a practice-centered point of view. Formal contracts are particularly interesting artifacts because they often have enormous symbolic and instrumental importance to both users (i.e., to the people or organizations referenced directly or indirectly in the contract) and producers (e.g., lawyers and their clients) of formal contracts. In this section, we focus attention on the conventional understandings that surround formal written contracts and the manner in which contracts come to be written and facilitate business interaction. In addition, we briefly address how formal contracts operate simultaneously in social and technical worlds and help to knit together organizations as these organizations act over time.

Though there has been some research on contracts and contracting, from a practice-centered perspective, the vast majority of this research has not fully explored the practice-centered, or performative, aspects of formal written contracts. Organizational economics research has assumed that a contract is an instrumentally efficient governance structure that emerges naturally through the bargaining of rational actors in the course of an economic transaction (Barzel, 1989; Masten, 1996; Polinsky, 1989; Williamson, 1985). The written contract is essentially treated as a prop that reflects the formally rational aspects of business interactions. Social structural/institutional and behavioral/cognitive researchers (Edelman, 1992; Macauley, 1963; MacNeil, 1981, 1985; Rousseau, 1995; Stinchcombe, 1990, chap. 6; Suchman, 2003) draw a more complex picture of the institutional and cognitive structures in which formal contracts and contracting processes are embedded. Yet, like organizational economists, these researchers continue to view formal written contracts as props in the performance of substantively rational (i.e., goal-oriented) interaction. The details of the manner in which users make sense of contracts and how producers make contracts sensible and the role of institutions in these sensemaking and sensegiving processes (Cappetta & Gioia, chap. 11, this volume) is neglected.

In contrast, a practice-centered perspective focuses on a written contract as an organizational artifact that is produced through some kind of institutionalized contracting process, and flexibly used to both orient and bind members of different occupations together by establishing and maintaining a state of collective mind in the context of a particular deal. To the extent that this state of collective mind can be maintained over time, a line of action (Blumer, 1969b; Strauss, 1993) can be carried through to completion. How written contracts are negotiated, drafted, and performed (i.e., the contracting process) is heavily influenced by both the customary practices and orientations of the people involved in these activities. In particular, to be "performable," a written contract must have a form and significance that makes it sensible both in the local context to which it applies and in the larger fields of activity in which it is contained.

In the U.S. legal system,[1] a valid contract exists between two or more parties when the parties reach a "meeting of the minds" on the particulars

---

[1]It is important that our discussion is restricted to the U.S. legal system. Legal systems in other nations have somewhat different institutional mechanisms for dealing with similar social situations. Reconciling differences between different legal systems is an important element of international law. Similarly, though all U.S. states have adopted some major standardized statutory frameworks such as the Uniform Commercial Code that help businesses regularize their contracting practices in interstate commerce, in some areas, important differences remain in the commercial codes of different states. In any complex contracting situation, the relationship between state, U.S. and international law is important. But for the sake of simplicity, we write as if only U.S. statutes are applicable.

along with the terms and conditions of an exchange between the two parties. This "meeting of the minds" provides a foundation on which a state of collective mind can be established and collective action performed. A "meeting of the minds" is deemed to be achieved when an offer has been made and the offer has been accepted. An offer is made when one party to a contract proposes to give something up (that they have a legal right to) in return for some other thing (that the other party has legal control over) subject to particular terms and conditions. An acceptance is made when the other party agrees to this proposal. In addition, to be legally binding and enforceable, the meeting of the minds must be deemed legitimate. This generally requires that both parties to a contract must be considered competent (i.e., minors and mentally impaired people cannot enter into contracts) and that the contract was not entered into due to fraud (on the part of one or both parties) or under coercion or duress (Schaber & Rohwer, 1990).

It is important to note that a formal written contract is not necessary for the law to recognize that a binding contract has been entered into. That is, artifacts other than formal written contracts may be produced and used in exchange processes. In fact, in "simple" contracting situations, a formal written contract would be unconventional and would be considered unnecessary. For example, written contracts are never composed in the context of a person buying an item at a supermarket. In this situation, the supermarket offers to give a consumer an item in return for money that the consumer hands over to a human or automated cashier. The cashier provides (or offers to provide) a written receipt (that may or may not be kept) as a record that an exchange has taken place. Customarily, these actions are sufficient to fulfill the contract. The parties to the transaction consider that mutual commitments have been satisfied and records of the transaction are filed. However, it is possible that a problem will develop after the exchange at the cash register has taken place (e.g., the grocer discovers that the money is counterfeit or the consumer discovers that the grocery item is spoiled). In this case, one or both parties may be judged to have not adequately performed their part of the agreement and the exchange may be reversed in some fashion.

In this simple case, the psychological understandings of both the consumer and grocer of the nature of the contracted exchange process are subsumed in routine buying and selling practices and orientations. A receipt is typically a sufficient artifact for handling any disputes that might arise and more complex artifacts such as written contracts serve no useful function. Even in a more complex transaction such as an agreement between a contractor and a homeowner for home improvements, a formal written contract is often not drafted or used. In these situations, there are more elements involved in the exchange and the relationships among the elements are more complex. Thus, the contracted agreement is open to a wider range of interpretations that often conflict with one another. Most of the negotiating takes place in the bidding process. The bidding process generally begins with a homeowner requesting bids from contractors. The homeowner and contractor discuss the details of the project and the contractor submits a written bid (another sort of artifact) to the homeowner. When the homeowner accepts a particular bid, a contract is entered into. Over time, the homeowner and contractor may continue to negotiate over particular aspects of their contracted relationship. If for some reason the homeowner and/or the contractor feel that the other has breached (i.e., not performed) the promises contained in the contract, the injured party may take the dispute to court and ask the court to resolve the dispute. The court will rely on artifacts (e.g., the written bid) and sworn oral testimony (based on memory) to determine the facts of the case and make a decision. In this case, the court supplies the final (and binding) interpretation.

In the most complex transactions such as an interorganizational exchange or an interorganizational collaboration, a formal written contract is conventional and sometimes required. A formal written contract provides a physical record that two or more parties have reached a meeting of minds with respect to some sort of exchange. The written contract provides evidence of an offer and acceptance (authorized signatures that have been dated), lays out the specifics of the exchange, and the terms and conditions that govern the exchange. More generally, a formal written contract memorializes the cognitive understandings of the parties to a bargained exchange. Presumably, when the contract is signed, it is sensible both in a specific business context (i.e., a specific business deal) and in the larger legal system that provides institutional assurances that the mutual promises embodied in a contract will be fulfilled (Rousseau, 2001). A written contract, therefore, is a "talking artifact" (Levy, 2001) that bears witness that a binding agreement has been reached. A written contract specifies the essential elements of the agreement, and provides general direction as to how the parties to a contract should orient their mutual interaction so as to achieve a common purpose. The written contract can be referred to as the parties perform or attempt to renegotiate the contractual relationship (Clegg, 1975). The formal written contract is also an important piece of evidence if the contractual relationship breaks down and the parties enter into some process of dispute resolution (e.g., suing each other in court).

The discussion above emphasizes the instrumental aspects of contracts—the role of contracts in organizing and governing economic action within legally legitimate boundaries. Yet as Vilnai-Yavetz and Rafaeli (chap. 1, this volume) argue, artifacts should be analyzed along three dimensions: instrumental, symbolic, and aesthetic. Like wedding rings, contracts also symbolize that the parties have entered into an important binding relationship. The symbolic import of that relationship can have a great effect on the behavior of the parties to the deal and on whether external observers of the deal consider the deal legitimate or illegitimate. In addition, the quality of formal written contracts is evaluated according to two important (and potentially competing) aesthetics.[2] From a business perspective, contracts are evaluated in line with a "rational aesthetic." Neoclassical economics with its concepts of individual utility maximization and Pareto optimal allocation of resources is built around a highly stylized version of this rational aesthetic. Economic actors who do not follow this aesthetic are considered irrational (Becker, 1976). From a legal/moral perspective, contracts are evaluated both in terms of their "efficiency" (i.e., how clear, minimal, and robust are the contractual terms) and their justice (i.e., do the terms correspond to accepted standards of appropriate business practice). These different aesthetics are reflected in both the institutional order and the cognitive structures of the parties to contract. Ideally, judgments made according to business and legal/moral standards reinforce each other. In practice, they often conflict.

Technology Transfer Managers and the Making of Technology Transfer Contracts[3]

In this section, we draw on empirical examples drawn from a study of professional university technology transfer managers to illustrate the role that one particular group of producers plays in the construction of formal contracts. We draw particular attention to the institutional residues embedded in all formal written contracts and the articulation work done by functional specialists like technology transfer managers through which concrete documents are imbued with these institutional residues in the context of a specific business deal. We focus particular attention on two topics, boilerplate contracts and technology transfer "legalese." Boilerplate contracts provide generic forms of contracts that can be applied effectively and sensibly in particular business deals. Boilerplate contracts are a resource that technology transfer managers draw on in doing their work and are a major mechanism through which institutional residues are

---

[2]We use the broad meaning of aesthetic to refer to formal and/or institutionalized evaluative standards generally rather than simply evaluative standards of beauty. These evaluative standards are, by definition, shared among a group of people and are thus not simply a matter of subjective taste.

[3]The material in this section is drawn from a three-year participant-observer field study conducted by one of the authors (Kaghan) at a technology transfer office at a major U.S. research university as part of his dissertation research (Kaghan, 1998). Published studies based on this material are Kaghan and Barnett (1997), Kaghan (2000), and Vogel and Kaghan (2001).

embedded in concrete contracts. Technology transfer "legalese" is a particular type of discursive practice (Boden, 1994; Jablin et al., 1987) that allows technology transfer managers to communicate sensibly both among themselves and to make formal contracts and the contracting process more sensible to their clients.

In their own words, university technology transfer managers are responsible for "arranging deals." What they mean by a "deal" is the network of relationships through which a particular line of action is accomplished along with a set of shared understandings that allow people and artifacts to be objectively coordinated and subjectively oriented toward their common goals. More specifically, in arranging technology transfer deals, university technology transfer managers work to assess the potential opportunities in and potential costs of developing the academic raw material described in invention disclosures.[4] Around the invention disclosures selected, technology transfer managers work to set up well-defined relationships between the university and an industrial firm and any third parties (such as government funding agencies) with an interest in the work and its outcomes. To the extent possible, technology transfer managers also work to create or reinforce the proper sort of work environment (both social and technical) in which the work can be jointly performed by university and industry employees. In doing this work, technology transfer managers help to preserve, to erect, or to lower buffers between the university and the industrial firm and to translate the invention from an academic format fit for journal publications into a commercial format suitable for patents and commercial development. In short, technology transfer managers work to formally articulate and clarify the sense of a deal so that margins of interpretation are well-defined and the parties whose work will be affected by the deal are oriented in a way that will encourage joint performance with a minimal amount of friction.

The central artifact produced by all this work is a technology transfer contract that has been signed by authorized representatives of the university and the industrial firm. Most typically, technology transfer contracts are documents through which industrial firms obtain a license to use or develop a university-generated invention for commercial purposes. In a business sense, a technology transfer contract is meant to facilitate the translation (Latour, 1987) of a set of skills, associated technological artifacts, and relevant protocols from a non-profit basic research environment to a for-profit applied research environment. In a legal sense, a technology

---

[4]Generally, faculty members, students, and staff are required to disclose inventions that they believe to have commercial potential that were developed using outside funds or within the scope of their university responsibilities. To disclose an invention, the members of a research and development team were required to fill out a standard disclosure form.

transfer contract represents an exchange of permission to make use of an invention in which a university possesses some form of intellectual property rights (i.e., patent, copyright, or trademark) in return for some form of payment. In a moral sense, a technology transfer contract represents the fulfillment of a social pledge that the fruits of basic research will be effectively transplanted into practical applications (Etzkowitz et al., 2000; Geiger, 1986). The goal of the university is to earn some form of monetary return on basic research activity and to use those funds to promote the health of the university community. The goal of industrial firms is to better absorb newly developed knowledge and technologies (Cohen & Levinthal, 1990). Written technology transfer contracts provide evidence that a meeting of the minds between a university and an industrial firm has been reached and provides some ground rules for progressively "disentangling" university-generated technologies from "unnecessary" university connections and "entangling" the technology in more commercially oriented arenas.

As discussed in the preceding section, when a deal involves two or more large complex organizations, both the formal and informal understandings that underpin deal performance are correspondingly complex. The object of the deal—normally a complex product or service—affects many parts of the organizations in a variety of ways that are more or less sensible to the people actually involved in performing the deal. The organizational "meeting of the minds" memorialized in the contract should, at least in principle, encompass and be sensible to all of these actors. However, in practice, additional work is typically required to insure that the participants involved in performing the contract have a "sufficient" level of shared understandings to sustain a particular line of action over an extended period of time. Participants need a clear idea of what is expected of them and of what they can reasonably expect of others. These shared understandings are the means through which collective mind comes into being and can endure over time. Without this state of collective mind, there can be no "reasonable" expectation that a deal can actually be enacted.[5]

Focusing on the work that technology transfer managers do to transform the raw data provided in an invention disclosure into a signed contract is important. This focus serves to emphasize the fact that, in the majority of cases, the elements of a deal fail to "coalesce" in the proper way. There are innumerable possible contingencies that may be faced in process of arranging deals. To bring the elements of a deal together and then

---

[5]Furthermore, courts adjudicating contract disputes rely on evidence that these "shared understandings" have been developed in the course of contract construction. Legally "binding commitments" must be both based on these "shared understandings" and be deemed to fall within the boundaries set by legal statutes and precedents.

bind the elements of a deal together in a contract, the contingencies that arise must be overcome or worked around. Often, important transformations in invention, inventor, university, industrial firm, or government agencies have to be brought about before a contract can be signed and a deal enacted. In addition, technology transfer managers operate in a number of highly institutionalized contexts that define the repertoire of actions that they can take to plan for or respond to the contingencies they encounter. The university that they work for has a set of procedures and practices that have developed over time and which reflect in some fashion shared understandings of appropriate procedures and practices within the population of research universities. Similarly, the industrial firms that they deal with have their own particular set of procedures and practices which reflect both the way that the firm does things and the general standards of practice of the industry that the firm belongs to. Perhaps most importantly for technology transfer managers, the artifacts that they are responsible for producing, formal written contracts, reflect the institutional context in which they are constructed. That is, formal written contracts reflect both the ways a university has learned to deal with industrial firms and the broader range of practices and procedures that have been institutionalized in the business and legal environments in which university–industry technology transfer takes place.

The vast majority of a technology transfer manager's time is spent trying to overcome barriers that arise and to transform a set of disparate elements into a "doable" deal that reflects both the contingencies found in a particular situation and the institutionalized mechanisms for handling "deal-arranging" situations. In particular, a "doable" deal requires an "enactable" contract. The concepts of institutional residue, articulation (Zollo & Winter, 2002), and articulation work (Fujimura, 1987; Strauss, 1988) are helpful for thinking about these deal-making processes. In practice, technology transfer managers take a disparate set of elements and articulate (i.e., specify, construct, and join together) a governance structure in which these elements can productively interact. They may also monitor the performance and possibly modify the structure based on observed outcomes. In doing this work, technology transfer managers formalize (i.e., reduce the margins of interpretation) of "informal agreements" associated with a deal. The formal written contract is the centerpiece of this articulation work.

In the process of doing this articulation work, technology transfer managers draw on institutionalized practices and artifactual standards (e.g., model contracts) so that the formal contracts that they write fit within the larger institutional environment within which technology transfer deals are negotiated (Strauss, 1978). The traces of these institutionalized practices that can be found in organizational artifacts such as formal written contracts are what we term institutional residues. One tool that is regularly used by technology transfer managers as a mechanism for imbuing formal contracts with institutionalized residues is a boilerplate (i.e., generic) contract. Boilerplate contracts provide an easily modified template that can serve as a basis for drafting a final signable contract. The institutional residues that are evident in a final contract can be traced back to the form and contents of the boilerplate contract. A boilerplate contract reflects the model of the university's preferred mode of dealing with industry organized and articulated in a way that is sufficiently sensible that they can be readily applied to a particular deal. At its worst, boilerplate is sensible only to legal professionals inside organizations and in the court system. At its best, boilerplate is relatively easy for the wider group of professionals involved in the deal to understand.

In practice, different managers employ resources like boilerplate contracts in different ways and the same manager may use these resources differently on different occasions. Some managers view legal templates as "formulaic" documents that can be easily modified or adapted to fit specific cases. Other managers view the templates in a less formulaic way and prefer to break down and rearticulate boilerplate contracts in terms of particular clauses that applied to particular sorts of contractual issues. These clauses—and even terms within clauses—might need to be carefully negotiated and carefully drafted. The final contract is thus an assemblage of well-constructed and well-fitting clauses that serve as a script for a deal. Within technology transfer offices, a number of different boilerplate contracts might be developed to fit particular situations that arose in deals with particular industries.[6]

Because of the highly technical nature of formal written contracts, technology transfer managers made use of a professional jargon which we term "technology transfer legalese."[7] As they learn their trade, technology transfer managers must become proficient in both "creole" and "pidgin" versions of technology transfer legalese. The concepts of pidgin and creole languages were initially developed in linguistic anthropology (Galison,

---

[6]Examples of genres of legal boilerplate are material transfer agreements (MTAs) covering the transfer of biological materials, patent licenses which granted an industrial firm to make use of a patented product or process in a commercial product, and software licenses which covered the allowable uses of copyrighted material.

[7]What is termed "technology transfer legalese" is best thought of as a particular dialect of a broader class of legal and bureaucratic languages. Charrow (1982) discusses these sorts of exceptional languages and makes reference to "legalese" as a particular trial oriented language. Kaghan's original use of the word "legalese" differed from hers only in noting that "legalese" comes in a wide variety of dialects that are used to connect everyday speech and common-sense concepts of law and justice with formal legal language and more "rationalized" systems of law and justice.

1997). They are conceptualized as primary types of "contact" languages that develop when two distinct social groups come into increasing contact with each other. Anthropologists (e.g., Bickerton, 1982; Crystal, 1994; Foley, 1988) have studied pidgins and creoles primarily in terms of language change in the face of colonization where colonizers and colonized have an interest in communicating about some restricted set of activities. However, closer to the context of our paper on technology transfer contracts, Galison (1997) extended the concept of pidgin and creole to analyze communication between members of different specialized occupations who need to collaborate on some kind of joint project.

In discussing boilerplate contracts and related technology transfer matters with their colleagues and others (e.g., legal counsel) who worked very closely with technology transfer managers in the work of managing intellectual property rights and drafting complex contracts, technology transfer managers used a creole version of "technology transfer legalese." This creole is a distinctive occupational language through which professionals can discuss with their professional colleagues how to apply institutional resources in the context of specific deals. Though sometimes dismissed as "meaningless" or "opaque" jargon" by "outsiders" (e.g., faculty inventors, university administrators, industry executives), this terminology has quite precise (and highly institutionalized) meaning for technology transfer managers. The terminology is important not only as single terms but also in the context of a wider system of terms and concepts dealing with the formal legal aspects of technology transfer work (Bowker & Star, 1999). To technology transfer insiders this creole serves as a mechanism for ready communication with other insiders about how to go about responding to contingencies and embedding institutional residues within formal written contracts.

However, in addition to mastering this technology transfer creole, technology transfer managers have to be masters of a number of different pidgin versions of technology transfer legalese to communicate with those significant outsiders who have little understanding of the "jargon" of the more developed creole version of technology transfer legalese. Where technology transfer professionals do use "technology transfer legalese" as an occupational "native tongue," their clients and other outsiders insufficiently schooled and/or experienced in the institutions of deal arranging cannot speak this creole fluently. However, these clients are often—after some work—able to recognize important terms and able to react in suitable ways to requests from technology transfer managers. As importantly, technology transfer managers recognize that their clients bring stereotyped understandings of the operation of the legal system to technology transfer activities. These stereotypical understandings are usually tied to representations common in their particular domain of activity—higher education, government, or private business or to general, everyday notions of justice. For a deal to be enacted, technology transfer managers may have to work to reduce any disjunction between the understandings embedded in these stereotypes and the institutional residues embedded in the formal contract in which an agreement on a deal is memorialized.

The relative importance of pidgin versions of technology transfer legalese is reflected in the hiring practices at university technology transfer offices. For instance, contrary to expectations, the employment of lawyers in technology transfer manager positions is often discouraged.[8] Rather than hiring lawyers, technology transfer offices often hire people who have strong backgrounds in particular technologies, a comfortable familiarity with the academic environment, the commercial environment or both, and good "management" skills. Though technology transfer managers must develop a solid grounding in the creole version of technology transfer legalese so that they can consult effectively with attorneys on highly technical legal issues, a formal legal education is not a mandatory requirement. In contrast to lawyers who were often more concerned with managing potential disputes, technology transfer managers were more concerned with using contracts to develop comfort or trust among transacting parties by insuring that the structural foundations of a deal were well articulated. To the extent that a "well-articulated deal" served to reduce the perception of "opportunism" (by increasing the experience of "trust"), this on-going work might be said to reduce "transaction costs" over the course of a deal (Williamson, 1985).

CONCLUSION

In rational models of bureaucratic organizations, a state of collective mind is assumed to be achieved through a formalization of ties and relationships on a functional basis, a standardization of procedures, and a modularization of specialized tasks (Callon, 1998; Simon, 1969; Stinchcombe, 1990). Professional managers using the tools of professional management were seen to be the "higher-order" functionaries through which a state of collective mind can be achieved and sustained. Theorists relying on cogni-

---

[8]However, the office studied did consult regularly with the university Attorney General's on specific legal issues. After the researcher left the field site, a full time legal counsel was hired. Nevertheless, the utility of formal legal training is a topic that is actively debated. The alleged disadvantages of formal legal training include an adversarial bias promoted by formal legal training and a lack of specific business related knowledge and negotiating skills. Another disadvantage of legal training was the relative expense of hiring a person with legal training and the other requisite qualifications versus that of hiring a person with no legal training but the ability to acquire sufficient skill in the use of "technology transfer legalese."

tive and institutional approaches have argued that these rational models—though parsimonious—neglect important aspects of human behavior and the institutionalized processes through which a sustainable state of collective mind is achieved.

In our paper, we have expanded on both these streams of research by focusing on how artifacts are constructed and used in processes of collective action and how artifacts are implicated in the development and maintenance of a state of collective mind. We have argued that rational models of organization and organizing by focusing exclusively on the monetary benefits and costs of artifacts neglect important aspects—instrumental, symbolic, and aesthetic—of artifacts. We focused particular attention on the problem of developing a state of collective mind that could be sustained over the entire course of large-scale collective action. We noted that in situations involving large-scale and sustained collective action bundles of tasks are typically distributed across a variety of specialized occupations whose members possess knowledge about some institutionalized set of occupational practices and orientations. We presented a general model of how organizational artifacts can be incorporated into the dynamics of an institutionalized field of activity.

More particularly, we have further argued that a deep understanding of the manner in which artifacts come to be connected to collective mind often requires a close examination of the "communities of practice" who are routinely involved with the artifact. To illustrate this argument, we developed a practice-centered view of contracting and formal written contracts and analyzed the work of a particular community of practice, technology transfer managers, who are intimately involved with producing formal written technology transfer contracts. In discussing the work of technology transfer managers we have remained cognizant that other communities of practice like faculty inventors and university administrators are involved with using or interpreting artifacts like technology transfer contracts. For collective action to have some effect, some level of "collective mind" among all the members of different communities of practice involved in the joint action must be reached so that the different actors "act together" in some more or less coordinated way (Dougherty, 1992). The skill of technology transfer managers lies in the manner in which they articulate institutional forms into concrete contracts so that a contract both provides a record of a legitimate "meeting of the minds" and promotes a sustainable state of collective mind in relation to a particular deal.

V

FUTURE RESEARCH DIRECTIONS

What have we learned? Where do we go from here?

15

Artifacts and Organizations: Understanding Our "Object-ive" Reality

Michael G. Pratt
Anat Rafaeli

> *A man's Self is the sum total of all he CAN call his, not only his body and his psychic powers, but his clothes and his house, his wife and children, his ancestors and friends, his reputation and works, his lands and yacht.*
> —William James (1890, p. 177)

It should be clear at this point that organizational life is infused with artifacts and that people understand themselves, their organizations, and their institutions through artifacts. However, their ubiquity leads to two paths in the treatment of artifacts. First, artifacts have been assigned to the realm "ordinary"—and by implication, the realm of the uninteresting or superficial. Second, there have been many narrow slices of the artifact phenomenon—viewing them through various lenses that mask their full complexity and power. But artifacts are neither superficial nor impotent. As Carlile (chap. 6, this volume) reminds us, "The material world, in one shape or form, always mediates human activity." So, as we hope this book has taught, there is lot to be said and a lot to yet be done toward a full understanding of artifacts.

What can we learn about artifacts from this volume? We learn that only through understanding the many facets of artifacts can we truly appreciate their power and significance in the multiple slices of organizational life in which they inhere. Building on this lesson, there are multiple avenues for research that we hope future scholars will travel in the study of artifacts.

WHAT ARE ARTIFACTS?

A key challenge to working with a concept is delineating its conceptual boundaries. In his foundational book on artifacts Gagliardi (1990, p. 3) identified artifacts as intentionally made *products* that are perceived by the senses. Similarly, each of the authors in this volume reminds us that artifacts are constructed. They are purposefully "made" by sentient beings. As such artifacts may be seen as anything that is "not natural"—a conceptualization that reminds us that in discussing artifacts we are discussing a very large category of "things"! However, the authors in this book add some texture to this broad description by separating two types of constructions of artifacts: *physical* and *social*.

This general distinction, however, is not unique to this volume. Fiell and Fiell (1997), for example, illustrate the physical and social divide in their photographs of 1,000 different chairs—some of which challenge the mere idea of what most of us would call "a chair." Their work, along with the classic work of Lakoff and Johnson (1980), challenges us to accept that the labels given to artifacts (e.g., chairs) are socially constructed and can be separate from the wood, leather, or other materials composing the artifact. Such a distinction may even have biological basis. Kahneman (2003), for example, argues that physical characteristics, such as size and loudness, are "natural assessments" and are quickly and automatically registered by human beings. Other properties of stimuli require more effortful processing, and may require language to understand. Characteristics of social stimuli range along a continuum from those that are automatically perceived to those that require more effortful processing. Using this distinction, the properties underlying artifacts' physical construction characteristics would tend to evoke more natural assessments than their social construction characteristics.

Artifacts as Physical Constructions

At their most basic, artifacts are *physically constructed*. Authors in this volume consider artifacts that are "built" (Kaghan & Lounsbury; Schultz, Hatch, & Ciccolella; Yanow) and arranged (Anand; Carlile; Elsbach; Fiol & O'Connor). Artifacts are noted as not only resulting from physical behaviors, but also as initiating new actions such as buying, selling, or talking (Cappetta & Gioia; Carlile; Harquail; Strati; Yanow).

Artifacts as physical constructions make salient the materials used in artifact construction: words, actions, or more tangible materials. By extension, we can therefore consider artifacts according to how *sturdy* or *durable* they are (i.e., their "shelf life" or "half life"). Artifacts can be ephemeral— fleeting unless they are repeated often or captured in some other artifactual medium (e.g., filming, writing, sculpting) as an artifact-simula-crum (Strati). The plays of William Shakespeare, for example, endure because they are constantly reproduced and staged. Other artifacts—by the nature of their materials—may endure for hundreds or thousands of years. The ruins of Ephesus, the pyramids in Egypt and South America, and the temples of Jerusalem make salient the powerful and lasting impact that "hardy" societal artifacts can have throughout time. Of course most artifacts, like the clothes we all wear, fall somewhere in between these two extremes (Rafaeli & Pratt, 1993).

Artifacts can also be considered according to how many of the senses they capture—that is, their *sensuality*. Some artifacts, such as stories or paintings, may engage one or two senses. Others, such as visual performances and a fine meal at a corporate gathering, may engage many others. Figure 15.1 depicts these aspects of artifacts as physical constructions.

The types of artifacts discussed in this book help illustrate the dimensions depicted in Fig. 15.1. A spoken name (e.g., "Fred's Bank" as analyzed by Glynn and Marquis) is highly ephemeral. If not repeated or written down, it is likely to be forgotten. It also engages a single sense (at least primarily)—the sense of hearing. The performance described by Strati is similarly ephemeral but engages multiple senses—one can see and hear (and possibly smell) the performance; some elements—like the iron cage—can be touched. Many senses may also come into play with the black medical bags described by Fiol and O'Connor: the sound of the zipper; the touch, feel, and smell of the leather. Left to itself, a leather bag is likely to last longer than a spoken word or a dramatic gesture, making this a less ephemeral artifact. Finally, the cartoons described by Anand depict an artifact that is more fragile than a black bag, but more hardy than a spoken word. And unlike a black bag, cartoons engage our sight more than our other senses.

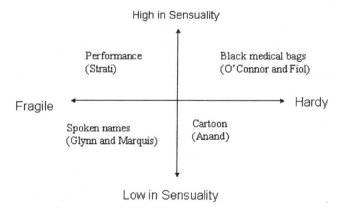

FIG. 15.1. Artifacts as physical constructions.

These dimensions illustrate how artifacts may be constructed and perceived, but not how they are interpreted. They relate to the medium (what artifacts are made of), but not necessarily the message (what they communicate). However, a recognition of artifacts as physical constructs is critical to the appreciation that some artifacts are fragile (e.g., a performance) and that artifacts may influence organizations only to the degree that they become "transposed" onto other materials. Such transposition suggests that organizational researchers might want to explore in greater detail how artifact-simulacrum are created, and the influence of such creations. Tracing the history of "hardy" symbols may help unravel artifacts that are simulacrum for more fragile ones.

A better understanding of the physical construction of artifacts may benefit from knowledge possessed by other disciplines, such as engineering. We know that even simple materials (e.g., denim) can hold a multitude of meanings (J. Fiske, 1989). However, if different materials are—by their very nature—better for some construction projects than others, might also certain artifactual materials be better to construct some meanings than others? For example, should some artifacts be made in materials that are pliable whereas others "set in stone"? The idea holds implications for both research and practice if, as Schultz et al. (chap. 8, this volume) suggest, the organizational pattern of shifting from physical objects to ideas parallels a move from product to corporate branding. To fully understand these types of issues, however, artifacts need to be examined as possessing a second type of construction: social construction.

Artifacts as Social Constructions

Artifacts—like many features of social life—have a life beyond their physicality: They are also socially constructed (Berger & Luckmann, 1966). At least three aspects of artifacts as social constructs surface in the chapters of this book. First, individuals and social groups may intend to convey meanings through artifacts, but the meanings perceived by various audiences may not be the meanings intended. As Gagliardi (1990) noted, artifacts can be imbued with meaning, but they exist independently of those who make and wield them. Thus, we can make plastic blocks (Schultz et al.), "specs" (Carlile), and contracts (Kaghan & Lounsbury); create performances (Strati), ride buses (Vilnai-Yavetz & Rafaeli), and display cartoons (Anand), names (Glynn & Marquis), logos, business cards (Baruch), and office decor (Cappella & Gioia, Elsbach). We—as individuals and social groups—may assume that our artifactual displays communicate particular messages (e.g., brands, identity, and legitimacy); however, as noted by several authors here, different or additional messages from those intended may be gleaned by others. The social construction of artifacts suggests an important separation between the intended and the perceived: sensegiving as distinct from sensemaking (Gioia & Chittipeddi, 1991; Pratt, 2000).

Second, the social construction of artifacts reminds us that intentions and interpretations may vary along at least three dimensions: instrumental, aesthetic, and symbolic (Vilnai-Yavetz & Rafaeli). Several of the chapters here considered at least two of these dimensions. In addition to their symbolic functions, some (e.g., Baruch; Elsbach; Schultz, Hatch, & Ciccolella; Strati; Yanow) focused heavily on the aesthetic judgments of perceivers in explaining the potency of certain artifacts. Others, such as Cappetta and Gioia, talked about the interrelationship among the three dimensions: Fashion artifacts are often created to be high on aesthetics and symbolism while minimizing attention to instrumentality. Still others talked about how separated sensegiving is from sensemaking along these dimensions. For example, Israeli buses can be painted green for symbolic reasons and Italian fashion items crafted for aesthetic ones, but this does not mean that they cannot be accepted or rejected along different lines (e.g., instrumental).

A third aspect of artifacts as social constructions is the types of conversations they evoke. As was apparent in the second part of our book, artifacts are potent conveyors of information. Artifacts can be used in creating (e.g., Fiol & O'Connor), marking (e.g., Elsbach), and traversing (e.g., Carlile) social categories and boundaries, but also in negotiating organizational roles (Harquail), responsibilities (Kaghan & Lounsbury), and prestige (Baruch). Artifacts and the conversations they inspire, all these authors suggest, facilitate the important process of communicating identity and legitimacy of individuals and collectivities—in addition to expressing culture (Schein, 1990; Trice & Beyer, 1993).

The use of artifacts in creating social markers has a long practical and theoretical tradition (Berger, Webster, Ridgeway, & Rosenholtz, 1986). Organizations throughout history have adopted particular symbols (e.g., blue or red crosses for medical organizations) to convey legitimacy (Rafaeli & Pratt, 1993). Similarly, organizations have long built and occupied buildings as a way of saying to the world: Here we are; we exist as a physical and social entity (Pratt & Rafaeli, 2001; Yanow, 1995). In the age of the virtual reality one cannot but wonder about the role or importance of hardy, sensual artifacts. For example, how critical is it for organizations to have a building that members can enter, see the corporate dress of coworkers, and hear the chatter of colleagues? What other artifacts may substitute for the important functions that these traditional artifacts have played in convincing constituents about a "real" corporate entity?

As the quote that opens this chapter suggests, an individual's personal possessions have long been seen as a way of creating and "extending" the self-concept (Belk, 1988; Csikszentimihalyi & Rochberg-Halton, 1981; Mc-Carthy, 1984; Prelinger, 1959). Anand further shows how individuals can use others' "identity artifacts" and tailor them to fit their own needs through the autoproduction of culture. However, do individuals use artifacts to convey more than identity? Fiol and O'Connor, as well as Glynn and Marquis, imply that individuals can use artifacts in an attempt to gain legitimacy. There are likely other uses of artifacts as well. In a global and diverse workforce, individuals may increasingly come up with creative conversations using artifacts as anchors (Pratt & Rafaeli, 2001).

An integration of the multiple chapters and analyses of this book thus suggests three aspects of artifacts as social constructs: *perspective* (sensemaker or sensegiver), *dimension* (instrumental, aesthetic, symbolic), and *conversation* (e.g., identity and legitimacy)—as depicted in Fig. 15.2. We use a triangle to try to show the aspects as interrelated but also uniquely contributing to the understanding of artifacts as social constructs, and of the social phenomena they represent. Important to note, the triangular model and the aspects it comprises hold within and across multiple levels of analysis—individual, organizational, institutional, and professional.

The chapters in this volume illustrate how aspects of artifacts as social constructions play out in organizations. The Figure, in turn, helps convey how the different pieces that each chapter presents weave together the organizational tapestry of artifact and its interpretation. Corporate branding (Schultz et al.) may be seen as the intended identity message of the sensegiver; but when viewed from the perspective of the sensemaker may be quite different—and may result in changes in how sensemakers view themselves, especially when they are the carriers of the message (Harquail). Al-

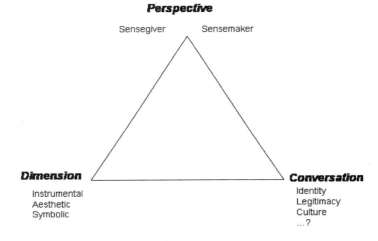

FIG. 15.2.   Artifacts as social constructions.

ternatively, humorous messages may be just one piece of the cultural milieu transformed via artifacts through the autoproduction of culture to create a unique identity (Anand); but here as well, others' interpretations of an office milieu may well vary from the intentions of the office bearer (Elsbach) due to symbolic, instrumental, or aesthetic considerations (Strati; Vilnai-Yavetz & Rafaeli). Artifacts can be used by sensegivers (e.g., doctors—see Fiol & O'Connor) to communicate the identity of individuals and of a profession, but sensetakers may respond by endowing either legitimacy or illegitimacy. And a name presented by a corporation (sensegiver) as a communicator of identity and legitimacy via symbolism may nonetheless be interpreted by the sensetaker—a stakeholder—aesthetically (Glynn & Marquis; Vilnai-Yavetz & Rafaeli).

In sum, we consider artifacts to be both physical and social constructs that integrate multiple perspectives, multiple conversations, and multiple dimensions. When examining artifacts, we suggest that researchers should be mindful of (a) the hardiness of the materials composing the artifact; (b) how many senses the artifact engages (sight, hearing, taste, touch, and smell); (c) the perspective on the artifact (sensegiver, sensemaker); (d) the dimension or dimensions of the artifact—instrumental, aesthetic, or symbolic; and (e) the conversations with or through the artifact—conversations about identity, about legitimacy, about culture, or about other notions.

WHERE DO WE GO FROM HERE?

Keeping in mind the physical and social aspects of artifacts should illuminate several new directions for future research on their role in organizations. We briefly offer a few suggestions here, hoping that these inspire many others:

1. *A broader range of artifacts can be examined.* Most research on artifacts anchors on the "hardy" end of the continuum, and on artifacts that engage a limited set of senses, leaving out many other types of artifacts. Strati, for example, suggests performance as artifacts, whereas Cappetta and Gioia suggest rites and ceremonials as artifacts. Common to both is their ephemeral nature and the engagement of multiple senses. Their sensuality suggests that they will be noticed, but their transient nature leaves doubt about what impact they might have on organizational life. How might such ephemeral artifacts be perceived and interpreted (Vilnai-Yavetz & Rafaeli)? How do their meanings change as members try to capture them in their own deep cognitive structures (Cunliffe & Shotter)? How does viewing a performance or a leader's visionary speech differ from a video-taped performance and a transcribed speech (Schultz et al.)?

The questions also raise the possibility of studying "linked" artifacts—artifacts that evolve from one another or are meant to replicate each other. For example, organizational routines may involve both written procedures and multiple "performances" (Feldman & Pentland, 2003; Feldman & Rafaeli, 2002; Pentland & Reuter, 1994). How do these multiple representations coevolve? And what happens to routines that are repeated over time? When using a photocopying machine, copying a previously copied image leads to a lower quality (degraded) but very similar copy. However, routines repeated over time tend to vary and adapt (Feldman & Rafaeli, 2002). What accounts for artifact degradation versus evolution? Do some artifacts "copy" better than others (e.g., hardier vs. more ephemeral)? What happens when routines get written down; how does the introduction of a new medium—a tangible artifact—that captures the routine, alter behavioral performance?

2. *Artifacts and dialogues.* We have suggested elsewhere (Pratt & Rafaeli, 2001) that physical symbols should be viewed as a language so that patterns of artifacts work together to convey a message. Building off this insight we suggest that perhaps a view of artifacts as monologues is too limited. Rather, sensemakers and sensegivers may both act and react to an artifact or set of artifacts in a process of double interact (Weick, 1969/1979). In this volume, Carlile shows how boundary objects serve the function of creating communities. Cunliffe and Shotter, as well as Kaghan and Lounsbury, talk about conversations and "talking artifacts" as processes that bring people together. The chapters on identity and branding (Schultz, Hatch, & Ciccolella; Cappetta & Gioia; Harquail) similarly connect organizational attempts to use artifacts to convey identity to the reaction of both members and nonmembers to such attempts.

Viewing artifacts as dialogues raises some new and interesting issues. For example, to what degree are the dialogues synchronous versus asynchronous? Because artifacts can have a life beyond their originators (Gagliardi, 1990), communication between sensegiver and sensemaker need not take place at the same time. Universities and corporations, for example, can display logos and names (Baruch; Glynn & Marquis), but reactions to the logos and names may not occur until years after the artifacts were originally crafted. Similarly, a cartoon on the door or the decoration of an office (as Anand and Elsbach analyze) may inspire reactions in the absence of the individual who designed the office or hung the cartoon. Response to the artifact—and by extension to the displayer—can be delayed, or asynchronous.

Such delays may be especially likely when artifacts span levels of analyses, and span organizational boundaries. Fiol and O'Connor illustrate how medical professionals used artifacts to create a dialogue with constituents about professional legitimacy. But such dialogues are not "clean" because even though sensegivers and sensemakers may talk "in turns," the period between turns may vary randomly over large stretches of time. These conversations may also involve errors of interpretation or myopia (Elsbach, Vilnai-Yavetz, & Rafaeli). Similarly, Cappetta and Gioia, as well as Schultz, Hatch, and Ciccolella, show how the production of organizational artifacts in the form of fashion or plastic bricks represents a call from the organization about who they are. However, the anxiety that plagues such steps is the lack of knowledge of how quickly or how well such calls will be answered.

A different type of asynchronicity may occur with the boundary objects described by Carlile and the contracts described by Kaghan and Lounsbury, which appear to involve serial dialogues. One person or group works on the object and passes it to another party, which eventually passes it back. How might these dialogues differ from the group of observers at a performance—described by Strati—who are also involved in some sort of dialogue of trying to make sense of what that performance means? These chapters just promise a hint of the richness that looking at artifacts as dialogues might reveal.

3. *Who might be best suited to study artifacts?* It may be that organizational science needs additional skills and perspectives to fully appreciate the role of artifacts in organizations. Focusing attention on the material side of artifacts suggests that we might learn something from those in the material sciences or engineering. Turning to the socially constructed aspects of artifacts, we are reminded that in addition to "classic" social science methods of interviews, surveys, or ethnography, we might also delve into areas of ergonomics (regarding instrumentality; cf. Gibson, 1979; Nielsen, 1994) and art (regarding aesthetics)—both of which are marginalized to various degrees even though they are occasionally represented in organizational studies. Viewing artifacts in dialogues further reminds to look to linguists and communication research to better understand the grammar and process of artifact use (Boden, 1994; Kasper & Blum-Kulka, 1993; Levinson, 1983). Such a view also reminds of the limitations of acting as archeologists; studies of artifacts necessarily position researchers as sensemakers attempting to understand something from the past. However, such past-oriented views often obscure the dynamic nature of artifacts-in-use.

4. *The management of artifacts matter in practice.* To this point, we have focused primarily on the theory of artifacts. But a resounding message from all authors is that the management of artifacts can have large consequences for organizations in terms of finances and human resources. Vilnai-Yavetz and Rafaeli begin this conversation in chapter 1 by showing the dramatic effects of artifact myopia. Their illustration of the "green bus" (Rafaeli & Vilnai-Yavetz, 2004) shows how the lack of attention to the

instrumental and aesthetic dimensions of artifacts can lead to losses in reputation and revenue among customers. Cappetta and Gioia further argue that organizations must simultaneously be in tune with the aesthetic and instrumental needs of their customers, while also considering symbolic messages conveyed through artifacts to customers and employees.

Carlile, Cunliffe and Shotter, as well as Kaghan and Lounsbury, further suggest that the management of artifacts can influence knowledge transfer and can impact the building of communities. This message is echoed by Schultz, Hatch, and Ciccolella, who discuss the importance of using artifacts in aligning an organization's vision, culture, and image, as well as by Fiol and O'Connor, who discuss the importance of artifacts in maintaining professional identity and legitimacy. For each of these authors, artifacts give community members "something to talk about." That is, they serve as focal points for discussing commonalities and marking community boundaries.

By contrast, artifacts may also exacerbate the breakdown of communities. Historically, the owing and branding of slaves in the United States nearly led to the destruction of the nation. Might organizations face similar dangers through the use of branding? Harquail warns of some of the dangers of transforming employees into brands. In our own research, we saw how the potential mismanagement of something as seemingly innocuous as a nurse's work dress caused incredible strife for a hospital unit (Pratt & Rafaeli, 1997). Given that artifacts, such as dress, are such a critical means of maintaining individual and organizational identity and legitimacy, we suggest that managers should be very aware of how artifacts are managed in their organizations.

Our goals for this volume were to raise awareness and advance our knowledge of the power of artifacts for understanding and shaping our corporate lives. Artifacts matter. In many ways, organizational realities are "object"-ive: mediated by artifacts. It is our hope that we have managed to inspire students of organizations to further explore this often overlooked aspect of organizational life.

References

Aaker, D. (1994). Building a brand: The "Saturn" story. *California Management Review, 36*(2), 114–133.

Aaker, D. (1994). *Building stronger brands.* New York: The Free Press.

Aaker, D. A., & Joachimstahler, E. (2000). *Global brand leadership.* New York: The Free Press.

Aaker, D. A., & Myers, J. G. (1987). *Advertising management.* New York: Prentice-Hall.

Abbott, A. (1988). *The system of professions: An essay on the division of expert labour.* Chicago: University of Chicago Press.

Adorno, T. W., & Horkheimer, M. (1972). *Dialectic of enlightenment.* New York: Herder & Herder.

Albert, S., & Whetten, D. (1985). Organizational identity. *Research in Organizational Behavior, 7,* 263–295. Greenwich, CT: JAI Press.

Aldrich, H. E., & Fiol, C. M. (1994). Fools rush in? The institutional context of industry creation. *Academy of Management Review, 19*(4), 645–670.

Altman, I. (1975). *The environment and social behavior.* Monterey, CA: Brooks/Cole.

Altman, Y., & Baruch, Y. (1998). Applying cultural analysis in organizational settings: Analytical method & two case studies. *Organization Studies, 19,* 769–785.

American Academy of Family Practice Physicians. (2003). http://www.aafp.org

Antorini, Y. M. (2003). *Brand communities* (Working Paper). Copenhagen: Copenhagen Business School.

Argyris, C. (1982). *Reasoning, learning, and action: Individual and organizational.* San Francisco: Jossey-Bass.

Argyris, C., & Schon, D. A. (1974). *Theory in practice.* San Francisco: Jossey-Bass.

Ashforth, B. E., & Humphrey, R. H. (1993). Emotional labor in service roles: The influence of identity. *Academy of Management Review, 18*(1), 88–115.

Ashforth, B. E., & Mael, F. (1989). Social identity and the organization. *Academy of Management Review, 14*(1), 20–39.

Ashforth, B. E., & Mael, F. A. (1998). The power of resistance: Sustaining valued identities. In R. Kramer & M. Neale (Eds.), *Power and influence in organizations* (pp. 89–119). Thousand Oaks, CA: Sage.

Atwood, G. E., & Stolorow, R. D. (1984). *Structures of subjectivity: Explorations in psychoanalytic phenomenology.* Hillsdale, NJ: Analytic Press.

Avraham, E., & First, A. (2003). "I buy American": The American image as reflected in Israeli advertising. *Journal of Communication, 53*(2), 282–299.

Bacharach, S. B., Bamberger, P., & Conley, S. C. (1991). Negotiating the "see-saw" of managerial strategy: A resurrection of the study of professionals in organization theory. *Research in the Sociology of Organizations, 8,* 217–238.

Bakhtin, M. M. (1981). *The dialogical imagination* (M. Holquist, Ed.; C. Emerson & M. Holquist, Trans.). Austin: University of Texas Press.

Bakhtin, M. M. (1984). *Problems of Dostoevsky's poetics* (C. Emerson, Ed. and Trans.). Minneapolis: University of Minnesota Press.

Bakhtin, M. M. (1986). *Speech genres and other late essays* (V. W. McGee, Trans.). Austin: University of Texas Press.

Bakhtin, M. M. (1993). *Toward a philosophy of the act* (M. Holquist, Ed.; V. Lianpov, Trans.). Austin: University of Texas Press.

Balmer, J., & Greyser, S. (Eds.). (2003). *Revealing the corporation: Perspectives on identity, image, reputation and corporate branding.* London: Routledge.

Bansal, P., & Roth, K. (2000). Why companies go green: A model of ecological responsiveness. *Academy of Management Journal, 43*(4), 717–736.

Barley, S. R. (1986). Technology as an occasion for structuring: Evidence from observations of CT scanners and the social order of radiology departments. *Administrative Science Quarterly, 31*(1), 78–108.

Barley, S. R. (1990). The alignment of technology and structure through roles and networks. *Administrative Science Quarterly, 35,* 63–105.

Barley, S. R., & Tolbert, P. S. (1991). At the intersection of organizations and occupations. *Research in the Sociology of Organizations, 8,* 1–13.

Barley, S. R., & Tolbert, P. S. (1997). Institutionalization and structuration: Studying the links between action and institution. *Organization Studies, 18,* 93–117.

Baron, R. A. (1994). The physical environment of work setting: Effects on task performance, interpersonal relations, and job satisfaction. *Research in Organizational Behavior, 16,* 1–46.

Barrett, T. G., & Booth, I. W. (1994). *Sartorial elegance: Does it exist in the paediatrician–patient relationship?* Retrieved February 18, 2003, from http://0-web5.infotrac.galegroup.com

Bartel, C., & Dutton, J. (2001). Ambiguous organizational memberships: Constructing organizational identities in interactions with others. In M. A. Hogg & D. J. Terry (Eds.), *Social identity processes in organizational contexts* (pp. 115–130). Philadelphia: Psychology Press.

Barthes, R. (1967). *Elements of semiology.* New York: Hill & Wang.

Barthes, R. (1972). *Mythologies.* New York: Hill & Wang. (Original work published 1970)

Barthes, R. (1982). *Empire of signs.* New York: Hill & Wang. (Original work published 1970)

Barthes, R. (1983). *The fashion system.* New York: Hill & Wang.

Barzel, Y. (1989). *Economic analysis of property rights.* Cambridge, England: Cambridge University Press.

Bateson, G. (1972). *Steps to an ecology of mind.* New York: Ballantine.

Baudrillard, J. (1978). *La précession des simulacres* [Simulations]. Paris: Editions de Minuit.

Baudrillard, J. (1997). *Art and artifact.* London: Sage.

Baumgarten, A. G. (1750–1758). *Aesthetica.* Frankfurt am Oder: Kleyb. (photostat: Olms: Hildesheim, 1986).

Bechky, B. (2003). Object lessons: Workplace artifacts as representations of occupational jurisdiction. *American Journal of Sociology, 109,* 720–752.

Becker, F. D. (1981). *Workspace: Creating environments in organizations.* New York: Praeger.

Becker, F., & Steele, F. (1995). *Workplace by design.* San Francisco: Jossey-Bass.

Becker, G. S. (1976). *The economic approach to human behavior.* Chicago: University of Chicago Press.

Becker, H. S. (1982). *Art worlds.* Berkeley: University of California Press.

Becker, H., Geer, B., Hughes, E., & Strauss, A. (1961). *Boys in white.* Chicago: University of Chicago Press.

Belch, G. E., & Belch, M. A. (2001). *Advertising and promotion* (5th ed.). New York: McGraw-Hill.

Belk, R. W. (1988). Possessions and the external self. *Journal of Consumer Research, 15,* 139–168.

Benedict, R. (1934). *Patterns of culture.* Boston: Houghton Mifflin.

Bennett, P. D. (1995). *Dictionary of marketing terms.* Lincolnwood, IL: NTC Business Books.

Berg, P. O., & Kreiner, K. (1990). Corporate architecture: Turning physical setting into symbolic resources. In P. Gagliardi (Ed.), *Symbols and artifacts: Views of the corporate landscape* (pp. 41–67). New York: Aldine de Gruyter.

Berger, J., Webster, M. J., Ridgeway, C., & Rosenholtz, S. J. (1986). Status cues, expectations, and behavior. *Advances in Group Processes, 3,* 1–22.

Berger, P. L., & Luckmann, T. (1966). *The social construction of reality.* New York: Anchor Books.

Berleant, A. (1988). Aesthetic perception in environmental design. In J. L. Nasar (Ed.), *Environmental aesthetics: Theory, research and applications* (1st ed., pp. 84–97). Cambridge, England: Cambridge University Press.

Berry, D. S., Hansen, J. S., Landry-Pester, J. C., & Meier, J. A. (1994). Vocal determinants of first impression of young children. *Journal of Nonverbal Behavior, 18,* 187–197.

Bevir, M. (forthcoming). How narratives explain. In D. Yanow & P. Schwartz-Shea (Eds.), *Interpretation and method: Empirical research methods and the interpretive turn.* Armonk, NY: M. E. Sharpe.

Bickerton, D. (1982). Learning without experience the Creole way. In L. K. Obler & L. Menn (Eds.), *Exceptional language and linguistics* (pp. 15–29). New York: Academic Press.

Biernat, M., Vescio, T. K., & Green, M. L. (1996). Selective stereotyping. *Journal of Personality and Social Psychology, 71,* 1194–1209.

Biggart, N. W., & Beamish, T. D. (2003). The economic sociology of conventions: Habit, custom, practice, and routine in market order. *Annual Review of Sociology, 29,* 443–464.

Biner, P., Butler, D., Lovegrove, T., & Burns, R. (1993). Windowlessness in the workplace: A reexamination of the compensation hypothesis. *Environment and Behavior, 25,* 205–227.

Bitner, M. J. (1992). Servicecapes: The impact of physical surroundings on customers and employees. *Journal of Marketing, 56,* 57–71.

Black, L., Carlile, P. R., & Repenning, N. (2004). Expanding theoretical insights from ethnographic evidence: Building on Barley's study of CT-scanning implementations. *Administrative Science Quarterly, 49*(4), 572–607.

Blumer, H. (1969a). Fashion: From class differentiation to social selection. *Sociological Quarterly, 10,* 275–291.

Blumer, H. (1969b). *Symbolic interactionism: Perspective and method.* Englewood Cliffs, NJ: Prentice-Hall.

Boden, D. (1994). *The business of talk: Organizations in action.* London: Polity Press.

Boorstin, D. J. (1961). *The image, or what happened to the American dream.* London: Weidenfeld and Nicolson.

Bourdieu, P. (1977). *Outline of a theory of practice* (R. Nice, Trans.). Cambridge, England: Cambridge University Press.

Bourdieu, P. (1984a). *Distinction: A social critique of the judgment of taste.* Cambridge, MA: Harvard University Press.

Bourdieu, P. (1984b). Haute couture et haute culture [High fashion: High culture]. In P. Bourdieu (Ed.), *Questions de sociologie* (pp. 196–206). Paris: Minuit.

Bowker, G. C., & Star, S. L. (1999). *Sorting things out: Classification and its consequences.* Cambridge, MA: MIT Press.

Breward, C. (2003). *Fashion.* Oxford, England: Oxford University Press.

Brewer, M. B. (1991). The social self: On being the same and different at the same time. *Personality & Social Psychology Bulletin, 17,* 475–482.

Brewer, M. B., & Gardner, W. (1996). Who is this "we"?: Levels of collective identity and self-representations. *Journal of Personality and Social Psychology, 71*, 83–93.

Brewer, M. B., Manzi, J. M., & Shaw, J. S. (1993). In-group identification as a function of de-personalization, distinctiveness, and status. *Psychological Science, 4*, 88–92.

Brickson, S. (2000). The impact of identity orientation on individual and organizational outcomes in demographically diverse settings. *Academy of Management Review, 25*, 82–101.

Brown, J. S., & Duguid, P. (1991). Organizational learning and communities-of-practice. *Organization Science, 2*(1), 40–57.

Brown, J. S., & Duguid, P. (2000). *The social life of information.* Cambridge, MA: Harvard Business School Press.

Brown, R. W. (1958). *Words and things.* Glencoe, IL: The Free Press.

Bunderson, J. S., Lofstrom, S. M., & Van de Ven, A. H. (2000). Conceptualizing and measuring professional and administrative models of organizing. *Organizational Research Methods, 3*(4), 366–391.

Burke, K. (1969). *A grammar of motives.* Berkeley: University of California Press. (Original work published 1945)

Burns, L. D., & Caughey, C. C. (1992). Category use in first impressions of restaurant interiors. *Perceptual and Motor Skills, 75*, 107–110.

Cairns, G. (2002). Aesthetics, morality and power: Design as espoused freedom and implicit control. *Human Relations, 55*(7), 799–820.

Callon, M. (1980). Struggles and negotiation to define what is problematic and what is not: The sociology of translation. In K. K. Cetina, R. Krohn, & R. Whitley (Eds.), *The social process of scientific investigation* (pp. 197–219). Boston: Reidel.

Callon, M. (1998). An essay on framing and overflowing: Economic externalities revisited by sociology. In M. Callon (Ed.), *The laws of the markets* (pp. 244–269). Oxford, England: Blackwell.

Campbell, D. E. (1979). Interior office design and visitor response. *Journal of Applied Psychology, 64*, 648–653.

Canter, D. (1977). *The psychology of place* (1st ed.). London: Architectural Press.

Canter, D. (1997). The facets of place. In E. H. Zube & G. T. Moore (Eds.), *Advances in environment, behavior, and design* (Vol. 4, pp. 109–147). New York: Plenum Press.

Cappetta, R., & Cillo, P. (2001). *Patterns of stylistic innovation: An empirical analysis of the evolution of style in prêt-à-porter between 1984 and 1999.* Paper presented at the 2001 Academy of Management Conference, Washington, DC.

Cappetta, R., Perrone, V., & Ponti, A. (2003, March/April). Competizione economica e competizione simbolica: Capacità organizzative per il fashion system [Economic and Symbolic Competition Organizational Capabilities for the Fashion System]. *Economia e Management, 2*, 73–88.

Cardy, R. L. (2001). Employees as customers? *Marketing Management*, pp. 12–16.

Carey, J. W. (1989). *Communication as culture: Essays on media and society.* Boston: Unwin Hyman.

Carlile, P. (1997). *Transforming knowledge in product development: Making knowledge manifest through boundary objects.* Unpublished doctoral dissertation, University of Michigan, Ann Arbor.

Carlile, P. R. (2002). A pragmatic view of knowledge and boundaries: Boundary objects in new product development. *Organization Science, 13*(4), 442–455.

Carlile, P. R. (2004). Transferring, translating and transforming: An integrative framework for managing knowledge across boundaries. *Organization Science, 15*(5), 555–568.

Casey, E. S. (1993). *Getting back into place.* Bloomington: Indiana University.

Cash, T. F., Gillen, B., & Burns, D. S. (1997). Sexism and "beautyism" in personal consultant decision making. *Journal of Applied Psychology, 62*, 301–310.

Charrow, V. R. (1982). Linguistic theory and the study of legal and bureaucratic language. In L. K. Obler & L. Menn (Eds.), *Exceptional language and linguistics.* New York: Academic Press.

Chia, R. (1996). *Organizational analysis as deconstructive practice*. Berlin: Aldine de Gruyter.

Christopher, A. N., & Schlenker, B. R. (2000). The impact of perceived material wealth and perceiver personality on first impressions. *Journal of Economic Psychology, 21*, 1–19.

Ciborra, C. (1996). Introduction: What does Groupware mean for the organizations hosting it? In C. Ciborra (Ed.), *Groupware & teamwork* (pp. 1–19). Chichester, England: Wiley.

Clark, K., & Wheelwright, S. (1995). *The product development challenge: Competing through speed, quality, and creativity*. Cambridge, MA: Harvard Business School Press.

Clarke, A., & Fujimura, J. (1992). Introduction. In A. Clarke & J. Fujimura (Eds.), *The right tools for the job: At work in twentieth-century life sciences* (pp. 3–46). Princeton, NJ: Princeton University Press.

Clegg, S. (1975). *Power, rule, and domination: A critical and empirical understanding of power in sociological theory and organizational life*. London: Routledge.

Clegg, S. (1994). Power relations and the resistant subject. In J. M. Jermier, D. Knights, & K. G. Smith (Eds.), *Resistance and power in organisations* (pp. 274–325). London: Routledge.

Clifford, J., & Marcus, G. (Eds.). (1986). *Writing culture: The poetics and politics of ethnography*. Berkeley: University of California Press.

Cohen, A. (1976). *The symbolic construction of community*. London: Tavistock.

Cohen, D. (1986). Trademark strategy. *Journal of Marketing, 50*, 61–74.

Cohen, J. B. (1989). An over-extended self? *Journal of Consumer Research, 16*, 123–128.

Cohen, W. M., & Levinthal, D. A. (1990). Absorptive capacity: A new perspective on knowledge and innovation. *Administrative Science Quarterly, 35*, 128–152.

Collins, J. C., & Porras, J. (1994). *Built to last*. New York: Harper Business.

Collinson, D. L. (1988). "Engineering humor": Masculinity, joking and conflict in shop-floor relations. *Organization Studies, 9*, 181–199.

Collinson, D. L. (2002). Managing humor. *Journal of Management Studies, 39*, 269–288.

Collinson, D. L. (2003). Identities and insecurities: Selves at work. *Organization, 10*(3), 527–547.

Cooley, C. H. (1902). *Human nature and the social order*. New York: Scribner's.

Cooper, C. (1976). The house as symbol of the self. In J. Lang, C. Burnette, W. Moleski, & D. Vachon (Eds.), *Designing for human behavior* (pp. 130–146). Stroudsburg, PA: Dowden, Hutchinson, & Ross.

Cooper, R. (1990). Organization/disorganization. In J. Hassard & D. Pym (Eds.), *The theory and philosophy of organizations* (pp.). London: Routledge.

Covaleski, M. A., Dirsmith, M. W., Heian, J. B., & Samuel, S. (1998). The calculated and the avowed: Techniques of discipline and struggles over identity in Big Six public accounting firms. *Administrative Science Quarterly, 43*(2), 293–327.

Crowston, K., & Kamerrer, E. E. (1998). Coordination and collective mind in software requirements development. *IBM Systems Journal, 37*, 227–245.

Crystal, D. (1994). Pidgins and Creoles. In V. P. Clark, P. A. Eschholz, & A. F. Rosa (Eds.), *Language: Introductory readings* (pp.). New York: St. Martin's Press.

Csikszentmihalyi, M., & Rochberg-Halton, E. (1981). *The meaning of things: Domestic symbols and the self*. Cambridge, England: Cambridge University Press.

Cunliffe, A. L. (2001). Managers as practical authors: Reconstructing our understanding of management practice. *Journal of Management Studies, 38*(3), 351–371.

Cunliffe A. L. (2002a). Reflexive dialogical practice in management learning. *Management Learning, 33*(1), 35–61.

Cunliffe, A. L. (2002b). Social poetics as management inquiry: A dialogical approach. *Journal of Management Inquiry, 11*(2), 128–146.

Czarniawska, B. (1997). *Narrating the organization: Dramas of institutional identity*. Chicago: University of Chicago Press.

Czarniawska-Joerges, B., & Joerges, B. (1990). Linguistic artifacts at service of organizational control. In P. Gagliardi (Ed.), *Symbols and artifacts: Views of the corporate landscape* (pp. 339–364). Berlin: Aldine de Gruyter.

Dalton, M. (1959). *Men who manage*. New York: Wiley.

Dandridge, C. T. (1983). Symbols' function and use. In L. R. Pondy, J. Frost, G. Morgan, & T. C. Dandridge (Eds.), *Organizational symbolism* (pp. 69–79). Greenwich, CT: JAI Press.

Davis, F. (1991). Clothing, fashion and the dialectic of identity. In D. R. Mains & C. Couch (Eds.), *Communication and social structure* (pp. 23–38). Springfield, IL: Thomas.

Davis, F. (1992). *Fashion, culture, and identity.* Chicago: University of Chicago Press.

Davis, S. M., & Dunn, M. (2002). *Building the brand-driven business: Operationalize your brand to drive profitable growth.* San Francisco: Jossey-Bass.

Davis, T. R. V. (1984). The influence of the physical environment in offices. *Academy of Management Review, 9*(2), 271–283.

Dean, J. W. J., Ramirez, R., & Ottensmeyer, E. (1997). An aesthetic perspective on organizations. In C. L. Cooper & S. E. Jackson (Eds.), *Creating tomorrow's organization* (pp. 419–437). New York: Wiley.

de Chernatony, L., & McDonald, M. (1998). *Creating powerful brands* (2nd ed.). Oxford, England: Butterworth-Heinemann.

Deephouse, D. L. (1996). Does isomorphism legitimate? *Academy of Management Journal, 39*(4), 1024–1039.

Deleuze, G., & Guattari, F. (1984). *Anti-Edipus.* London: Athlone Press.

Dell, D., Ainspan, N., Bodenberg, T., Troy, K., & Hickey, J. (2001). *Engaging employees through your brand.* The Conference Board, Research Report 1288-01-RR. New York.

Derrida, J. (1967). *De la grammatologie* [Of grammatology]. Paris: Minuit.

Descamps, M.-A. (1979). *Psychosociologie de la mode.* Paris: PUF.

Devine, P. G. (1989). Stereotypes and prejudice: Their automatic and controlled components. *Journal of Personality and Social Psychology, 56,* 5–18.

DiMaggio, P. J., & Powell, W. W. (1983). The iron cage revisited: Institutional isomorphism and collective rationality in organizational fields. *American Sociological Review, 48,* 147–160.

DiMaggio, P. J., & Powell, W. W. (1991). Introduction. In W. W. Powell & P. J. DiMaggio (Eds.), *The new institutionalism in organizational analysis* (pp. 1–38). Chicago: University of Chicago Press.

Dines-Levy, G., & Smith, G. W. H. (1988). Representation of women and men in *Playboy* sex cartoons. In C. Powell & G. Paton (Eds.), *Humour in society: Control and resistance* (pp. 234–259). London: Macmillan.

Dittmar, H. (1992). Perceived material wealth and first impressions. *British Journal of Social Psychology, 31,* 379–391.

Djelic, M. L., & Ainamo, A. (1999). The coevolution of new organization forms in the fashion industry: A historical and comparative study of France, Italy and the United States, *Organization Science, 10*(5), 622–637.

Dougherty, D. (1992). Interpretive barriers to successful product innovation in large firms. *Organization Science, 3,* 179–202.

Douglas, M. (1986). *How institutions think.* Syracuse, NY: Syracuse University Press.

Douglas, M., & Isherwood, B. (1979). *The world of goods.* New York: Basic Books.

Doxtater, D. (1990). Meaning of the workplace. In P. Gagliardi (Ed.), *Symbols and artifacts: Views of the corporate landscape* (pp. 107–127). New York: Aldine de Gruyter.

Durgee, J. F., & Stuart, R. W. (1987). Advertising symbols and brand names that best represent key product meanings. *Journal of Consumer Marketing, 4,* 16–23.

Durkheim, E. (1965). *The elementary forms of religious life* (J. W. Swain, Trans.). New York: The Free Press.

Dutton, J. E., Dukerich, J. M., & Harquail, C. V. (1994). Organizational images and member identification. *Administrative Science Quarterly, 39,* 239–263.

Eco, U. (1976). *A theory of semiotics.* Bloomington: University of Indiana Press.

Edelman, L. B. (1992). Legal ambiguity and symbolic structures: Organizational mediation of law. *American Journal of Sociology, 97,* 1531–1576.

Edelman, M. J. (1964). *The symbolic uses of politics.* Urbana: University of Illinois Press.

Edelman, M. J. (1995). *From arts to politics: How artistic creations shape political conceptions.* Chicago: University of Chicago Press.

Ehn, P. (1988). *Work-oriented design of computer artifacts.* Stockholm: Arbetslivscentrum.

Eisenman, M. (2004). *Aesthetic interfaces: A theory of symbolic differentiation.* Manuscript in progress. Columbia University, New York.

Elliott, R., & Wattanasuwan, K. (1998). Brands as symbolic resources for the construction of identity. *International Journal of Advertising, 17,* 131–144.

Elsbach, K. D. (2003a). Organizational perception management. In R. M. Kramer & B. M. Staw (Eds.), *Research in organizational behavior* (Vol. 25, pp. 297–332). Oxford, UK: Elsevier.

Elsbach, K. D. (2003b). Relating physical environment to self-categorizations: A study of identity threat and affirmation in a non-territorial office space. *Administrative Science Quarterly, 48,* 622–654.

Elsbach, K. D. (2004). Interpreting workplace identities: The role of office décor. *Journal of Organizational Behavior, 25,* 99–128.

Elsbach, K., & Glynn, M. A. (1996). Believing your own PR: Embedding identification in strategic reputation. *Advances in Strategic Management, 13,* 65–90.

Elsbach, K. D., & Kramer, R. M. (1996). Members' responses to organizational identity threats: Encountering and countering the *Business Week* rankings. *Administrative Science Quarterly, 41,* 442–476.

Elsbach, K. D., & Kramer, R. M. (2003). Assessing creativity in Hollywood pitch meetings: Evidence for a dual process model of creativity judgments. *Academy of Management Journal, 46,* 283–301.

Emery, F., & Trist, E. (1965). The causal texture of organizational environments. *Human Relations, 18,* 21–32.

Engestrom, Y. (1990). *Learning, working and imagining.* Helsinki: Orienta Konsultit Oy.

Entwistle, J. (2000). *The fashioned body: Fashion, dress and modern social theory.* Cambridge, England: Polity Press.

Erickson, E. H. (1950). *Childhood and society.* New York: W. W. Norton & Co., Inc.

Erlandson, D. A., Harris, E. L., Skipper, B. L., & Allen, S. D. (1993). *Doing naturalistic inquiry.* Newbury Park, CA: Sage.

Etzkowitz, H., Webster, A., Gephardt, C., & Branca, R. C. T. (2000). The future of the university and the university of the future: Evolution of ivory tower to entrepreneurial paradigm. *Research Policy, 29,* 313–328.

Feldman, M. S. (1989). *Order without design.* Stanford, CA: Stanford University Press.

Feldman, M. S. (1995). *Strategies for interpreting qualitative data.* Newbury Park, CA: Sage.

Feldman, M. S., & Pentland, B. T. (2003). Reconceptualizing organizational routines as a source of flexibility and change. *Administrative Science Quarterly, 48,* 94–118.

Feldman, M. S., & Rafaeli, A. (2002). Organizational routines as sources of connections and understandings. *Journal of Management Studies, 39*(3), 309–331.

Fiell, C., & Fiell, P. (1997). *1000 chairs.* Koln, Switzerland: Benedikt Taschen Verlag.

Fineman, S. (2000). *Emotion in organizations* (2nd ed.), London: Sage. (Original work published 1993)

Firth, R. (1973). *Symbols public and private.* London: George Allen & Unwin.

Fischer, F., & Forester, J. (Eds.). (1993). *The argumentative turn in policy analysis and planning.* Durham, NC: Duke University Press.

Fiske, J. (1989). The "jeaning" of America. In J. Fiske (Ed.), *Understanding popular culture* (pp. 1–32). New York: Routledge.

Fiske, S. T., & Neuberg, S. L. (1990). A continuum of impression formation, from category-based to individuating processes: Influences of information and motivation on attention and interpretation. In L. Berkowitz (Ed.), *Advances in experimental social psychology* (Vol. 23, pp. 1–74). San Diego: Academic Press.

Fiske, S., & Taylor, S. (1991). *Social cognition.* New York: McGraw-Hill.

Flanders, V. (2002). *Son of web pages that suck: Learn good design by looking at bad design.* San Francisco: Sybex.

Foley, W. A. (1988). Language birth: The processes of Pidginization and Creolization. In F. J. Newmeyer (Ed.), *Language: The sociocultural context* (pp. 162–183). Cambridge, England: Cambridge University Press.

Fombrun, C. J. (1996). *Reputation: Realizing value from the corporate image.* Boston: Harvard Business School Press.

Fombrun, C., & Shanley, M. (1990). What's in the name? Reputation building and corporate strategy. *Academy of Management Journal, 33,* 233–255.

Fombrun, C., & Van Riel, C. (2003). *Fame and fortune: How successful companies build winning reputations.* London: Prentice-Hall.

Ford, C. M., & Gioia, D. A. (2000). Factors influencing creativity in the domain of managerial decision making. *Journal of Management, 26,* 705–732.

Foucault, M. (1972). *The archaeology of knowledge* (Sheridan Smith, Trans.). New York: Pantheon Books.

Fournier, S. (1998). Consumers and their brands: Developing relationship theory in consumer research. *Journal of Consumer Research, 24,* 343–373.

Frank, M. G., & Gilovich, T. (1988). The dark side of self- and social perception: Black uniforms and aggression in professional sports. *Journal of Personality and Social Psychology, 54*(1), 74–85.

Frank, R. (1985). *Choosing the right pond: Human behavior and the quest for status.* New York: Oxford University Press.

Freud, S. (1960). *Jokes and the relation to the unconscious.* Harmondsworth, England: Penguin.

Friedland, R., & Alford, R. (1991). Bringing society back in: Symbols, practices, and institutional contradictions. In P. DiMaggio & W. W. Powell (Eds.), *The new institutionalism in organizational analysis* (pp. 232–263). Chicago: University of Chicago Press.

Frost, P., & Morgan, G. (1983). Symbols and sense-making: A realization of a framework. In L. R. Pondy, P. Frost, G. Morgan, & T. Dandridge (Eds.), *Organizational symbolism* (pp. 207–237). Greenwich, CT: JAI Press.

Fujimura, J. H. (1987). Constructing doable problems in cancer research: Articulating alignment. *Social Studies of Science, 17,* 257–293.

Fujimura, J. H. (1996). *Crafting science: A sociohistory of the quest for the genetics of cancer.* Cambridge, MA: Harvard University Press.

Gabriel, Y. (1999). *Organizations in depth.* London: Sage.

Gabriel, Y. (2000). *Storytelling in organizations.* Oxford, England: Oxford University Press.

Gagliardi, P. (Ed.). (1990). *Symbols and artifacts: Views of the corporate landscape.* New York: Aldine de Gruyter.

Gagliardi, P. (1996). Exploring the aesthetic side of organizational life. In S. R. Clegg, C. Hardy, & R. W. Nord (Eds.), *Handbook of organization studies* (pp. 565–580). London: Sage.

Galison, P. (1997). *Image and logic: A material culture of microphysics.* Chicago: University of Chicago Press.

Gans, H. (1976). Personal journal: B. On the methods used in this study. In M. P. Golden (Ed.), *The research experience* (pp. 49–59). Itasca, IL: F. E. Peacock.

Garfinkel, H. (1967). *Studies in ethnomethodology.* Englewood Cliffs, NJ: Prentice-Hall.

Garling, T., & Golledge, R. G. (1989). Environmental perception and cognition. In E. H. Zube & G. T. Moore (Eds.), *Advances in environment, behavior, and design* (Vol. 2, pp. 203–236). New York: Plenum Press.

Gecas, V. (1982). The self-concept. In R. H. Turner & J. F. Short (Eds.), *Annual review of sociology* (Vol. 8, pp. 1–33). Palo Alto, CA: Annual Reviews.

Geertz, C. (1973). *The interpretation of cultures: Selected essays.* New York: Basic Books.

Geiger, R. L. (1986). *To advance knowledge: The growth of American research universities, 1900–1940.* Oxford, England: Oxford University Press.

Gelder, K., & Thornton, S. (1997). *The subcultures reader.* London: Routledge.

Gergen, K. J. (1985). The social constructionist movement in modern psychology. *American Psychologist, 40,* 266–275.

Gherardi, S., & Strati, A. (Eds.). (2003). *The iron cage. Dialogues from Max Weber about Loris Cecchini's installation "Density Spectrum Zone 1.0"* [DVD/VHS, 19']. Performance by Anna Scalfi, April 2. Trento, Italy: Faculty of Sociology.

Gibson, J. J. (1979). *The ecological approach to visual perception.* Boston: Houghton Mifflin.

Giddens, A. (1984). *The constitution of society: Outline of the theory of structuration.* Berkeley: University of California Press.

Gilbert, D. T. (1989). Thinking lightly about others: Automatic components of the social inference process. In J. S. Uleman & J. A. Bargh (Eds.), *Unintended thought* (pp. 189–211). New York: Guilford.

Gioia, D. A., & Chittipeddi, K. (1991). Sensemaking and sensegiving in strategic change initiation. *Strategic Management Journal, 12,* 443–448.

Gioia, D. A., Schultz, M., & Corley, K. (2000). Organizational identity, image and adaptive instability. *Academy of Management Review, 25,* 63–82.

Gioia, D., & Thomas, J. B. (1996). Image, identity and issues interpretation: Sensemaking during strategic change in academia. *Administrative Science Quarterly, 41,* 370–403.

Glynn, M. A., & Abzug, R. A. (1998). Isomorphism and competitive differentiation in the organizational name game. In J. A. C. Baum (Ed.), *Advances in strategic management* (Vol. 15, pp. 105–128). Greenwich, CT: JAI Press.

Glynn, M. A., & Abzug, R. (2002). Institutionalizing identity: Symbolic isomorphism and organizational names. *Academy of Management Journal, 45,* 267–280.

Glynn, M. A., & Marquis, C. (2004). When good names go bad. In C. Johnson (Ed.), *Research in the sociology of organizations* (pp. 147–170). Amsterdam: Elsevier.

Goffman, E. (1961). *Encounters.* Indianapolis, IN: Bobbs–Merrill.

Goodman, N. (1978). *Ways of worldmaking.* Indianapolis, IN: Hackett.

Goodman, N., & Elgin, C. Z. (1988). How buildings mean. In *Reconceptions in philosophy and other arts and sciences* (pp. 31–48). Indianapolis, IN: Hackett.

Goodrich, R. (1982). Seven office evaluations: A review. *Environment and Behavior, 14*(3), 353–378.

Goodrick, E., Meindl, J. R., & Flood, A. B. (1997). Business as usual: The adoption of managerial ideology by U.S. hospitals. In J. J. Kronenfeld (Ed.), *Research in the sociology of health care, the evolving health care delivery system: Necessary changes for providers of care, consumers, and patients* (Vol. 14, pp. 27–50). Greenwich, CT: JAI Press.

Goodrick, E., & Salancik, G. R. (1996). Organizational discretion in responding to institutional practices: Hospitals and cesarean births. *Administrative Science Quarterly, 41,* 1–28.

Goodsell, C. T. (1988). *The social meaning of civic space.* Lawrence: University Press of Kansas.

Goodsell, C. T. (1993). Architecture as a setting for governance—introduction. *Journal of Architectural and Planning Research, 10*(4), 271–272.

Gordon, W. H. (1950). *The doctor's bag—what should be in it?* Retrieved February 18, 2003, from www.aafp.org/afp/20000415/afp.html

Gottdiener, M., & Lagopoulos, A. P. (Eds.). (1986). *The city and the sign.* New York: Columbia University Press.

Gouldner, A. W. (1970). *The coming crisis in Western sociology.* New York: Basic Books.

Greenberg, J. (1988). Equity and workplace status: A field experiment. *Journal of Applied Psychology, 73,* 606–613.

Greenhouse, S. (2003). Going for the look, but risking discrimination. *The New York Times,* July 13, p. 12 (national edition).

Griswold, W. (1994). *Cultures and societies in a changing world.* Thousand Oaks, CA: Pine Forge Press.

Guillet de Monthoux, P. (2000). Performing the absolute. Marina Abramovic organizing the unfinished business of Arthur Schopenhauer. *Organization Studies, 21,* 29–51.

Guillet de Monthoux, P. (2004). *The art firm. Aesthetic management and metaphysical marketing.* Stanford, CA: Stanford University Press.

Gusfield, J. R. (1989). Introduction. In K. Burke (Ed.), *On symbols and society.* Chicago: University of Chicago Press.

Hackley, C. (2003). We are all customers now: Rhetorical strategy and ideological control in marketing management texts. *Journal of Management Studies, 40*(5), 1325–1352.

Hafferty, F. W., & Light, D. W. (1995). Professional dynamics and the changing nature of medical work. *Journal of Health and Social Behavior* (Extra issue), 132–153.

Hall, E. T. (1966). *The hidden dimension.* Garden City, NY: Doubleday.

Hamilton, J. R. (2001). *Theater.* In B. Gaut & D. M. Lopes (Eds.), *The Routledge companion to aesthetics* (pp. 557–568). London: Routledge.

Harquail, C. V. (2003). *Sustaining organizationally-based identities through identity work.* Manuscript under review.

Harquail, C. V., & King, A. W. (2003, August). *Organizational identity and embodied cognition.* Paper presented at the annual meeting of the Academy of Management, Seattle, WA.

Hart, A. J., & Morry, M. M. (1997). Trait interferences based on racial and behavioral cues. *Basic and Applied Social Psychology, 19*, 33–48.

Hartsock, N. C. M. (1987). The feminist standpoint. In S. Harding (Ed.), *Feminism and methodology* (pp. 157–180). Bloomington: Indiana University.

Hatch, M. J. (1990). The symbolics of office design: An empirical exploration. In P. Gagliardi (Ed.), *Symbols and artifacts: Views of the corporate landscape* (pp. 129–146). New York: Aldine de Gruyter.

Hatch, M. J. (1993). The dynamics of organizational culture. *Academy of Management Review, 18*, 657–693.

Hatch, M. J. (1997a). Irony and the social construction of contradiction in the humor of a management team. *Organization Science, 8*, 275–288.

Hatch, M. J. (1997b). *Organization theory: Modern symbolic and post modern perspectives.* New York: Oxford University Press.

Hatch, M. J., & Jones, M. O. (1997). Photocopylore at work: Aesthetics, collective creativity and the social construction of organizations. *Studies in Cultures, Organizations and Society, 3*, 263–287.

Hatch, M. J., & Schultz, M. (1997). Relations between organizational culture, identity and image. *European Journal of Marketing, 31*, 356–365.

Hatch, M. J., & Schultz, M. (2000). Scaling the tower of Babel: Relational differences between identity, image, and culture in organizations. In M. Schultz, M. J. Hatch, & M. H. Larsen (Eds.), *The expressive organization: Linking identity, reputation, and the corporate brand* (pp. 11–35). Oxford, England: Oxford University Press.

Hatch, M. J., & Schultz, M. (2001, February 1). Are the strategic stars aligned for your corporate brand? *Harvard Business Review*, pp. 128–134.

Hatch, M. J., & Schultz, M. (2002). Organizational identity dynamics. *Human Relations, 55*(8), 989–1017.

Hatch, M. J., & Schultz, M. (2003). Bringing the corporation into corporate branding. *European Journal of Marketing, 37*, 1041–1064.

Hatch, M. J., & Yanow, D. (2003). Organizational studies as an interpretive science. In C. Knudsen & H. Tsoukas (Eds.), *The Oxford handbook of organization theory: Meta-theoretical perspectives* (pp. 63–87). New York: Oxford University Press.

Hawkesworth, M. E. (1989). Knowers, knowing, known. In M. R. Malson, et al., *Feminist theory in practice and process* (pp. 327–352). Chicago: University of Chicago.

Heath, C., & Button, G. (Ed.). (2002). Special issue on workplace studies. *British Journal of Sociology, 53*(2), 157–161.

Hebdige, D. (1979). *Subculture: The meaning of style.* London: Methuen.

Heidegger, M. (1966). *Discourse on thinking: A translation of Gelassenheit* (J. M. Anderson & E. H. Freund, Trans.). New York: Harper & Row.

Helander, M. G., Khalid, H. M., & Po, P. M. (Eds.). (2001). *The International Conference on Affective Human Factors Design (CAHD 2001).* Singapore: ASEAN Academic Press.

Helman, B., & de Chernatony, L. (1999). Exploring the development of lifestyle brands. *The Service Industries Journal, 19*(2), 49–69.

Henderson, K. (1991). Flexible sketches and inflexible data-bases: Visual communication, conscription devices and boundary objects in design engineering. *Science, Technology, & Human Values, 16*(4), 448–473.

Henderson, P. W., & Cote, J. A. (1998). Guidelines for selecting or modifying logos. *Journal of Marketing, 62,* 14–30.

Herman, D. (2002). *The making or faking of emotionally significant brands* (Self-published E-book). Herman Strategic Consultants, Main@danherman.com.

Hershberger, R. G., & Cass, R. C. (1988). Predicting user responses to buildings. In J. L. Nasar (Ed.), *Environmental aesthetics: Theory, research and applications* (1st ed., pp. 195–211). Cambridge, England: Cambridge University Press.

Herzberg, E. (1966). *Work and the nature of man.* Cleveland, OH: World Publishing.

Heskett, J. (1980). *Industrial design.* London: Thames & Hudson.

Heskett, J. (2002). *Toothpicks and logos: Design in everyday life.* Oxford, England: Oxford University Press.

Hiley, D. R., Bohman, J. F., & Shusterman, R. (1991). *The interpretive turn.* Ithaca, NY: Cornell University Press.

Hirsch, P. M. (1986). From ambushes to golden parachutes: Corporate takeovers as an instance of cultural framing and institutional integration. *American Journal of Sociology, 91,* 800–837.

Hirschman, E. C. (2003). Men, dogs, guns, and cars: The semiotics of rugged individualism. *Journal of Advertising, 32*(1), 9–22.

Hochschild, A. (1983). *The managed heart.* Los Angeles: University of California Press.

Hodge, R. (2002). Myths and realities of electronic medical records: 9 vital functions combine to create comprehensive EMR. *The Physician Executive, 28,* 14–19.

Hofstede, G. (1991). *Culture and organizations: Software of the mind.* London: McGraw-Hill.

Holstein, J. A., & Gubrium, J. F. (1995). *The active interview.* Thousand Oaks, CA: Sage.

Höpfl, H., & Linstead, S. (1993). Passion and performance: Suffering and the carrying of organizational roles. In S. Fineman (Ed.), *Emotion in organizations* (pp. 76–93). London: Sage.

Hornby, A. S. (1974). *Oxford advanced learner's dictionary of current English.* Oxford, England: Oxford University Press.

Hornsey, M. J., & Hogg, M. A. (2002). The effects of status on subgroup relations. *British Journal of Social Psychology, 41,* 203–218.

Howell, W. C. (1994). Human factors in the workplace. In M. Dunnette, L. Hough, & H. Triandis (Eds.), *Handbook of I/O psychology* (2nd ed., pp. 209–269). Chicago: Rand-McNally.

Hughes, E. C. (1971). *The sociological eye: Selected papers.* Chicago: Aldine-Atherton.

Hughes, T. (1983). *Networks of power: Electrification in Western society, 1880–1930.* Baltimore: Johns Hopkins University Press.

Ibarra, H. (1999). Provisional selves: Experimenting with image and identity in professional adaptation. *Administrative Science Quarterly, 44,* 764–791.

Ickes, W. J. (1984). Compositions in black and white: Determinants of interactions in interracial dyads. *Journal of Personality and Social Psychology, 47,* 230–241.

Ind, N. (2001). *Living the brand: How to transform every member of your organization into a brand champion.* London: Kogan Page.

Ingersoll, V. H., & Adams, G. B. (1992). *The tacit organization.* Greenwich, CT: JAI Press.

Iser, W. (1989). *Prospecting: From reader response to literary anthropology.* Baltimore: Johns Hopkins University Press.

Jablin, F. M., Putnam, L. M., Roberts, K. H., & Porter, L. (Eds.). (1987). *Handbook of organizational communication: An interdisciplinary perspective.* Newbury Park, CA: Sage.

Jackson, J. B. (1980). *The necessity for ruins, and other topics.* Amherst: University of Massachusetts Press.

Jackson, J. B. (1984). *Discovering the vernacular landscape.* New Haven, CT: Yale University Press.

Jacobson, S., & Jacques, R. (1990, August). *Of knowers, knowing and the known.* Presented at the Academy of Management Annual Meeting.

James, W. (1890). *The principles of psychology* (Vol. 1). New York: Henry Holt.

Jauss, H. R. (1982). *Ästhetische Erfahrung und literarische Hermeneutik* [Question and answer: Forms of dialogic understanding]. Frankfurt am Main: Suhrkamp Verlag.

Jobling, P., & Crowley, D. (1996). *Graphic design: Reproduction and representation since 1800.* Manchester, England: Manchester University Press.

Jones, E. E., & Nisbett, R. E. (1972). The actor and the observer: Divergent perceptions of the causes of behavior. In E. E. Jones, D. E. Kanouse, H. H. Kelley, R. E. Nisbett, S. Valins, & B. Weiner (Eds.), *Attribution: Perceiving the causes of behavior* (pp. 79–94). Morristown, NJ: General Learning Press.

Jones, M. O. (1996). *Studying organizational symbolism.* Thousand Oaks, CA: Sage.

Jones, V. A. (1999). The white coat: Why not follow suit? *The Journal of the American Medical Association, 281*(5), 478.

Jost, J. T., & Banaji, M. R. (1994). The role of stereotyping in system-justification and the production of false consciousness. *British Journal of Social Psychology, 33,* 1–27.

Jung, G. G. (1964). *Man and his symbols.* London: Aldus Books.

Kaghan, W. N. (1998). *Court and spark: Studies in professional technology transfer management.* Unpublished doctoral dissertation, University of Washington, Seattle.

Kaghan, W. N. (2000). Harnessing a public conglomerate: Technology transfer managers and the entrepreneurial university. In J. Croissant & S. Restivo (Eds.), *Degrees of compromise: Industrial interests and academic values* (pp.). Albany: State University of New York Press.

Kaghan, W. N., & Barnett, G. B. (1997). The desktop model of innovation in digital media. In H. Etzkowitz & L. Leydesdorff (Eds.), *Universities and the global knowledge economy: A triple helix of university–industry–government relations.* London: Pinter.

Kaghan, W. N., & Bowker, G. C. (2001). Out of the machine age?: Complexity, sociotechnical systems and actor network theory. *Journal of Engineering and Technology Management, 18,* 253–269.

Kaghan, W. N., & Phillips, N. (1998). Building the Tower of Babel: Communities of practice and paradigmatic pluralism in organization studies. *Organization, 5,* 191–215.

Kahneman, D. (2003). A perspective on judgment and choice: Mapping bounded rationality. *American Psychologist, 58,* 697–720.

Kant, I. (1968). *Kritik der Urteilskraft.* In I. Kant, *Werke in zwölf Bänden* [The critique of judgment]. (Vol. X, W. Weischedel, Ed.). Frankfurt am Main: Suhrkamp. (Original work published 1790)

Kanter, R. M. (1977). *Men and women of the corporation.* New York: Basic Books.

Kaplan, S., & Kaplan, R. (1983). *Cognition and environment: Functioning in an uncertain world.* Ann Arbor, MI: Ulrich's.

Karliner, J. (2001). *A brief history of greenwash* (CorpWatch). Retrieved July 2002 from http://www.corpwatch.org/campaigns/PCD.jsp?articleid=243

Kasper, G., & Blum-Kulka, S. (Eds.). (1993). *Interlanguage pragmatics.* New York: Oxford University Press.

Kassin, S. M. (1979). Consensus information, prediction, and causal attribution: A review of the literature and issues. *Journal of Personality and Social Psychology, 37,* 1966–1981.

Kaufman, H. (1960). *The forest ranger: A study in administrative behavior.* Baltimore: Resources for the Future, Johns Hopkins Press.

Keller, K. L., Sternthal, B., & Tybout, A. (2002). Three questions you need to ask about your brand. *Harvard Business Review, 80*(9), 80–86.

Kelman, H. C. (1958). Compliance, identification, and internalization: Three processes of attribute change. *Journal of Conflict Resolution, 2,* 51–60.

Kemper, T. D. (1990). *Social structure and testosterone.* New Brunswick, NJ: Rutgers University Press.

Kets de Vries, M., & Miller, D. (1987). Interpreting organizational texts. *Journal of Management Studies, 24,* 233–247.

King, A. R., & Pate, A. N. (2002). Individual differences in judgmental tendencies derived from first impressions. *Personality and Individual Differences, 33*, 131–145.

Kirshenblatt-Gimblett, B. (1998). *Destination culture: Tourism, museums, and heritage.* Berkeley: University of California Press.

Kling, R. (2000). Learning about information technologies and social change: The role of social informatics. *Information Society, 16*, 217–232.

Knorr Cetina, K. (2003). *Posthumanist challenges to the human and social sciences.* Paper presented at the International Conference on The Role of Humanities in the Formation of New European Elites, Venice, Italy.

Koller, M. R. (1983). *Humor and society: Explorations in the sociology of humor.* Houston, TX: Cap & Gown.

Kropp, H. R., French, W. A., & Hillard, J. E. (1990). Trademark management—not brand management. *Business, 40*, 17–24.

Kunda, G. (1992). *Engineering culture.* Philadelphia: Temple University Press.

Kyl-Heku, L., & Buss, D. M. (1996). Tactics as units of analysis in personality psychology: An illustration using tactics of hierarchy negotiation. *Personality and Individual Differences, 21*, 497–517.

Lakoff, G., & Johnson, M. (1980). *Metaphors we live by.* Chicago: University of Chicago Press.

Lakoff, G., & Johnson, M. (1999). *Philosophy in the flesh: The embodied mind and its challenge to Western thought.* New York: Basic Books.

Lang, J. (1988). Symbolic aesthetics in architecture: Toward a research agenda. In J. L. Nasar (Ed.), *Environmental aesthetics: Theory, research and applications* (1st ed., pp. 11–26). Cambridge, England: Cambridge University Press.

Lasswell, H. (1979). *The signature of power.* Piscataway, NJ: Transaction.

Latour, B. (1987). *Science in action: How to follow scientists and engineers through society.* Milton Keynes: Open University Press.

Latour, B. (1992). Where are the missing masses? Sociology of a few mundane artifacts. In W. Bijker & J. Law (Eds.), *Shaping technology—building society: Studies in sociotechnical change* (pp. 225–259). Cambridge, MA: MIT Press.

Latour, B. (1996). *Aramis, or the love of technology.* Cambridge, MA: Harvard University Press.

Laumann, E. O., & Hase, J. S. (1969). Living room styles and social attributes: The patterning of material artifacts in a modern urban community. *Sociology and Social Research, 53*, 321–342.

Lave, J. (1988). *Cognition in practice: Mind, mathematics, and culture in everyday life.* Cambridge, England: Cambridge University Press.

Lave, J., & Wenger, E. (1991). *Situated learning: Legitimate peripheral participation.* Cambridge, England: Cambridge University Press.

Lavie, T., & Tractinsky, N. (2004). Assessing dimensions of perceived visual aesthetics of web sites. *International Journal of Human–Computer Studies, 60*(3), 269–298.

Law, J., & Hassard, J. (Eds.). (1999). *Actor network theory and after.* Oxford, England: Blackwell.

Leather, P., Pyrgas, M., Beale, D., & Lawrence, C. (1998). Windows in the workplace: Sunlight, view, and occupational stress. *Environment and Behavior, 6*(30), 739–762.

Lepore, L., & Brown, R. (1999). Exploring automatic stereotype activation: A challenge to the inevitability of prejudice. In D. Abrams & M. A. Hogg (Eds.), *Social cognition and social identity* (pp. 141–163). Oxford, England: Blackwell.

Levinson, S. (1983). *Pragmatics.* Cambridge, England: Cambridge University Press.

Levy, D. M. (2001). *Scrolling forward: Making sense of documents in the digital age.* New York: Arcade.

Lieberson, S., & Bell, E. O. (1992). Children's first names: An empirical study of social taste. *The American Journal of Sociology, 98*(3), 511–554.

Lieberson, S., Dumais, S., & Baumann, S. (2000). The instability of androgynous names: The symbolic maintenance of gender boundaries. *The American Journal of Sociology, 105*(5), 1249–1287.

Linstead, S., & Höpfl, H. (Eds.). (2000). *The aesthetics of organization.* London: Sage.

Litterer, J. A. (1973). *The analysis of organizations* (2nd ed.). New York: Wiley.

Locke, V., & Walker, I. (1999). Stereotyping, processing goals, and social identity: Inveterate and fugacious characteristics of stereotypes. In D. Abrams & M. A. Hogg (Eds.), *Social cognition and social identity* (pp. 164–182). Oxford, England: Blackwell.

Loomis, G. A., Ries, J. S., Saywell, R. M., & Thakker, N. R. (2002). If electronic medical records are so great, why aren't family physicians using them? *The Journal of Family Practice, 51*(7), 636–641.

Lord, C. G., & Saenz, D. S. (1985). Memory deficits and memory surfeits: Differential cognitive consequences of tokenism for tokens and observers. *Journal of Personality and Social Psychology, 49,* 918–926.

Lounsbury, M., & Kaghan, W. N. (2001). Organizations, occupations and the structuration of work. In S. P. Vallas (Ed.), *Research in the sociology of work* (Vol. 10, pp. 25–50). Oxford, England: JAI Press.

Lounsbury, M., & Rao, H. (2004). Sources of durability and change in market classifications: A study of the reconstitution of product categories in the American mutual fund industry, 1944–1985. *Social Forces, 82*(3), 969–999.

Lounsbury, M., & Ventresca, M. (2003). The new structuralism in organizational theory. *Organization, 10,* 457–480.

Lynn, L. A., & Bellini, L. M. (1999). Portable knowledge: A look inside white coat pockets. *Annals of Internal Medicine, 130*(3), 247–250.

Lyotard, J. F. (1984). *The postmodern condition: A report on knowledge.* Minneapolis: University of Minnesota Press.

Macaulay, S. (1963). Non-contractual relations in business: A preliminary study. *American Sociological Review, 28,* 55–67.

MacNeil, I. R. (1981). Economic analysis of contractual relations: Its shortfalls and the need for a rich classificatory apparatus. *Northwestern University Law Review, 75,* 1018–1063.

MacNeil, I. R. (1985). Relational contract: What we do and do not know. *Wisconsin Law Review, 3,* 483–525.

Macrae, C. N., & Bodenhausen, G. V. (2000). Social cognition: Thinking categorically about others. *Annual Review of Psychology, 51,* 93–120.

Malinowski, B. (1953). *Sex and repression in primitive society.* London: RKP.

Mangham, I. L. (1996). Beyond Goffman: Some notes on life and theatre as art. *Studies in Cultures, Organizations and Societies, 2*(1), 31–41.

March, J. (1994). *A primer on decision making. How decisions happen.* New York: The Free Press.

March, J. G., & Olsen, J. P. (1989). *Rediscovering institutions: The organizational basis of politics.* New York: The Free Press.

March, J. G., & Simon, H. A. (1958). *Organizations.* New York: Wiley.

Marks, G., & Miller, N. (1987). Ten years of research on the false consensus effect: An empirical and theoretical review. *Psychological Bulletin, 102,* 72–90.

Markus, H., & Wurf, E. (1987). The dynamic self-concept: A social psychological perspective. *Annual Review of Psychology, 38,* 299–337.

Markus, T. A. (1987). Buildings as classifying devices. *Environment and Planning B* (Journal previously called *Planning and Design*), *14,* 467–484.

Martin, J. (1990). Deconstructing organizational taboos: The suppression of gender conflict in organizations. *Organization Science, 1,* 339–359.

Martin, J. (1992). *Perspectives on organizational culture.* Oxford, England: Oxford University Press.

Masten, S. E. (Ed.). (1996). *Case studies in contracting and organization.* Oxford, England: Oxford University Press.

Mayer, J. P. (1956). *Max Weber and German politics. A study in political sociology.* London: Faber & Faber.

Mazumdar, S. (1988). *Organizational culture and physical environments.* Unpublished doctoral dissertation, MIT, Cambridge, MA.

McCall, M., & Belmont, H. J. (1996). Credit card insignia and restaurant tipping: Evidence for an associative link. *Journal of Applied Psychology, 81*(5), 609–613.

McCarthy, D. (1984). Towards a sociology of the physical world: George Hubert Mead on physical objects. *Studies in Symbolic Interaction, 5,* 105–121.

McCracken, G. (1988). *Culture and consumption: New approaches to the symbolic character of consumer goods and activities.* Bloomington: Indiana University Press.

Meeks, K. (2000). *Driving while Black: Highways, shopping malls, taxicabs, sidewalks: What to do if you are a victim of racial profiling.* New York: Broadway Books.

Mehrabian, A. (1972). *Nonverbal communication.* Chicago: Aldine.

Meinig, D. W. (Ed.). (1979). *The interpretation of ordinary landscapes.* New York: Oxford University Press.

Merrick, A. (2003, March 10). May I show you something I can't afford? *The Wall Street Journal,* pp. B1, B3.

Meyer, J. W., & Rowan, B. (1977a). The effects of education as an institution. *American Journal of Sociology, 83,* 55–77.

Meyer, J. W., & Rowan, B. (1977b). Institutionalized organizations: Formal structure as myth and ceremony. *American Journal of Sociology, 83,* 440–463.

Meyers-Levy, J., & Peracchio, L. A. (1995). Cognitive impact of banner ad characteristics: An experimental correspondence between available and required resources affect attitudes. *Journal of Consumer Research, 22,* 121–138.

Mildon, J., & Cohen, T. (2001). Drivers in the electronic medical records market. *Health Management Technology, 22*(5), 14.

Millward, L., & Kyriakidou, O. (2004). Linking pre- and post-merger identities through the concept of career. *Career Development International, 9*(1), 12–27.

Mitchell, C. (2002, January 1). Selling the brand inside. *Harvard Business Review,* pp. 99–103.

Mohr, J. W. (1998). Measuring meaning systems. *Annual Review of Sociology, 24,* 345–370.

Montuori, A. (2003). The complexity of improvisation and the improvisation of complexity: Social science, art and creativity. *Human Relations, 56*(2), 237–255.

Moore, M. C., & Harquail, C. V. (2003). *Creating the brand at Land Rover NA* (Teaching case, working draft). Charlottesville, VA: The Darden Graduate School of Business Administration.

Morgan, G. (1997). *Images of organization.* Thousand Oaks, CA: Sage.

Morgan, G., Frost, P. J., & Pondy, L. R. (1983). Organizational symbolism. In L. R. Pondy, P. J. Frost, G. Morgan, & T. C. Dandridge (Eds.), *Organizational symbolism* (pp. 3–35). Greenwich, CT: JAI Press.

Morita, A. (1987). *Made in Japan.* London: Collins.

Mosse, G. (1975). *The nationalization of the masses.* New York: Howard Fertig.

Muniz, A. M., & O'Guinn, T. C. (2001). Brand community. *Journal of Consumer Research, 27,* 412–432.

Murnighan, J. K., & Conlon, D. E. (1991). The dynamics of intense work groups: A study of British string quartets. *Administrative Science Quarterly, 36,* 165–186.

Nasar, J. L. (1994). Urban design aesthetics: The evaluative qualities of building exteriors. *Environment and Behavior, 26*(3), 377–401.

Nasar, J. L. (1997). New developments in aesthetics for urban design. In E. H. Zube & G. T. Moore (Eds.), *Advances in environment, behavior, and design* (Vol. 4, pp. 149–193). New York: Plenum Press.

NetEducation. (2003). http://www.sytty.net/nice/esittely/elogo.htm

Neuman, W. R., Just, M. R., & Crigler, A. N. (1992). *Common knowledge.* Chicago: University of Chicago Press.

Nicolini, D., Gherardi, S., & Yanow, D. (Eds.). (2003). *Knowing in organizations: A practice-based approach.* Armonk, NY: M. E. Sharpe.

Nielsen, J. (1994). *Usability engineering.* San Francisco: Morgan Kaufman.

Nielsen, J. (2000). *Designing web usability.* Indianapolis, IN: New Riders.

Nissley, N., Taylor, S., & Houden, L. (2004). The politics of performance in organizational theatre-based training and interventions. *Organization Studies, 25*(5), 817–839.

Nonaka, I. (1994). A dynamic theory of organizational knowledge creation. *Organization Science, 5,* 14–37.

Norman, D. (2004). *Emotional design.* New York: Basic Books.

Noschis, K. (1987). Public settings of a neighborhood: Identity and symbolism. *Architecture and Behavior, 3*(4), 301–316.

O'Connor, E. J., & Fiol, C. M. (2002). *Reclaiming your future: Entrepreneurial thinking in health care.* Tampa, FL: American College of Physician Executives.

Olins, W. (1989). *Corporate identity.* Boston: Harvard Business School Press.

Olins, W. (2000). Why brands are taking over the corporation. In M. Schultz, M. J. Hatch, & M. H. Larsen (Eds.), *The expressive organization—Linking identity, reputation, and the corporate brand.* Oxford, England: Oxford University Press.

Olins, W. (2000). *On brands.* London: Thames & Hudson.

Orenstein, J. (2003). Where have all the Lisas gone? *New York Times Magazine.*

Orlikowski, W. J. (1992). The duality of technology: Rethinking the concept of technology in organizations. *Organization Science, 3,* 398–427.

Orlikowski, W. J. (2000). Using technology and constituting structures: A practice lens for studying technology in organizations. *Organization Science, 11,* 404–428.

Orlikowski, W. J., & Barley, S. R. (2001). Technology and institutions: What can research on information technology and research on organizations learn from each other? *MIS Quarterly, 25,* 145–165.

Ornstein, S. (1986). Organizational symbols: A study of their meanings and influences on perceived psychological climate. *Organizational Behavior and Human Decision Processes, 38,* 207–229.

Ornstein, S. (1989). Impression management through office design. In R. A. Giacalone & P. Rosenfeld (Eds.), *Impression management in the organization* (pp. 411–426). Hillsdale, NJ: Lawrence Erlbaum Associates.

Orr, J. (1992, September). *Ethnography and organizational learning: In pursuit of learning at work.* Paper presented at the NATO Advanced Research Workshop, "Organizational Learning and Technological Change," Siena, Italy.

Orr, J. (1996). *Talking about machines: An ethnography of a modern job.* Ithaca, NY: Cornell University Press.

Owens, D. A., & Sutton, R. I. (2002). Status contests in meetings: Negotiating the informal order. In M. E. Turner (Ed.), *Groups at work: Advances in theory and research* (pp. 299–316). Mahwah, NJ: Lawrence Erlbaum Associates.

Pareyson, L. (1954). *Estetica. Teoria della formatività* [Aesthetics. Theory of formativeness]. Torino: Giappichelli.

Pentland, B. T., & Rueter, H. H. (1994). Organizational routines as grammars of action. *Administrative Science Quarterly, 39*(3), 484–510.

Perrow, C. (1984). *Normal accidents.* New York: Basic Books.

Peters, T., & Waterman, R. (1982). *In search of excellence.* New York: Harper & Row.

Peterson, R. A., & Anand, N. (2004). The production of culture perspective. *Annual Review of Sociology, 30,* 311–334.

Pettigrew, A. M. (1979). On studying organizational culture. *Administrative Science Quarterly, 24,* 570–581.

Pinch, T., & Bjiker, W. (1984). The social construction of facts and artifacts: Or how the sociology of science and the sociology of technology might benefit each other. *Social Studies of Science, 14,* 399–441.

Pine, B. J., & Gilmore, J. H. (1999). *The experience economy: Work is theatre and every business a stage.* Cambridge, MA: Harvard Business School Press.

Polanyi, M. (1962). *Personal knowledge. Towards a post-critical philosophy.* London: Routledge & Kegan Paul. (Original work published 1958)

Polanyi, M. (1966). *The tacit dimension.* New York: Doubleday.

Polinsky, A. M. (1989). *An introduction to law and economics* (2nd ed.). Boston: Little, Brown.

Pondy, L. R., Frost, P. J., Morgan, G., & Dandridge, T. C. (Eds.). (1983). *Organizational symbolism.* Greenwich, CT: JAI Press.

Postrel, V. (2001, July 12). Aesthetics and instrumentality: Can good looks guarantee a product's success? *The New York Times.* Retrieved from http://www.nytimes.com/2001/07/12/business/companies/12SCEN.html?ex995970994&ei=1&en=bdb495aaa2d11fc7

Prasad, P. (1993). Symbolic processes in the implementation of technological change: A symbolic interactionist study of work computerization. *Academy of Management Journal, 36,* 1400–1429.

Pratt, M. G. (2000). The good, the bad, and the ambivalent: Managing identification among Amway distributors. *Administrative Science Quarterly, 45*(3), 456–493.

Pratt, M. G., & Rafaeli, A. (1997). Organizational dress as a symbol of multilayered social identities. *Academy of Management Journal, 40*(4), 862–898.

Pratt, M. G., & Rafaeli, A. (2001). Symbols as a language of organizational relationships. *Research in Organizational Behavior, 23,* 93–133.

Prelinger, E. (1959). Extension and structure of the self. *The Journal of Psychology, 47,* 13–23.

Preston, S. H. (1998). Time to hang up the white coat? *Medical Economics, 75*(20), 149–150.

Preziosi, D. (1979). *Architecture, language, and meaning.* New York: Mouton.

Pringle, H., & Gordon, W. (2001). *Brand manners: How to create the self-confident organization to live the brand.* Chichester, England: Wiley.

Putnam, L. L., & Fairhurst, G. T. (2001). Discourse analysis in organizations: Issues and concerns. In F. M. Jablin & L. L. Putnam (Eds.), *The new handbook of organizational communication: Advances in theory, research, and methods* (pp. 78–136). Thousand Oaks, CA: Sage.

Putnam, L. L., & Pacanowsky, M. E. (Eds.). (1983). *Communication and organizations: An interpretive approach.* Beverly Hills, CA: Sage.

Putnam, L., Phillips, N., & Chapman, P. (1996). Metaphors of communication and organization. In S. R. Clegg, C. Hardy, & W. R. Nord (Eds.), *Handbook of organization studies* (pp. 375–408). London: Sage.

Quart, A. (2003). *Branded: The buying and selling of teenagers.* Cambridge, MA: Perseus.

Radcliffe-Brown, A. R. (1965). *Structure and function in primitive society.* New York: The Free Press.

Rafaeli, A., Barron, G., & Haber, K. (2002). The effects of queue structure on attitudes. *Journal of Service Research, 5*(2), 125–139.

Rafaeli, A., Dutton, J., Harquail, C. V., & Mackie-Lewis, S. (1997). Navigating by attire: The use of dress by female administrative employees. *Academy of Management Journal, 40*(1), 9–45.

Rafaeli, A., Kedmi, E., Vashdi, D., & Barron, G. (2003). *Queues and fairness: A multiple study investigation.* Unpublished manuscript, Faculty of Industrial Engineering and Management, Technion, Haifa, Israel.

Rafaeli, A., & Pratt, M. J. (1993). Tailored meaning: On the meaning and impact of organizational dress. *Academy of Management Review, 18*(1), 32–55.

Rafaeli, A., & Sutton, R. (1987). Expression of emotion as part of the work role. *The Academy of Management Review, 12*(1), 23–38.

Rafaeli, A., & Vilnai-Yavetz, I. (2003). Discerning organizational boundaries through physical artifacts. In N. Paulsen & T. Hernes (Eds.), *Managing boundaries in organizations: Multiple perspectives* (pp. 188–210). Basingstoke, Hampshire, England: Palgrave (Macmillan).

Rafaeli, A., & Vilnai-Yavetz, I. (2004a). Instrumentality, aesthetics, and symbolism of physical artifacts as triggers of emotions. *Theoretical Issues in Ergonomics Science, 5*(1), 91–112.

Rafaeli, A., & Vilnai-Yavetz, I. (2004b). Emotion as a connection of physical artifacts and organizations. *Organization Science, 15*(6), 671–686.

Rafaeli, A., & Worline, M. (2000). Symbols in organizational culture. In N. Ashkenazy, C. Wilderom, & M. Peterson (Eds.), *Handbook of organizational culture and climate* (pp. 71–84). Thousand Oaks, CA: Sage.

Ramirez, R. (1991). *The beauty of social organization.* Munich: Accedo.

Rapoport, A. (Ed.). (1976). *The mutual interaction of people and their built environment.* Paris: Mouton.

Rapoport, A. (1982). *The meaning of the built environment.* Beverly Hills, CA: Sage.

Raz, E. A. (1997). The slanted smile factory: Emotion management in Tokyo Disneyland. *Studies in Symbolic Interaction, 21,* 201–217.

Reynolds, B. (1987). *Material anthropology: Contemporary approaches to material culture.* Berkeley: University of California Press.

Richardson, J. (1996). Vertical integration and rapid response in fashion apparel. *Organization Science, 7*(4), 400–412.

Ricoeur, P. (1971). The model of the text: Meaningful action considered as text. *Social Research, 38,* 529–562.

Ritzer, G. (1996). *The McDonaldization of society* (Rev. ed.). Thousand Oaks, CA: Pine Forge Press.

Robertson, K. R. (1989). Strategically desirable brand name characteristics. *Journal of Consumer Marketing, 6,* 61–71.

Rosen, M. (2000). *Turning words, spinning worlds: Chapters in organizational ethnography.* Amsterdam: Harwood.

Rosen, M., Orlikowski, W. J., & Schmahmann, K. S. (1990). Building buildings and living lives. In P. Gagliardi (Ed.), *Symbols and artifacts: Views of the corporate landscape* (pp. 69–84). New York: Aldine de Gruyter.

Ross, L. (1977). The intuitive psychologist and his shortcomings: Distortions in the attribution process. In L. Berkowitz (Ed.), *Advances in experimental social psychology* (Vol. 10, pp. 174–221). New York: Academic Press.

Rothman, E. L. (2000). *White coat: Becoming a doctor at Harvard Medical School.* New York: HarperCollins.

Rousseau, D. M. (1995). *Psychological contracts in organizations: Understanding written and unwritten agreements.* Thousand Oaks, CA: Sage.

Rousseau, D. M. (2001). Schema, promise and mutuality: The building blocks of the psychological contract. *Journal of Occupational and Organizational Psychology, 74,* 511–541.

Rust, R. T., & Kannan, P. K. (2002). *E-service: New directions in theory and practice.* Armonk, NY: M. E. Sharpe.

Sassoon, J. (1990). Colors, artifacts, and ideologies. In P. Gagliardi (Ed.), *Symbols and artifacts: Views of the corporate landscape* (pp. 169–183). New York: Aldine de Gruyter.

Scalfi, A. (2003). *Performance, estetica e studi organizzativi* [Performance, aesthetics and organization studies]. Trento, Italy: University of Trento, Facoltà di Sociologia.

Schaber, G. D., & Rohwer, C. D. (1990). *Contracts* (3rd ed.). St. Paul, MN: West.

Schaffer, F. (forthcoming). Ordinary language interviewing. How narratives explain. In D. Yanow & P. Schwartz-Shea (Eds.), *Interpretation and method: Empirical research methods and the interpretive turn.* Armonk, NY: M. E. Sharpe.

Scheflen, A. E. (1974). Quasi-courtship behavior in psychotherapy. In S. Weitz (Ed.), *Nonverbal communication: Readings with commentary* (pp. 182–198). New York: Oxford University Press. (Original work published 1966)

Scheiberg, S. L. (1990). Emotions on display: The personal decoration of work space. *American Behavioral Scientist, 33*(3), 330–338.

Schein, E. (1984). Coming to a new awareness of organizational culture. *Sloan Management Review, 25*, 1–25.

Schein, E. (1985). *Organizational culture and leadership.* San Francisco: Jossey-Bass.

Schein, E. (1990). Organizational culture. *American Psychologist, 45*, 109–119.

Schein, E. (1991). What is culture? In P. Frost, L. F. Moore, M. R. Louis, C. C. Lundberg, & J. Martin (Eds.), *Reframing organizational culture* (pp. 243–253). Newbury Park, CA: Sage.

Schein, E. (1992). *Organizational culture and leadership* (2nd ed.). San Francisco: Jossey-Bass.

Scherer, A. G. (2003). Models of explanation in organizational theory. In H. Tsoukas & C. Knudsen (Eds.), *The Oxford handbook of organization theory* (pp. 310–344). Oxford, England: Oxford University Press.

Schlenker, B. R. (1980). *Impression management.* Monterey, CA: Brooks/Cole.

Schlenker, B. R., & Trudeau, J. V. (1990). Impact of self-presentations on private self-beliefs: Effects of prior self-beliefs and misattributions. *Journal of Personality and Social Psychology, 58*, 22–32.

Schmidt, R., Sr. (forthcoming). Value-critical policy analysis: The case of language policy in the U.S. How narratives explain. In D. Yanow & P. Schwartz-Shea (Eds.), *Interpretation and method: Empirical research methods and the interpretive turn.* Armonk, NY: M. E. Sharpe.

Schmitt, B., & Simonson, A. (1997). *Marketing aesthetics—the strategic management of brands, identity, and image.* New York: The Free Press.

Schön, D. A. (1983). *The reflective practitioner: How professionals think in action.* New York: Basic Books.

Schön, D. A., & Rein, M. (1994). *Frame reflection.* New York: Basic Books.

Schultz, M. (1994). *On studying organizational cultures.* Berlin: Walter de Gruyter.

Schultz, M. (2000, August 6). *Constructing symbols: New interfaces between management and design.* Paper presented at the annual meeting of The Academy of Management, Toronto, Canada.

Schultz, M., & De Chernatony (Eds.). (2002). *Corporate Reputation Review, 3–4.* Special Issue on Corporate Branding.

Schultz, M., & Hatch, M. J. (2003). Cycles of corporate branding: The case of LEGO Company. *California Management Review, 46*(1), 6–26.

Schwartz-Shea, P. (forthcoming). Judging quality: Evaluative criteria and epistemic communities. In D. Yanow & P. Schwartz-Shea (Eds.), *Interpretation and method: Empirical research methods and the interpretive turn.* Armonk, NY: M. E. Sharpe, ch. 5.

Scott, J. C. (1998). *Seeing like a state: How certain schemes to improve the human condition have failed.* New Haven, CT: Yale University Press.

Scott, W. R. (2001). *Institutions and organizations* (2nd ed.). Newbury Park, CA: Sage.

Scott, W. R., Ruef, M., Mendel, P., & Caronna, C. (2000). *Institutional change and healthcare organizations: From professional dominance to managed care.* Chicago: University of Chicago Press.

Serres, M. (1974). *La Traduction. Hermes III* [The translation]. Paris: Editions de Minuit.

Sevon, G. (1996). Organizational imitation in identity transformation. In B. Czarniawska & G. Sevon (Eds.), *Translating organizational change* (pp. 49–68). Berlin: Walter de Gruyter.

Sheridan, J. E. (1992). Organizational culture and employee retention. *Academy of Management Journal, 35*, 1036–1056.

Shim, S., & Bickle, M. C. (1994). Benefit segments of the female apparel market: Psychographics, shopping orientations, and demographics. *Clothing and Textiles Research Journal, 12*, 1–12.

Shortell, S. M., Morrison, E. M., & Friedman, B. (1990). *Strategic choices for America's hospitals: Managing change in turbulent times.* San Francisco: Jossey-Bass.

Shotter, J. (1993a). *Conversational realities: Constructing life through language.* London: Sage.

Shotter, J. (1993b). *Cultural politics of everyday life: Social constructionism, rhetoric, and knowing of the Third Kind.* Milton Keynes: Open University Press. London: Sage.

Shotter, J. (2003). Cartesian change, chiasmic change B the power of living expression. *Janus Head: Journal of Interdisciplinary Studies in Literature, Continental Philosophy, Phenomenological Psychology and the Arts, 6*(1), 6–29.

Shotter, J., & Cunliffe, A. L. (2002). Managers as practical authors: Everyday conversations for action. In D. Holman & R. Thorpe (Eds.), *Management and language: The manager as practical author* (pp. 15–37). London: Sage.

Shumaker, S. A., & Pequegnat, W. (1989). Hospital design, health providers, and the delivery of effective health care. In E. H. Zube & G. T. Moore (Eds.), *Advances in environment, behavior, and design* (Vol. 2, pp. 161–199). New York: Plenum Press.

Simmel, G. (1998). *Die Mode* [Fashion]. La moda, Arnoldo Mondadori Editore, Milano. (Origin work published in 1895)

Simmel, G. (1904). Fashion. *International Quarterly, 10*(1), 130–155. (Reprinted 1957, *American Journal of Sociology, 62*(6), 541–558)

Simon, H. A. (1969). The architecture of complexity. In *The sciences of the artificial* (pp. 192–229). Cambridge, MA: MIT Press.

Snow, D. A., & Anderson, L. (1987). Identity work among the homeless: The verbal construction and avowal of personal identities. *American Journal of Sociology, 92*(6), 1336–1371.

Solomon, S. M. R. (1983). The role of products as social stimuli: A symbolic interactionism perspective. *Journal of Consumer Research, 10*, 319–329.

Spinosa, C., Flores, F., & Dreyfus, H. L. (1997). *Disclosing new worlds: Entrepreneurship, democratic action, and the cultivation of solidarity*. Cambridge, MA: MIT Press.

Sproull, L. S. (1981). Beliefs in organizations. In P. C. Nystrom & W. H. Starbuck (Eds.), *Handbook of organizational design* (pp. 203–224). Oxford, England: Oxford University Press.

Stanovich, K. E., & West, R. F. (1998). Individual differences in rational thought. *Journal of Experimental Psychology, 127*, 161–188.

Star, S. L. (1989). The structure of ill-structured solutions: Boundary objects and heterogeneous distributed problem solving. In M. Huhns & L. Gasser (Eds.), *Readings in distributed artificial intelligence* (Vol. 2, pp. 37–54). Menlo Park, CA: Morgan Kaufman.

Star, S. L., & Ruhleder, K. (1996). Steps toward an ecology of infrastructure: Design and access for large information spaces. *Information Systems Research, 7*, 111–134.

Starr, P. (1982). *The social transformation of American medicine*. New York: Basic Books.

Staw, B. M., Sandelands, L. E., & Dutton, J. E. (1981). Threat-rigidity effects in organizational behavior: A multilevel analysis. *Administrative Science Quarterly, 26*, 501–524.

Steele, C. M. (1988). The psychology of self-affirmation: Sustaining the integrity of the self. In L. Berkowitz (Ed.), *Advances in experimental social psychology* (Vol. 21, pp. 261–302). New York: Academic Press.

Steele, F. I. (1973). *Physical settings and organization development*. Menlo Park, CA: Addison-Wesley.

Steele, F. I. (1981). *The sense of place*. Boston: CBI.

Steele, K. M., & Smithwick, L. E. (1989). First names and first impressions: A fragile relationship. *Sex Roles, 21*, 517–523.

Stein, S. J. (2001). "These are your Title I students": Policy language in educational practice. *Policy Sciences, 34*, 135–156.

Steinem, G. (1983). *Outrageous acts and everyday rebellions*. New York: Holt, Rinehart & Winston.

Stephenson, R. M. (1951). Conflict and control functions of humor. *American Journal of Sociology, 56*, 569–574.

Stern, S. (1988). Symbolic representation of organizational identity: The role of emblem at the Garrett Corporation. In M. O. Jones, M. D. Moore, & R. C. Snyder (Eds.), *Inside organizations: Understanding the human dimension* (pp. 281–295). London: Sage.

Steyaert, C., & Hjorth, D. (2002). Thou art a scholar, speak to it—on spaces of speech: A script. *Human Relations, 55*(7), 767–797.

Stinchcombe, A. L. (1990). *Information and organizations*. Berkeley: University of California Press.

Strang, D., & Meyer, J. W. (1994). Institutional conditions for diffusion. In R. Scott & J. W. Meyer (Eds.), *Institutional environments and organizations* (pp. 100–112). Thousand Oaks, CA: Sage.

Strati, A. (1992). Aesthetic understanding of organizational life. *Academy of Management Review, 17*(3), 568–581.

Strati, A. (1996). Organizations viewed through the lens of aesthetics. *Organization, 3*(2), 209–218.

Strati, A. (1999). *Organization and aesthetics* (1st ed.). London: Sage.

Strati, A. (2000). *Theory and method in organization studies. Paradigms and choices.* London: Sage.

Strati, A., & Guillet de Monthoux, P. (2002). Organizing aesthetics. Introduction to the special issue. *Human Relations, 55*(7), 755–766.

Strauss, A. L. (1978). *Negotiations: Contexts, processes, and social order.* San Francisco: Jossey-Bass.

Strauss, A. L. (1988). The articulation of project work: An organizational process. *Sociological Quarterly, 29,* 163–178.

Strauss, A. L. (1993). *Continual permutations of action.* New York: Aldine de Gruyter.

Strauss, A. L., Bucher, R., Ehrlich, D., Schatzman, L., & Sabshin, M. (1964). *Psychiatric ideologies and institutions.* New York: The Free Press.

Suchman, L., Trigg, R., & Blomberg, J. (2002). Working artifacts: Ethnomethods of the prototype. *British Journal of Sociology, 53*(2), 163–179.

Suchman, M. C. (1995a). *The contracting universe: Law firms, venture capital funds and the institutionalization of new-company financing in Silicon Valley* (Working Paper). Madison: University of Wisconsin, Department of Sociology.

Suchman, M. C. (1995b). Managing legitimacy: Strategic and institutional approaches. *Academy of Management Review, 20,* 571–610.

Suchman, M. C. (2003). The contract as social artifact. *Law & Society Review, 37*(1), 91–142.

Sundstrom, E., & Altman, I. (1989). Physical environments and work-group effectiveness. In L. L. Cummings & B. M. Staw (Eds.), *Research in organizational behavior* (Vol. 11, pp. 175–209). Greenwich, CT: JAI Press.

Sundstrom, E., Bell, P. A., Busby, P. L., & Asmus, C. (1996). Environmental psychology 1989–1994. In J. T. Spence, J. M. Darley, & D. J. Foss (Eds.), *Annual review of psychology* (Vol. 47, pp. 485–512). Palo Alto, CA: Annual Reviews Inc.

Sundstrom, E., & Sundstrom, M. G. (1986). *Work places: The psychology of the physical environment in offices and factories.* Cambridge, England: Cambridge University Press.

Sundstrom, E., Town, J., Brown, D. Forman, A., & McGee, C. (1982). Physical enclosure, type of job, and privacy in the office. *Environment and Behavior, 14,* 543–559.

Swann, W. B., Jr. (1987). Identity negotiation: Where two roads meet. *Journal of Personality and Social Psychology, 6,* 1038–1051.

Swartz, T. A. (1983). Brand symbols and message differentiation: Viable tools for product differentiation? *Journal of Advertising Research, 23*(5), 59–64.

Swidler, A. (1986). Culture in action: Symbols and strategies. *American Sociological Review, 51,* 273–286.

Takahashi, S. (1995). Aesthetic properties of pictorial perception. *Psychological Review, 102*(4), 671–683.

Taylor, C. (1971). Interpretation & the sciences of man. *Review of Metaphysics, 25,* 3–51.

Taylor, S. E. (1981). A categorization approach to stereotyping. In D. L. Hamilton (Ed.), *Cognitive processes in stereotyping and intergroup behavior* (pp. 88–114). Hillsdale, NJ: Lawrence Erlbaum Associates.

Temple, L. E., & Loewen, K. R. (1993). Perceptions of power: First impressions of a woman wearing a jacket. *Perceptual and Motor Skills, 76,* 339–348.

Thatcher, S. M. B., Doucet, L., & Tuncel, E. (2003). Subjective identities and identity communication processes in information technology teams. In M. A. Neale, E. A. Mannix, & J. T. Polzer (Eds.), *Research on managing groups and teams* (Vol. 5, pp. 53–90). London, UK: Elsevier Science, Ltd.

Thomas, J. B., Clark, S. M., & Gioia, D. A. (1993). Strategic sensemaking and organizational performance: Linkages among scanning, interpretation, action, and outcomes. *Academy of Management Journal, 36,* 239–270.

Toulmin, S. (1982). The genealogy of consciousness. In P. F. Secord (Ed.), *Explaining human behavior: Consciousness, human action, and social structure.* Beverly Hills, CA: Sage.

Tractinsky, N., & Zmiri, D. (in press). Exploring attributes of skins as potential antecedents of emotion in HCI. In P. Fishwick (Ed.), *Aesthetic computing.* Boston, MA: MIT Press.

Tracy, S. J. (2000). Becoming a character for commerce: Emotion labor, self-subordination, and discursive construction of identity in a total institution. *Management Communication Quarterly, 14*(1), 90–128.

Trethewey, A. (1999). Disciplined bodies: Women's embodied identities at work. *Organization Studies, 20*(3), 432–450.

Trice, H. M., & Beyer, J. M. (1984). Studying organizational culture through rites and ceremonials. *Academy of Management Review, 9*(4), 653–669.

Trice, H. M., & Beyer, J. M. (1993). *The cultures of work organizations.* Englewood Cliffs, NJ: Prentice-Hall.

Turner, B. (1990). *Organizational symbolism.* Berlin: de Gruyter.

Tyler, T. R. (1999). Why people co-operate with organizations: An identity-based perspective. In B. M. Staw & R. Sutton (Eds.), *Research in organizational behavior* (Vol. 21, pp. 201–246). Greenwich, CT: JAI Press.

The ultimate LEGO book. (1999). London: Dorling Kindersly.

van Buskirk, W., & McGrath, D. (1999). Organizational cultures as holding environments: A psychodynamic look at organizational symbolism. *Human Relations, 52,* 805–832.

Van der Weyden, M. B. (2001). White coats and the medical profession: Time to rediscover the symbol of our purpose and our pride? *Medical Journal of Australia, 174,* 324–325.

Van Maanen, J. (1978). Observations on the making of policemen. *Human Organization, 32,* 407–418.

Van Maanen, J. (1991). The smile factory: Work at Disneyland. In P. J. Frost, L. F. Moore, M. R. Louis, C. C. Lundberg, & J. Martin (Eds.), *Reframing organizational culture* (pp. 58–76). Newbury Park, CA: Sage.

Van Maanen, J. (1995a). The smile factory: Work at Disneyland. In B. M. Staw (Ed.), *Psychological dimensions of organizational behavior* (pp. 290–302). Englewood Cliffs, NJ: Prentice-Hall.

Van Maanen, J. (1995b). Style as theory. *Organization Science, 6,* 133–143.

Van Maanen, J. (1996). Commentary: On the matter of voice. *Journal of Management Inquiry, 5,* 375–381.

Vaughan, D. (1996). *The Challenger launch decision: Risky technology, culture, and deviance at NASA.* Chicago: University of Chicago Press.

Veblen, T. (1979). *Theory of the leisure class.* New York: Viking Penguin. (Original work published 1899)

Veblen, T. (1992). *The theory of the leisure class.* London: Transaction. (Original work published 1899)

Vico, G. (1968). *The new science of Giambattista Vico* (T. G. Bergin & M. H. Fisch, Eds.). Ithaca, NY: Cornell University Press. (Original work published 1725)

Vilnai-Yavetz, I., Rafaeli, A., & Ramati, T. (2004). *The influence of appearance of service providers on customers.* Manuscript under review.

Vilnai-Yavetz, I., Rafaeli, A., & Schneider-Yaacov, C. (2005). Instrumentality, aesthetics and symbolism of office design. *Environment and Behavior, 37*(4), 533–551.

Vitruvius. (1934). *Vitruvius on architecture.* Boston: Harvard University Press.

Vitruvius. (1960). *The ten books on architecture.* New York: Dover.

Vogel, A., & Kaghan, W. N. (2001). Bureaucrats, brokers and the entrepreneurial university. *Organization, 8*(2), 358–365.

von Hippel, E., & Tyre, M. (1996). The mechanics of learning by doing: Problem discovery during process machine use. *Technology and Culture, 37,* 312–329.

Waibel, M. C., & Wicklund, R. A. (1994). Inferring competence from incompetence: An ironic process associated with person description. *European Journal of Social Psychology, 24,* 443–452.

Warner, W. L. (1959). *The living and the dead.* New Haven, CT: Yale University Press.

Webb, E. J., Campbell, D. T., Schwartz, R. D., Sechrest, L., & Grove, J. B. (1981). *Nonreactive measures in the social sciences* Boston: Houghton Mifflin (Original work title *Unobtrusive measures* and published 1966).

Weber, M. (1922). *Wirtschaft und Gesellschaft. Grundriß der verstehenden Soziologie* [Economy and society: An outline of interpretive sociology]. Tübingen: Mohr.

Weber, M. (1956). On bureaucratization. In J. P. Mayer (Ed.), *Max Weber and German politics. A study in political sociology* (pp. 125–131). London: Faber & Faber.

Weick, K. E. (1979). *The social psychology of organizing.* Reading, MA: Addison-Wesley. (Original work published 1969)

Weick, K. E. (1995). *Sensemaking in organizations* (Foundations for Organizational Science Series). Beverly Hills, CA: Sage.

Weick, K. E. (2001). *Making sense of the organization.* Oxford, England: Blackwell.

Weick, K. E., & Roberts, K. H. (1993). Collective mind in organizations: Heedful interrelating on flight decks. *Administrative Science Quarterly, 38,* 357–381.

Weitz, S. (1974). *Nonverbal communication: Readings with commentary.* New York: Oxford University Press.

Wenger, E. (1999). *Communities of practice: Learning, meaning, and identity.* Cambridge, England: Cambridge University Press.

Wernick, A. (1994). Vehicles for myth: The shifting image of the modern car. In S. Maasik & J. Solomon (Eds.), *Signs of life in the U.S.A.: Readings on popular culture for writers* (pp. 78–94). Boston: Bedford Books.

Whalen, J., Whalen, M., & Henderson, K. (2002). Improvisional choreography in teleservice work. *British Journal of Sociology, 53*(2), 239–258.

Whetten, D. (2003, October). *Identity* (Working Paper). Provo, UT: Brigham Young University, Marriott School of Management.

White, J. D. (1992). Taking language seriously: Toward a narrative theory of knowledge for administrative research. *The American Review of Public Administration, 22,* 75–88.

Whyte, W. F. (1955). *Street corner society.* Chicago: University of Chicago Press. (Original work published 1943)

Wicklund, R. A., Braun, O. L., & Waibel, M. C. (1994). Expertise in performance or interest in the performing person? Some evidence for mutual exclusiveness. *European Journal of Social Psychology, 24,* 425–441.

Williamson, O. E. (1985). *The economic institutions of capitalism.* New York: The Free Press.

Willmott, H. (1993). Strength is ignorance, slavery is freedom: Managing culture in modern organizations. *Journal of Management Studies, 30*(4), 512–552.

Wittgenstein, L. (1953). *Philosophical investigations.* Oxford, England: Blackwell.

Wittgenstein, L. (1980). *Culture and value* (P. Winch, Trans.). Oxford, England: Blackwell.

Wittgenstein, L. (1981). *Zettel* (2nd ed.) (G. E. M. Anscombe & G. H. V. Wright, Eds.). Oxford, England: Blackwell.

Yanow, D. (1992). Supermarkets and culture clash: The epistemological role of metaphors in administrative practice. *American Review of Public Administration, 22,* 89–109.

Yanow, D. (1993). Reading policy meanings in organization-scapes. *Journal of Architectural and Planning Research, 10,* 308–327.

Yanow, D. (1995). Built space as story: The policy stories that buildings tell. *Policy Studies Journal, 23*(3), 407–422.

Yanow, D. (1996). *How does a policy mean? Interpreting policy and organizational actions.* Washington, DC: Georgetown University Press.

Yanow, D. (1998). Space stories: Studying museum buildings as organizational spaces while reflecting on interpretive methods and their narration. *Journal of Management Inquiry, 7*(3), 215–239.

Yanow, D. (2000). *Conducting interpretive policy analysis.* Newbury Park, CA: Sage.

Yanow, D. (2001). Learning in and from improvising: Lessons from theater for organizational learning. *Reflections* (The Society for Organizational Learning Journal), *2*(4), 58–62.

Yanow, D. (2003, December 7–10). *Privileging text, ignoring context: On the importance of "objects" in the communication of organizational meaning.* Paper presented in the "Discourse analysis and management practice" stream, 10th APROS International Colloquium, Oaxaca, Mexico.

Yanow, D., & Schwartz-Shea, P. (Eds.). (forthcoming). *Interpretation and method: Empirical research methods and the interpretive turn.* Armonk, NY: ME Sharpe.

Yates, J., & Orlikowski, W. J. (1992). Genres of organizational communication. *Academy of Management Review, 17,* 299–326.

Yun, M. H., Han, S. H., Kim, K. J., Kwahk, J., Hong, S. W., & Kim, J. S. (2001). Incorporating user satisfaction into the look-and-feel of wireless phones. In M. G. Helander, H. M. Khalid, & P. M. Po (Eds.), *Proceedings of The International Conference on Affective Human Factors Design* (pp. 423–429). Singapore: ASEAN Academic Press.

Zeisel, J. (1981). *Inquiry by design.* Monterey, CA: Brooks/Cole.

Zenardelli, H. A. (1967). Testimonial to life in a landscape. *Office Design, 5,* 30–36.

Zollo, M., & Winter, S. G. (2002). Deliberate learning and the evolution of dynamic capabilities. *Organization Science, 13,* 339–351.

Zucker, L. G. (1988). Where do institutional patterns come from? Organizations as actors in social systems. In L. G. Zucker (Ed.), *Institutional patterns and organizations* (pp. 23–49). Cambridge, MA: Ballinger.

Zucker, L. G. (1991). The role of institutionalization in cultural persistence. In W. W. Powell & P. J. DiMaggio (Eds.), *The new institutionalism in organizational analysis* (pp. 83–107). Chicago: University of Chicago Press.

Author Index

Note: Page numbers followed by "n" refer to footnotes.

A

Aaker, D. A., 14, 15, 142, 149, 150
Abbott, A., 264
Abzug, R. A., 182, 192, 223, 225, 226, 227, 229, 230, 231
Adams, G. B., 48
Adorno, T. W., 86
Ainamo, A., 201
Albert, S., 185, 196, 212, 229
Aldrich, H. E., 243
Allen, S. D., 46
Altman, I., 63, 64
Alvesson, M., 173
American Academy of Family Practice Physicians, 254
Anand, N., 86
Anderson, L., 171
Antorini, Y. M., 151
Argyris, C., 46, 122
Ashforth, B. E., 62, 173, 242
Asmus, C., 63
Atwood, G. E., 44
Avraham, E., 14, 15

B

Bacharach, S. B., 249
Bakhtin, M. M., 125, 130–131, 132, 133

Balmer, J., 142, 149
Bamberger, P., 249
Banaji, M. R., 69
Bansal, P., 19, 20
Barley, S. R., 103, 260, 261
Barnett, G. B., 268n
Baron, R. A., 10
Barrett, T. G., 244, 247
Barron, G., 18
Bartel, C., 171, 241
Barthes, R., 201, 202
Barzel, Y., 265
Bateson, G., 132, 132n
Baudrillard, J., 37
Baumann, S., 224
Baumgarten, A. G., 38
Beale, D., 10
Beamish, T. D., 263
Bechky, B., 261
Becker, F. D., 23, 42, 56
Becker, G. S., 268
Becker, H. S., 38, 47n, 259, 260, 262
Belch, G. E., 189, 192
Belch, M. A., 189, 192
Belk, R. W., 171, 173, 244, 254, 256, 284
Bell, E. O., 229
Bell, P. A., 63
Bellini, L. M., 244
Belmont, H. J., 10
Benedict, R., 86

Bennett, P. D., 183
Berg, P. O., 14
Berger, P. L., 45, 282
Berleant, A., 15
Beyer, J. M., 10, 13, 14, 189, 210, 283
Bickerton, D., 273
Bickle, M. C., 174
Biggart, N. W., 263
Biner, P., 64
Bitner, M. J., 21
Bjiker, W., 103
Black, L., 102
Blomberg, J., 23
Blumer, H., 201, 260, 265
Blum-Kulka, S., 287
Boden, D., 269, 287
Bodenhausen, G. V., 68, 80
Bohman, J. F., 42
Boorstin, D. J., 216
Booth, I. W., 244, 247
Bourdieu, P., 103, 202, 210, 259, 260, 262
Bowker, G. C., 101, 260, 261, 273
Branca, R. C. T., 270
Braun, O. L., 69
Breward, C., 201, 202
Brewer, M. B., 62, 245
Brickson, S., 62
Brown, D., 63
Brown, J. S., 102, 262
Brown, R., 67, 80
Brown, R. W., 226
Bucher, R., 264
Bunderson, J. S., 248, 249
Burke, K., 48
Burns, R., 64
Busby, P. L., 63
Buss, D. M., 71
Butler, D., 64
Button, G., 23

Carlile, P. R., 102, 103, 105
Caronna, C., 248
Cass, R. C., 11
Chapman, P., 25
Charrow, V. R., 272n
Chia, R., 122, 125
Chittipeddi, K., 211, 283
Christopher, _, 65
Ciborra, C., 23
Cillo, P., 203
Clark, K., 102
Clark, S. M., 215
Clarke, A., 101
Clegg, S., 173, 267
Clifford, J., 122
Cohen, A., 146, 147
Cohen, D., 182, 183
Cohen, J. B., 173
Cohen, T., 250
Cohen, W. M., 270
Collins, J. C., 149
Collinson, D. L., 94, 97, 173
The Conference Board, 163
Conley, S. C., 249
Conlon, D. E., 94
Cooley, C. H., 171
Cooper, C., 44
Cooper, R., 122
Corley, K., 151, 212, 214
Cote, J. A., 183
Covaleski, M. A., 173
Crigler, A. N., 48
Crowley, D., 202
Crowston, K., 262
Crystal, D., 273
Csikszentmihalyi, M., 14, 284
Cunliffe, A. L., 119, 120, 122, 131, 135, 136
Czarniawska, B., 152
Czarniawska-Joerges, B., 185

C

Cairns, G., 26
Callon, M., 23, 274
Campbell, D. E., 211
Campbell, D. T., 57n
Canter, D., 11, 12
Cappetta, R., 201, 203, 259, 265
Cardy, R. L., 161
Carey, J. W., 90

D

Dandridge, T. C., 11, 146, 182, 185
Davis, F., 166, 170, 171, 174, 201, 201n
Davis, S. M., 161, 162
Davis, T. R. V., 10, 14, 211
Dean, J. W. J., 13
de Chernatony, L., 143, 175, 189
Deleuze, G., 146
Derrida, J., 24

Descamps, M.-A., 201
Devine, P. G., 65
DiMaggio, P. J., 242
Dines-Levy, G., 97
Dirsmith, M. W., 173
Dittmar, H., 62, 65, 70
Djelic, M. L., 201
Doucet, L., 171
Dougherty, D., 109, 275
Douglas, M., 90, 260
Doxtater, D., 56
Dreyfus, H. L., 136
Duguid, P., 102, 262
Dukerich, J. M., 176, 182, 200, 212
Dumais, S., 224
Dunn, M., 161, 162
Durgee, J. F., 182
Durkheim, E., 87, 259
Dutton, J., 16, 56, 64, 168, 171, 172, 200,
    212, 241
Dutton, J. E., 176, 182, 250

E

Eco, U., 201
Edelman, L. B., 260, 265
Edelman, M. J., 44, 59, 60, 88, 211, 217
Ehn, P., 23
Ehrlich, D., 264
Eisenman, M., 13, 19
Elgin, C. Z., 44
Elliott, R., 174
Elsbach, K. D., 61, 62, 63, 65, 66, 69, 71, 73,
    79, 80, 81, 165
Emery, F., 261
Engestrom, Y., 101
Entwistle, J., 166, 171
Erickson, E. H., 218
Erlandson, D. A., 46
Etzkowitz, H., 270

F

Fairhurst, G. T., 229
Feldman, M. S., 48, 50, 260, 286
Fiell, C., 280
Fiell, P., 280
Fineman, S., 38
Fiol, C. M., 45, 243, 249, 260

First, A., 14, 15
Firth, R., 149
Fischer, F., 42
Fiske, J., 282
Fiske, S. T., 65, 66, 67, 68, 79
Flanders, V., 12
Flood, A. B., 243, 248
Flores, F., 136
Foley, W. A., 273
Fombrun, C. J., 142, 195, 212
Forester, J., 42
Forman, A., 63
Foucault, M., 122
Fournier, S., 142, 150
Frank, M. G., 10
Frank, R., 62
French, W. A., 182
Freud, S., 89
Friedman, B., 248
Frost, P. J., 11, 146, 185, 229
Fujimura, J., 101
Fujimura, J. H., 259, 271

G

Gabriel, Y., 182, 183, 185
Gagliardi, P., 10, 13, 14, 15, 23, 42, 86, 146,
    147, 186, 210, 259, 280, 282, 286
Galison, P., 272, 273
Garfinkel, H., 122
Garling, T., 12
Gecas, V., 172
Geer, B., 47n
Geertz, C., 86, 251, 259
Geiger, R. L., 270
Gelder, K., 86, 93
Gephardt, C., 270
Gergen, K. J., 120
Gherardi, S., 25, 38
Gibson, J. J., 12, 19, 287
Giddens, A., 260
Gilbert, D. T., 65
Gilmore, J. H., 161
Gilovich, T., 10
Gioia, D. A., 151, 183, 211, 212, 214, 215,
    259, 265, 283
Glynn, M. A., 165, 182, 192, 223, 225, 226,
    227, 229, 230, 231
Goffman, E., 91, 128, 129
Golledge, R. G., 12

Goodman, N., 44, 45n
Goodrich, R., 11
Goodrick, E., 243, 244, 248
Goodsell, C. T., 44, 51
Gordon, W., 161, 165, 166
Gordon, W. H., 245
Gottdiener, M., 44
Gouldner, A. W., 122

Greenhouse, S., 166
Greyser, S., 142, 149
Griswold, W., 86
Grove, J. B., 57n
Guattari, F., 146
Gubrium, J. F., 57n
Guillet de Monthoux, P., 24, 27, 39, 186, 196
Gusfield, J. R., 48

H

Haber, K., 18
Hackley, C., 161
Hafferty, F. W., 248, 253
Hall, E. T., 55
Hamilton, J. R., 24
Han, S. H., 13
Harquail, C. V., 16, 56, 64, 167, 168, 171,
        172, 175, 176, 178, 182, 200, 212, 259
Harris, E. L., 46
Hassard, J., 23
Hatch, M. J., 10, 11, 14, 23, 42, 43, 56, 86,
        97, 103, 141, 142, 143, 144, 145, 146,
        149, 151, 176, 185, 188, 194, 196, 259
Heath, C., 23
Hebdige, D., 91
Heian, J. B., 173
Heidegger, M., 122
Helander, M. G., 15
Helman, B., 175
Henderson, K., 24
Henderson, P. W., 183
Herman, D., 174
Hershberger, R. G., 11
Herzberg, E., 16
Heskett, J., 10, 182, 187
Hiley, D. R., 42
Hillard, J. E., 182
Hipple, E., 104
Hirsch, P. M., 226
Hirschman, E. C., 10, 14, 15

Hjorth, D., 27
Hochschild, A., 16
Hodge, R., 250
Hofstede, G., 186
Hogg, M. A., 250
Holstein, J. A., 57n
Hong, S. W., 13
Höpfl, H., 24, 38
Horkheimer, M., 86
Hornby, A. S., 10
Hornsey, M. J., 250
Houden, L., 24
Howell, W. C., 15
Hughes, E., 47n
Hughes, E. C., 260
Hughes, T., 103
Humphrey, R. H., 173

I

Ibarra, H., 64, 172
Ickes, W. J., 67
Ind, N., 143, 161, 162, 163, 165
Ingersoll, V. H., 48
Iser, W., 48
Isherwood, B., 90

J

Jablin, F. M., 269
Jackson, J. B., 44
James, W., 244, 279
Jauss, H. R., 25
Joachimstahler, E., 142, 149
Jobling, P., 202
Joerges, B., 185
Johnson, M., 21, 52, 280
Jones, E. E., 68
Jones, M. O., 56, 85
Jones, V. A., 244, 245, 246, 247, 249
Jost, J. T., 69
Jung, G. G., 185
Just, M. R., 48

K

Kaghan, W. N., 260, 261, 268n
Kahneman, D., 280
Kamerrer, E. E., 262

Kannan, P. K., 20
Kant, I., 38
Kanter, R. M., 48
Kaplan, R., 17
Kaplan, S., 17
Karliner, J., 20
Kasper, G., 287
Kassin, S. M., 71
Kedmi, E., 18
Keller, K. L., 162
Kelman, H. C., 172
Kemper, T. D., 56n
Kets de Vries, M., 88
Khalid, H. M., 15
Kim, J. S., 13
Kim, K. J., 13
King, A. R., 64
King, A. W., 178
Kirshenblatt-Gimblett, B., 44
Kling, R., 262
Knorr Cetina, K., 24
Koller, M. R., 89, 96
Kramer, R. M., 62, 79
Kreiner, K., 14
Kropp, H. R., 182
Kunda, G., 48, 149
Kwahk, J., 13
Kyl-Heku, L., 71
Kyriakidou, O., 185

L

Lagopoulos, A. P., 44
Lakoff, G., 21, 52, 280
Lang, J., 11
Lasswell, H., 44, 56
Latour, B., 23, 103, 259, 262, 269
Lave, J., 102, 104, 122, 262
Lavie, T., 15
Law, J., 23
Lawrence, C., 10
Leather, P., 10
Lepore, L., 67, 80
Levinson, S., 287
Levinthal, D. A., 270
Levy, D. M., 267
Lieberson, S., 224, 229
Light, D. W., 248, 253
Linstead, S., 24, 38
Litterer, J. A., 183
Locke, V., 67, 80

Lofstrom, S. M., 248, 249
Loomis, G. A., 250
Lord, C. G., 67
Lounsbury, M., 260
Lovegrove, T., 64
Luckmann, T., 45, 282
Lynn, L. A., 244
Lyotard, J. F., 122

M

Macaulay, S., 265
Mackie-Lewis, S., 16, 56, 64, 168, 172
MacNeil, I. R., 265
Macrae, C. N., 68, 80
Mael, F., 62, 173, 242
Malinowski, B., 102
Mangham, I. L., 24
Manzi, J. M., 62, 245
March, J., 36
March, J. G., 229, 260
Marcus, G., 122
Marks, G., 71
Markus, H., 96
Markus, T. A., 11
Martin, J., 94, 145, 149
Masten, S. E., 265
Mazumdar, S., 54
McCall, M., 10
McCarthy, D., 284
McCracken, G., 170
McDonald, M., 189
McGee, C., 63
McGrath, D., 183
Meeks, K., 81
Mehrabian, A., 42, 51
Meindl, J. R., 243
Meinig, D. W., 44
Mendel, P., 248
Merrick, A., 166
Meyer, J. W., 226, 227, 242, 251
Meyers-Levy, J., 190
Mildon, J., 250
Miller, D., 88
Miller, N., 71
Millward, L., 185
Mitchell, C., 162, 163, 164, 165
Mohr, J., 227, 260
Montuori, A., 25
Moore, M. C., 167, 168, 175
Morgan, G., 11, 146, 185, 186, 229

Morita, A., 195
Morrison, E. M., 248
Muniz, A. M., 150
Murnighan, J. K., 94
Myers, J. G., 14, 15

N

Nasar, J. L., 10, 12, 15
NetEducation, 186–187
Neuberg, S. L., 65
Neuman, W. R., 48
Nicolini, D., 25
Nielsen, J., 12, 15, 287
Nisbett, R. E., 68
Nissley, N., 24
Nonaka, I., 105
Norman, D., 15, 19
Noschis, K., 44

O

O'Connor, E. J., 45, 249, 260
O'Guinn, T. C., 150
Olins, W., 142, 149, 192, 196
Olsen, J. P., 260
Orenstein, J., 224
Orlikowski, W. J., 56, 88, 98, 103, 261
Ornstein, S., 11, 14, 63, 216
Orr, J., 48, 59
Ottensmeyer, E., 13
Owens, D. A., 189

P

Pacanowsky, M. E., 48
Pareyson, L., 26, 38, 39
Pate, A. N., 64
Pentland, B. T., 260, 286
Pequegnat, W., 12
Peracchio, L. A., 190
Perrone, V., 201
Perrow, C., 261
Peters, T., 185
Peterson, R. A., 86
Pettigrew, A. M., 184, 198
Phillips, N., 25, 260
Pinch, T., 103
Pine, B. J., 161

Po, P. M., 15
Polanyi, M., 25, 42, 52, 105
Polinsky, A. M., 265
Pondy, L. R., 11, 146, 185, 229
Ponti, A., 201
Porras, J., 149
Porter, L., 269
Postrel, V., 13, 18, 20
Powell, W. W., 242
Prasad, P., 21
Pratt, M. G., 10, 21, 38, 51, 56, 58, 64, 103,
        168, 178, 185, 196, 210, 211, 223, 224,
        225, 226, 238, 244, 259, 281, 283, 284,
        286, 288
Prelinger, E., 284
Preston, S. H., 246, 247, 249
Preziosi, D., 44
Pringle, H., 161, 165, 166
Putnam, L. L., 25, 48, 229, 269
Pyrgas, M., 10

Q, R

Quart, A., 175
Radcliffe-Brown, A. R., 86, 92
Rafaeli, A., 9, 10, 11, 12, 13, 16, 17, 18, 19,
        20, 21, 38, 51, 56, 58, 64, 103, 168,
        172, 173, 178, 184, 185, 196, 210, 211,
        216, 223, 224, 225, 226, 229, 238, 244,
        259, 267, 281, 283, 284, 286, 287, 288
Ramati, T., 16
Ramirez, R., 13, 23
Rao, H., 260
Rapoport, A., 44
Raz, E. A., 17, 19
Rein, M., 60
Repenning, N., 102
Reynolds, B., 102
Richardson, J., 201
Ricoeur, P., 44
Ridgeway, C., 283
Ries, J. S., 250
Ritzer, G., 183
Roberts, K. H., 262, 269
Robertson, K. R., 183
Rochberg-Halton, E., 14, 284
Rohwer, C. D., 266
Rosen, M., 48, 56
Rosenholtz, S. J., 283
Ross, L., 67
Roth, K., 19, 20

Rothman, E. L., 247
Rousseau, D. M., 265, 267
Rowan, B., 226, 242, 251
Ruef, M., 248
Rueter, H. H., 286
Ruhleder, K., 109
Rust, R. T., 20

S

Sabshin, M., 264
Saenz, D. S., 67
Salancik, G. R., 244
Samuel, S., 173
Sandelands, L. E., 250
Sassoon, J., 10
Saywell, R. M., 250
Scalfi, A., 28
Schaber, G. D., 266
Schaffer, F., 48
Schatzman, L., 264
Scheflen, A. E., 41, 58
Scheiberg, S. L., 10, 97
Schein, E., 10, 14, 85, 98, 145, 146, 185, 188, 196, 198, 200, 210, 283
Scherer, A. G., 186, 196
Schlenker, B. R., 64, 65, 173
Schmahmann, K. S., 56
Schmidt, R., Sr., 60
Schmitt, B., 182, 188, 193, 194
Schneider-Yaacov, C., 16, 18
Schon, D. A., 46, 60, 122
Schultz, M., 11, 141, 142, 143, 144, 145, 149, 151, 176, 194, 212, 214, 259
Schwartz, R. D., 57n
Schwartz-Shea, P., 43, 46
Scott, J. C., 124
Scott, W. R., 242, 243, 244, 248, 257, 260
Sechrest, L., 57n
Serres, M., 25
Sevon, G., 194
Shanley, M., 195
Shaw, J. S., 62, 245
Sheridan, J. E., 185
Shim, S., 174
Shortell, S. M., 248
Shotter, J., 119, 121, 122, 125, 132n, 133, 135, 136
Shumaker, S. A., 12
Shusterman, R., 42

Simmel, G., 199, 201, 202
Simon, H. A., 229, 274
Simonson, A., 182, 188, 193, 194
Skipper, B. L., 46
Smith, G. W. H., 97
Snow, D. A., 171
Solomon, S. M. R., 174
Spinosa, C., 136
Sproull, L. S., 183
Stanovich, K. E., 17
Star, S. L., 101, 102, 109, 110, 273
Starr, P., 245, 246
Staw, B. M., 250
Steele, C. M., 172
Steele, F., 42, 56, 64
Steele, F. I., 23, 56, 63
Stein, S. J., 51, 53
Steinem, G., 16, 17
Stephenson, R. M., 88, 93, 97
Stern, S., 10, 14, 185
Sternthal, B., 162
Steyaert, C., 27
Stinchcombe, A. L., 265, 274
Stolorow, R. D., 44
Strang, D., 227
Strati, A., 11, 13, 15, 23, 25, 26, 27, 38, 39, 186, 196, 211, 216
Strauss, A. L., 47n, 101, 259–260, 264, 265, 271
Stuart, R. W., 182
Suchman, L., 23
Suchman, M. C., 86, 93, 225, 227, 265
Sundstrom, E., 63, 64
Sundstrom, M. G., 63
Sutton, R., 173, 189
Swann, W. B., Jr., 171
Swartz, T. A., 15
Swidler, A., 238

T

Takahashi, S., 15
Taylor, C., 44
Taylor, S., 24, 65, 66, 67, 68, 79
Taylor, S. E., 67
Thakker, N. R., 250
Thatcher, S. M. B., 171
Thomas, J. B., 183, 215
Thornton, S., 86, 93
Tolbert, P. S., 260
Toulmin, S., 123, 134

Town, J., 63
Tractinsky, N., 15
Tracy, S. J., 175
Trethewey, A., 173
Trice, H. M., 10, 13, 14, 189, 210, 283
Trigg, R., 23
Trist, E., 261
Trudeau, J. V., 173
Tuncel, E., 171
Turner, B., 23
Tybout, A., 162
Tyler, T. R., 182
Tyre, M., 104

V

van Buskirk, W., 183
Van der Weyden, M. B., 246, 249, 251
Van de Ven, A. H., 248, 249
Van Maanen, J., 17, 42, 48, 52, 56
Van Riel, C., 142
Vashdi, D., 18
Vaughan, D., 262
Veblen, T., 201, 259
Ventresca, M., 260
Vico, G., 38
Vilnai-Yavetz, I., 9, 10, 11, 12, 13, 16, 17, 18, 19, 20, 21, 70, 210, 216, 224, 225, 259, 267, 287
Vitruvius, 15
Vogel, A., 268n

W

Waibel, M. C., 69
Walker, I., 67, 80
Warner, W. L., 41
Waterman, R., 185

Wattanasuwan, K., 174
Webb, E. J., 57n
Webster, A., 270
Webster, M. J., 283
Weick, K. E., 133, 185, 186, 262, 286
Weitz, S., 51, 57n
Wenger, E., 102, 122, 262
Wernick, A., 18
West, R. F., 17
Whalen, J., 24
Whalen, M., 24
Wheelwright, S., 102
Whetten, D., 144, 151, 185, 196, 212, 229
White, J. D., 42
Whyte, W. F., 46, 47n
Wicklund, R. A., 69
Williamson, O. E., 265, 274
Willmott, H., 173
Winter, S. G., 271
Wittgenstein, L., 119, 126, 132, 136
Worline, M., 184, 210, 224, 225, 229, 238
Wurf, E., 96

Y

Yanow, D., 10, 25, 41, 42, 43, 44, 45, 46, 47, 48, 49, 50, 51, 52, 54, 55, 58, 59, 283
Yates, J., 88, 98
Yun, M. H., 13

Z

Zeisel, J., 44
Zenardelli, H. A., 63
Zmiri, D., 15
Zollo, M., 271
Zucker, L. G., 246

Subject Index

Note: Figures in *italics* refer to figures; those in **boldface** refer to tables. Figures followed by "n" refer to footnotes.

A

Abercrombie & Fitch, 166
Action-adventure cartoons, 97
Actor network theory, 23–24
Actor/observer effect, 68, 70–71
Aesthetics
  in artifact errors, 17–19
  in contracts, 268
  described, 11–13, 23–24
  in Iron Cage performance, 24–25, 38–39
  in logos, 182–183, 185, 186–188
  other artifact dimensions and, 20–21
  in performance artifact, 24–27, 38–39
  validity of, 14–17
Apple computers, 13, 18
"Argento" example, 206–208
Articulation work, 271
Artifact errors, described, 17–19
Artifact myopia
  artifact dimensions and, 10–17
  artifact errors and, 17–21
  defined, 9, 17
  effect on work performance, 19–20
Attribute change, in employee branding, 172, 175–176
Attribution biases
  displayers', 70–71
  observers', 67–68
Autoproduction of culture, 85–86

B

Bath & Body Works, 164
Behavioral identity markers, 66–67
Being-in-use, 25–27
"Bianco" example, 203–206
Black bag (medical artifact), 245–247, 255–256
Boilerplate contracts, 272–273
Boundary objects
  characteristics of
    described, 114–116
    illustrative story, 111–114
  defined, 110
  paradox of, 101–102, 109
  relational properties of, 116–117
  types of, 110–111
Brands and branding. *See also* Corporate branding; Employee branding; Product branding
  defined, 162
  organizational identity and, 212–215

as sensemaking tools, 162–163
Built space research
    comparative analysis in, 57–58
    data access in, 47–50
    data analysis in, 50–57
    interpretive approach to, 58–60
    lack of, 42

C

Calvin and Hobbes, 97
Cartoon displays
    as artifact, 86
    as autoproduction of culture, 86
    content analysis of, 88
    demographics of, 87–88, **87**
    genres of
        comic relief, 96–97
        communion, 89–93
        crusade, 93–95
        missing, 97
        overview of, 88–89, **89**, 98
        persona, 95–96
    sources of, 97
    study limitations of, 98
Categorization, of artifacts, 10–11
Categorization biases
    displayers', 71–72
    observers', 70
Cell phone design, 13
Cognitively-biased interpretations, 67
Collective mind
    concept of, 262, 274–275
    in contracts, 265–267, 270
Collegial conflicts, 94
Comic relief cartoons, 89, **89**, 96–97
Communication
    as employee branding, 165
    through artifacts, 283
Communion cartoons (genre), 88–93, **89**
Condensation symbols, 88
Conflicts, in cartoon displays, 93–95
Conformity
    in organizational names, 224, 227–228,
        237–239
    in social identity, 255–256
Consumer desires, and employee brand-
        ing, 175–176
Consumers, employees as, 176
Contracts, as artifacts

practice-centered view of, 264–268
    technology transfer example of, 268–274
Cooperative learning, 23–24
Corporate branding. *See also specific ele-*
        ments
    approaches to, 142
    elements of, 144–146, *145*
    versus product branding, 142–143
Corporate offices. *See* Office design and
        decor
Creole language, 272–274
Crusade cartoons (genre), 89, **89,** 93–95
Cultural meanings, in built space, 53–55
Culture. *See* Organizational culture
Culture production theories, 85–86

D

Definition of artifacts, 210
Demographics, of cartoon displayers,
        87–89, **88**
Design gestures, 53–55
Design proxemics, 55–56
Design vocabularies, 52–53
Dialogues, artifacts as, 286–287
Differences and dependencies, of bound-
        ary objects, 115
Dimension, of artifacts
    in artifact errors, 17–19
    described, 10–14
    relations among, 20–21
    in social artifacts, 284
    validity of, 14–17
Direct influence, 12
Distinctiveness markers, described, 62. *See*
        also Physical identity markers
Dress and dress codes
    as employee branding (*See* Employee
        branding)
    individual differences and, 17
    as physical identity marker, 64, 78–79,
        246–247

E

Ecological approach, 12
Edsel car, 17–18
Employee branding
    described, 163–164

forms of, 164–165
implications of, 179–180
organization–employee relationship and,
    176–178
wearing the brand
    described, 165–167
    employee sense of self and, 170–176
    Land Rover example, 167–168
    work involved in, 168–170
Employee dress. *See* Dress and dress codes
Employee identity, 171, 173
Employee relations
    business cards and, 188–189
    employee branding and, 176–178
EMRs, 250–253, *254*
Environmental psychology, of physical
    identity markers, 63–64
Ephemeral artifacts, 27–35, 280–282, 285
Espoused values, 145. *See also* Organiza-
    tional values
Ethics, in linguistic artifacts, 127–130
Exchange process, in contracts, 266–267

F

False consensus effect, 71
Far Side, 97
Fashion industry. *See* Fine fashion indus-
    try
Fashion magazines, 202
Fine fashion industry
    artifacts in, 210–212, **213,** 217
    defined, 201–202
    paradox of success in, 202n
    sensemaking and sensegiving in, *209,*
        215–216, 218
    style and identity in
        comparative examples of, 203–209
        expression of, 202–203
        image and, 212–215, 217–218
        symbolic nature of, 202
First impressions, 64–65
Fundamental attribution error, 67–68

G

The Gap, 166
Gender issues
    in cartoon displays, 87, 94, 97–98

in wearing the brand, 173
Gestures, spatial, 53–55
Green Bus Case, 9, 19, 20
Group identification, cartoon displays and,
    90–91
Gucci, 220–221

H

Hierarchical conflicts, 93–94
Humor. *See* Cartoon displays

I

Identity artifacts. *See* Employee identity; Or-
    ganizational identity; Social identity
Identity categorization, described, 61–62.
    See also Physical identity markers
Image. *See* Organizational identity
Impression management
    identity claiming as, 171
    logos as, 183
    physical identity markers and, 64–65
Independence, of physical identity mark-
    ers, 66–67
Indirect influence, 12
Individual differences
    artifact myopia and, 17
    organizational names and, 228–230,
        238–239
Institutional residues, 272–274
Institutional theory, 225, 242
Instrumentality
    in artifact errors, 17–20
    of contracts, 266–267
    described, 12
    in fine fashion artifacts, 211–212
    in logos, 185
    other artifact dimensions and, 20–21
    validity of, 14–17
Interpretive approach. *See also* Built space
    research
    flexibility in, 58
    presuppositions of, 43–47
Interviewing, in interpretive research, 48
Iron Cage performance
    aesthetics in, 24–27, 38–39
    artifacts from, 37–38
    description of, 27–31, *30*

insights from, 38–39
organizational spaces of, 35
rehearsal of, 36–37
transcriptions of, 31–34

J

Joking relationships, 92–93

K

Knowing
ethics and, 127–130
versus knowledge, 120–126, **127**
in management, 134–136
relational responsiveness and, 130–134
Knowledge transformation, of boundary
objects, 115

L

Land Rover NA, 167–168, 170, 173, 175
Legalese, 272–274
Legitimacy
in medical profession, 247–255, *252, 254*
in organizational names, 225, 227–228,
237–238
in social identity, 243–245
LEGO Brand School, 157–158
LEGO company artifacts
in corporate-brand strategy, 153–155, *155*
cultural, 147
development of, *148*
employee use of, 155–158
identity, 152, *153*
stakeholder, 151
strategic-vision, 149
LEGO Interactive, 156–157
Linguistic artifacts. *See also* Organizational
names
described, 119–120
ethics and, 127–130
as "knowing of third kind," 121–126, **127**
in management, 134–136
relational responsiveness and, 130–134
Linked artifacts, 286
Logos
as artifacts, 188–189

described, 181–183
limitations of, 184, 196–197
as symbols, 184–188
of UK universities, 189–195, *190, 191,
192, 193*
uniqueness of, 183–184

M

Management of artifacts, 287–288
Maps of interdependencies, 111
Marketing, role of logos in, 188
Mass-mediated artifacts. *See* Cartoon dis-
plays
Material artifacts. *See* Physical artifacts
Material possessions. *See* Physical identity
markers
Medical profession
identity claiming versus granting in,
241–245
legitimacy in, 247–255, *252, 254*
physical identity markers of, 245–247
Models, as boundary objects, 110

N

NetEducation logo, *187*
New Yorker, 97
Nonverbal communication
in interpersonal exchanges, 42
of space data, 50–57

O

Objects, as artifacts, 101–103. *See also*
Boundary objects
Office design and decor
versus behavioral identity markers,
66–67
biased interpretations of
framework for, 65–72
study of, 73–79, *74,* **76, 77**
as employee branding, 165
as physical identity marker, 62–65
spatial language of, 52–57
On-brand behaviors, 163
Ontology, in linguistic artifacts, 130–134

Organizational boundaries, in employee
        branding, 176–177
Organizational culture
    in corporate branding, 144–147
    linguistic artifacts in, 134–135
    logos in, 184–189, *186*
    Schein's typology of, 200
Organizational identity
    in corporate branding, 144–146, 151–152
    employee branding and, 178
    in fine fashion industry
        comparative examples of, 203–209
        defined, 212
        image and, 201, 212–215, 217–218
    in logos, 182–183, 185
    in organizational names, 225, 237–238
    research in, 64
    significance of artifacts in, 200
Organizational names
    dual influences on, 224–226
    individual differences and, 228–230,
        238–239
    institutional norms and, 226–228
    study of
        methods, 230–233
        results, 233–237, **234–236**
Organizational values
    corporate branding and, 145, 147, 152
    employee branding and, 177, 178

P

Paradoxes
    of boundary objects, 101–102, 109
    in fashion industry, 202n, 217
Paralanguage, 57n
Participatory design, 23–24
Perceived brand image, 212
Performance. *See* Work performance;
        Work performance reviews
Performance artifact. *See* Iron Cage per-
        formance
Permanence, of physical identity markers,
        66, 78–79. *See also* Ephemeral artifacts
Persona cartoons (genre), 89, **89,** 95–96
Personal identities, 62
Person perception biases, 69–70
Physical artifacts. *See also* Built space
    defined, 10
    dimensions of
        in artifact errors, 17–19

    described, 10–14
    relations among, 20–21
    validity of, 14–17
    in organizational studies, 102–103
Physical identity markers
    biased interpretation of
        framework for, 65–72, 79–81
        study of, 73–79, *74,* **76, 77**
    defined, 61–63
    identity perceptions and, 62–65
    in medical profession, 245–247
    organizational regulation of, 81
    unique characteristics of, 66–67
Pidgin language, 272–274
Power relationships, in employee brand-
        ing, 178
Practice-centered approach
    to formal written contracts
        versus conventional approach to,
            264–268
        technology transfer example of,
            268–274
    framework for, 260–264, *261, 263*
Prada, 216
Product branding, 142–143
Product design, aesthetics in, 13
Product development
    boundary objects in
        characteristics of, 114–116
        illustrative story, 111–114
        types of, 110–111
    design engineering in, 105–107
    manufacturing engineering in, 107–109
    problem-solving in, 103–105, *104,* 109
Production of culture theory, 86
Projected brand image, 212
Proxemics analysis, 55–56

Q

Qualitative research, 47

R

Racial profiling, 81
Rank. *See also* Physical identity markers
    cartoon displays and, 87, 97
    office design and decor and, 53–55, 63
Relational properties, of boundary objects,
        116–117

Relational responsiveness, 130–134
Repositories, 110
Role distance, 91–92
Role performance, 171–172
Romance cartoons (genre), 97

S

Salience, of physical identity markers,
        66–67, 76–78
Self-beliefs, 172
Self-consistency pressures, 173–174
Sensemaking and sensegiving. *See also*
        Knowing
    in branding, 162–163
    in employee branding, 170–176
    in fine fashion industry
        artifacts' function in, 211–212, 215–216,
        218
        comparative examples of, 203–209
        processes in, *209*
    in social artifacts, 282–283
Sense of self
    employee branding and, 170–176
    social identity and, 244
Sensuality, of artifacts, 281, *281*
Shareable qualities, of boundary objects,
        115
Social identity
    claiming versus granting of, 241–245
    defined, 61–62
    legitimacy and, 247–255
    physical markers of, 245–247
Social-identity theory, 242
Sociotechnical systems, 261–262, *261, 263*
Spatial design language, 50–57
Stakeholder image artifacts, 144, 150–151
Standardized form and methods, 110
Status and distinctiveness markers, de-
        scribed, 62. *See also* Physical identity
        markers
Stereotypes, from physical identity mark-
        ers, 69, 81
Strategic-vision artifacts, 144, 147–150
Style, in fashion industry, 202–203
Symbols and symbolism
    in artifact errors, 17–19
    in artifact myopia, 11

versus artifacts, 146, 185–186, *186*
    artifacts as, 210
    in contracts, 268
    described, 13–14
    in fine fashion industry, 202, 217
    in logos, 182–188, 185
    other artifact dimensions and, 20–21
    validity of, 14–17

T

Tactile behavior, 57n
Taken-for-granted state, 101
Technology transfer legalese, 272–274
Threat-rigidity theory, 250–251
Tokyo Disneyland, 19
Training, as employee branding, 164–165

U

UK universities
    logos of
        examples of, 190–194, *190, 191, 192,*
        193
        meanings of, 194–195
    types of, 189–190, 195

V

Vocabularies, spatial, 52–53

W

Wait queues, 18
Wal-Mart, 165
Wearing the brand. *See* Employee brand-
        ing
Web sites, as artifacts, 12
White coat (medical artifact), 246–247, 249,
        250–253, *254,* 255–256
Work performance
    artifact myopia and, 19–20
    office size and location and, 63
Work performance reviews, 69, 81
Workplace studies, 23–24